ORTHODOXIES IN MASSACHUSETTS

Thomas J. Wilson Prize

The Board of Syndics of Harvard University Press has awarded this book the twenty-second annual Thomas J. Wilson Prize, honoring the late director of the Press. The Prize is awarded to the book chosen by the Syndics as the best first book accepted by the Press during the calendar year.

ORTHODOXIES IN MASSACHUSETTS

Rereading American Puritanism

Janice Knight

Harvard University Press
Cambridge, Massachusetts
London, England

Copyright © 1994 by the President and Fellows of Harvard College
All rights reserved
Printed in the United States of America
Second printing, 1997

First Harvard University Press paperback edition, 1997

Library of Congress Cataloging-in-Publication Data

Knight, Janice
    Orthodoxies in Massachusetts : rereading American Puritanism /
Janice Knight
        p.   cm.
    Includes bibliographical references and index.
    ISBN 0-674-64487-5 (cloth)
    ISBN 0-674-64488-3 (pbk.)
    1. Puritans—New England. 2. New England—Church history.
    I. Title.
BR520.K55 1994
285'.9'.097409032—dc20
93-6398

For my parents, Doris and Julius

Acknowledgments

What I know of the communion of saints I have learned from the goodness and wisdom of my friends, teachers, and colleagues. It is a pleasure to acknowledge their gifts to me.

At an early stage, Bernard Bailyn, Robert Gross, David Hall, and David Watters read parts of this manuscript, providing valuable advice. William Hutchison, Harry Stout, Mark Valeri, and John Wilson commented on an earlier version of the chapter on Jonathan Edwards. Andrew Delbanco and Emory Elliot gave timely and essential criticism on the entire text. I am grateful to Stephen Foster for reading Chapter 2, not only correcting some errors but also sharing his copious knowledge of English religious culture. Sargent Bush helped me decipher a particularly difficult letter to John Cotton, graciously offering his own transcription.

Over the years, conversations with Jesper Rosenmeier, Teresa Toulouse, and Susan Howe have greatly deepened my appreciation for and understanding of my subject. Chicago colleagues Jerald Brauer, James Chandler, Laura Rigal, and Richard Strier offered judicious advice on the penultimate draft. Lisa Ruddick proved an insightful reader and more. Her unflagging support and friendship during the final phase of writing sustained me.

Three colleagues deserve special thanks for their help and encouragement. Janel Mueller read and critiqued the entire manuscript. Her knowledge of the period, her precision as a critic, and her thoroughness as an editor made this a better book. In conversation and in the classroom she serves as a model of humane collegiality and intellectual rigor. I have also been the lucky recipient of David Levin's expert advice. I thank him not only for his insightful comments on this manuscript, but also for his many kindnesses during my first years as an assistant professor. Finally, Michael McGiffert has been very generous in reading my work with a critical and benevolent eye.

The love and understanding of my family during my years of obsession with the Puritans and neglect of them deserve special thanks. With great good humor and devotion, my mother, Doris Knight, partnered me in final proofreading. My friends Barbara DeWolfe, Ruth DiPietro, Pat Gill, Mark Massa, and Janice Moulton believed in me and helped me to believe in my work. The memory of Maria Kostello remains an inspiration. And for over twenty years, Michael Franco has been a spiritual anchorhold—his friendship is nothing short of miraculous.

A number of institutions have helped at crucial stages and in material ways. Harvard University's Program in the History of American Civilization and the Giles Whiting Foundation provided early funding. The American Studies Association award of the Ralph Henry Gabriel Prize was another source of early encouragement. A fellowship year at the Charles Warren Center for Studies in American History offered not only time for revisions but also good colleagues and conversation during a critical period. I owe special thanks to Bernard Bailyn and David Donald for their encouragement. Two summer grants from the University of Virginia and a fellowship from the Chicago Humanities Institute allowed time for polishing the manuscript.

Several libraries shared their treasures with me. For their patience and many courtesies, I thank the staffs of Houghton Library, Beineke Library, the American Antiquarian Society, the Massachusetts Historical Society, the New England Historic Genealogical Society, and the Rare Books Room of the Boston Public Library. A portion of Chapter 3 appeared in *Amerikastudien,* and parts of the epilogue were published in the *William and Mary Quarterly.*

At Harvard University Press Aida Donald and Elizabeth Suttell have been unusually supportive; Kate Schmit has proven a patient and discerning copy editor. I am also grateful to the Board of Syndics for honoring this book with the Thomas J. Wilson Prize.

Jeff Gross and Maureen McLane deserve special praise and thanks for their scrupulous work in checking references; Paula McQuade, Peter Sattler, and Barbara Anderson also provided valuable assistance in preparing the manuscript.

Finally, it is a great pleasure for me to acknowledge my debt to Alan Heimert. As his many friends and students will recognize, his readings of Sibbes and Cotton, Davenport and Preston resonate throughout the pages of this text. Honoring his "father in the gospel," Paul Baynes, Richard Sibbes observed, "He was a man of much communion with God, and acquaintance with his own heart . . . one that had not all his learning out of books; of sharp wit, and clear judgment: though his meditations were of a higher strain than ordinary, yet he had a good dexterity, furthered by his love to do good, in explaining dark points with lightsome similitudes." Alan Heimert is such a teacher. For his compassion, wisdom, generosity, and more, I thank him.

Contents

ORTHODOXIES IN MASSACHUSETTS

Introduction

I WRITE the WONDERS of the CHRISTIAN RELIGION, flying from the depravations of Europe, to the American Strand." This strange and evocative declaration sets the agenda for Cotton Mather's majestic *Magnalia Christi Americana*. Published in 1702, this account of "the mighty works of Jesus Christ in America" initiates the project of reading the first Puritan generation as a sacred origin of American culture. Though his tale of the *"Actors"* and *"Actions"* of the Puritan plantation includes ample description of the differences of opinion, social conflicts, and political contests that were an important part of the drama of the early decades of settlement, Mather holds true to his grand design and unified purpose. These differences are subsumed into a vision of New England as the progressive unfolding of the sacred idea of God: "the wonderful displays of His infinite Power, Wisdom, Goodness and Faithfulness, wherewith His Divine Providence hath irradiated an Indian Wilderness."[1]

Cotton Mather himself stands as something of a type for modern interpreters of the Puritans. Perhaps more than other scholarly communities, early Americanists read their subjects as a point of origin for the present day—we read ourselves against, and we read "America" out of, the Puritan past. Of his own inspiration for writing of New England, the distinguished critic Perry Miller describes an "epiphany," a sudden realization of "the pressing necessity for expounding my America to the twentieth century." Miller's narrative, like Mather's, traced the "movement of European culture into the vacant wilderness."[2] Reading for emergent social and ideological formations that he identified with the modern period, Miller found a Puritanism identified by its celebration of divine power, its elabo-

rated system of contractual covenants, and its tribal nationalism. His interest in the continuity of the New England past with twentieth-century
America necessarily produced a history of the dominant group within that
religious culture. Many scholars have recapitulated this discovery of
"America"—for better or worse—in the Puritan past, producing studies of
great interpretive power, interest, and even beauty.[3] As with Mather's
history, however, the variations, conflicts, and alternative voices within
early New England culture are often suppressed in these narratives tracing
our imagined homogeneous Puritan origin.

I am less interested in such a genealogy of modern America than in a
local history of New England Puritanism in the first decades of settlement—less interested in what emerged as the dominant religious culture
than in the shifting compromises, articulated resistances, and exercises of
power that preceded the establishment of orthodoxy in New England.
Rather than discovering a univocal origin, I find significant differences and
alternative voices within Puritan culture. When I read Richard Sibbes and
John Cotton, John Preston and John Davenport, for example, I find a
passionate mysticism in place of the divine power described by Miller; an
emphasis on charity at odds with the logic of contract; an expansive
communalism counter to tribal nationalism. This book offers a reading of
New England's first Puritans in terms of a set of values, experiences, and
expressions alternative to those currently identified with the Puritan orthodoxy. Working within regnant constructions of the "dominant" culture,
I find diversity within that familiar group of Puritan elites that has seemed
most homogeneous. Even there, experience was divergent and volatile. My
interests in this reading are satisfied in describing a Puritan culture that
is contested from within. In the first decades of plantation the edges of
events were rougher, experiences less predictable, the outcomes less inevitable than our genealogical histories have allowed.

❧

This book attempts to recover varieties of religious experience within
Puritanism, then, by giving voice to an alternative community within what
is usually read as the univocal orthodoxy of New England. My purpose is
to retrace the social, intellectual, theological, and aesthetic signatures distinguishing two communities within the larger Puritan household—
groups I identify as the "Intellectual Fathers" and the "Spiritual Brethren."[4]

The first group, familiar to readers of *The New England Mind,* is composed of Perry Miller's "orthodoxy": Thomas Hooker, Thomas Shepard,
Peter Bulkeley, John Winthrop, and most of the ministers of the Massachusetts Bay Colony; in England, William Perkins and William Ames

were their authorities. These preachers identified power as God's essential attribute and described his covenant with human beings as a conditional promise. They preached the necessity of human cooperation in preparing the heart for that promised redemption, and they insisted on the usefulness of Christian works as evidence of salvation.* They were less interested in the international church than in their local congregation and their tribal faith. In general, they were pre- or a-millennial, in that they had little sense of participating in a prophetic errand into the wilderness and had no particular commitment to advancing the coming of Christ's kingdom. Miller, among others, has lamented that these religionists developed structures of preparationism and an interlocking system of contractual covenants that diminished the mystical strain of piety he associated with Augustinianism.

The second party closely embodies that Augustinian strain.[5] Originally centered at the Cambridge colleges and wielding great power in the Caroline court, this group was led by Richard Sibbes and John Preston in England; in America by John Cotton, John Davenport, and Henry Vane. Neither a sectarian variation of what we now call "orthodoxy" in New England nor a residual mode of an older piety, this party presented a vibrant alternative within the mainstream of Puritan religious culture. In a series of contests over political and social dominance in the first American decades, this group lost their claim to status as an "official" or "orthodox" religion in New England. Thereafter, whiggish histories (including Cotton Mather's own) tell the winner's version, demoting central figures of this group to the cultural sidelines by portraying their religious ideology as idiosyncratic and their marginalization as inevitable.

As this book will show, these preachers differed from their so-called orthodox counterparts in significant ways. More emotional and even mystical, their theology stressed divine benevolence over power. Emphasizing the love of God, they converted biblical metaphors of kingship into ones of kinship. They substituted a free testament or voluntary bequeathing of grace for the conditional covenant described by the other orthodoxy. Richard Sibbes speaks of this testament in affective terms as God's legacy given "merely of love."[6]

Such a view argues against a doctrine of preparation by refusing human

---

* Because these theologians put the greatest stress on the importance of preparing the heart for the reception of grace, they are often here termed "preparationists," in contrast to the identification of their opponents as "spiritists." These designations should be understood primarily as a form of polemical economy, however. All Puritan preachers placed a high value on spiritual exercises, but the "Intellectual Fathers" (or Amesians) made preparationism the center of their pastoralism, while the "Spiritual Brethren" (or Sibbesians) more often focused on the immediacy of God's transformative love.

performance as a sign of salvation and pastoral discipline as a mode of social order. Recalling Augustine and anticipating Jonathan Edwards, these preachers construed sin not as a palpable evil but as an absence of good. They preached that grace was a new taste for divine things, that it "altereth the rellish" and is immediately infused into the passive saint by God alone. For the Spiritual Brethren the transformation of the soul was neither incremental nor dependent on exercises of spiritual discipline. In this piety, there are no steps to the altar.[7] Labor is the joyful return for grace already received. Love, not anxiety, is the hallmark of this piety, a difference that has consequences for Max Weber's thesis concerning the marriage of Protestantism with the work ethic.

The coherence of the Cambridge group challenges theories of American exceptionalism, whether that construct is understood as describing a special New England self or a prophetic national destiny. This group's ideas were formed in England well before the Great Migration and persisted, relatively unchanged, afterwards. On the whole, the Cambridge preachers rejected a typology of national mission. They remained devoted to the international church, whose members "God in heavenly wisdom scatters . . . as jewels, as the lights of the world."[8] Moreover, these preachers were avid millennialists: they believed in the unfolding of the kingdom of Christ within history rather than in an apocalyptic shattering of creation. They worked zealously on behalf of this second coming.

As I will show, these doctrinal differences had literary consequences as well. The Cambridge preachers evolved a distinctive rhetoric of grace and embodied it in identifiable tropes, literary forms, and conceptions of reader and text. Significantly, they rejected the *ordo salutis* as a sermonic plot. Most often presupposing a regenerate audience, they were less interested in instruction than edification. Their texts trade on incantation, hovering over single words or verses of scripture. Lyrical, these sermons privilege affect over logic, sensibility over meaning, sometimes even sound over sense.

❧

My purpose is to put in question the scholarly representation of a monologic Puritan culture, then, not by tracing dissent at the sectarian margins of the culture but by challenging the myth of consensus at the center. "Orthodoxy" figures here not as a stable category describing either transcendent truth or doctrine sanctioned by prior articulation within the Protestant tradition, but as a mutable, socially produced category—a description of the official structures and codes designed to mark lawful from illegitimate opinion in Puritan New England. Its contents were polemically constructed to set boundaries and establish dominance, in terms of defining both key words and practices.[9]

Many historians, including Cotton Mather himself, have observed dissension among members of America's founding generation.[10] The records of New England's first three decades reveal an unsettling amount of debate, controversy, and even violent confrontation. I would maintain that these events reveal abiding conflicts within the Puritan leadership itself, not simply contests between a unified theocracy and its sectarian opponents, as is often argued. These significant party divisions within moderate Puritanism were neither born on American soil nor limited to the opinions of single figures like John Cotton or his lay disciple, Anne Hutchinson. By 1630 two powerful parties had formed within the Puritan leadership— fellowships gathered into distinctive personal, social, and political networks holding disparate views on matters of doctrine and expression. In America these differences became the source of heated contestations over the status of orthodoxy in New England.

I argue that while an orthodoxy was established in early America, its status was contested and partial. Adapting from Raymond Williams's model of counter-hegemony, I would observe that the conflicts in early New England proved a concrete instance in which orthodoxy emerged as dominant, but its dominance was neither absolute nor exclusive. There were alternatives and oppositions *within* the Puritan mainstream, forces that—despite pressures of prohibition, exclusion, or assimilation—succeeded in counteracting suppressions, exile to positions at the social margin, and mechanisms of neutralization.[11]

❧

This claim about competing parties within the Puritan leadership arises within a set of academic conversations. Participants in those debates will recognize the implications of my argument; for others, I will briefly sketch the context that has given shape to my reading of the Puritans.

In 1933 Perry Miller offered what has become the standard account of New England's religious elite, *Orthodoxy in Massachusetts*. Identifying Puritanism with "that group of men who wished to replace the [church] hierarchy with another ecclesiastical system," Miller put forward a definition of orthodoxy that involved the construction of a proper institutional model for church organization. For New England Puritans that model was non-separating congregationalism: its intellectual genealogy traced to Holland and the originary influence of William Ames. In the series of studies that followed, Miller expanded his original definition of orthodoxy to include the structures of thought and expression that constituted his New England "mind." The doctrine of preparationism, the set of religious and social covenants, and an elaborated system of logic (based on the writings of Petrus Ramus) characterized this version of Puritanism. But even as he specified varieties of opinion that complicated his portrait of Puritan culture, Miller posited an essential intellectual unity among patriarchal founders—indeed, his conviction was so powerful that he could make a now infamous declaration of method: "I have taken the liberty of treating the whole literature as though it were the product of a single intelligence." This Puritan consensus was derived as a heritage from the "Learned Dr. Ames."[12]

Despite errors and misreadings, despite the criticism leveled at him by subsequent scholars and the undoubted value of their correctives, Miller's analysis remains the most persuasive and subtle discussion of New England religious ideology. Perhaps more than anyone before or since, Miller appreciated the nuances and contradictions within Puritan culture. Yet, because his focus was always on its internal homogeneity and the continuity of that culture with our own, the vital difference between contesting Puritan ideologies often was blurred and sometimes even erased—disputes were minimized in Miller's portrait of conflicts as minor fluctuations in an otherwise stable world. It was most often on the shoulders of radicals like Anne Hutchinson or Roger Williams—individuals clearly positioned on the social margin—that Miller placed both credit and responsibility for originating and sustaining a dissenting tradition.[13]

The half-century of scholarship since Miller first published his magisterial studies has proved the Puritans to be among the most fascinating actors of American history.[14] Challenges to Miller's monolithic view of Puritan culture have come from multiple sources. Religious scholars have complicated our understanding of Puritan theology and church organization.[15] Practitioners of the new social history have challenged the focus on the clerical elite, unearthing the daily lives of those designated as the "inarticulate"; studies of popular religion have joined pulpit to pew.[16] Feminist scholarship has challenged the patriarchal bias of Puritan studies, revising the portrait of a monolithic culture from yet another vantage.[17] Moreover, critics of British colonialism have challenged the depiction (presented not only by the Puritans themselves but also by subsequent historians) of America as a vacant wilderness, exposing the fatal impact of Puritan land policies on Amerindian populations.[18]

Though assessments of Puritanism have become more complex as our image of the broader culture has diversified, readings of the so-called dominant or elite culture remain surprisingly monologic. Let me be clear that I am interested in the issue of difference within the sphere critics identify as the "dominant" culture of early New England; within that context, Miller's model of consensus still obtains. My project is to demonstrate the existence and persistence of opposition even within that most homogeneous group of male ministers and magistrates. Therefore, I adopt the working definition of Puritanism as well as the patriarchal bias of traditional Puritan historiography, but do so in order to interevene and realign aspects of the field as it stands. To elaborate briefly, I will describe revisions of Miller's thesis that I argue nonetheless reinstate his claims regarding consensus among the ruling elite of the first Puritan generation.

First, compelling rereadings of Miller have come from ideological critics—most prominently, Sacvan Bercovitch—who adopt and extend Miller's assertion of consensus among Puritan patriarchs. Though importantly revising specific formulations of Miller's understanding of the Puritan errand and the issue of tribal exceptionalism, Bercovitch argues even more vigorously than Miller for the univocality of Puritan culture, minimizing the significance of even the limited range of conflict Miller recorded. Bercovitch's account of the consensus model focuses on Puritan ideology, exposing the rhetorical strategies by which the dominant culture neutralized conflict and transformed dissent into an affirmation of its official structures. Central to this process was the Puritans' reading of their experiment not just as an errand in this world but as a turning point in "the preordained scheme of redemption."[19] From this marriage of sacred and secular purpose, personal and tribal identity, follows America's claim to an exceptional destiny and the concomitant yet delusive claim of every citizen to share in the American dream of success. The *ordo salutis* converts into everyman's way to wealth; America's prophetic destiny transforms into an affirmation of secular progress.[20] The union assured America of its place in the center of history as the chosen New Jerusalem; its sacred prophetic role would be realized as a secular manifest destiny: "In other words," Bercovitch writes, the Puritans "used the biblical myth of exodus and conquest to justify imperialism before the fact."[21]

To be sure, Bercovitch acknowledges diversity as it is articulated by social historians of New England and as it emerges in later periods of American literature, but his exposition of the "rituals of socialization" and the "cultural myth" informing Puritan ideology claims an original consensus.[22] In this model, dissent figures as the creature of a hegemonic Puritan culture, the margin that confirms the dominance of the orthodox center. My rather schematic redaction of Bercovitch's claims does not do justice to the power or richness of his argument, but it does suggest that his predominant concern is with mapping the symbolic structures that produce and reproduce cultural hegemony.

While I might agree that as an outcome of conflict in the first decades of New English settlement "official" religious and political structures were produced, I do not believe that consensus obtained in the first instance. I argue that Bercovitch projects consensus onto first-generation Puritan culture when it did not exist, erasing significant differences and converting volatile events into inevitable outcomes. His analysis effectively details some of the intellectual and rhetorical complexities of Puritan ideology, but only for that hemisphere of the New England "mind" most properly designated as "preparationist"—the same half that interested Miller. Yet even as it emerged as dominant, the repeated controversies in the first decades attest to strong countervoices within the religious culture that predated and persisted after the establishment of the preparationist orthodoxy. By no means was all opposition silenced, transformed into assent, or put in service of social revitalization. Insisting on the actuality of something "other," I invoke Raymond Williams's observation that there are "at least in part significant breaks beyond [hegemonic limits], which may again in part be neutralized, reduced, or incorporated, but which in their most active elements nevertheless come through as independent and original."[23]

One might expect that more substantive challenges to the consensus model might be lodged by scholars whose cultural-analytic foregrounds conflict. Yet recent studies of sectarians, women, and other disenfranchised groups are governed by an interpretive model that positions dissent at the cultural margins. In so doing, these works tend to confirm, even reify, the seamless coherence of the orthodox center.[24] Though such studies bring pressure to bear on the monologic model of the culture at large, they strengthen the consensus thesis with respect to the spectrum of so-called moderate Puritans. Though they argue that "*heterogeneity*, not unanimity, actually characterized the colony's religious life," their "heterogeneity" is largely confined to marginalized or excluded cultural "others."[25] Important sites of difference within the dominant culture are themselves effaced within this dynamic of margin and center, with the result that dominance is totalized and the possibility of dissent from within the cultural mainstream is precluded.[26]

Each of these models has demonstrable explanatory power. Miller and Bercovitch, true to the dominant mode in Puritan ideology and culture, eloquently describe the general contours of that tradition. Equally, Philip

Gura and others have illuminated the hidden corners of the world of sectaries and other marginalized peoples. While their findings serve their specific concerns, their analytic models inevitably obscure or rather erase the phenomena that interest me.

A third approach, more in sympathy with my own, focuses on the peculiar career of John Cotton. I am pleased to join such scholars as John Coolidge, Teresa Toulouse, Jesper Rosenmeier, and Andrew Delbanco who have sympathetically registered the ways that Cotton's piety counters the preparationist orthodoxy. I have learned a great deal from their splendid readings of Cotton's doctrine of the covenant, his understanding of the process of salvation, and his aesthetics and stylistics.[27] In one matter, however, I dissent from their findings. These studies often portray Cotton as unique, the author of a utopian discourse that was discredited and discarded by an oppressive or unappealing orthodox regime. Stressing Cotton's distinctiveness, however, marginalizes him even in the work of recuperation. This approach leaves untouched, indeed confirms, the centeredness of the centered orthodoxy. As a result, when we look at the so-called Puritan mainstream, we are left to trace a lineage from Ames and Perkins to Hooker and Shepard, with Cotton a reluctant fellow-traveler or a prophet in the wilderness, either coopted or tragically silenced.

I want to recognize the larger context and tradition in which Cotton resides—a discursive community that existed as a second orthodoxy both in New England and in Old. The existence of an alternative tradition within the Puritan mainstream has been suggested by such scholars as Geoffrey Nuttal, James Maclear, Alan Heimert, and more recently Michael Schuldiner, who have noted Cotton's mysticism and hinted at its place within a larger pietistic tradition.[28] The scope and complexity of the proposed alternative vision and its roots in pre-migration English culture are still to be discovered, however. Situated within a doctrinal context, this alternative piety extended well beyond such boundaries to inform social structures and political practices, as well as expressive styles and modes of feeling. The composition of the New England mind in this minor key is yet to be fully performed; Cottonian piety was a far more ancient and persistent countervoice within "moderate" Puritanism than has been recognized. It was neither the product of specifically American conditions, nor was it banished to sectarian groups in the aftermath of the Antinomian Controversy.

❦

Given the structural difference I claim to discover, a question arises: how has the existence of twin orthodoxies within American Puritanism gone so long unremarked or refigured by scholars as the singular position of John Cotton and his radical followers? One possible answer involves the politics of the Puritan archive itself.

A curious yet largely unexamined contradiction in the early scholarship of the field may prove instructive. Just one year before Miller published the first volume of *The New England Mind,* William Haller published his classic account of *The Rise of Puritanism* (1938). Though many scholars treat these two works as founding texts for modern Puritan studies, few have remarked that they bear surprisingly little resemblance to one another.

Like Miller, Haller constructs a genealogy of Puritan "fathers," but he does so from the perspective of English intellectual history. Interestingly, Ames, William Bradshaw, and Hooker—central figures in Miller's Puritan pantheon—have a lesser place in Haller's universe. They are briefly mentioned as "the intellectual fathers of Independency." Haller's interest attaches to the prominent group of Puritans who moved in circles of power at court and the colleges. The roll call of that leadership—Sibbes, Cotton, Preston, Thomas Goodwin, Philip Nye—constitute my Spiritual Brethren. As prominent actors in the salient events of the prewar period, these men achieved a reputation that eclipsed Ames's and Hooker's and continued to do so in subsequent historical accounts of the British national past. Haller's reading, drawing on the *Lives* of Samuel Clarke, in some measure imported the whiggish bias of that early hagiography.[29]

Conversely, the victors of the early disputes in New England have been given a disproportionate place in our national history. In the aftermath of the Antinomian Controversy, men like Shepard and Winthrop began the task of writing apologies regarding the disputes, naturalizing their own authority as inevitable, as "orthodox," and rewriting opposition as "heresy." Shoring up their authority not just by exiling dissenters or by marginalizing Cotton and Davenport, they also engaged in literary acts of self-justification. The volatility of the events was represented as the inevitable emergence of "right opinion," a history later rehearsed by Cotton Mather, among others. While admitting of rupture and dissonance, this Puritan archive inscribed the winner's tale in the very act of narrating difference as dissent. Drawing on this written record, even wary historical reconstruction of the "original" context runs the risk of re-authorizing the myth of inevitable origin by redeploying this triumphalist dynamic of margin and center.

The Winthrop orthodoxy has dominated American hagiography, theirs is the theology that has become synonymous with the univocal Puritan piety. Drawing on this record and from an Americanist perspective, Miller could conclude that with respect to the "fundamental point" of preparationism "Hooker's influence eclipsed Cotton's and his share in the formation of American Puritanism is correspondingly the larger."[30] This bias is reflected in a subsequent focus on the preparationist orthodoxy in succeeding historical interpretations and a romanticizing of Cotton's piety as the lost, best part of ourselves.

❧

My study is offered as an effort of recovery—one that seeks return to the period before orthodox modes were secured in New England in order to restore a sense of drama and volatility to our early history. A corrective to triumphalist histories, this study offers a thick description of the ideas, associations, and experiences that bound the Sibbesian party together and describes the set of compromises, dialogic exchanges, and heated conflicts that ultimately set them apart from the "orthodox" culture. Rather than acquiescing in a description that locates them as dissenters from an orthodox center, this study places them at the center and considers the production of a single "orthodoxy" as a volatile process that has only come to seem inevitable in subsequent narrative accounts.

Beginning with a narrative of the Antinomian Controversy of 1636–1638, the first chapter of this book describes the moment of visible rupture in New England culture that concluded with the establishment of orthodox structures and practices. The second chapter returns to England to describe the political, social, professional, and personal allegiances binding the two parties. An analysis of contrasting doctrinal positions and rhetorical styles—differing views of divine and human nature, versions of God's covenant, of the ontology of conversion, of doctrines of the pure church and the ideal society—will be undertaken in succeeding chapters. How these contrasting religious ideologies informed conceptions of audience and sermonic structure and style will be considered through rhetorical analysis of the writings of members of both groups. Finally, I will trace the recurrence of similar modes of opposition in the controversy surrounding the Half-Way Covenant and in John Davenport's final reading of the fate of spiritist aspirations in New England. My epilogue considers the possibilities and problems of interpreting Edwardsean pietism of the next century in light of a Sibbesian tradition.

The early history of New England must be rewritten in terms of a continuing contest between these two orthodoxies. Religious and institutional conflicts, including the Antinomian Controversy, the quarrels over

Harvard College, and the Half-Way Covenant debates, must be reconsidered as moments in which these inherent ideological strains became visible and volatile. Rather than chronicling the successes of co-optation, this study focuses on the persistence and vitality of difference. One lesson the Cambridge Brethren teach is the possibility of pragmatic, tactical opposition. On another level, they imagine an alternative to a spiritual economy of the *quid pro quo*.

I

🌿

New England Ways

> I end, dear Christian, with the proposal of two Christian knots
> or riddles, not unsuitable to these present times and spirits.
> First, why is the heart of a David himself (Psalm 30) more apt
> to decline from God upon the mountain of joy, deliverance,
> victory, prosperity, than in the dark vale of the shadow of death,
> persecution, sickness, adversity, etc.? Secondly, why is it, since
> God worketh freely in us to do and to will of his own good
> pleasure, that yet he is pleased to command us to work out our
> own salvation with fear and trembling? Let us all humbly beg
> the finger (the spirit) of the Lord to untie these knots for us.
>
> Roger Williams

From his lonely vantage in exile Roger Williams surveyed the Bible Commonwealth of Massachusetts with some bitterness and no little insight, puzzling over two riddles that his early experiences in the Bay had seemed to prove though not to explain. His first "Christian knot"—that zeal seems vouchsafed to saints only in adversity while it inevitably declines in times and places of free enjoyment—had a special poignancy for Puritan immigrants. Indeed, Williams had touched on the irony of New England itself. Scholars have long attended colonists' laments over their declining faith, especially by members of New England's second generation. But even as they made landfall, the first Puritans had to reckon with the sense of disappointment and disillusionment, had to confront the ambiguities propounded in Williams's puzzle.

Puritanism was a movement shaped in a crucible of persecution, a piety cherished by men and women who paid a high price for disaffection from the English church. The visible threat of the high churchmen combined with harassment by the Crown confirmed these dissenters in their resistance. In Old England chains of persecution were transformed into communal bonds. Motives for colonization have long been debated; though voyagers to New England set sail for a variety of reasons, strong among them was the hope of discovering a place where they could enjoy an untroubled communion of saints. The colonists intended to plant pure churches in what they saw as a vacant land; they dreamed of establishing a New Jerusalem in the wilderness.[1]

A mere six years after landfall, however, Governor John Winthrop felt compelled to admit the collapse of this "holy experiment." Reporting on the state of the Commonwealth in 1636, Winthrop found little to praise.[2] Controversy raged as religious and political dissent disrupted nearly every community. Originating "first, in the Church," disputes quickly spread "into Civill and publike affaires" and "bred great disturbance there." Not only were civic and religious orders threatened, but even the structure of family life was put at risk: "divisions between husband and wife, and other relations" proliferated, to be resolved only if "the weaker give place to the stronger." "Otherwise," Winthrop observed, "it turnes to open contention." "Every occasion increased the contention, and caused great alienation of minds," so that church gatherings and public assemblies proved failures rather than models of Christian charity. Declaring this "plague" of controversy "the sorest tryall that ever befell us since we left our Native soyle," Winthrop despaired that his world was "turned upside down."[3]

Winthrop here describes the turmoil which has come to be called the Antinomian Controversy, perhaps the best-known episode of New England's early history.[4] By most contemporary accounts, Winthrop's fears were justified. Edward Johnson, captain of Woburn's militia, suspected that "Satans Malignity to the truths of Christ" was the real author of the "Errours and Heresies" that, "sliding the darke like the Plague," were "proving very infectious" to the church. Neither the "cruell savages," the "Prelates Prisons," nor even the "perillous Seas" they had crossed seemed "so terrible in the apprehension of some as was this floud of errors violently beating against the bankes of Church and civill Government."[5] Clerics like Thomas Shepard knew whom to blame as well—the "evangelical hypocrisy and deceit" of John Cotton, Anne Hutchinson, and members of the Boston churches proved Satan's plan to "send delusions" to trouble the saints.[6]

At the close of the century, when the passage of years should have made for cooler heads, Cotton Mather still insisted that the real enemy in 1636 had been "the cunning and malice of Satan," whose intent was nothing less than to "break the prosperity of the churches."[7] To men like Johnson, Winthrop, Shepard, and Mather, it seemed as if New England's fate hung by a slender thread in these tumultuous years and, like Jonathan Edwards's famous spider, was preserved from destruction by God's condescending favor.

As hyperbolic as such assessments seem, they were largely accurate. By the late 1630s New England was in disarray; Winthrop's city on the hill had been transformed into a doctrinal battlefield. The "ligaments of love" which were to bind the colonists into a harmonious social body were all but severed. Originating in Boston, religious discontent quickly spread to other churches; by 1636 the entire population was embroiled in controversy. "All men's mouths were full" of debates about theological and political legitimacy.[8]

Nor was dissatisfaction limited to words. Church quarrels quickly transformed into political struggles, manifesting themselves in a variety of dramatic and sometimes violent acts of rebellion. According to Winthrop, Boston saints made a habit of disrupting neighboring churches and haranguing their ministers. They insulted duly elected magistrates (including Winthrop himself), rejected orders of the General Court, and in an act that supposedly threatened the survival of the Massachusetts colony, they refused to serve in military expeditions against the neighboring Pequots. In these and other ways, Boston congregants expressed open revolt against what was fast becoming the ruling orthodoxy.[9]

Describing his return to New England during this turbulent period, Giles Firmin reported that *"before our Ship came into Harbour, a Shallop coming of Shore to us, the Men told us, the Churches were on fire."* No friend of the dissenters, Firmin recorded the general fear that *"the Heat, the Animosities were so high, that they were ready to lay Hands on their Swords, to draw one against another."*[10] The May 1637 court of elections proved just how volatile these ideological divisions would become. Ostensibly a routine election, this contest between Henry Vane and John Winthrop incarnated the conflict between the Boston church and the rest of the colony. Points of procedure were so hotly contested that, as Firmin predicted, "some laid hands on others."[11] Although the outcome of the election spelled defeat for Henry Vane, political leader of the Boston rebels, and reestablished the power of Winthrop's party, subsequent events proved this victory partial. Resistance persisted throughout the decade in disputes over legislation of the General Court, the founding and supervision of Harvard College, and the gathering of new churches.

When Winthrop was chronicling the controversy for an Old English audience in his "Short Story," he tended to minimize the involvement of leaders like Cotton in this schism. His more forthright *History*, however, reveals how profoundly radicalism circulated among the cultural elite. In their acts of contestation, the Boston saints did not work alone. The laity joined hands with some of the most prominent ministers and magistrates of the colony in what might be called an outright revolt.[12] Support—indeed encouragement—for the dissenters came from Vane, the deputies of the General Court, and such ministers as John Cotton, John Wheelwright, and John Davenport. These leaders did not hesitate to censure preparationist ministers like John Wilson publicly, nor to chastise openly the practices of secular leaders they disapproved, including Winthrop himself.[13]

The events surrounding the December 1636 session of the General Court prove a case in point. At that session Pastor Wilson "made a very sad speech" lamenting the theological divisions and asserting his own "orthodoxy" by "la[ying] the blame upon these new opinions" of the Cottonians. Not surprisingly, the speech "was taken very ill" by Cotton, Vane, and other members of the First Church. According to Winthrop, "they called [Wilson] to answer publickly . . . pressed it violently against him . . . with much bitterness and reproaches." Cotton "joined with the church in their judgment" against Wilson, but finally intervened to prevent formal censure of his fellow clergyman.[14]

In these skirmishes, the Boston ministers did not attempt to hide the source of disagreement from their English friends. To Winthrop's dismay, in February 1637 Cotton addressed a shipload of saints returning to England, spelling out the differences that divided the colony and instructing them to tell friends "that would strive for grace, they should come hither." Some scholars have suggested that Cotton's speech was an accommodationist gesture, minimizing the conflicts as matters of emphasis rather than substance. To the theological combatants, however, Cotton's explanation of the differences was significant: "all the strife amongst us was about magnifying the grace of God; one party seeking to advance the grace of God within us, and the other to advance the grace of God towards us, (meaning by the one justification, and by the other sanctification;)." While it is true that Cotton cast all disagreements as disputes over grace, John Winthrop knew such differences of emphasis cut to the heart of the matter. Winthrop concludes this journal entry by observing, "Thus every occasion increased the contention, and caused great alienation of minds . . ."[15] Had Cotton's invitation to "come hither" been accepted by his English supporters, the balance of power in New England well might have tipped in favor of the dissenters and the new "orthodoxy" itself displaced!

These astonishing events did not measure the full extent of the protesters' zeal, however. Divisions between ministers became more pronounced when the Bostonians refused to attend first the gathering of Concord Church and then the ordination of Concord's ministers, Peter Bulkeley and John Jones. Scholars often minimize the divisiveness of these events as well, arguing that Cotton supported the orthodoxy's regulation of church gathering, clerical ordination, and admission testimonies, interpreting them as concessions to popular spiritism. Yet these claims are countered by the participants' own commentaries on the normalizing procedures.[16] John Winthrop records that "the governour [Vane], and Mr. Cotton, and Mr. Wheelwright, and the two ruling elders of Boston, and the rest of that church, which were of any note, did none of them come to this meeting" in April 1637 to witness the ordination of Concord's ministers. Giving the lie to claims of Cotton's approval of and complicity with the emergent orthodoxy's regulation of such ceremonies, Winthrop shrewdly observed that Bostonians refused attendance "because they accounted these as legal preachers, and therefore would not give approbation to their ordination."[17]

Nor was 1637 the first time Bostonians had slighted these ministers. In the previous year, the elders of Concord took the first step in the long process of church formation. On July 5, 1636, Winthrop reports that Bulkeley and Jones "appointed this day to gather a church at Newtown, to settle at Concord. They sent word, three days before to the governour and deputy, to desire their presence; but they took it in ill part, and thought not fit to go." Governor Vane refused to attend this church gathering, as he avoided the ordination, ostensibly taking offense at some breach of protocol.[18] A surviving letter from John Cotton to Bulkeley and Jones reveals that he, too, declined the July ceremony. To be sure, Cotton's letter is apologetic, filled with assurances of loving support. Yet given Vane's refusal and Cotton's later absence at the ordination, his excuse that he was "restreyned by an vnexpected Occasion from Coming" to Newtown seems forced; his plea to Bulkeley, "Impute not I pray you my necessary Absence to voluntary Estrangement," perhaps less than candid.[19]

On March 31, 1637, a few days before his ordination, Bulkeley wrote to Cotton, informing him of the ceremony. Tension rides just beneath the surface of this seemingly cordial communiqué. Converting Cotton's complaint of the "want of brotherly love" into a lament for the disrespect he himself has suffered, Bulkeley observes:

> I doe confesse I haue found as ^little [love] toward myselfe^ here, as euer I did in any place that god brought me vnto. It is the place that I haue desired to shew loue vnto . . . and yett haue I found soe much

stangenes, alienation, and soe much neglect from some whoe would sometimes haue visited me with diverse myles going, (yett here, will passe by my dore, as ^if^ I were the man that they had not knowen) . . . that I haue sometimes maruelled where the cause of the change should be: whether in myselfe or in them.[20]

Begging Cotton "to lay aside all Jealousys" at the outset of this letter, Bulkeley concludes with a postscript informing Cotton of the ordination and soliciting his presence. In light of the prior truancy of the Bostonians, however, Bulkeley's addendum seems to anticipate disappointment: "if it be necessary to giue any other notice, to other persons or in another way, we would nott be wanting therein for auoyding of offence."

Yet, while the tone of the letter is deferential, the content was antagonistic. Raising again the relationship of justification to sanctification, the doctrine of assurance, and the explosive topic of Wheelwright's preaching, Bulkeley persisted in asserting his disagreement with Cotton: "There must be some difference betwixt Christ righteousness, and that which dothe manifest it unto me as mine. but those 2 yow seeme to confonde." His hope "that we may all thinke and speake the same thing" proved less a prayer for unity than a plan for coercion. And, while Cotton seemed to have the upper hand in April of 1637, the tables quickly turned.[21]

Little wonder, with such precedents, that the Boston congregation walked out of Wilson's sermons, "contemptuously turning their backs upon the faithfull Pastor." Nor is it remarkable that they questioned local ministers after their sermons about points of faith, or that the intransigent conservative Thomas Weld should characterize such inquiries as "halfe a dozen Pistols discharged at the face of the Preachers"—Wilson among them. The Boston spiritists' refusal to fight in the Pequot campaign is made more comprehensible when one registers that the disliked Wilson had been named pastor to the troops.[22] In this climate of revolt, it is not surprising that radicals like Hutchinson felt free to accuse local clergy of preaching a doctrine of works. What they did not anticipate was the fury and fullness with which their opponents would eliminate their opposition.

On January 19, 1637, at Cotton's invitation, John Wheelwright mounted Boston's pulpit to preach the sermon that became central to the final confrontation in the November trials. He instructed the ready auditors to "prepare for a spirituall combate," to "contend for the faith once delivered to the saynts," even if so doing "cause a combustion in the Church and common wealth."[23] Though the weapons were to be spiritual ones *only*, the "orthodoxy"—recalling the violence of Munster and perhaps anticipating the zeal of English radicals a few years hence—feared open rebellion. As Winthrop nervously observed, "In every place we find that the contentions began first by disputations and Sermons, and when the minds of the people were once set on fire by reproachfull termes of incendiary spirits, they soone set to blowes, and had alwayes a tragicall and bloudy issue."[24] In March, 1637, the General Court charged Wheelwright with sedition; in November he was banished as an enemy to the commonwealth. That same November Anne Hutchinson, Wheelwright's sister-in-law and a learned exponent of spiritist piety, was called to Court to answer for her opinions. After a dramatic exchange with Winthrop and the clerics, she, along with her followers, was also banished. Opposition would now be practiced in secret or in exile, as the emergent orthodoxy took steps to outlaw overt expressions of dissent.

Cataloging these familiar events reminds the modern reader of a tenet that no Puritan could accept: structures of orthodoxy are polemically constructed. Throughout the early period in New England, these rival versions of the "true faith" at times cohabited peacefully, accommodating each other through a series of shifting compromises. In 1636, however, the right to define normative belief became hotly contested. Rehearsing the events of 1636–1638 discovers a Puritanism divided within itself.

❧

Central to this internal struggle were issues springing directly from Roger Williams's second riddle, which asked "why is it, since God worketh freely in us to do and to will of his own good pleasure, that yet he is pleased to command us to work out our own salvation with fear and trembling?"[25] This Pauline riddle energized Reformation theology, framing the paradoxical relationship between justification and sanctification, election and merit, God's free pleasure and human response.

Not everyone resolved this theological puzzle in the same way, however, and the solution reached by Boston's First Church divided it from the rest of the Bay. Whether the crucial issue of the controversy involved the nature and effects of grace, the doctrine of assurance, the efficacy of preparation, the order of salvation, or the nature of the covenant is still debated.[26] But regardless of how *the* central issue is defined, the fevered pitch of events confirms that these questions were argued for mortal and immortal stakes. The conflicts revealed that Cotton, Wheelwright, and Davenport preached a doctrine of salvation opposed to that of most of the ministers of the Bay, including Wilson, Hooker, Shepard, Bulkeley, and Hugh Peter.[27] The first public articulation of differences began in early 1636, when

John Cotton was forced into a dialogue with other ministers of the Bay, most notably Shepard and Bulkeley, on the whole range of these issues. While all Puritans allowed that the saint prepares the heart for Christ, disagreements emerged over the order of salvation, the relationship between preparation and assurance, God's complete prevenience and the efficacy of human cooperation, and the nature of God's covenantal promise. Though each of these topics will be fully examined in the chapters to follow, for clarity's sake I will briefly sketch the major points of difference here.

As set forth by Hooker and Shepard, preparationism presupposed the seeds of faith and therefore some degree of human cooperation or initiative *before* God's full imputation of merit, the moment of justification. This issue turned on whether or not God acted by absolute or conditional promises—in other words, whether grace was bestowed directly and immediately, without the mediation of church ordinances to *remake* the soul, or whether God always worked mediately, through the created order, to *restore* human holiness by degrees. Implicitly this involved the choice of biblical models—whether the saint was restored to the image of Adam before the Fall or was utterly reconstituted into a new Christic likeness. In terms of covenantal doctrine, the question was whether faith precedes or results from union with the Holy Spirit—that is, whether understanding of the covenant somehow filtered through an Adamic lens of reciprocity or rested on a conception of a free *testament* in which the individual depends solely on God's action.[28]

Though they began by arguing that faith was the fruit of grace already received, by 1636 nearly every minister of the Bay insisted on the conditionality of God's promise, advocating some form of prior preparation. They argued that God gradually bestowed his grace, usually through the ordinary means of the ministry. In this process the saint must undergo a period of humiliation that culminates in a true sight of sin before the heart is readied for the reception of saving faith. No minor felon or disobedient child, as frequently described by Cotton, the human being here was often figured as a "vile creature" who deserved nothing but eternal torment. As Thomas Shepard declared to his auditors: "wonder then at God's patience, that thou livest one day longer, who hast all thy lifetime, like a filthy toad, spit thy venom in the face of God." For the preparationists, sin was an active presence, a blot on the human heart that had to be removed before Christ could consent to enter.[29] Conviction of sin under the Law was an essential prerequisite to reception of the "good news" of grace under the Gospel.

This was an outlook and a depiction that Cotton consistently modified. To his mind, sin was an absence of good rather than active malignity—in true Augustinian fashion, evil was privative. Drawing on Canticles, Cotton counseled the auditor to wait like an eager bride for the moment when Christ would "be-sprinkle you with the blessing of his grace"; to attend the moment when this gentle Bridegroom would come to "the bed of loves" and shed "the seeds of his grace . . . abroad in your hearts." Cotton's auditor resembled no lowly washerwoman scrubbing a filthy rag of a heart. Instead, like the Shulamite, Cotton's saint was the comely bride waiting for the pleasures of union. More mundanely stated, Cotton believed there are no "steps to the altar," that the soul was passive until the moment that grace was infused.[30]

While not disallowing divine influence through mediate causes, Cotton insisted on preserving an aspect of what had been orthodox teaching but that the other ministers now refused to admit: the possibility of God's immediate regeneration of even the most sinful soul.[31] Even in his most preparatory sermons, in which the injunctions to "labor to bring your heart to godly sorrow" sounded like utterances more characteristic of Hooker, John Cotton insisted that "the ignorance and scornfulnesse of carnall hearts doth not, nay cannot hinder the Lord, from piercing or pricking them."[32]

This insistence on God's immediate and arbitrary action undermined the assertion of *necessary* preparation upon which the other ministers increasingly based their conception of the *ordo salutis*. And they were in some measure correct to claim that Cotton's prescription left no room either for an effective process of mediation or for an ordered soteriology. Cotton's conception of grace as a new perception or sensibility, a new relish for divine things, really could not be reconciled with the gradualist processes of preparationism or with the conception of regeneration as a new ability. Although these were differences of emphasis rather than of kind, they became increasingly significant in the 1630s.

In the end, Cotton compromised on some issues and became circumspect and judicious in his articulation of others. Though he could have avoided such measures by retreating to Davenport's New Haven, Cotton remained committed to reform within the Bay Colony. As in England, he took the necessary measures to retain his pulpit and his influence. He never retreated, however, from an insistence on grace as a new aesthetic and spiritual sense passively infused; nor did he abandon his commitment to the church international. This last concern, in fact, may have determined him to stay in Boston in the aftermath of the controversy, just as it served in 1668 to recall John Davenport to Massachusetts on a mission to reform the churches of New England. Thomas Shepard bears witness to Cotton's intransigence on the essential issues of the controversy, observing with exasperation, "Mr. Cotton repents not, but is hid only."[33] Along with Cotton, Henry Vane, John Davenport, John Wheelwright, and (one suspects) the majority of the Boston congregation remained unrepentant.

It must be stressed that Cotton's party was not at all unorthodox, much less "heretical," on the major points of disagreement, in so far as that term is meant to measure deviation from doctrines sanctioned by prior exposition within the Reformed tradition. Cotton was a high Calvinist, just as Hooker articulated doctrines sanctioned by William Perkins and William Ames. In this sense, Cotton and his opponents were equally "orthodox."[34]

Just as English high churchmen in earlier decades found in *puritanism* a covering term for a multitude of sins, so the term *antinomian* became a label by which the conservative clergy in America sought to proscribe the opinions of their opponents, exiling them beyond the bounds of acceptability. Indeed, Cotton's model of conversion was rooted in Lutheran and Calvinist texts; only by linking these doctrines to the more obviously radical opinions of his followers could Cotton's theology be impugned. Only when Anne Hutchinson confessed faith in direct revelation and defended the opinion known as mortalism was the Synod able to find sufficient grounds for censure.[35]

Yet the preparationist opposition was also operating from within the framework of orthodoxy as received opinion. Just as the label *antinomian* functioned as a broad brush for tarring the Cottonians, so the accusation of proto-Arminianism, of preaching a covenant of works, was strategically leveled against men like Wilson and Hooker. The modification of high Calvinism inherent in their assertion of conditional promises and the doctrine of preparation were adaptations made within the boundaries of traditionally defined Reformation "orthodoxy." Patrick Collinson has asserted that "the theological achievement of the Puritans, from William Perkins onwards, can be roughly interpreted as the adaptation and domestication of Calvinism to fit the condition of voluntary Christians."[36] This adaptation consisted largely in the evolution of the conditional covenant and, with it, the doctrine of preparationism.

The antinomian conflict, then, engaged two legitimate heirs of the magisterial reformers, two traditions which might have coexisted as orthodox*ies* within the commonwealth. But *orthodoxy* has a different meaning as a description of the processes that legitimate or establish normative structures of faith and expression, and the disputes of these years were less about discovering heresy than about establishing dominance. It is fair to say that before the controversy of 1636 there were at least two religious parties within the New England churches, each with an equal claim to legitimacy. Although many historians have noted a conservative drift in 1636, the degree to which this transformation represents not a weeding out of heretics but a violent redefinition of orthodoxy itself has not been appreciated.

❧

There was more at stake than doctrine in these years, however; battles were not fought over theological principles alone. Political parties formed around these issues and the 1636 controversy was not the only example of conflict. Even a cursory glance at the records reveals an informal partnership of interest and sympathy between competing political and clerical groups from these earliest days of settlement and continuing beyond the Antinomian Controversy itself. In 1636 the competition for hegemony in the Bay pitted the party of Winthrop and Wilson against that of Vane and Cotton, but these were not the only entanglements in the complex web of secular and sacred, political and theological allegiances.

Lines of division within the Puritan colony are visible almost from the outset—perhaps as early as the hotly contested debate over the location of the capital in 1632. This dispute, involving Thomas Dudley and Winthrop, seems to have been a forthright competition for political influence, uncomplicated by abstruse theological issues, dissociated from partisan structures within old English Puritanism, and resolved long before 1636. As the trial of Hutchinson would prove, Dudley was certainly no friend to the spiritists. Yet, in January 1636, when Henry Vane initiated his political war with Winthrop he courted an alliance with Dudley, invoking this old quarrel as a prehistory for what Vane diagnosed as a general divisiveness in the colony. At a meeting convened by Vane, Hugh Peter, and John Haynes, Winthrop was called to account for the early dispute, as well as for his general conduct as magistrate and governor. In his *History*, Winthrop insinuated that his opponents seized on his conflict with Dudley as a pretext for forming new allegiances in the Bay.[37]

Asked to testify about the earlier dispute, Dudley himself denied the validity of Vane's contentions about a continuing conflict, declaring that "he came thither a mere patient, not with any intent to charge his Brother Winthrop with any thing." Dudley reported that "though there had been formerly some differences and breaches between them, yet they had been healed, and, for his part, he was not willing to renew them again." Nonetheless, Vane claimed to discern ancient causes for the present "distraction in the commonwealth," for hostilities that seemed to arise "from some difference in judgment, and withal some alienation of affection among the magistrates and some other persons of quality." Implicitly, Winthrop stood accused of maleficence. The upshot was a public examination of Winthrop's policies, which were condemned for "over much lenity and remissness." Like John Wilson, Winthrop was publicly humiliated at the hands of Vane's coalition, a slight that discovered ancient enmity and fueled new animus.[38]

Thus, sometime before Shepard began his informal interrogation of Cotton or the points of so-called heresy were enumerated against Hutchinson, "factions began to grow among the people," factions supposedly rooted in ancient divisions.[39] The discontent may have animated other seemingly tangential disputes, particularly those involving struggles over the planting of new colonies. As Perry Miller first suggested, resentment against the leadership of Winthrop, Vane, and Cotton may well have been the motive force behind Haynes's and Hooker's migration to Connecticut. Haynes's discontent with Winthrop is suggested by his participation in the public censure described above. His departure followed upon Vane's election to governor in 1636. And the record bears ample testimony to Hooker's dismay in discovering "the great influence which Mr. Cotton had in the colony" and to his subsequent refusal to compete with this other theological "star" who was offered the premier pulpit in New England. Thomas Hutchinson declares flatly that these reasons "inclined Mr. Hooker and his friends to remove to some place more remote from Boston than Newtown." Though Cotton and Vane proved the nominal victors in this first struggle, Hooker was to return to the Bay in 1637 as Winthrop's ally, joining forces with his future son-in-law, Thomas Shepard, to head the Synod that unseated Cotton and scapegoated Hutchinson.[40]

The founding of New Haven Colony was similarly enmeshed in the theo-political divisions of these years. By 1637 John Davenport and his mentor Theophilis Eaton found insufficient room either for their brand of pietism or for the exercise of economic or political power in a colony now dominated by the new alliance of Winthrop with Wilson, Shepard, and, at some remove, Thomas Hooker. Davenport's and Eaton's departure to New Haven came in the immediate aftermath of the Synod in which Davenport steadfastly stood by Cotton and tried to draw Hutchinson to a moderated position. His colony would indeed prove a haven for radicals—Cotton considered removal to the plantation in 1637–38, and it later provided shelter for the regicides Edward Whalley and William Goffe.[41]

But as the events of the late 1630s were to show, not all opponents of the New England Way as defined by the Winthrop/Shepard party undertook to resolve their differences by migration. Many dissenters decided to stand their ground, to fight Wheelwright's spiritual war on Massachusetts soil. Hutchinson, John Coggeshall, William Coddington—indeed many of the most prominent citizens and merchants of the Bay—were determined to make their objections heard.[42] This open opposition was made nearly impossible, however, by the swift and thorough measures taken by the Winthrop party. The strength and popular appeal of the "antinomians" is suggestively attested by the extensive measures taken to thwart them.

In the heated climate of the controversy, "orthodox" magistrates were initially cautious in exercising their power, aware of potential schisms within the Court itself. In the March 1637 session, for example, Winthrop reported that "when any matter about these new opinions was mentioned, the court was divided," but he reassuringly concluded "yet the greater number far were sound." This "sound" majority commanded sufficient votes to revisit the earlier condemnation of Wilson's "sad speech" delivered at the December session, declaring it "to have been seasonable advice." Nonetheless, the magistrates apparently remained fearful of reprisals from their local congregations. They were vividly aware of the Boston church's near censure of Wilson.[43]

Before they felt free to proceed, therefore, officers of the Court drafted official measures to protect themselves from the public questioning visited on Wilson and earlier on Winthrop at the hands of Vane. Remarkably, the Bay ministers agreed to limit their own clerical prerogatives in order to empower the magistrates in these actions. To protect Winthrop and encourage others in proceeding against the dissenters, these ministers yielded to "the authority of the court in [two] things concerning the churches": "that no member of the court ought to be publickly questioned by a church for any speech in the court"; and "in all such heresies . . . as are manifest and dangerous to the state, the court may proceed without tarrying for the church." The general wording and broad application of this measure suggest that other magistrates felt the need of such protection, but more particularly it allowed John Winthrop to denounce and even to prosecute the spiritists in his own congregation without fear of church censure. The immediate consequence was the Court's condemnation of Wheelwright's January fast-day sermon, which supposedly "tend[ed] to sedition." Not surprisingly, Winthrop reports there was "much heat of contention . . . between the opposite parties" within the Court over the issue of Wheelwright's guilt. Nor was it unexpected that the "highly offended" Boston church later tried to "have [Winthrop] called to account" for his part in these actions. Due to the concessions made by the ministers, however, the Bostonians were thwarted in the attempted discipline of Winthrop.[44]

The popular appeal of Cottonian piety within the churches may be gauged indirectly by considering the trepidation displayed by the magistrates in acting against the dissenters. Throughout the first years of colonization, magistrate and minister alike had puzzled over the proper balance between church and state, each jealously guarding his own preserve. That the ministers willingly sacrificed hard-won prerogatives in order to secure the Cottonians' defeat testifies to the magnitude of their anxiety. For an extraordinary moment, "orthodox" ministers were willing to side with "sound" magistrates against fellow clerics and against their own congregations.

Thus safeguarded, the magistrates quickly moved against the Cottonian opposition, establishing their dominance and constructing additional institutional structures to protect their authority.[45] The means by which they achieved control remain somewhat mysterious; the staging of the May 1637 election in which Winthrop supplanted Vane as governor provides a case in point. Over Governor Vane's objections, Winthrop's "sound majority" voted in the March session to move the elections from Cotton's Boston to Newtown, where Shepard held sway. Here as elsewhere, the scholar seeking fuller explanation for such actions is thwarted by curious omissions and frustrating silences in the official records.[46]

However the change of venue was managed, the election gave the advantage to the Winthrop faction and infuriated the Cottonians. Since Harvard was to become an arm of the emergent orthodoxy, it seems fitting that when the freemen gathered on Cambridge Common to cast their votes, they spilled over into "what, a year later, became the College Yard." It is reported that the once humiliated Wilson "'in his zeal gat up upon the bough of a tree' and harangued the multitude" into submission.[47] So often smoothing the rough edges of events, Winthrop here recorded the full drama of this civil revolt: "There was great danger of a tumult that day; for those of that side grew into fierce speeches, and some laid hands on others; but seeing themselves too weak, they grew quiet."[48]

Vane's ouster as governor signaled the defeat of the Cottonian party, politically and theologically. In high-handed fashion, the Winthrop Court subsequently refused to recognize Boston's legitimate representatives, Vane and Coddington. After the determined Bostonians elected them a second time, though, "the court not finding how they might reject them, they were admitted."[49] This seeming concession was short-lived, however. By

November the Winthrop Court again dismissed three of Boston's elected deputies—Aspinwall, Coggeshall, and Coddington. Resisting these usurpations, the outraged freemen planned to "send the same Deputies which the Court have rejected," but an increasingly wary John Cotton realized there would be consequences for what was sure to be regarded as "rash and contemptuous behaviour." He persuaded his followers to select new candidates, but the now confident magistrates saw fit to reject even one of these alternates. Disheartened or perhaps defiant, the spirited Bostonians refused to send another candidate to the Court. Thus, within the legislative body of the colony, the newly empowered Winthrop party insured its hegemony by an extralegal exclusion of opposition.[50]

Immediately following their May victory, the leaders of the emergent orthodoxy consolidated power by a number of means. Their first tactic for subverting oppositional strength was to impose restrictions on settlement. As both Wheelwright and Vane protested, this new law imposed "a penalty upon all such as should retain any, &c. above three weeks, which should not be allowed by some of the magistrates," thus insuring that all newcomers receive the approval of the Winthrop Court before being allowed to settle in the Bay. As Winthrop admitted, "it was very probable that [the dissenters] expected many of their opinion to come out of England."[51] The law was intended to inhibit the very immigrants Cotton had invited to New England to contend for the faith!

Understandably, Bostonians challenged the justice of these restrictions, but to no avail. With full confidence in his power, Winthrop dismissed objections that "this law was made of purpose to keep away such as are of Mr. Wheelwright's judgment" with the disingenuous query "(admit it were so which yet I cannot confess,) where is the evil of it?" Asserting the new Court's prerogative to determine right opinion, he argued: "If we conceive and find by sad experience that his opinions [are] such as will cause divisions, and make people look at their magistrates, ministers, and brethren as enemies to Christ and Antichrists, &c. were it not a sin . . . to receive more of those opinions, which we already find the evil fruit of"? And indeed, mere acquaintance with Wheelwright proved sufficient cause for exclusion from the colony.[52]

To further insure their dominance, the "orthodox" ministers convened a synod in August 1637 to discuss and dismiss alternative views. Winthrop reports that while Wheelwright resisted the advice of the ministers, Cotton came to agreement on several of the key points of difference—an observation that must be modified in light of Cotton's continued support for Hutchinson and his unrepentant commitment to the spiritist understanding of the *ordo salutis*. Whether agreement was reached may be debatable, but the concrete measures established by the synod were unambiguous assertions of power. Lay assemblies and women's meetings were restricted, public questioning of ministers banned, and mechanisms for disciplining dissenters were strengthened.[53]

These measures proved ineffective in quelling the spiritist movement, however, prompting the General Court to institute formal proceedings against Wheelwright, Hutchinson, and the Bostonians who supported them. Determining that "two so opposite parties could not [continue] in the same body, without apparent hazard of ruin to the whole," the Winthrop Court determined on November 2, 1637, to "send away some of the principal." The petition tendered in support of Wheelwright some eight months before (to the different constituency of the March Court) served as the "fair opportunity" for this unprecedented exiling of the dissenters. Stigmatized as antinomians, opponents to the emergent orthodoxy were dispersed—some were disfranchised and disarmed; many were banished. In what amounted to a coup, the Winthrop party thus guaranteed against their possible ouster by election or by violence.[54] Truly extraordinary by any standard, these tactics of exiling the opposition, restricting new settlement, and limiting eligibility for public office to those residing in the Bay for at least one year (meaning that only survivors of this partisan scrutiny would be allowed the privileges of freemanship) insured that the party elected in 1637 would hold power for a good time to come.

Nor were outright exiles like Hutchinson and Vane the only ones to feel the bitter sting of this policy. Years later, in a text designed to smooth the still rough edges of controversy, Cotton nonetheless felt compelled to register his opposition to these measures. In "The Way of the Congregational Churches Cleared" he admits that the high-handed restrictions nearly forced his own removal from the Bay, because he saw clearly that "by this means, we should receive no more members into our church, but such as must profess themselves of a contrary judgment to what I believed to be a truth."[55]

Yet Cotton was able to ride out the storm, abandoning his plan for removal to New Haven. With his political ally Henry Vane "outed" and with Winthrop now firmly aligned with Shepard and Wilson, Cotton recognized the vulnerability of his position and of his hopes for church reform. Wisely, he retreated in order to salvage what he could of those hopes. As Sargent Bush has recently argued, in the aftermath of the controversy Cotton tutored Wheelwright on the wisdom of strategic self-revisions. Cotton's advice was that Wheelwright repent his want of discretion in order to appease the Court, leaving differences of doctrine unspoken.[56] As in Old England, outward compliance could secure an essential freedom of opinion. Though Wheelwright was too headstrong to take heed, by these means Cotton kept his pulpit, chastening his rhetoric without revising the substance of his own doctrine.

In light of these oppressive measures, Winthrop's condemnation of Anne Hutchinson for violating the commandment to "honor thy father and mother" in her acts of civil disobedience takes on a special irony. Since compliance could not be secured by this attempt to naturalize their authority, these "fathers of the commonwealth" resorted to extralegal seizure of power. They could exercise little claim to her filial loyalty.[57]

Yet, despite the Court's high-handed measures and the decimation of their numbers by voluntary and forced migration, a radical party persisted in feeling and expressing themselves in opposition to the new regime. Though Cotton's strategic advice to exercise discretion suggests that the archive of the "official" culture would contain fewer and more modest expressions of dissent in subsequent years, the strength of the opposition within the Bay after the expulsion of Hutchinson may be deduced from the reflected anxiety of the orthodoxy itself. Throughout the 1640s Shepard, Bulkeley, and others produced a barrage of sermons and treatises to counteract radical opinion. These texts express continued fear of "the fickle minds of a heady multitude," "exceeding apt to be led . . . by lures, & golden pretenses which Innovators ever have." Shepard voiced this worry in an election sermon of 1638; it was still being rehearsed in 1650 by Peter Bulkeley. In a letter to none other than John Cotton, Bulkeley condemned the "heady or headless multitude," who have "too much liberty and power . . . which they are too weak to manage, many growing conceited, proud, arrogant, self-sufficient, as wanting nothing." These charges are similar to the ones lodged against the enthusiasts of 1636. One suspects that what they "wanted" in Bulkeley's judgment was the discipline of an orthodox clergy.[58] Bulkeley's *Gospel-Covenant* insisted on the points of doctrine that could provide such training—the conditional covenant and an elaborated preparationism.

The victory over Cottonian piety was never complete. Resistance to the new orthodoxy continued into the 1650s and 1660s as quarrels over the founding of new institutions like Harvard College and Boston's Third Church, as well as in opposition to doctrinal innovations like the Half-Way Covenant.[59] In 1668 John Davenport returned to Boston to contest what he saw as the apostasy of New England and the final erosion of a utopia of free grace and a pure church of saints. Launching a full assault on the

Half-Way Covenant measures, he commanded the loyalty of stalwart congregants who still yearned for an earlier pietism and railed against the pastoral discipline of the standing orthodoxy.[60] In short, it is no exaggeration to hold that, although "Orthodoxy in Massachusetts" was defined in these years, this definition failed to reflect a full consensus among the ministers or the laity. Rather it was a hard-won status, always partial, ceaselessly contested.

It would be hard to overestimate the importance of the party alignments of the 1630s; indeed the history of the commonwealth in these years must be written as the attempted suppression of the spiritual radicalism originating in the Boston congregation—in large measure this is Winthrop's own version of the first decades of settlement. Yet his account insists that this radicalism was a form of heresy, a characterization by no means as accurate as it was expedient. Theological "correctness" was not the only or perhaps even the central issue at stake in this controversy. The preceding discussion only hints at the degree to which religious ideas emerged from distinctive social networks, were wedded to specific political ideologies and programs, and were expressed in unique stylistic modes. In a real sense worlds—or world views—collided in 1636. To be sure, religion was at the heart of New England life and of the contentions of these decades; but the debates about divine essence and human nature, about the underlying meaning of history and the constitution of the church in the world, involved larger questions than doctrine alone could embrace. Personal allegiances, political affiliations, convictions about the self and society, utopian ideals, and practical politics were enmeshed in the events here described.

⚘

I have begun with the Antinomian Controversy as a proof and illustration of the radical division within the New England mind from the outset, one that had a prehistory in England. Only in hindsight does the outcome of the antinomian dispute seem inevitable, the contours of orthodoxy foreordained. This controversy brings into focus a subset of party divisions within the spectrum of moderate Puritanism, traceable in lines of allegiance that thread across the Atlantic, predating the Great Migration by a decade or more. These heretofore unremarked connections comprise a nexus of two groups linked by personal, social, and political bonds—believers united by common principles of piety and of sensibility.

The first group, which became the ruling orthodoxy in New England, was composed of those men who adamantly preached the necessity of

preparation and the usefulness of sanctification as an evidence of faith—
Hooker, Shepard, Wilson, Bulkeley, Winthrop, and most of the ministers
of the Bay. These "Intellectual Fathers" of American church polity looked
to William Perkins and most especially to William Ames as their theological authorities.

The second group, the "Spiritual Brethren," encompassed Cotton, Davenport, Wheelwright, Eaton, and Vane in New England. These men found
a spiritual and temperamental home in the so-called Cambridge circle in
Old England, where John Preston and most importantly Richard Sibbes
presided.

In Old England, confrontation with the more tangible threats of Ca-
tholicism and high Anglicanism had safeguarded the communion of saints;
under extreme external pressures, differences remained nuances of temperament and thought within the framework of a more cohesive Puritanism.[61] But in New England, in the absence of external opponents, these
divisions became visible and volatile. If, as many have suggested, New
England was a laboratory of pure Puritanism, it was precisely because it
provided the place where latent internal stresses within the movement
became manifest in the very incarnation of a Bible commonwealth. The
splintering that occurred in New England in the 1630s adumbrated divisions that would emerge in Old England when the victories of the Civil
War removed the threat posed by high churchmen. As with the golden
bowl of Henry James, there was an almost invisible fissure, a division
within Puritanism, which held together for a time. But when external
pressures no longer forced cohesion, there came an inevitable shattering, a
division of sensibilities.

In New England this shattering came with the Antinomian Controversy.
The drama of the moment made manifest and to some extent produced
differences that had been only half sensed; now the participants realized
the divide between them.[62] Hitherto, men like Cotton had phrased their
opinions—almost—in the language of what was to become the dominant
group; they presumed some degree of essential agreement. Kai Erikson has
said that "the deviant and the conformist . . . are creatures of the same
culture, inventions of the same imagination."[63] How much more true was
this observation for Cotton's alternative stance within the Puritan social
order; how much more applicable to a religious ideology rooted in like
principles but variant in their exfoliation.

A concept of essential difference within seeming similarity helps to
elucidate the power of the monolithic or consensus model that Miller and
other historians have adopted. For it is true that from one perspective—as

the proponents of this model have urged—the differences that separated the parties in New England are far fewer and in some ways less important than the broad range of issues on which they agreed. On man's depravity, on God's transcendence, and on the primacy of the doctrines of *sola scriptura* and *sola fides*, the clergy of New England spoke with a single voice—the voice of the Reformed theologians. For decades men like Hooker and Cotton had joined in a common struggle to define and refine the tenets of the Reformation, to rephrase them in an English tongue. Common sense and experience confirm that this deeply shared struggle to forge a local idiom of religious experience produced an overlapping of tenets, and more importantly, of terminology. Nevertheless, this overlapping has obscured real and significant differences of judgment. Though Hooker and Cotton both spoke of God's *covenant*, Hooker's contract was not the same as Cotton's testament.[64] And the modifications of God's sovereignty into rational structures on the one hand, into affective modes on the other, chart real and significant differences in religious sensibility.

Although these differences were as much matters of tone and sensibility as of doctrine, by 1636 they could no longer be ignored. Nor could they be easily reconciled or rooted out. Cotton must have been astonished by his opponents' implacability, shocked to discover he had almost as much to fear from the Boston Synod as he ever had from the Star Chamber. Similarly, Hooker and Shepard must have been disheartened—indeed outraged—to discover what a tenacious hold Cottonian piety had on the hearts of New England saints. Despite all their efforts to weed it out, this oppositional religion flowered again and again. Indeed its resilience may be precisely due to their shared principles, to Cotton's phrasing of resistance in nearly the same language of orthodoxy. His proved a far more difficult religious ideology to banish from the life of the culture than those more easily defined and therefore discredited opinions of so-called deviants. It is possible that Cottonian piety proved a more effective counter-voice because it could simulate outer agreement while in important ways remaining substantively other. Rather than merely consolidating orthodoxy as sectarian groups have been shown to do, this oppositional mode of piety may have proved a ground from which to challenge orthodoxy from within—may have provided a language to articulate the experience of feeling "other."[65]

In constructing my alternative genealogy, I take to heart Emily Dickinson's observation that it is in "internal difference, / Where the Meanings, are—"[66] Despite the vast contours of shared doctrine, there were internal differences in what our critics have described as the New England mind and the American self—differences that cut to the heart and divided that mind. Though men like Cotton and Hooker read the same Bible, they fetched different treasures from its leaves. When they looked upward they did not see the same God; when they looked inward they did not see the same creature. Covenant, grace, telos, communitas, had a different taste on the tongue, a different claim on the heart of these first preparationists and pietists. Sorting out these differences became the work of the first decades of settlement in America. And in large measure, the outcome of this process was wholly unanticipated. For, as the next chapter will show, the victory of the preparationists overturned patterns of dominance that had been established in Old England.

2

❦

Societies of Saints

Nor is it to be doubted but that there have been many famous
in their Generations, whose Memories are buried in the dust.

Increase Mather

S piritual Brethren" and "Intellectual Fathers"—names adapted from
William Haller—are the descriptive titles I have given to the circles
of Sibbes and Ames, respectively. Along with such terms as *preparationist*
and *spiritist,* these familial metaphors suggest the differences between the
two groups while still acknowledging their membership in the larger
Protestant fellowship. All of these preachers belonged to the Puritan
household, yet they also gathered into more particular and intimate group-
ings. This chapter will explore the personal and professional ties that
united the ministers and project a speculative genealogy for these two
Puritan clans.

An initial caveat is in order. In constructing this genealogy, I do not
mean to exclude the possibility—indeed the reality—of affiliations and
affections that complicate easy division along party lines. Exile in the
Netherlands, for example, provided preachers like Hooker and Davenport
with a shared past. Similarly, the timing of emigration may have established a certain like-mindedness among such men as Cotton and Hooker,
distinguishing them from dissenters who migrated a few years later.[1]
Moreover, the decision to flee to America rather than stay in England or
choose a nearer exile in the Netherlands defines an important difference
within the groups, one that has underwritten histories based on national
identities.

During the agonized premigration period there were numerous associations across party lines that problematize drawing firm boundaries. And
just as threats from the high churchmen produced a united Puritan front
in the premigration period, so the proliferation of radical sectaries and

theological liberals provoked consolidation of the Puritan center in the 1650s.[2] These coalitions witness a general concordance within the Puritan movement; recognition of that consensus must precede any evaluation of internal differences. My purpose is not to discredit consensus readings, but to supplement them with an interpretation that registers diversity.

I argue that general agreement on fundamental issues neither obviated the experience and expression of difference between the Amesians and Sibbesians, nor did it diminish their sense of allegiance within their chosen group. Since mine is primarily a literary history of the affections, the interest of this volume is in mapping the ideational structures and rhetorical signatures of these two groups. Yet there were more tangible marks of this affinity, registered in pastoral and political practices, personal and social networks, and the general patterning of professional careers. This chapter will briefly suggest the possibility of an alternative social history, first by tracing some of the modes of affiliation and then by reconstructing the exemplary career pattern for each group.

One way of suggesting the differences between Sibbesians and Amesians would be to adopt and adapt classic formulations of difference. Just as the Spiritual Brethren more closely fit the model of Augustinian piety articulated in Perry Miller's opening of the *New England Mind*, so too they conform to Peter Lake's portrait of moderate Puritans of an earlier generation.[3]

Flexible on issues of nonconformity in the interests of an uninterrupted ministry and persuaded above all of the importance of the word preached to a gathering of believers, the Spiritual Brethren more often adopted a moderate stance on questions of ecclesiastical discipline. Their commitment was to the affective dimensions of piety, and in general they aspired to a more egalitarian community formed by preachers and saints. Early in their university careers, preachers like Cotton and Preston recognized their common cause with moderates like Sibbes and Laurence Chaderton.

Since they placed as much value on the international community of saints as on local congregational purity, the Brethren were often willing to hedge on minor issues of conformity. Committed to fighting larger battles against the Catholic "menace," they became pragmatic and tactical in their programs for reform. Throughout their careers these men were willing to be both "in and out of the game," willing to disguise their nonconformity in order to remain active in the church. Except in the extreme instance, pulpit was never to be sacrificed to polity. In general, they were more fortunate in their enjoyment of powerful patrons and benevolent episcopal administrations.

These issues were important to the Intellectual Fathers, but their own emphasis rested on other aspects of religious life. Generally conforming to Miller's portrait of preparationist piety, these ministers also fit more comfortably with Lake's description of radical nonconformists.[4] Less flexible on issues of ecclesiology and formal purity, these men often chose suspension from preaching before yielding on polity. Many were denied pulpits, silenced, or exiled early in their careers; some went to the Low Countries, many found their way to New England.

While the gathering of saints was part of their utopian aspiration, they focused on local congregations rather than on the church international. More often than the Cambridge Brethren, the Amesians were subjected to the scrutiny of exacting churchmen in their local region. The misfortunes of these preachers had impressed them with a greater sense of hierarchy—social and churchly—as evidence of God's organizing hand. Accordingly, their emphasis on the pedagogy of preparationism distinguished them from their auditors, marking that relationship as more paternal than fraternal.

With respect to typical career patterns within each group, the obvious observation is also an essential one—despite their nonconformity, nearly every member of the Cambridge circle managed to occupy and retain highly visible and influential pulpits for a longer period of time. They fit the classic pattern of moderate Puritans of an earlier generation who hoped to maintain both Puritan principles and churchly power through the fine arts of compromise, seeming conformity, and/or secrecy.

The Intellectual Fathers, by contrast, subscribed to a more radical program of Puritan reform, standing their ground ideologically but often forced to cede it literally. Unwilling to conform or to dissemble, they had difficulty securing pulpits and were suspended earlier (sometimes by several years). These preachers remained loyal reformers of the English Church, steadfastly resisting the lure of separatist ideology despite years of persecution. Yet, their rejections of moderate accommodationism as a tactic effectively placed them out of church office. They learned early on that expulsion was the bitter fruit of a too scrupulous loyalty to formal purity. Exiled, Amesians found alternative ways to disseminate their doctrine; publishing often became an important part of their ministry. While the Cambridge preachers emphasized the efficacy of the word preached, Amesians argued that the imperative of hearing the word could be as easily achieved through circulation of printed texts.

Scholarly celebrations of the power and influence of Ames and his disciples have obscured the degree to which they suffered personal defeat in Old England. As ecclesiastical radicals, early on they found themselves targets of intransigents like Laud; they became marginal men in an already marginal movement. Their status was made all the more poignant by the comparative success of the Sibbesians. Indeed, the Cambridge Brethren occupied a more central place in the religious life of the English saints—an observation that makes the preparationist victories of the 1630s all the more remarkable. The surprise for students of American Puritanism is that the history of first plantation involves a tale of status reversal in which the less powerful became dominant, as Sibbesians were forced to yield their traditional privilege to the emergent preparationist orthodoxy.

Though many scholars have retraced the Amesian network, less effort has been made to discover the thick web of associations binding the Cambridge divines. Moreover, since it is so often assumed that all these preachers held identical positions on questions of nonconformity and church polity, important differences of affiliation remain unexamined. This chapter will map these divergences first by tracing some of the personal and professional allegiances that constituted partisan identity; second, by analyzing individual careers to establish the latent yet paradigmatic professional patterns that mark the two groups. The scope of the chapter must be modest; the interested reader is referred to the wealth of biographical and historical studies that document the cultural context of the period. My aim is to identify exemplary instances rather than to attempt an exhaustive group biography.

❧

Cotton Mather reported that his grandfather's veneration for Richard Sibbes was so "particular and perpetual" that "it caused him to have the *picture* of that Great Man, in that part of his house, where he might oftenest look upon it." John Cotton's affection was requited: his biographer, John Norton, reported that he was "answerably beloved" by Sibbes.[5] Begun in the early days of Cotton's university career, this friendship proved a powerful, lifelong influence. Far from espousing a singular theology, John Cotton spoke from within a community of like-minded preachers and friends, among whom Sibbes figured prominently.

As was often the case, this affinity was discovered in Cotton's experience of conversion, when his "singular and constant love of Doctor Sibbs" was born.[6] Susceptibility to a particular style of preaching often reflected latent religious sympathies. Indeed, the history of conversion becomes a first chapter in the prosopography of these two groups. While the preparation-ists characteristically experienced conversion as a protracted process, incre-mental and sometimes incomplete, the Brethren often seem to have ex-perienced a more dramatic transformation of the heart. Though they, too, suffered periods of spiritual doubt and anguish in the early phases of their conversion, the Brethren more often achieved an assurance that was full and complete.

Cotton's conversion narrative is instructive because it suggests an early sensitivity to these two experiential modes and expressive styles. As a young preacher and scholar at Emmanuel, Cotton struggled to suppress the first "motions and stirrings of his heart." Attributing this resistance to scholarly ambition, the fear that "if he became a *godly* man, 'twould spoil him for being a *learned* one," Cotton's biographers ignore a more plausible explanation—that he had not yet discovered the preacher who could melt his heart. In these years, Cotton was a resistant auditor of William Perkins. Legend has it that upon hearing Perkin's death bell Cotton was "secretly glad in his heart" to be rescued from a ministry that had troubled him but had never offered spiritual peace.[7]

One of the most influential and powerful preachers of his day and the catalyst for Ames's awakening, Perkins might justly be called the intellec-tual grandsire of the entire Amesian circle. His understanding of the covenant as both absolute and conditional, along with his doctrine of weak or temporary faith, provided a place for human activity in the order of salvation, establishing the foundations for preparationism. Though Perkins insisted on the doctrine of prevenience, he also allowed that moral behavior might serve as a preliminary sign of God's favor. Implicit in Perkins's sermons was the thin edge of legalism that Cotton was to contest in New England. It is understandable, then, that Cotton would resist his ministry. Though his sermons had "laid siege to and beleaguered his heart," they could not win Cotton for the church.[8]

After a long period of spiritual doubt, the word as preached by Sibbes turned Cotton's affections. Known as the "sweet dropper" and "honey-mouthed," Sibbes was considered the most effective converting preacher of his day.[9] Giles Firmin claimed that the hardened sinner "would not hear Dr. Sibbes, for fear he should convert him." John Dod described Sibbes's sermons as so "full of heavenly treasure" that weak Christians would find "their temptations answered, their fainting spirits revived, their understandings enlightened, and their graces confirmed."[10] This diagnosis proved accurate for Cotton.

According to Cotton Mather, a Sibbes sermon "wherein was discoursed the misery of those who had only a *negative righteousness,* or a civil, sober, honest *blamelessness* before men," first awakened Cotton's new spiritualism.[11] Though no Puritan would equate blamelessness before men with grace in God, Perkins's preaching apparently came too close for Cotton's comfort. He preferred Sibbes's stress on God's prevenience and on grace as a transformation of the heart. This change was evidenced by the saint's lively affections, by "a sweet relish in all divine truths . . . a spiritual taste, which the Spirit of God puts into the soul of his children."[12] For three years Cotton attended Sibbes's instruction, until at last he became sensible of the graciousness that "made him a thoroughly renewed Christian," filling him "with a sacred joy, which accompanied him unto the fulness of joy for ever."[13]

When next he preached at St. Mary's, Cotton witnessed his conversion to a surprised congregation. Abandoning the ornate rhetoric and learned allusions for which he was revered, Cotton spoke in the simple and affecting words of the Puritan plain style. Young John Preston, soon to emerge as one of the leaders of the 1620s, was immediately converted.[14] Having come with a scholar's relish of high oratory, Preston was instead "pierced at the heart" by Cotton's delivery of the spiritual lessons learned from Sibbes. Cotton thus became "*spiritual father* unto one of the greatest men of his age."[15] Preston discovered kinship with Sibbes as well, reverencing him "with a love that was something wonderful."[16]

From Richard Sibbes to John Cotton to John Preston—the converting Word was passed from mouth to mouth, heart to heart. These men formed a chain of believers joined in apostolic succession—one generation bringing forth the next in spiritual rebirth.[17] Along the way they supplied the church with succeeding generations of sympathetic preachers. By Cotton's agency John Owen was converted; Sibbes and Preston rescued Thomas Goodwin from his flirtation with Arminianism. These preachers exercised an equally formative influence on such New World luminaries as John Norton and Henry Vane. John Davenport, who joined Sibbes in many of his evangelical activities, regarded him as "a bosom friend."[18]

In Old England, their circle of friends and benefactors included most of the notable Puritans of the day. The Cambridge Brethren numbered among their patrons the Pembrokes, Veres, Conway, Warwick, Manchester, Say and Seale, Yelverton, Brooke, and briefly the king's own favorite, Buckingham.[19] Among their preaching contemporaries, Chaderton, Arthur Hildersam, Dod, Ussher, William Gouge, Philip Nye, Jeremiah Burroughs, and Simeon Ashe were counted intimates.[20] These names constitute a roll call of the most influential spiritual leaders of the prewar years, including many of those destined to dominate at Westminster. The Cambridge Brethren exercised more power and influence than other contingents within Puritanism; in large measure, they shaped the policy of moderate Puritans in the two decades preceding the rise of Laud.

The ties that joined these preachers extended over the years and across the Atlantic. Most were Emmanuel graduates, whose shared college years first established loyalty and like-mindedness among them. Of course, Emmanuel was home to Puritans of both groups; Cotton and Hooker were fellows at the same time. Yet, the Brethren seem to have established closer ties, and their friendships were regularly renewed.[21] When Cotton left Emmanuel in 1612, for example, Preston paid annual visits to his mentor's home until his own death in 1628.[22] The Brethren regularly corresponded, consulted on issues of church polity, collaborated on publications, helped each other find and retain preaching posts within an increasingly conservative and repressive church, and gathered together in political organizations designed to challenge and reform policies of church and state. Coming of age in the most troubled years of that Church, they decided issues of faith and practice through consultation and debate, evolving common policy and tactics, and a shared doctrine and rhetoric.

One example serves to illustrate this collaborative process. In 1632, when Cotton finally decided to abandon his moderate stance on conformity and lost his pulpit, Davenport, Goodwin, and Nye called him to account for this new intransigence. They demanded "the ground of his judgment and practice, whereby the Church was in danger to be deprived of him." They still believed that hidden resistance was preferable to silencing, and that schism was a greater sin than compromised conformity. Cotton's reasoning prevailed, however; the others were converted to visible noncompliance with ceremonies. Careers were changed as a result of this single meeting; in that moment, Davenport and Goodwin were fated to become exiles. This outcome reflects not only the intimacy of their fellowship but also the flexibility of mind that characterized the group.[23]

In addition to these mutual ministrations, the Brethren worked together to extend their influence and numbers. They sought converts not just from their pulpits but from university posts as well. Almost all of the Brethren held academic fellowships early in their careers—Cotton at Emmanuel; Davenport at Magdalen; Preston at Queens'. Later, Sibbes and Preston presided as masters of St. Catherine's and Emmanuel, respectively, drawing gifted students into their orbit and referring them to members of the brotherhood for advanced study. Alexander Grosart observed that with their assumption of these offices, Preston and Sibbes became "the two great centres of influence in Cambridge." Moreover, their mutual zeal made them "as Luther and Melanchthon . . . They were never found apart when anything was to be done for THEIR MASTER." Grosart's affection for his subjects may have led him to hyperbole; there was a strong Arminian influence at Cambridge as well.[24] However, control of Emmanuel and St. Catherine's did give Sibbes and Preston a unique advantage in furthering the Puritan cause.[25] Cotton was an integral part of this plan for reform. Preston referred so many students to Cotton that he became known as "Dr. Preston's seasoning vessel."[26] And of the thirteen students Preston brought with him to Emmanuel from Queens', five were sent to study at Gray's Inn under Sibbes.[27] This tradition of spiritual and intellectual mentorship continued throughout the 1620s.

A brief look at the publishing history of the group similarly witnesses their fellowship. The Brethren collected and preserved each other's sermons, supplied them with prefaces, and saw them into print. Though rarely published in his own lifetime, after his death Preston's sermons were edited by Davenport and Sibbes, Goodwin and Thomas Ball.[28] Sibbes's own works drew prefaces from Dod, Burroughs, Nye, and Goodwin; his funeral sermon was preached by William Gouge. Both Davenport and Norton penned a biography of Cotton; and in New England, Cotton wrote the introduction to Norton's *Orthodox Evangelist*. Such literary collaboration not only announced their common agenda but insured its dissemination.[29]

Examples of their affiliation could be multiplied, mapping the private correspondences, public displays of support, shared tactics for reform, and the cultivation of mutual patrons (the Veres, Conway, Say and Seale) that reenforced the fellowship.[30] In addition to these manifest traces, however, a common pattern marks their careers in Old England and distinguishes them from the Amesians. These prominent Puritan divines developed tactics of noncompliance that allowed them to exercise power within the increasingly hostile national church.

At the center of this apostolic family stood Richard Sibbes, preacher at Gray's Inn, Trinity Lecturer and Master of St. Catherine's Hall.[31] Sibbes's career models success based on moderation. Privileging the doctrine of the spirit over the letter of conformity, Sibbes kept his pulpit while preaching his spiritist brand of Puritanism. In part, he evaded the disciplining arm of the churchmen precisely by stressing the affections, leaving aside ecclesiastical reform for a more propitious moment. He followed the advice he gave his flock to keep private counsel: "let us labour to be good *in secret*. Christians should be as minerals, rich in the depth of the earth." In this way, he retained his power.[32]

Receiving his M.A. in 1602 from St. John's College, Sibbes became the first preacher to hold the influential lectureship at Trinity, later held by Preston and then Goodwin before it returned to Sibbes in 1633.[33] Through the influence of powerful friends Sibbes was also appointed lecturer at prestigious Gray's Inn in 1617, where he stayed until his death in 1635.[34] From that forum, Sibbes addressed prominent lawyers, future leaders of the Long Parliament, and important intellectuals of the day.[35] When other preachers were being "outed," Sibbes was receiving more calls than he could accept. In 1626 Archbishop Ussher offered Sibbes the post of Provost of Trinity College, Dublin.[36] Despite Laud's determination to be rid of Puritan dissidents, Sibbes still held, at the end of his career, three of the most coveted posts in all England: he had served nine years as Master of St. Catherine's, almost twenty years at Gray's Inn, and over seven years at Trinity.

In large measure, Sibbes's success was due less to his own political acuity than to the shrewd maneuverings of friends. Buckingham, Preston, and Goodwin, for example, were probably responsible for securing the mastership of St. Catherine's Hall for Sibbes in 1626.[37] At the time, St. Catherine's was neither a Puritan stronghold nor a prestigious college. Under Sibbes's leadership, however, it joined Emmanuel as a favored training ground for sons of the Puritan gentry.[38] As we will see, far from being anomalous, Sibbes's remarkable career was in fact representative of the success enjoyed by other members of the Cambridge brotherhood.

While Sibbes stood as the spiritual center of the brotherhood and the very type of moderation, John Preston acted as tactician and model of political pragmatism. Often regarded as "the outstanding figure among the younger tutors at Cambridge," Preston seemed destined for a great career in commerce or the court until the fateful day in 1612 when he heard John Cotton preach. By 1614 Preston was ordained, accepting a post at Peterborough. In less than ten years he would be named Prince Charles's chaplain, preacher at Lincoln's Inn, Trinity Lecturer, and Master of Emmanuel. He had been offered and rejected several other posts, including Provost of Trinity College, Dublin.[39] Together Sibbes and Preston—one through his long pastoral career and the other through his brief but shrewd management of patronage and power at court—proved the effectiveness of tactical moderation in orchestrating the Puritan cause.

Indeed, Preston was a model politician, cultivating patronage wherever it was to be had and by any means necessary. Surprisingly for a reforming zealot, Preston began his meteoric rise to power with a frivolous display of wit. In a debate staged for James I on the question of "whether dogs could make syllogisms," Preston successfully defended canine rationality. Thomas Ball joked that "the King's Hound had opened a way for Master Preston at Court." James, the animal fancier, was so pleased with Preston's defense that he brought him into the inner circles of power.[40] Pragmatic, witty, and wily, Preston was not above exploiting even absurd situations to his own advantage and to advance the Puritan cause.

Preston combined this understanding of political pragmatics with a native talent for intrigue. The ultimate triumph of the church militant justified compromise, even subterfuge, in the daily management of power in church and court. As one of Prince Charles's chaplains, Preston set himself the task of changing foreign and domestic policy. His biographers tell us that during the 1620s he secured aid for the Palatinate, undertook covert missions abroad, arranged secret conferences with the Queen of Bohemia, and spied on Catholic operations at The Hague and elsewhere. He even sought to arrange a royal marriage amenable to the Puritan party. That Preston worked against the Spanish match without alienating Buckingham, once a strong supporter of the Catholic union, testifies to his political acumen.[41]

It has been argued that Preston's influence on the politics of the period has been exaggerated in traditional accounts of the Puritan movement. In some measure Preston's prominence may require reevaluation; it may well be that he was as much a pawn as a power broker in the complex political games and shifting allegiances at court. Indeed, the period of Preston's ascendancy was rather brief, waxing and waning in tandem with Buckingham's pursuit of Puritan favor. Though Preston's influence on the wider world of royal politics and policy may stand revised, the claim for Preston's importance to his Puritan contemporaries remains undiminished by such objections. Just as Sibbes demonstrated the gains of moderation, so Preston proved the value of tactical politics within a hostile regime. His reputation is celebrated in partisan hagiographies of the period; his death in 1628 was seen by many as a mortal blow to the Protestant cause.[42]

During the years of his leadership, Preston was zealous in pressing church reform from within. Accordingly, he supported unions in prayer, fast-days, and most importantly an organization for establishing Puritan pulpits throughout the countryside. In a study of Puritan lectureships, Paul Seaver observed that "even in sophisticated London the popular preachers attracted larger audiences week after week than Shakespeare or Jonson in their prime."[43] Preston coveted control of church offices as much as Laud feared Puritan domination of England's pulpits. He actively sought preferments for preachers of his liking and conspired to secure them. In 1614 when William Tyndale was dying, for example, it appeared that the mastership of Queens' might fall to a non-Puritan, George Mountain (Mountaigne). Preston staged a coup to instate his own favorite, John Davenant. Standing watch at Tyndale's bedside, Preston arranged for the election the instant he died, before formal announcements were issued or appeals on Mountain's behalf could be made.[44]

With Queens' under Davenant and St. Catherine's under Sibbes, Preston aimed at nothing less than Puritan control of the universities; he even began stocking the grammar schools with his own appointees.[45] In 1622 when it was feared that Emmanuel might pass out of Puritan hands, should the aging Laurence Chaderton suddenly die, Preston's disciples unceremoniously urged Chaderton to retire, making way for Preston's own appointment to the mastership. Though contemporary accounts suggest that the great leader of the previous generation was chagrined by this forced retirement, he agreed that personal sacrifice was part of a pragmatic political agenda. Again, to circumvent the nomination of other candidates, Chaderton's resignation was kept secret until Preston's election was secure.[46] In all these activities, Preston hedged on traditional standards of personal loyalty, compromised on conformity, pressed the bounds of integrity, and masterfully managed the available sources of power to advance the Puritan agenda at home and abroad.

The careers of many of the Cambridge Brethren rehearse a marriage of Sibbes's high spiritism with Preston's tactical wisdom. Cotton, for example, began his career at Emmanuel, where he rapidly advanced, becoming first a fellow, then "Head Lecturer, the Dean and the Catechist, in that famous College."[47] As Preston's agent, Cotton instructed the next generation of advanced scholars. Like Sibbes, however, Cotton made his greatest contribution in the pulpit, fulfilling the intention of Emmanuel's founder, Sir Walter Mildmay. Often called the nursery of Puritanism, Emmanuel was intended to supply all of England with pious ministers. To that end, Mildmay reserved fellowships for students entering the ministry and limited their term to twelve years from commencing the M.A. He was determined to produce ministers, not academics; even in times of persecution, he argued "we would not have any Fellow suppose that we have given him a permanent home in this college."[48]

Cotton more than exceeded these expectations. He left Emmanuel long before his fellowship expired to minister to the largest parish church in England. And though he was questioned for nonconformity, circumstances always conspired to secure his liberty. When he was first harassed for nonconformity in 1615, Thomas Leverett, later a ruling elder in Boston's First Church, acted as Cotton's advocate. According to Norton, Leverett "so far insinuated himself into one of the Proctors of that high-Court, that Mr. Cotton was treated by them as if he were a conformable man" and returned to his pulpit.[49]

In 1621, when his congregants at St. Botolph's destroyed statuary and shattered the stained glass of the church, Cotton was suspended by George Mountain, then bishop of Lincoln. Fortuitously, or perhaps with an eye to courting Preston's favor, Mountain invited the sympathetic John Davenant to join him in Cotton's examination. Not surprisingly, Cotton was restored to his pulpit. When Mountain was appointed bishop of London, John Williams succeeded him as bishop of Lincoln. Moderate and mild-mannered, Williams practiced a benevolent toleration of nonconformists like Cotton. With London under the administration of Mountain, with Lincoln supervised by Williams, with Preston at court, and with friends like Thomas Leverett in his congregation, Cotton's liberty was assured. As was often the case, the success of the Sibbesians relied on a fortuitous combination of personal flexibility and the enjoyment of powerful patrons and benevolent bishops.[50] Cotton occupied his influential pulpit a full twenty years, managing to develop and then practice his doctrine of the purified church by establishing an inner congregation of visible saints.[51] Only after Preston's death, Laud's appointment as bishop of London, and the eclipse of moderates like George Abbot and John Williams did Cotton convert to a radical nonconformity that required separation. Until then, he successfully and covertly practiced his nonconformity within the conservative church.[52]

Despite John Davenport's conversion to covert nonconformity in the 1620s and to more open resistance after his 1632 conference with Cotton, he also held influential preaching posts. He served first as chaplain at Hilton Castle, then lecturer at St. Lawrence, Jewry in 1619, finally settling at St. Stephen's, Coleman Street from 1624 until 1633, where he presided over more than 1,400 communicants. A special favorite of the Veres and Edward Conway, Davenport fled only after Laud became Archbishop of Canterbury. Preston was a staunch ally and friend throughout these years, quite probably securing Buckingham's support of Davenport's Coleman Street appointment.[53]

Like his fellows, Davenport used his position to advance the greater cause; along with Preston and Sibbes he organized the feoffees at home and aid for the Protestant cause abroad. Even after his suspension Davenport remained sanguine about these tactics for reform, removing no further than the Netherlands and hoping to fight the good fight on native soil.[54] Finally events, along with Cotton's importunings, led Davenport to postpone his hopes for reform in England and migrate to New English shores. Well into the 1630s, however, Davenport remained a favorite of the Puritan gentry; when he laid plans for New Haven Colony, he secured support from Warwick, among others.[55]

Though my concern is to chart the American genealogy of the brotherhood, it should be noted that Brethren who remained in England achieved similar successes in the period before the war. Thomas Goodwin and William Gouge, for example, enjoyed powerful patrons and held influential posts. Jointly editing Preston's papers with Sibbes and Davenport, Goodwin was a student at St. Catherine's and was Trinity lecturer from 1628 to 1634. Along with Davenport, Goodwin surrendered his pulpit upon converting to a more radical nonconformity in 1632. Yet he remained in England until the late 1630s and when he did flee, it was to the nearer exile of the Netherlands. Goodwin, of course, would return to become a key figure at Westminster. In 1650 he became President of Magdalen College, thus carrying on the tradition of university leadership established by Sibbes and Preston. In the 1620s Gouge joined Davenport and Sibbes as an organizer of the feoffees and fundraiser for Protestants in the Palatinate. He, too, enjoyed a long and relatively secure career, residing at Blackfriars from 1608 until his death in 1653. Like Sibbes, Gouge survived Laud's regime and maintained influence by a shrewd compliance.[56]

In an era of increasing persecution of dissenting churchmen, it is surely remarkable that so many of the Cambridge Brethren were succeeding. While Ames and Hooker had found it necessary to flee, Sibbes and Cotton, Gouge and Davenport remained active soldiers in the Christian warfare at home. In large measure, it would seem that Sibbes's brand of pastoralism combined with Preston's example of resistance by subterfuge enabled this triumph. Though all Puritans opposed corrupt church forms, the Brethren learned to exploit the space between "being" and "seeming" oppositional, a stratagem that produced the necessary freedom and ground from which to undermine the requirements of church officials while still enjoying the union of saints.

This subversive position has rarely been discussed as a strategic and useful alternative to more radical reforms. Most scholars have disdained Cotton's deployment of such tactics, attributing his retreat from controversy to weakness of character.[57] But Cotton rehearsed the essential lesson of Sibbes's and Preston's public careers: he placed highest value on the communion of saints and he was determined to remain on the battlefield. Although he adopted the dissenter's rejection of church authority over things indifferent by 1618, Cotton practiced his nonconformity covertly until 1632. Writing on church ceremonies, he concluded that "if it be a sin in church-governours to command especially upon so strict a penalty, indifferent, decent things; it shall be a sin also in ministers and other private christians to subscribe *ex animo*, and to yield obedience to such command."[58] Cotton never abandoned his opposition, but he did argue that while nonconformity was practiced, it neither had to be advertised nor admitted.

In his early sermons, Cotton establishes these lawful strategies of secret nonconformity in a prose/poetry similar to that of Sibbes: the league of friendship between God and his saints is one of "secret communication," or "secret counsell" that "others shall never be acquainted with."[59] As he explained more pragmatically to Davenport, there were practical applications of this poetic truth: when "church governors" "call us to know our opinions in private (intending to bring us into trouble,) or publicly, rather as captious questioners than judicial governers, in such a case I suppose we may conceal our minds, and put our adversaries upon proof, as our Savior did." Persecuted saints are entitled to tell "part of the truth" and conceal the rest. True Christians "would take no offence, but would understand" the stratagem. As Cotton explained, even St. Paul "scape[d] by this devise." Anne Hutchinson would have profited from following this advice.[60]

Davenport, however, made good use of this strategy. In order to accept the call to St. Stephen's in 1624, for example, he presented himself as a conformable man, a claim supported by Vere and Conway. In a letter to radical Alexander Leighton in the same year, Davenport argued that in these times of "Atheisme, Libertinisme, papisme, and Arminianisme," Puritans should not fight "amongst our selves about Ceremonialls." Adopting Cotton's wider view, Davenport asked, "is it not worke enough to preach unles we dispute also? or, if we must dispute, were it not better to unite our forces against those who oppose us in Fundamentalls than to be divided amongst our selves about Ceremonialls?" He lamented that enemies "both at home, and abroad have stolen in, and taken possession of the house, whilest we are at strife about the hangings and paintings of it."[61] For the Sibbesians, remaining part of the church outweighed the discomfort they felt with these compromises.

Thus, until his departure for the Low Countries, Davenport practiced nonconformity with sufficient craft to avoid suspension. In 1631 objections were made to his practices by his curate Timothy Hood, who charged Davenport was irregular in his wearing of the surplice, refused to admit strangers to communion, and declined to administer the sacrament to the kneeling. It is not wholly clear from the record, but Davenport apparently issued tokens for the sacrament only to congregants he knew, thus suggesting the existence of an inner congregation of saints not unlike that at Cotton's church. The rest were ministered to by his curate.

Davenport displayed Prestonian casuistry in defending this practice, arguing that the enormous size of his congregation (1,400) meant there was no room for kneeling: "it is impossible that many should receive it kneeling, whereby he is constrayned to administer it them in such gestures as they can receive it in." It was Davenport, not Hood, who won the argument. It is interesting to note Cotton successfully practiced a similar casuistry, arguing that the enormous size of his congregation prohibited kneeling for the sacrament![62]

As remarked above, the help of numerous friends and his own wily strategies allowed Cotton to "scape" his various interlocutors as well. Norton claims that "when he was Lord keeper of the great Seal," Williams made a personal appeal to the king, who "was willing notwithstanding his non-conformity, to give way that [Cotton] should have his liberty without interruption in his Ministry." The Earl of Dorchester also "put himself forth what he could in the time of Mr. Cottons troubles to deliver him out of them."[63] Samuel Ward remarked Cotton's good fortune: "Of all men in the world I envy Mr. Cotton, of Boston, most; for he doth nothing in way of conformity, and yet hath his liberty, and I do everything that way, and cannot enjoy mine."[64]

It might well be argued that secrecy was finally more corrosively radical than a more visible nonconformity. To remain hidden meant refusing to engage the dominant culture on its terms; openly declaring opposition resulted in immediate expulsion. This was the path taken by the Amesians (and later the Hutchinsonians), whose concern for ideological consistency and personal purity brooked no compromise. For Sibbesians, preserving the community of saints took precedence over issues of formal purity, allowing them the freedom to be duplicitous. As Laud recognized, their practices of disguise and/or misrepresentation was potentially more subversive because it rejected all disciplinary structures exacting self-incrimination. Cotton and his congregants were more than happy to declare themselves in the subjunctive—the "as if" of conformity that guaranteed their freedom and effectiveness.[65]

Only when such stratagems failed did migration become an acceptable course. Since the Cambridge brothers believed in the word *preached*, in the last extreme, flight was preferable to silencing.[66] In a letter defending his choice to immigrate, Cotton tells Davenport: "What service myself and brother Hooker might do to our people or other brethren in prison (especially in close prison which was feared) I supposed we both of us (by God's help) do the same and much more, and with more freedom, from hence."[67] Note that here Cotton speaks for Hooker, who traveled with him to America. That they fled England together in 1633 recalls their solidarity in opposition to the Church of England. Yet it is also important to remember that Hooker had been silenced since 1629 and in exile since 1631. The choice to leave England came later for the Brethren; only Laud's elevation to archbishop in 1633 signaled that the end of their wily and pacific reformation of the church was at hand.

A final and important chapter needs to be added to this history of moderation and/or the duplicitous staging of conformity. In the early 1620s the Brethren had successfully positioned themselves to work through and around the establishment. As the decade unfolded, however, it became clearer that compliance and manipulation of court patronage was producing neither the domestic nor the foreign policies they desired. Anticipating the disappointments to come, Preston determined to establish "Buttresses to underprop him in the Countrey," should "his standing at Court [be] undermined."[68] Accordingly, in the aftermath of the York House conference, the Brethren adopted more active strategies of resistance and shifted their focus from the court to the House of Commons. One historian has speculated that "Preston and the Puritans decided that, instead of forming a part of the 'Court' party as they had up until the York House conference, they would increase their influence and support in the 'Country.'" Broadening their strength, the Brethren hoped to accomplish their goals by other means, including direct appeals to their patrons and garnering influence in Parliamentary elections. Their early cultivation of the Puritan gentry and their high visibility enabled these crucial oppositional programs.[69]

Together the Brethren mounted a two-pronged assault on crown and church, organizing for reform at home and aid for the cause abroad. These two actions—establishing the "Corporation of Feoffees for Buying of Impropriations to the Church" (1626) and sponsoring a circular letter soliciting funds for exiled Protestants in the Palatinate (1627)—drew largely from the Cambridge circle. Such activities incarnated their ideological positions into practical political programs. Later chapters will discuss the philosophical foundations of these programs; more relevant here is the partisan constituency of the organizers and the material consequences of their utopian plans.

The general disappointment with the crown's failure to support the Protestant cause in the Palatinate is well known.[70] The war was universally regarded by Puritans as an attempt by the Antichrist to destroy God's church. Failure to enter the fray seemed a capitulation to Satan, risking the destruction of England itself. Sibbes spoke for his generation in lamenting "how little support hath the church and cause of Christ at this day! how strong a conspiracy is against it!" He warned that "the spirit of antichrist is now lifted up," and that "the church of God now abroad . . . is in combustion."[71] Counseling auditors to "go to Bohemia, go to the Palatinate, and see what God hath done there," he urged that "judgments of God abroad" were "fair warning" to contend for the faith or risk God's abandonment.[72] This message was, of course, echoed by the Amesians; one of Hooker's most famous sermons laments the current crisis and warns of the dangers of God's desertion of England.[73]

But Sibbes and Preston, Cotton and Davenport focused intensely on the Christian's duty to work for the world church and formulated specific practical programs for change. Insisting that the "common good is to be preferred before private good," they consistently expanded the sphere of Christian concern, from the personal to the congregational, the national to the international church. And in the current crisis of international, indeed cosmic proportions, action rather than lamentation or retreat was the only adequate response.[74]

Withdrawal from religious corruption at home was insufficient; the Spiritual Brethren joined together to act, to apply their carefully cultivated political resources. These men organized prayer unions linking congregations and supported John Dury's irenic plan for Christian union. Prominent among the signatories of Dury's many petitions on behalf of peace are the names of the Cambridge brotherhood: Sibbes, Davenport, Goodwin, Nye, Owen, Baxter, Gouge, Ussher, Cotton.[75]

Prayers and petitions did not altogether satisfy the claims of Christian duty, however. Despairing of royal intervention, at Preston's instigation, Sibbes joined with Thomas Taylor, Davenport, and Gouge to organize a collection for Protestants suffering "the furie of the mercilesse papists in the Upper Palatinate." In 1627 they issued a circular letter to "all godly Christians . . . as fellowe feelinge members of the same body of Jesus Christ," urging contribution of funds from the private sector "till some publique means (which hereafter may be hoped) may be raised for their releife." This letter reveals not only the determination of such men to fulfill their duties to their fellows, but their recognition that action must be undertaken without crown support, indeed in defiance of royal policy. These men who had been trained in administrative posts and had held reins of power were well equipped to organize and mobilize their patrons. By the late 1620s, however, they also learned the consequences of such actions. All four signatories were questioned and reprimanded before the Star Chamber.[76]

Advancing the Kingdom also meant a call for action at home—just as the true Christian must commit to the cause of the church international, so he or she must take a hand in comforting and rousing the saints in England. Again, violence was not "the way to hinder popery from prevailing," but "preaching, and writing, and such good means." Reform came about in "one main way, the planting of an able ministry; for this painted harlot, she cannot endure the breath of the ministry."[77] This position was axiomatic of the entire Puritan community, including Ames and his disciples. But again, what distinguished the Cambridge brotherhood was not their willingness to be silenced for preaching the true word of God, but their determination to find ways around scrutiny and suppression in order to speak.

By means of the feoffees for the purchase of impropriations, the Brethren hoped to "maintain a constant, able, and painful Ministry, in those parts of the Kingdom where there was most want."[78] One might characterize the plan for purchasing clerical livings as an attempt to plant safe colonies of Puritanism within the church at home. By establishing lectureships the Brethren increased the number of preaching posts with fewer onerous duties than church appointments entailed—nor were preachers as immediately scrutinized by church officials for what they said.[79]

The campaign to engross feoffments emerged as a response to Buckingham's betrayal at York House, when interventions in court policy were rendered unlikely. By amassing lectureships and advowsons, the Brethren hoped to find places for preachers of their liking, shape opinion in the country, and influence the outcome of parliamentary elections. The outlines of this scheme require no new recounting here.[80] It is enough to say that before their dissolution the feoffees had collected £7,000 and engrossed over thirty advowsons, fifty impropriations, and two schools in some twenty-six parishes. They also controlled the prized St. Antholin Lectures, which Laudians fearfully looked on as a "seminary" where, "bringing up youth as they please," the Puritans would "after 6. yeares, then . . . disperse them in the Country."[81] Considering attempts the Brethren had already made toward dominating education from the local grammar schools to the colleges at Cambridge, the Star Chamber had more than enough reason for concern. Though no mention of their control of Emmanuel and St. Catherine's was made at the time the feoffees were dissolved, it could not have escaped official notice.

Laud himself accused these London preachers of finding "a cunning way, under a glorious pretense, to overthrow the Church Government, by getting into their power more dependency of the clergy, than the King, and all the Peers, and all the Bishops in all the kingdom had."[82] This charge is all the more trenchant, since the feoffees focused their attention on securing livings in market towns "which send forth Burgesses to the Parliament, the Deputies of the realm."[83] Accordingly, with his rise to power in 1633, Laud made dissolution of the feoffees one of his top priorities.[84]

From 1627 to 1629 Sibbes served as president of this group, which met as often as twice a week to plan their strategy for reform.[85] What has not been pointed out in studies of this organization is that the leadership was composed largely of the Cambridge preachers. The dissolution of the feoffees forced the Spiritual Brethren to reckon with a new and more virulent policy of suppression that rendered impossible the peaceful refor-mation of the church from within.[86] Yet, while Goodwin and others fled to the Netherlands, and Cotton and Davenport cast their lots with the planters of New England, Sibbes and Gouge remained in their preaching posts, never abandoning hope for a pure English Church or for success of irenic strategies in achieving it. Regardless of the option chosen, all of the Brethren faced the agony of deciding how best to further the Reformation in what appeared to be the twilight of Puritanism, at least on English shores. But the seeds of reform that had been planted during these years of subversive ministries were soon to flower in the Civil War.

Meanwhile, for the Spiritual Brethren two choices remained—to leave behind the corruptions of the church in the hopes of planting purer congregations on the American strand, or to stay and fight for the good cause in Old England. Each of the Brethren would in time choose his alternative. But as long as it was possible they stayed in Old England and first by secrecy and craft, then by vocal and visible means, effected a reformation without tarrying.

❧

The Cambridge fellowship found its counterpart in the circle of William Ames, a group joined together by similar bonds of affection and affiliation. A shared professional profile can be constructed for this group as well— one reversing the success enjoyed by the Brethren.

If a single patriarch were to be sought among the Intellectual Fathers of Puritanism, the honor would fall to William Ames. Converted by William Perkins, Ames adopted and elaborated the covenantal theology and voluntarist emphasis preached by Perkins.[87] Blending this religious orientation with the pragmatic rationalism of Petrus Ramus, Ames produced a systematic theology that defined the marrow of faith as practical divinity and that articulated the first principles of congregational polity, covenantal theory, and preparationist practices. Published in its full edition in 1627, the *Medulla* became the classic textbook of theology for generations of Puritan divines.[88]

Ames reversed the emotional emphasis of preachers like Sibbes to stress the rational dimension of religious practice. While Sibbes was known by such affective names as "sweet dropper" and "honey-mouthed," Ames was warned to "beware . . . of a strong head and a cold heart." His rationalism was expressed in a rhetoric of divine contract and human activity and in a tenacious consistency on issues of polity. Ames was invested in a radical nonconformist agenda, privileging the purity of the local congregation over compromise in the interests of the church international. As a corollary, his pastoralism emphasized personal preparation more than the gathering of saints. The epithets he most often drew denote intellection and foundationalism—"the learned Doctor Ames" or "Ames of famous memory."[89]

Cotton Mather stretched the limits of his florid vocabulary to memorialize Ames as "that *profound,* that *sublime,* that *subtil,* that *irrefragable*— yea, that *angelical doctor;*" "one of the most eminent and judicious persons that ever lived in this world." Just as John Wilson paid homage to Sibbes, so Ames was admired by all New England divines, including the Brethren. Partisan differences did not diminish feelings of respect or obviate larger areas of agreement. However, Ames was claimed as the particular mentor of those New England preachers associated with high preparationist doctrine: Hooker, Wilson, Winthrop, Peter, and Shepard expressed a more singular love for Ames, regarded him as their intellectual father, and claimed he was himself "*intentionally* a New England man."[90]

The Amesian fellowship was bound together by intellectual and emotional ties similar to those joining the Brethren. Tracing the genealogy of New England divines, one historian has remarked that "from Ramus to Ames to seventeenth-century Puritanism is one line of Ramist-Puritan descent." While this observation would have to be qualified for the Brethren, most of the Amesians were devoted to the teachings of Ramus and many of them were students of Alexander Richardson at Cambridge.[91]

Personal bonds of friendship also joined the learned Doctor to the company of American divines. Cotton himself memorialized the affection between Ames and Hooker in his eulogy of the Hartford preacher.[92] Although Ames was not the catalyst in Hooker's anguished and protracted conversion, their relationship began quite early in Hooker's career (probably sometime before 1610) and continued until Ames's death.[93] This friendship was strengthened during years of mutual exile in Holland, where Hooker, legend has it, aided Ames in his pastoral duties, consulted with him on issues of polity, wrote the preface to Ames's *Fresh Suit Against Ceremonies,* and perhaps even "assisted him in composing some of his discourses."[94]

Hooker so admired Ames that he declared "if a scholar was but well studied in Dr. Ames his *Medulla*" he would make a "*good divine,* though he had no more books in the world." In return Ames professed that "though he had been acquainted with many scholars of divers nations, yet he never met with Mr. Hooker's equal, either for preaching or for disputing."[95] Hooker remained Ames's loyal disciple, first encouraging him to emigrate to New England, then serving as protector to his widow and children, who transplanted after Ames's death.[96] Beyond such personal bonds, Hooker's debt to Ames was inscribed in his sermonic texts; the doctrines of preparation and conditional covenant that appeared in seed in Perkins were cultivated by Ames and harvested in the sermons of Thomas Hooker.

Hooker was not Ames's only disciple; the adherents of his theology virtually constituted the preparationist party of New England. It was no accident that these men joined hands against Cotton and Hutchinson— they had already felt themselves to be a community of like-minded divines during the premigration period.[97] John Wilson, for example, sought Ames's counsel while he was at Cambridge, and upon his advice began to confer with congenial ministers who influenced his early theological development.[98] Wilson's affection for Ames was warmly returned; Ames declared "That if he might have his option of the best condition that he could propound unto himself this side heaven, it would be that he might be the teacher of a congregational church, whereof Mr. Wilson should be the pastor." Cotton Mather with unintended irony observed that "this happiness, this privilege" had been instead accorded Mr. Cotton in the church of Boston.[99] As the Antinomian Controversy proved, never was there such an unhappy marriage of pastor and teacher in a single church; it served as the battleground for the differences dividing the Brethren and the Fathers.

John Winthrop, Hugh Peter, and Nathaniel Eaton round out the New England group who had religious and personal ties with Ames. The stream of nonconformists who found themselves in the Netherlands all came under the influence of this patriarch. In exile, these men consulted on issues of polity, establishing the same sort of dialogue as the Sibbes group. Peter, later a virulent opponent of Cotton's, developed his ideas of congregationalism under Ames's tutelage, preached his funeral sermon, and became the literary executor of his works in 1633.[100] It is said that Eaton, a student of Ames in the Low Countries, was appointed master of the infant college in New England on the strength of that single credential.[101]

Loyalties were also forged through the secondary associations of Ames's disciples. Another key figure in the New England controversies, Thomas Weld, was brought into the intellectual orbit of Ames through his Essex associations with Wilson and Hooker. Weld was to become one of the most aggressive inquisitors of 1637, representing the preparationist position in England as solicitor for the Court-controlled Harvard College and serving as editor of Winthrop's "Short Story." Weld also sheltered Thomas Shepard after his departure from Emmanuel, drawing one of most important New England divines into the fellowship.[102]

Shepard is the most complex of the preachers in this group—a man whose experiences bound him to both the Intellectual Fathers and the Spiritual Brethren, and whose temperament remained divided throughout his lifetime.[103] His first religious awakening, around 1624, was through the agency of Preston and Goodwin, those pillars of the Cambridge school, whom Shepard declared "the most able men for preaching Christ in this latter age."[104] Shepard confessed a son's affection for Preston: "And the Lord made me honour him highly, and love him dearly."[105] But these were neither the only nor the most powerful influences on Shepard.

Upon leaving the university, Shepard entered the social world of Weld, Wilson, and Hooker. These proved the stronger ties, though Shepard's attraction to a hotter piety remained a troubling part of his mental world. After 1627 Shepard's allegiances shifted; within six months of leaving college "he went to reside in the family of Thomas Weld" in Terling, Essex, where he entered the sphere of Thomas Hooker. Shepard's biographers report that just at that time Dr. Wilson, thought to be the brother of John Wilson, had decided to fund a lectureship in the region. Many of the local ministers hoped to establish the appointment in Cogshall, with Shepard as preacher. Hooker, however, intervened, arguing that Shepard "was altogether too young and inexperienced" for a post in such a large city and arranging instead for Shepard to settle in Earles-Colne.[106] Hooker willingly became the younger man's practical advisor and spiritual mentor. Some years later, Shepard confided to his journal that when Hooker "preached about contentedness . . . I was confirmed in the faith."[107] This attachment was formalized when Shepard took Hooker's daughter as his second wife in 1637, in the midst of the Antinomian Controversy. When Henry Vane returned to England, becoming an influential figure in the

Puritan regime, Shepard began to fear reprisal for his part in the anti-nomian dispute; it was to Hooker's Hartford that he contemplated flight.[108]

Shepard quite literally embodied in nearly equal measure the competing affections marking the two fellowships. He serves as an important reminder that the issue of difference does not involve binary oppositions, even though the act of description sometimes presses in that direction. Questions must be framed in terms of emphasis rather than exclusion; affinities were always mixed. Shepard's conversion, seasoned in equal measure with convictions of positive evil and a faith in infusion based on privative sin stands as a testament to this psychic ambivalence.[109] Throughout his private writings one finds expressions of the ecstatic piety characteristic of the Sibbes circle. His personal record is of a heart ravished: "the Lord made himself sweet to me and to embrace him and give myself up to him."[110] Though his attraction to Sibbesian piety remained, after the Antinomian Controversy Shepard often consigned it to his spiritual closet, to the private ejaculations of the personal notebook. In his public utterances, he adopted the cooler, contractual language of high preparationism. Acting as an arbiter of orthodox expression, Shepard preached against hotter sorts of piety and actively disciplined spiritists like Anne Hutchinson.

It is ironic that Hutchinson, at least according to Cotton, "esteemed best of Mr. Shepard," of all the other Bay ministers.[111] Whether Shepard was attracted to both styles of piety because of an initial psychic dexterity, or whether his divided consciousness was the product of his peculiar career—converted by one contingent, nurtured by another—is impossible to say, but his subsequent public repudiation of the Cambridge spiritism was perhaps the most vehement of any New England divine. Rejecting his own early spiritism as a flirtation with familism, Shepard became New England's most diligent advocate of the new orthodoxy. In the early 1630s, he joined with Bulkeley to interrogate Cotton's theology; along with Hooker, Bulkeley, and Winthrop, he directed the Antinomian Synod. Shepard was instrumental in developing and enforcing the policies of the emergent New England orthodoxy. In 1646 he gave his imprimature, in the form of an introductory preface, to Peter Bulkeley's explication of the new preparationist orthodoxy, *The Gospel Covenant*.[112]

To complete this sketch of personal histories of affiliation, I should mention John Winthrop's involvement with the preparationist patriarchs. Membership in both groups extended beyond the black regiment both in New and Old England. Just as Henry Vane became connected to the Cambridge circle through Wheelwright and Cotton, so John Winthrop formed an early allegiance to the Ames group, originating with personal and social connections as well as religious sympathies and consolidated by correspondence before and after the migration. Preaching at the town of Boxford, near the Winthrop family home, Ames came to know the future governor through various social connections. Both participated in the New England Company at London, where Ames was consulted about the plans for plantation.[113] Winthrop joined Hooker in encouraging Ames to emigrate—an invitation Ames accepted in 1629, writing to Winthrop that "I longe to bee with yow, though I doe not see how I should satisfie the opinion and expectation which you have conceyved of mee." Had he lived, those expectations might have included serving as President of Harvard College.[114]

Winthrop's ties to the circle were strengthened by his associations in America, not only with Hooker and Shepard but with John Wilson. The governor's loyalty to Wilson was described in the first chapter. Neighbors in Old England and allies in America, Winthrop stood with his pastor against Cotton and the entire Boston congregation; he alone blocked Wheelwright's appointment as co-pastor to the church. As so often in these two societies of fellows, family ties soon confirmed philosophical ones; through marriage Wilson's and Winthrop's children formalized their parents' political and religious allegiances.[115]

Like their Cambridge counterparts, the Amesians tried to widen their circle, ministering and counseling each other. On Ames's advice, Wilson gathered a group of fellow students to meet regularly and discuss matters of faith and polity, for example.[116] Thomas Hooker also gathered a group of ministers during his years as lecturer at Chelmsford. Mather's *Magnalia* records that "the godly ministers round about the country would have recourse unto [Hooker] to be directed and resolved in their *difficult cases;* and it was by his means that those godly ministers held their *monthly meetings,* for *fasting* and *prayer,* and profitable *conferences.*"[117] Apparently, Hooker, Wilson, Weld, and Shepard formed a nucleus of Amesians in the Essex region.

As they were able, these men helped each other find preaching posts. Hugh Peter made a temporary place in Rotterdam for the exiled Hooker (as he did for Davenport). As noted, John Wilson's brother seems to have been a patron of the Essex region, relying on Shepard and Hooker for advice concerning the disposition of his lectureship. By his agency Samuel Stone, soon to become Hooker's co-pastor at Hartford, was maintained at Towcester.[118] Such arrangements reveal a network of Puritan lectureships in the region consistent with the efforts of the Cambridge group. Indeed

Essex was an important center of lay patronage and power; in addition to such lectureships, the Puritan country gentry controlled a number of livings in the region. Yet, it must be noted that preachers like Hooker and Shepard occupied less prestigious pulpits than those of Sibbes or Cotton and that they were unable to sustain them for as long a tenure. The appointment of Laud as bishop of London in 1628 meant that unless they were willing to practice a compromised conformity, the Essex confreres could expect suspension under his exacting administration. Early in their careers it became evident that they could not expect the security nor enjoy the limelight of a St. Botolph's or Coleman Street.[119]

Given that the opponents of Cotton's doctrines in the 1637 Synod had already established informal allegiances in Old England (most of them attached to the Essex circle), it is perhaps less surprising that Shepard and Hooker, Wilson and Weld, should have grouped with such unanimity against Vane and Cotton, Wheelwright and Davenport. Shepard's immediate alliance with Hooker upon his arrival in 1635 is rendered more comprehensible, as is his initiation of the questioning of Cotton. These constellations of loyalty and belief seem to have preceded the events of the 1630s; that turbulent decade made the differences manifest.

As a group, the Amesians shared a similar career profile, one that differed from the success of the Brethren. The history of Ames's disciples in Old England is more often one of early silencing, exile, and prolonged and frequently frustrated searches for pulpits. As a group these men wielded less real power than the Sibbesians, a point that must be underscored because the importance and fame of these preachers has been so strongly foregrounded in the subsequent histories of New English Puritanism. The preachers of Ames's circle were suspended earlier and from less prominent pulpits. Circumstances often forced them to exercise their influence by way of the printed word, in contrast to the Brethren whose beliefs required and whose good fortune allowed for emphasis on the word *preached.*

The premier example of such relative powerlessness is Ames himself, whose fame has been celebrated throughout the literature of Puritanism and whose influence is claimed to have dominated the intellectual life of the movement. While there can be no doubt that his systematic theology was tremendously influential, the degree to which Ames's thinking was *formative* for the whole Puritan contingent may require reconsideration. Although the *Medulla* was first delivered as a series of lectures in Leyden in the early 1620s, its first printing in Latin in abbreviated form waited until 1623; a full English edition was printed in 1627. Widely circulated by the end of the decade, this text did exert an extraordinary influence over members of the Puritan party. It was, no doubt, all the more important and suggestive for having been written in exile, where the nonconformist agenda could be expressed more directly than was possible for those in a compromised position within the church.[120] Like Perkins, Ames was universally revered; Cotton as well as Hooker cited him when they needed canonical support in the theological disputes of the 1630s.[121]

It must be observed, however, that the *Medulla* appeared long after the formative moments of spiritual awakening and conversion to nonconformity for most of the divines here discussed—after Cotton had formulated his position with respect to things indifferent and had gathered his inner congregation; after Preston had begun shaping the party to fit his prophetic plan; after Sibbes had awakened a generation of students and lawyers and citizens from his various pulpits.

John Eusden, Ames's modern translator, has observed that though Ames was influential in England (despite a ban on his writings until the 1640s) it was in New England that he had "his greatest influence"; in New England "where his covenant theology, church polity, Ramist thought, understanding of the Scriptures, and conception of faith and religious experience were accepted as canonical."[122] I would speculate that Ames's prominence in New England is due in part to the dominance of his disciples, who came into power in 1637 and could determine for themselves which texts would speak for the orthodoxy.

But in Old England, in the formative years of the 1610s and 1620s, there is reason to question what has been portrayed as Ames's formative influence. Among the circles at the Inns and at court, the example and preaching of Sibbes and his spiritual kin surely had far greater impact. Even at Dort, where Ames's claim to leadership is rooted, other English emissaries, including Preston's friend John Davenant, spoke for the cause as well.[123] These particulars are not cited to diminish Ames but to suggest that measuring his impact or asserting his intellectual hegemony within the Puritan party is more problematic than scholars have allowed.

When one looks beyond the impact of the printed text to the power of appointment or to influence directly exercised through an active ministry, one must conclude that Ames's stature appears more modest. More than two decades before Sibbes came under the scrutiny of the Star Chamber or a single member of the Spiritual Brethren had been silenced, Ames was harried from the land. An early convert to nonconformity, Ames was also one of the most intransigent of the dissenters. Suspended for noncompliance in 1610 (the very year Sibbes assumed the Trinity lectureship), Ames began his twenty-year exile in the Low Countries—an exile during which he was denied both the comfort of a regular congregation and the coterie of students enjoyed by the Cambridge Brethren.

Nothing could more dramatically demonstrate the disparity of professional fates than to compare the careers of Sibbes and Ames at the close of their lives. In 1633, when Sibbes held three of the most coveted posts in England, Ames's fortunes were only beginning to improve. Up to that time his career was mixed at best, his successes amply seasoned with disappointment and deprivation.

Ames began his religious career when he entered Christ's College in 1593 or 1594, where he remained until his unceremonious ouster in 1610. Unlike Emmanuel, which continued to enjoy Chaderton's Puritan administration, Christ's College came under the conservative supervision of Valentine Cary in 1609. Cary's appointment as master ensured that Ames was to be among the first of a new generation of silenced preachers.[124]

This circumstance serves to remind that the success or misfortune of the dissenters was in good measure determined by the generosity or intransigence of their immediate superiors. While Cotton enjoyed the benevolent neglect of John Williams and Laurence Chaderton, Ames was subjected to the implacable scrutiny of men like Cary. Yet it is also true that Ames's own rigidity contributed to his suspension. Keith Sprunger speculates that "had he not been so militant, [Ames] could have survived at the college," citing the example of Thomas Goodwin, who found Christ's a congenial home as late as 1613. But survival would have meant practicing a style of covert noncompliance that Sibbes allowed but Ames and his followers could not countenance. Sprunger rightly concludes that Ames turned "toward radical Puritanism 'of the rigidest sort.'"[125]

Nor was Cary Ames's only nemesis. George Abbot, Archbishop of Canterbury from 1611 to 1633, who could be persuaded to look the other way in so many other instances of nonconformity, blocked Ames's appointment to a lectureship at Colchester in the period after his departure from Christ's. Under Abbot's tenure the term *conformable Puritan* was used to describe men like Sibbes—preachers who held their convictions about the spirit while remaining supple on the letter of conformity.[126] While Abbot tolerated such moderates, he remained Ames's irreconcilable enemy, refusing to license him as a lecturer in London, urging his dismissal from The Hague in 1612, and thwarting his appointments in the aftermath of the Synod of Dort.[127]

There can be no doubt that Ames's radical noncompliance contributed to his misfortune. Even after exile, he remained as adamant as the Cambridge Brethren were supple. Having settled in The Hague as chaplain to Sir Horace and Lady Mary Vere, Ames was warned to abandon his criticism of the bishops or risk silencing again. For a time he redirected his criticisms to the Separatists, but his reputation for intransigence once again ruined his chance for a peaceful ministry. According to Matthew Nethenus, his seventeenth-century biographer, by 1619 Ames was again under suspicion for anti-episcopal writing, forcing an unwilling Vere to dismiss him.[128] Perhaps these repeated silencings helped produce the unpleasant pessimism that Ames's biographers remark.[129]

Although in later years Ames did meet with success, enjoying an eleven-year tenure at Franeker (during which time he produced numerous influential treatises), his biographers report that Ames was bitter about his fate. Off the beaten track of European intellectual life, a teaching post at Franeker was a poor substitute for the mastership of Christ's, the office Ames had early dreamed of holding. Moreover, like all Puritans, Ames hungered for a devoted congregation, for the pulpit that had been denied him for most of his career.

One is led to speculate that the bitterness Ames expressed reflects an awareness of his precarious position and a disappointment in the effectiveness of his patrons. He must have known that while the Veres proved unable to protect him, Sibbes's patrons (including the Veres) successfully shielded him throughout the 1620s, managing even to reinstall Sibbes at Trinity after the feoffees had been officially rebuked.[130] In the increasingly chastened world of Puritan politics, influence had to be conserved—expended in protecting those favorites of the Puritan gentry who were also sufficiently conformable. Despite his prominence in the Puritan cause in 1618, Ames could not command the kind of patronage lavished on the likes of Sibbes and Preston, nor the protection extended to Cotton by the Bishop of Lincoln. One observer has remarked that the "very eminence" of men like Preston and Sibbes "brought with it the powerful patrons and the firm connections in Court, country, and university that must have given them virtual immunity from episcopal interference." Nothing could be further from the truth of Ames's experience![131]

In 1633, having wearied of bitter winters and the even more chilling and endless disputations with his university colleagues, he finally left Franeker, intending to answer the call to Hugh Peter's Rotterdam church or to Winthrop's Boston. However, he was taken ill and died before he could assume either post; in the end he was never to receive the honors due to a man of his piety and intellect, honors that would have been lavished upon him at either destination.[132]

In light of the celebrity enjoyed by Ames in the literature of the Puritan movement, it is worth underscoring that even after his famed advisory role at the Synod of Dort, Ames was unable to find a post worthy of his talents. Sprunger remarks that "unfortunately for Ames, he had become so outspoken in his Puritanism" that all avenues of appointment were blocked. For three years after the conference, Ames was forced to take a "lowly tutorial assignment," the only employment offered him. The ignominy he was thus forced to endure fanned "old flames of anger and bitterness" in him.[133] Thereafter, Ames would never regain the pulpit or enjoy patronage in his long history as a dissenter.

Just as Sibbes's success was replayed in the careers of Cotton and Preston, so Ames's tragic history of disappointment was rehearsed in the careers of men like Hugh Peter, Thomas Shepard, and Thomas Hooker. I do not mean to suggest that these preachers were without their successes or without patrons. Indeed, as noted above, many of them benefitted from the clerical patronage of the Puritan country gentry. While the feoffees cultivated patronage in the city and at court, men like the Earl of Warwick established Puritan power in the country; he alone controlled twenty-two livings in Essex. Warwick's complex allegiances again testify to the unity of purpose within the Puritan resistance generally. Benefactor of Sibbes and Preston, Warwick lent his support to ministers like Hooker, Wilson, Peter, and Weld as well. A frequent auditor of Hooker's, Warwick is also said to have "had a room specially built overlooking the chapel at Gray's Inn to hear Sibbes" and to have sponsored Preston's various activities.[134]

Yet historians tracing his activities also mark differences among the kinds of support Warwick provided, distinguishing between his efforts "to extricate ministers from trouble" and his cultivation of "close and enduring relations with a select group of eminent Puritans." In her study of Warwick's patronage, Barbara Donagan groups Hooker, Wilson, and Peter under the first category as ministers receiving Warwick's protection; Sibbes and Preston are identified as the "eminent Puritans" and "special friends" with whom he consulted. This is not to suggest that Warwick did not develop strong friendships with Hooker and Wilson—indeed he did—but that even within a single patronage network distinctions between types of ministers and their circumstances were also remarked.[135]

Moreover, Donagan recognizes that in the two decades before the war strains emerged among Warwick's associates: "there were already within the relatively restricted ranks of Warwick's clients in the 1620s and 1630s the seeds of Puritan faction and dissension." I would argue that this antagonism, emerging over the issue of conformity "in the interests of church unity," is an indication of latent partisan allegiances here described. Moreover, when their intransigence over issues of conformity was combined with the austere administration of Laud in the region, the Essex Amesians, "Warwick's more flamboyant early proteges," suffered repeated harassment and early suspension.[136]

The career of Thomas Hooker proves an exemplary case. It is said that Hooker could put a king in his pocket—yet the pattern of his career transforms this observation into something of an irony.[137] Preston could and indeed did hold Charles in his hand, at least for a time; Sibbes always found a way to escape beyond the reach of the bishops. Hooker could do neither. In fact, his peripatetic ministry dramatizes his relative lack of position or effective patronage. While Cotton left Emmanuel in 1612 to assume responsibility for the largest noncathedral church in Old England, Hooker remained at the college until 1618, nearly exhausting the tenure established by Mildmay.[138]

After leaving Cambridge, it is assumed that Hooker settled in the village of Esher. There he preached to the small congregation and joined the household of Thomas Drake, where his own agonized conversion was reprised in the spiritual torment of Drake's wife, Joan. It was through his ministry to her that Hooker's preparationism was confirmed and his reputation as a physician to anguished souls was born. Yet despite Cotton Mather's report of Hooker's well-deserved fame "for his ministerial abilities," he nonetheless found it difficult to find a satisfactory pulpit. According to some historians, he "spent the first half of the 1620s as an itinerant preacher in Essex and London." And though he sought an appointment in Dedham with John Rogers, Hooker complained that mysteriously "the providence of God gave an obstruction to that settlement."[139]

Indeed, Hooker's precarious status is reflected in the relative paucity of the records of his early life. Cotton Mather appends his sketch of Hooker to *Johannes in Eremo,* the lives of Cotton, Norton, Wilson, and Davenport, "confessing that through want of information I have underdone in this, more than in any part of the composure." Modern biographers are also left to speculate about much of Hooker's early career—reporting that to a surprising extent Hooker drops from the records for seven years after leaving Emmanuel, until he settled in the market town of Chelmsford in 1625. To be sure, Hooker's career in Chelmsford has been described as "brief but spectacular," drawing auditors county-wide. Cotton Mather reports that "the light of his ministry shone through the whole county of Essex," that Hooker was regarded as "a teacher sent from God," and that "a great reformation [was] wrought, not only in the town, but in the adjacent country." Yet, as Mather also observes, "the joy of the people in this light was 'but for a season,'" and a very short season at that.[140] Hooker probably sustained his office only four years before being silenced in 1629. Indeed, this was apparently "time enough to establish himself as a major Puritan presence in Essex," as one biographer remarks, but there is a poignancy to such a brief term of freedom from harassment.[141] How different a fate Cotton enjoyed in his twenty long years at St. Botolph's!

It is not my intention to diminish Hooker's deserved fame—as noted, he was a central figure in the Essex circle. Moreover, his sermons of the period were fiercely political and obviously effective. Yet, Hooker's difficulty in finding and keeping a satisfactory pulpit must be seriously weighed in our assessments of his English career. Cotton Mather reports that Hooker had a reputation as "a man of cholerick disposition," as well as being "a very condescending spirit." This is in vivid contrast to the meekness of Cotton, who confessed "angry men have an advantage above me." Charting his course through the small pastorates of Essex during the early part of his career, one can imagine Hooker's frustration. Even during his glorious few years at Chelmsford, Hooker's sermons read as the remarks of a beleaguered minister. In "The Faithful Convenanter," he voices disappointment and irritation over the antiministerial sentiment he sensed in his auditors. In his criticism of congregants who have "set [their] mouths against heaven," and who "will outface God and minister and gospel and all (and think to go away scot-free)," we sense traces of bitterness.[142]

Buried in his recurrent refrains against Dedham sinners who rebel against a convicting and converting ministry, we hear the outraged and poignant cry of a preacher struggling for souls during the dark period of Laud's ascendancy and on the eve of his own silencing. It was as an "itinerant evangelist," one already "insecure" in his Chelmsford pulpit, that Hooker delivered "The Faithful Convenanter" to the Dedham congregation.[143] There is pathos in Hooker's pleas for understanding: "Brethren, you may think I deal somewhat harshly with you, but I deal for the best for you."[144] How different are these sermons from the mild and at times blissful salutations Cotton offered to his familiar and responsive congregation!

The story of Hooker's silencing offers another point of contrast with the Brethren's career pattern. Sibbes and Gouge remained in their pulpits until their deaths. With the help of Leverett, his powerful patrons, and the mild administration of John Williams, Cotton escaped silencing until 1632, when he determined to adopt a more radical stance. Davenport was similarly blessed. Despite Warwick's efforts on his behalf, however, Hooker enjoyed only three years of freedom from persecution. In 1629, when Laud began his final campaign against Hooker, Warwick prompted local ministers to petition on Hooker's behalf—"no less than seven-and-forty conformable ministers of the neighboring towns" testified "that they esteem and know the said Mr. Thomas Hooker to be for doctrine, orthodox; for life and conversation, honest; for disposition, peaceable, and in no wise turbulent or factious." To Cotton Mather this expression of lay and clerical support made "the silencing of Mr. Hooker more unaccountable."[145]

While the powerful patrons of Sibbes, Davenport, and Cotton succeeded in swaying their more sympathetic local authorities, the ministrations of Warwick availed nothing with Laud, then bishop of London. However, the benignity of local officials was not the only factor in these misfortunes. The difficulties the Amesians experienced in finding and holding pulpits is also attributable to their visible and unyielding nonconformity.[146]

Again replicating the difficulties experienced by Ames, even in exile these men found little respite; Hooker never succeeded in resolving the disputes with John Paget that blocked his installation in the congregation at Amsterdam. He was similarly thwarted at Delft. Hooker's 1633 letter to Cotton offers a bleak picture of Protestantism abroad and laments his personal misfortunes, the "pursuits and banishments, which have waited upon me, as one wave follows another." Hooker summed up his English career in the negative, justly complaining that "the providence of God often diverted him from employment in such places as he himself desired, and still directed him to such places as he had no thoughts of."[147]

Even within the liminal group of the dissenting clergy, these preachers experienced an extra measure of bitterness and disaffection. Wilson was deprived of his college fellowship in 1610, also through Valentine Cary's agency. Though he found a congenial pulpit among the Essex circle in 1618, he was repeatedly persecuted until he emigrated in 1630. Hugh Peter had been suspended as early as 1627. Shepard was silenced in 1630; Weld was ousted soon after. None enjoyed Cotton's long tenure; none remained in their pulpits into the mid-1630s as did Goodwin, Gouge, and Sibbes; none held appointments of like influence.[148]

The surprising uniformity of career patterns within the Ames group is matched by its remarkable deviation from the Sibbesian paradigm. One fundamental reason for this difference of fortune seems to rest with their relative stances on nonconformity. The success of the Cambridge men was built upon their willingness to compromise. After 1632, when Cotton, Davenport, and Goodwin became intransigent and the power of their benefactors (including Abbot and Williams) was on the wane, they too were put to flight.[149] It must be recalled, however, that tactical compliance was not wholly alien to the Amesians. Hooker, too, was willing to have colleagues swear to his conformity, but the ruse was ineffectual—due, no doubt, in equal parts to Laud's austerity and to Hooker's flamboyance.

A reputation for conformity or noncompliance, local structures of episcopal authority, and the power and prestige of one's patrons combined, then, in deciding the fortunes of Puritan divines. Yet, the contrasting fates of Sibbes and Ames under the patronage of the Veres also suggests that the gentry acted most vigorously—or at least most effectively—on behalf of the Cambridge circle. These are the preachers that the Warwicks and the Veres, Say and Seale, Conway, Ussher, Buckingham, and others succeeded not just in protecting but in elevating.[150]

Why one group more than the other drew such devoted patronage is not clear, but many considerations join to suggest an explanation. Like all other Puritans, the dissenting gentry had an intense spiritual hunger for the preached word; this appetite they, however, were fortunate enough to satisfy through private, extra-churchly offices. Family chaplains, locally endowed lecturers, and access to private grammar schools and colleges allowed them to practice their nonconformity with lessened danger. Thus the Puritan gentry were able to partake of the pleasures of spiritual fellowship in a somewhat purified ecclesiastical structure while also enjoying relative safety from crown harassment.

Because of their economic stake in England, migration remained an unappealing alternative for the Puritan gentry, who were anxious to pursue all possible measures to stave off an open breach with the crown.[151] Thus, to insure continued Puritan ministry within a troubled church, they might have encouraged or welcomed the compromise on ceremonials that characterized the Brethren's practice. Like Vere's counsel to Ames in Holland, these gentlemen urged their chaplains to "conform sufficiently" to avoid silencing.[152] The goal was to enjoy pure religion while avoiding reprisal—a dual purpose not easily attained in the circumstances, but one made particularly difficult by men like William Ames. In this light, the seemingly modest support extended to the Amesians, along with the warm embrace of Sibbes's disciples, is somewhat more understandable.

Similarly, the Sibbesians' rejection of "negative righteousness" as a mark of religious virtue may have proved more compatible with the manners and mores of a leisured class. While the Amesians exacted rigorous standards, the Sibbesians may have exercised some lenience with respect to matters of dress, diet, and gaming. Despite their zeal, the Puritan gentry were, by and large, more liberal in philosophy and practice on such issues.

Though all preachers would have condemned excess, it seems likely that in material matters the Cambridge Brethren may have been flexible, as they were with ceremonials. Moreover, a preparationism that stressed not the affective experience of immediate infusion, but marked instead the slow accumulation of moral virtue as proof of regeneration, may have jarred more significantly with gentry sensibilities.

We are told, for example, that John Wilson became unpopular with one patron precisely because he insisted on exacting standards of behavior. As chaplain to Lord Scudamore, Wilson objected to certain gentlemanly practices that he deemed not properly respectful of the Sabbath. Mather reports that "Mr. Wilson observing the discourse of the gentry at the table, on the Lord's day, to be too disagreeable unto the devout frame to be maintained on such a day, at length he zealously stood up at the table" to deliver a reprimand. This admonition failed to forestall talk of hawking and gaming on future Sabbaths, occasioning more rebukes from Wilson and invoking the fury of his patron.[153] Wilson was dismissed, and at least one modern historian has speculated that his stridency may have converted Scudamore into a loyal disciple of Laud.[154] This incident contrasts with Sibbes's own practice of making summer tours of the homes of his wealthy friends, where he was warmly welcomed and "was an instrument of much good."[155]

Of course, not all of the gentry were as lax as Lord Scudamore, nor is it to be inferred that men like Sibbes or Preston would have countenanced inordinate liberalism (indeed this accusation is often lodged against advocates of unconditional grace—that it leads first to liberalism and then the libertinism of the antinomian). But it may be that preachers of their persuasion simply were less interested in scrutinizing the behavior of their patrons and congregants or in making "negative righteousness" a standard of virtuous piety. This might have allowed a certain freedom of practice the Puritan gentry found appealing.

A tantalizing speculation for the Brethren's appeal that is more difficult to prove is the greater compatibility between their style of piety and the economic privilege enjoyed by the Puritan gentry and the most successful members of the new merchant class. The theology of transformative faith, of the sudden infusion of freely bestowed grace, may have been a better psychological "fit" for these beneficiaries of a new, burgeoning world of investment capitalism.[156]

The convergence of the Protestant ethic with the spirit of capitalism has been a bedrock of sociological analysis beginning with Weber and continuing with Tawney; it has also been the resurrected subject of many recent studies of Puritanism. As one scholar has pointed out, however, the rhetoric of diligence in one's calling and the asceticism of deferred pleasure (as well as the pessimism of an unrealized eschatology) does not quite fit with the piety of a wealthy or a rising class—with men and women not driven by anxiety over assurance but instead resting in a confirmed and ebullient self-confidence.[157] Sibbes's exegesis of grace as an abundant infusion, signaling a sudden ontologic transformation, may have been more in keeping with the life of privilege, either as inherited or as rapidly attained in the marketplace. And it may not be accidental that the most prosperous immigrants were Cottonians or that "the merchants, with striking uniformity, backed the dissenters" in 1637.[158]

The incremental progress, self-reflexivity, and asceticism of the preparationist doctrine simply may not have appealed to this stratum of society; instead, its rhetoric of diligence, of modest and gradual change may have resonated more fully with the workingman's world depicted by Shepard and with the more static social vision of *A Modell of Christian Charity*.[159] Cotton, instead, seems to be speaking to and for the Puritan merchants and gentry, whose economic activity is of a different sort—far more fluid and dynamic.[160]

If the Cambridge piety was to have greater appeal for Puritan entrepreneurs and the gentry, one might ask whether successful patronage and the good fortune of their long careers did not also in some way confirm these ministers in their mode of piety. It seems reasonable to presume that a theology resting on God's free love and benevolence, an assurance of the perseverance of the saints in adversity, and a millennial optimism would find affirmation in a pastoral career supported by uninterrupted patronage. Men like Vere extended their support abundantly and unconditionally and remained loyal even in the dark days of persecution.

And, as an empowered group successfully effecting the reformation of the church from within (until the rise of Laud), such men had a stronger faith in the *possibility* of ushering in the kingdom and in the idea of history as progressive rather than apocalyptic. These two issues will of course require detailed analysis in later chapters; but for now one might ask: what, after all, were the organizations for the Palatinate and the feoffees if not expressions of faith in the possibility of reformation here and now?

In reading through the descriptions of the Brethren, one is struck by how frequently the words *sweet, meek, honied, irenic,* and the like are used. With loyal and powerful patrons and benevolent or at least tolerant bishops, devoted congregants gathered within stable pastorates, with concrete plans for reformation put into practice, it is no wonder that the Cambridge circle felt confirmed in their postmillennial hopes, at least until 1633. Given all this, it is not surprising that through the darkest days sweetness of temper and assurance of God's final glory were the hallmarks of the Cambridge piety.

By contrast, Ames's disappointment and Hooker's choler may have been by-products of a life of hardship and deprivation, in which faith in a realized reformation here and now always seemed thwarted. If there is a certain coldness in Ames, a sense of defensiveness in Hooker, and a measure of violent language in the sermons of Shepard, it is perhaps not surprising. Such feelings may to some degree be the results of their professional setbacks and struggles throughout this period.

These were men upon whom little was freely bestowed or even granted as a reward for merit. Rather, they learned the lessons of self-reliance, of incremental and sometimes undetectable progress of the kingdom, and of continued struggle in the face of disappointment. They learned these lessons in adversity, often deprived of the joys of congregation and community. Their experiences must have confirmed their sense of isolation, of the impossibility of change without an apocalyptic shattering, and of the necessity of daily and continuous struggle to improve one's estate—spiritual and worldly.

One might speculate that Hooker's repeated persecutions contributed to his sense of the minister as beleaguered, at odds with the larger church and his own congregants. His deprivations may have contributed to a more individualistic rather than communitarian piety—one all the more aware and respectful of established hierarchy for being at the lower end of it. These experiences may have gravitated against faith in the free bestowal of benefits without some form of effort, may have contributed to the Arminian drift that preparationism was to exhibit after 1640. It is not surprising that men like Hooker, without power to effect change, had less faith in the positive outcome of contending for the true religion than did Sibbes's adherents.

At the close of this exposition of career patterns, it seems appropriate to mark the shifting fates of these men once they arrived on New English shores. Given the preceding discussion, it seems surprising that scholars have made such vigorous claims concerning Ames's influence or Hooker's preeminence within the Puritan party. But of course, the patterns of success and failure traced here describe events only in Old England. These patterns were to be inverted in the New World, where the Amesian piety became normative as the voice of an empowered orthodoxy. In New England, it was the Cambridge Brethren who were forced to the marginal edge, that uncomfortable position so thoroughly familiar to Hooker and his peers.

Originally it had not seemed that this would happen. John Cotton's arrival set the stage for a replay of the Cambridge group's dominance. Called to the most influential pulpit in the colony and granted a salary that exceeded the incumbent Wilson's, Cotton seemed ready to resume the role of religious leader he had enjoyed in England. He brought with him many of the most well-to-do citizens of old Boston, men and women who immediately set about to challenge Winthrop and establish their own dominance. In an early dispute over land distribution, the victory went to the Cottonians, who won concessions from Winthrop in return for agreeing to settle in Boston.[161] After this skirmish, dominance within the congregation became an issue: two of Cotton's most loyal advocates, Leverett and Firmin, were appointed ruling officers of the church. All of this occurred well in advance of the arrival of Vane or Wheelwright; thereafter the claims of the party to power and influence were magnified.

The situation seemed so much to replicate the English pattern that jealousies may have flared. Just as Cotton reprised his role as leader, Hooker once again reprised his pilgrim. Many reasons, no doubt, informed Hooker's choice to depart, but among them is an argument about personal rivalry. Some scholars contend that, weary of the "great influence which Mr. Cotton had in the Colony," and convinced that his own "light would shine more brightly, and be more conspicuous, if it were farther from the golden candlestick of the church in Boston," Hooker resumed his peripatetic course and replanted in Hartford.[162] This was to be only a temporary retreat, however. Decades of struggle and exile seem to have reinforced the native tenacity and intransigence of men like Hooker, and this disposition served them very well during the years of the Antinomian Controversy. In Old England they had been outcasts within an already embattled group, a status they did not accept in the New World. Nor were they any more willing to accept compromise of their vision of church organization in New England than they were in Old. These were the men who ceded their pulpits rather than compromise on their notions of polity; in 1636 they yielded neither. By the end of the decade they had wrested control of the court, the pulpit, and the college from the party of Cotton, and they intended to keep it.

"Strenuous Puritan"—the epithet once given to Hugh Peter—was equally applicable to Hooker, to Winthrop and Wilson, to Shepard. These men contended for the faith in New England with the single-mindedness of the disaffected—those who had been on the outside and did not intend to be put there again. Cumulative adversity makes their stance in 1636 entirely understandable. Yet to insist on reading the events of the 1630s only in light of their past experiences is far too crude. These were first and foremost men of ideas and of unwavering commitment to the religious life, as they defined it. They had an absolute faith in the justness of their own beliefs that consciously inspired their dogged tenacity.

Faced with such intransigence, Cotton and Davenport learned with heavy hearts that their old strategies for perseverance within a hostile orthodoxy were going to be as necessary in New England as in Old. Only three years after fleeing the oppressive policies of the bishops, they realized that caution and craft still had to be exercised if one was to survive silencing. But training on the battlefield of Old England served them as well as it did their opponents: by reprising the flexibility that had proved so effective, they again successfully made the compromises necessary to stay in the game. Dissembling if necessary, staging temporary retreats, yielding on inessentials, again they became the wily spokesmen for an alternative discourse. Shepard indeed was prescient; Cotton and his company (with the notable exception of Anne Hutchinson and the radical spiritists) once again tended their spiritual gardens in secret, harvesting their fruits in silence, and remaining "hid only," like Sibbes's underground treasure of true Christians. Thus, they preserved their affectionate faith, husbanded its heat, and survived the cold years of controversy.

In conclusion, it must be observed that, though their experiences in Old England may have thus contributed to the hostility of the controversy, what divided these preachers most profoundly were ideas—they were a generation animated by religious and philosophical problems. Having limned their careers, one must go beyond and beneath biographical fact to the ideas that inspired allegiances and actions. And in this enterprise of theological explication, two primary matters absorbed their attention—unraveling the mystery of God's being and measuring the depravity of human nature. They spent themselves in endlessly weighing two quantities—God's love and human sin—and arrived at very different conclusions concerning the balance between the two. It is to their calculations that we must now attend.

3

✣

Measuring Sin and Love

Philosophers have measur'd mountains,
Fathom'd the depths of seas, of states, and kings,
Walk'd with a staffe to heav'n, and traced fountains:
But there are two vast, spacious things,
The which to measure it doth more behove:
Yet few there are that sound them; Sinne and Love.

George Herbert, "The Agonie"

Probably an auditor at Gray's Inn, certainly a spiritual kinsman of the Brethren, George Herbert defined the Christian's duty as measuring sin and love. How one could fathom these "two vast, spacious things" was a poignant question for the Puritans, who felt anew the Augustinian sense of what it meant to be a fallen creature in a sinful world. Despairing the power of natural reason and rejecting the authority of human tradition, these believers were cast back upon God's revealed word as the single reliable source of truth. *Sola Fides* and *Sola Scriptura* were the axioms of Reformation.

While accepting the limits of human knowledge, that saints on earth can know God only "through a glass, darkly, after a fashion," the Puritans nonetheless refused despair. Instead, they trusted the sufficiency of scripture, praising the Bible as "a glass that changeth us." The fundamental tenets of the Reformation can be understood by means of this metaphor: reflected "in the glass of the law" we see ourselves convicted of sin, but in the lens of the gospel we find a savior. The Bible's "transforming power" healed deformities, as sinners were "changed into the likeness of Christ."[1]

Modern readers recognize the Bible as a multivocal text, a storehouse of metaphors supporting a variety of readings and interpretations. God is figured simultaneously as a harsh sovereign and an indulgent father; human beings appear as willful servants or loving children. The balance struck between them is imagined variously as a truce, a bargain, or a family bond. These competing representations stand side by side, without mediation. Through selection and emphasis of one metaphor over another, the theologian unavoidably refracted revelation through the lens of his own temperament, giving doctrine a personal resonance.

Such textual variations produced a serious challenge for Puritan ministers, who trusted in a single "right reading" of scripture. As the disputes with Roger Williams and Anne Hutchinson demonstrated, reading practices varied widely within the Puritan community. Consensus was never achieved; the Bible could and did become the site of wars of interpretation.

All preachers acknowledged this potential for schism; they anguished over the possibility of a theology tainted by their own imperfect understanding and by human projection. Yet they also defined their duty as explaining and systematizing the mysteries of faith. To this end, theologians developed "a manner of speaking called anthropopathy," in which God's being "is explained as manifold, that is to say, as if consisting of many attributes"—justice, mercy, love, power, will, etc.[2]

As William Ames explained, since "God, as he is in himself, cannot be understood by any save himself . . . the things which pertain to God must be explained in a human way." Theologians of both camps employed this mode of discourse, cautioning themselves and their auditors that the attributes are "not distinguished from the Essence really, but notionally; that is, they are not distinguished at all in God, but only to us-ward, according to our manner of conceiving."[3] Yet, like selective readings of scripture, the doctrine of attributes inevitably produced partial and partisan representations of divinity. Caveats notwithstanding, the preachers routinely privileged certain of God's attributes and spoke as if they revealed his nature more fully than others.

It has long been supposed that the Puritans were of one mind with respect to the doctrine of attributes. Most scholars, following Miller, argue that the Puritans conceived of God first and foremost in terms of sovereignty.[4] Subsequent academic debates over preparationism, millennialism, and the *ordo salutis* have rested on this initial assumption of implacable power at the center of the Puritan godhead, to which human energy was pitched both in reverence and in attempts at containment by means of covenant legalism.[5]

While such a reading is generally true for the circle of Ames, whose fundamental understanding of God as sovereign was followed by an assertion of covenantal obligation, it is a less accurate description of the figural imagination of the circle of Sibbes, for whom God was first understood as overflowing love.

Reminding the reader of the common ground held by these ministers, however, is a necessary prerequisite to a reading of the texts that is sensitive to the question of difference. A comparativist method inevitably minimizes differences *within* groups in order to foreground differences *between* them; the element of distortion inherent in this method needs to be acknowledged and remembered. On any given issue, the knowledgeable reader will be aware of examples that complicate and at times contradict the general conclusions drawn. For example, a claim that Hooker and Shepard focus less on ecstasy than discipline in their pastoral texts is not meant to suggest that these texts were monolithic, affect-free; mine is an argument about emphasis. While my argument presses toward dichotomy by the very logic of its comparativist method, I wish to affirm clearly and strongly the mixed, ambivalent, and multivocal elements to be discovered in all of these preachers. Emphasis on religious affections was part of the heritage shared by all Puritan divines.[6]

While understood within the frame of a broader doctrinal consensus, a reading of the relevant texts that is attentive to the question of difference, however, does reveal the persistence of important rhetorical emphases that should not be underestimated. More than a mere literary exercise, linguistic preferences within religious discourse extend their significance beyond immediate issues of theodicy and shed light on a wide range of doctrinal issues and institutional practices. Whether God acts primarily by power—pure or as bound by contract—or whether he acts from unconditional love determined for these Puritans not just matters of doctrine but theories of civil society and individual subjectivity. Definitions of sainthood and citizenship, relations of anxiety to confidence, and discipline to piety, were imbricated in these structures of rhetoric. And in practice, the balance preachers struck between divine love and power varied to a surprising degree; there was no univocal orthodox position.[7]

❧

When William Ames read the Bible, he found on nearly every page a testimony to the lordship of God. The most compelling representation of the divine is not as brother or as bride, but the Kyrios of Paul or the Old Testament "Jehovah, or the Lord." While Cotton and Sibbes celebrated the new age of the gospel in which "the poorest believers . . . were taught to say, Our Father," Ames emphasizes that "God is called throughout in the Old Testament, *Mighty God* . . . also *God all-sufficient* . . . And in the New Testament he is called *The Lord Almighty* . . . and *The only potentate.*"[8]

In keeping with scholarly claims, sovereignty does occupy the center of Ames's theology. Even the metaphors by which he described the character

of the covenant—master/servant, king/subject—are rooted in a fundamental recognition of a necessary human submission to godly omnipotence.
Despite his preliminary caveats about the dangers of emphasizing one
attribute over another, Ames makes clear the order in which God's faculties
are to be understood: "the proper order for conceiving these things is, first,
to think of God's *posse*, his power, second, his *scire*, knowledge; third, his
velle, will."[9]

Obviously, this preference for images of domination does not fully characterize Amesian theology. He and his disciples spoke warmly of the
fatherhood of God and the brotherhood of Christ. Moreover, Hooker and
Shepard joined Ames in modifying absolute power by means of covenantal
obligations and an elaborated pneumatology. Yet, their primary interest was
always in the application of power to the human subject, not a meditation
on God's unconditional mercy.

Indeed, the master trope of sovereignty informs *The Marrow of Theology*,
dictating its structure and suffusing Ames's presentation of the offices of
the trinity and of God's working in the world. At the outset of the treatise
Ames adopts traditional theological categories for describing God's being:
essence, subsistence, and efficiency.[10] God's essence is described as his
indivisible or inherent nature. Subsistence is understood as God's manner
of being, that is, as his manifestation in the persons of the trinity. Essence
and subsistence together constitute God's sufficiency, "his quality of being
sufficient in himself for himself and for us." Lastly, the efficiency of God
is his "working all that he hath willed," the power by which God executes
his decree. While essence and subsistence constitute God's nature *ad intra*,
God's efficiency describes "God in action," his working *ad extra*.[11]

Though the ostensible purpose of *The Marrow of Theology* is to provide
a full explication of the whole of theology, in practice Ames focuses quite
intensely on efficiency or the operations of power. His discussion of God's
essence, that "by which he is absolutely the first being," is surprisingly brief,
considering that the doctrine of attributes was invented to contain just this
mystery.[12] In the hands of a mystic, God's essence becomes the object of
worship. In the discourse of a Sibbesian theologian like John Norton, it is
the subject of extended meditation and ecstatic explication. A pragmatic
theologian like Ames, however, acknowledges mystery only to move on to
the surer ground of divine things that can be known, and moreover applied
to the daily practice of Christian life. Eupraxia supplants metaphysical
reverie in this style of piety.[13]

This practical focus is reflected in the brevity of Ames's discussion of
God's ontological essence and by the curious spareness in his diction. I

would argue that Ames's reticence should be partially understood as an expression of humble submission to mystery; the rhetorical consequence, nonetheless, is emphasis on human activity and virtual silence about God's essence.[14] A representative passage serves to illustrate this point. Describing the vitality of God's nature, Ames employed the common metaphor of the living fountain: "He is called living, first, because God works by himself . . . ; second, because the vital action of God is his essence; third, because he is the fountain of all being and of vital operation in all other living things . . . Therefore our faith, seeking eternal life, rests in God alone because God is the fountain of all life, John 5:26."[15]

This passage is a model of Puritan plainstyle, which insists on the division of large topics into smaller, more comprehensible units and which favors useful explication over inspirational rhetoric. The austerity of this description is unrelieved in the following passages; the trope of the fountain remains as unadorned as it is here presented. It might be argued that such plain speech is the appropriate and predictable style of systematic discourse, especially when compared with the figural richness of the sermon form. Yet this claim is complicated by comparison with similar writings of the Cambridge Brethren.

When a Sibbesian preacher like John Norton unfolds God's essence, he breathes life into the abstract metaphor, converting it into an elaborate trope for God's vitality:

> God is a full Fountain, or rather a Fountain which is fulness it self; willing to communicate, as the Sun send forth its light, a fountain its streams, and the prolifical virtue in plants inclineth . . . them to fruitfulness; as the seminal virtue in living creatures, disposeth them to generation: the peculiar affection in parents towards their children, renders them propense to do them good . . . so is the Lord affected to do good.[16]

Rather than division and reduction, Norton compounds and expands his description of God's effulgent nature. The difference between his treatment and that of Ames is not simply in the degree of exfoliation, but in the tone. In these organic metaphors of warmth, wetness, and semen, Norton flirts with neoplatonist visions of divine plenitude and effulgence.

By contrast, Ames simply enumerates God's qualities by means of simple and abstract statements. His exegetical and rhetorical energy is instead reserved for discussions of the legal and operational nature of the sacrifice and covenant. This emphasis is not surprising in a book of practical divinity, where living to God supplants meditation on the living God, but that choice itself reflects Ames's temperamental bias.

Similarly, in his explication of the trinity (God's subsistence), Ames stresses both the primacy of divine power and the vast distance between God and humankind. It is not the incarnated Christ, but the ascended savior, the agent of the covenant, who commands his attention. Ames figures the trinity as distant and functional, rather than as personal and affective. The creator is transcendent, the son ascended, and the Spirit becomes the active agent in the application of redemption.[17]

Students of the period have long regarded this preference for the functional rather than the personal Christ as characteristic of all Puritan preachers. John Eusden, for example, draws a sharp distinction between Lutheran and Reformed christology, arguing that Luther's emphasis on the mystery of incarnation was never of crucial importance to English divines: "The Christocentrism of Martin Luther is not shared by most English Puritans . . . The incarnation . . . was not a mystery in which man should lose himself."[18] A chorus of scholars has echoed this conclusion, arguing that Puritans "minimized the role of the Savior in their glorification of the sovereignty of the Father." Their means was to focus on the ascended Christ and their purpose was "as far as mortals could" to emphasize the distance between heaven and earth.[19] The only bridge was the contractual covenant, not the personal Christ.

This argument is confirmed by the structure as well as the content of the *Marrow*. The person and life of Christ are only briefly treated, and again in language that is figurally abstract.[20] Christ as agent of the covenant assumes center stage in the *Marrow*.[21] This emphasis on Christ's legal function effectively forces Ames's discussion away from godly essence and toward divine omnipotence.

Ames's real interest is indeed the efficiency or the "working power of God by which he works all things in all things."[22] Other aspects of God's nature are subordinated to this application of power: "the meaning both of the essence of God and of his subsistence shines forth in his efficiency." In this somewhat surprising move, Ames collapses distinctions he had been careful to establish: "The power of God, considered as simple power, is plainly identical with his sufficiency." In these statements Ames shifts the focus of divinity from a meditation on the being of God *(esse)* to his performance *(operati)* in the world—from God's nature *ad intra* to his being *ad extra*.[23]

This stress on the exercise of power is inscribed in the works of Ames's disciples as well. Again, the caveat obtains: while they celebrated the beauty of Christ and the blessings of grace, on balance preachers like Hooker, Shepard, and Bulkeley focused on the functional application not the indwelling of Christ. It is not God as he is in himself, but as he deals with the sinner that engages them—God as exacting lord, implacable judge, or demanding covenanter. God is imagined as the creditor who will "have the utmost farthing" due him, or the landlord pressing his claim.[24] Repeatedly, Hooker refers to Christ as "Lord Jesus," or "Lord Christ"—terms which are found with far less frequency in the writings of Sibbes and Cotton. To be sure, this is a loving God, but he is also a "dreadful enemy," an "all-seeing, terrible Judge," "a consuming infinite fire" of wrath.[25]

And when these preachers use familial tropes to describe God's dealings, they often warn that loving fathers are also harsh disciplinarians: there is "no greater sign of God's wrath than for the Lord to give thee thy swing, as a father never looks after a desperate son, but lets him run where he pleases."[26] Though God is merciful, it is a mercy with measure, "it is to a very few . . . it is a thousand to one if ever . . . [one] escape this wrath to come."[27] Such restriction of the saving remnant is of course an axiom of Reformed faith, but one that Sibbes rarely stressed.[28] On the other hand, Hooker and Shepard's God often acts by "an holy kind of violence," holding sinners over the flames or plucking them from sin at his pleasure.[29] This God wounds humankind, hammers and humbles the heart until it is broken.[30]

Divine sovereignty also animates Hooker's description of conversion as royal conquest and dominion: Christ is like "the King [who] taketh the Soveraigne command of the place where he is, and if there be any guests there they must be gone, and resigne up all the house to him: so the Lord Jesus comes to take soveraigne possession of the soule."[31] With sins banished and the heart pledged to a new master, the saint begins the long journey of sanctification. This repetition of the language of lordship insists not only on the centrality of domination in conversion but in the general tenor of human/divine relations—abjection replaces the melted heart so often imagined by Cotton and Sibbes.[32]

It is not surprising that these were the preachers who enforced preparationist discipline among their congregants and who introduced official procedures for monitoring church formations in New England. In the aftermath of the Antinomian Controversy, Hooker and Shepard preached even more vigorously that depravity can be healed only by God's power, not his mercy. Just as he policed ecstatic expression in church gatherings, so by the mid-1630s Shepard restricted expression of his own high emotion to the private pages of his journal. To be sure that journal offers ample proof of Shepard's capacity for mystical experience and expression. Publicly, however, he preached a frightening message of human sin that could only be offset by absolute power: for him, only "by my vileness I may Understand Christ's glory."[33] And when Hooker explained why God saves such vile sinners, he argued, "The reason is taken from the Lords Almighty goodnesse and power, the Lord is able to supply all wants and amend that which is amisse." Hooker assured his auditors that they need not worry that God would prove as impotent in the face of sin as they were themselves: "When the Lord made heaven and earth he did not spend all his strength, that he was able to helpe no more. No, no; he is All-sufficient still, he is not only able to continue that good, which the creature hath, but to make a glorious supply of whatsoever is wanting."[34]

In this passage, the word *goodness* is hedged around by references to power: "Lord," "Almighty," "strength," "all-sufficient." This is the same litany of titles which Ames ascribed to God; and, like Ames, Hooker used tropes designed to make omnipotence manifest. While Sibbes more characteristically spoke of God's uncontainable love as the cure for sin, Hooker proved God's power to make good on what his benevolence promised. He concludes this passage with the assertion that sin only magnifies God's sovereignty: "if our sinnes were more than God could pardon, or if our weaknesses were more able to overthrow us, then his strength to uphold us, hee were not All-sufficient."[35]

There is a certain aesthetic symmetry in the inverse relation of sin and power—the deeper the depravity, the greater God's glory: "the more and greater our sinnes and wickednesses are, the more will the strength and glory of his power appear in pardoning of them, and where sinne abounds, there grace abounds much more in the pardoning of the same."[36] Finally, though, it was not the measure of God's spacious nature but the vastness of human sin that dominated the writings of Amesian theologians. In fact it might be argued that, contrary to Miller's assertion, one practical effect of maximizing the remoteness of God was to focus attention less on divine majesty than on human depravity, subsequently producing an emphasis on pastoral discipline.

Concerned with the dangers of hypocrisy and self-delusion, preachers like Shepard bent their talents to driving home the vileness of the natural man "born full of all sin, as full as a toad is of poison, as full as ever his skin can hold." His "mind is a nest of all the foul opinions, heresies." His heart "is a foul sink of all atheism." Not content with this general condemnation, Shepard enumerates the human sins of "sodomy, blasphemy, murder, whoredom, adultery, witchcraft, buggery." This "filthy toad" dedicates his days to sin, to spitting "venom in the face of God." Shepard concludes with a final tally which leaves nothing unscathed: "so that, if thou hast any good thing in thee, it is but as a drop of rosewater in a bowl of poison; where fallen it is all corrupted."[37]

In contrast to the spareness of Ames's discussion of God's essence, the variety and originality of these metaphors and their lengthy exfoliation testify to the rich imaginative energies dedicated to a vigorous exposition of sin. To be sure, these preachers assured sinners that the smallest labor cleansed the heart, but they also insisted that before that first preparatory work, the heart was all sin. As their epithet would suggest, the preparationists dilated on that sequence of time before union with Christ—the period between God's initial and effectual call. Guaranteed by covenant promises, the process of conversion worked a miraculous transformation in the heart, now likened to a watch whose mechanism could be repaired, a bolted door to be unlocked, a shop to be reordered. These measured metaphors succeeded the hectic depictions of the spotted, soiled heart. The rational sequence of the *ordo salutis* provided the theological ground for metaphors bespeaking an ordered and incremental process of spiritual reformation that always fell short of consummation.

When they did speak of union with Christ, preparationists deployed the trope of marriage so fully and affectively elaborated by the Sibbesians. As with the treatment of God's essence, however, the Amesian rhetoric of consummation tended to be far less ecstatic than that of the Cambridge group.[38] Though his title promises an emotional treatment of union, Hooker explains in *The Soules Exaltation* that his "purpose is not to meddle with the particulars at this time, but only with the generall nature of the communion of the soul with Christ." In fact he rarely dilated on the fruits and pleasures of consummation, remaining rather obscure about "the particulars" throughout his corpus. What is rarely vague in preparationist writings is the true and terrifying sight of sin.[39]

These preachers judged that their auditors were stranded in the first stages of contrition and humiliation, and the path to salvation was long. Hooker characteristically addressed his auditor as an "old weather-beaten sinner" who "hast wallowed in . . . filthinesse," whose heart "hath beene a thorow-fare, to all wickedness." These were the "proud hearts" who erred if they thought "the soule stains of sinne [were] washed away with a few teares." Before these sinners could improve their condition "there must be a true sight of sinne."[40]

Given this prescription, the surest path to salvation was by means of painful introspection. Perhaps the most fundamental observation to be made about preparationists is that their presentation of God's sovereignty worked to encourage this inward turn and the logic of preparationism. Faced with the terrifying abyss of irrational power and immeasurable sin, these preachers invented a doctrine to limit and contain both. They moved with agility from this initial terror to the comforting rationality of the covenant bond.[41]

Everett Emerson has remarked: "The most significant departure from Calvin's teachings in seventeenth-century Reformed theology in general and Puritan theology in particular was the shift in emphasis from God to man."[42] But again, such generalizations require qualification: if Amesians redirected theology to the heart's chamber, Sibbesians remained focused on the image of Christ. In *The Soules Preparation* Hooker remarked: "There are two things hardly knowne; what God is, and what our sinnes are, or else we hardly apply the knowledge of them to our selves."[43] It is really to this last task, the application of knowledge, that the preparationists devoted themselves.

A theocratic humanism ultimately underwrites Amesian doctrine. These preachers were pragmatists rather than pietists; their sermons rest on the efficacy of the conditional covenant, the necessity of antecedent faith, and the importance of human cooperation with divine process. This pastoral message offered comfort to many doubting Christians and proved a powerful stabilizing force in church life and civil society. Yet one must add that for these spiritual pilgrims happiness was always deferred; the path to salvation was long, and union with Christ postponed. Preparation, not consummation, marked this style of piety and made it the hallmark of Puritan social discipline. This was a pastoral method and message rarely employed by the preachers who gathered at Cambridge to worship with Richard Sibbes.

❧

When Richard Sibbes represented God's essence through his attributes, divinity was transformed. In such treatises as *The Excellency of the Gospel above the Law*, Sibbes argues for mercy rather than justice as the center of theology. His purpose, unlike Ames's, is to modify rather than to celebrate the primacy of power. Sibbes argues that "the several attributes of God shine upon several occasions," that "they have as it were several theatres whereon to discover their glory." Like Ames, he argues that in the first days of creation "there was power most of all." And "in governing the world, wise providence." So, for the unregenerate, "in hell, justice in punishing sinners." But for Sibbes the most important theater of God's action is not the first world of creation, or the future world of hell, but life now "to man in a lapsed estate." To such a man Sibbes posed the question, "what attribute shines most, and is most glorious," and he responded without hesitation, "Oh it is mercy and free grace."[44] And his disciples Cotton, Davenport, Norton, and Preston echoed this sentiment, declaring that God is a "God of all comfort," *the Father of mercies, and God of all consolations.*[45] Theirs was a God whose mercy was a fountain flowing without limit; a God who was a lord but, more importantly, a lover; one who melted the heart instead of hammering it; whose concern was as a shepherd to tend a flock, a gardener to prune the plant, a musician to tune the breast.

This is not to suggest that Ames's God of power has no place in their thought, but rather that it is not the primary attribute in the theology of the Sibbes circle. Mercy "churlishly refused" produced pastoral warnings that "the Lamb can be angry, and they that will not come under his sceptre of mercy, shall be crushed in pieces by his sceptre of power."[46] To sinners "out of Christ," the "devil shall present God . . . in a terrible hideous manner, as an avenging God, and 'consuming fire.'" Yet even then, wounded saints have a "prop and foundation of comfort,"—the knowledge that "God sets forth himself, not only in that sweet relation as a Father to Christ, but our father."[47]

This master trope of benevolence is manifest in Cotton's explanation of regeneration. It will be recalled that Hooker's bloody sinner is washed clean as proof of God's ability to do his will. For Cotton, salvation demonstrates instead "an abundant measure of the love of God." Drawing from Paul's assurance that "where sinne hath abounded, there grace hath abounded much more," Cotton turns sin into God's opportunity to bestow his love and to produce the saint's requiting affection: "they who have but a little forgiven them, will love but a little, but they who have much forgiven them will love much."[48] Here, effulgent love counters measureless sin.

Mercy and the constellated attribute of love define the Sibbesian deity. Sibbes asserts that "it is nature in him to be merciful . . . Mercy is his nature." Invoking the surety of the Bible, Sibbes argues that "there is not one attribute set down more in Scripture than mercy." Sibbes asks again and again, "what is the name of God?" and answers with consoling certitude: Mercy. Indeed, "it is the name whereby he will be known, Exod. xxxiv.6, where he describes it, and tells us his name."[49]

Confidence in the primacy of benevolence over sovereignty, justice, or any other attribute leads these theologians to cast knowledge of God in terms of comfort rather than awe: "The best way to trust in God is to know him as he is."[50] Here meditation is directed away from God's power or efficiency and toward his essence. Auditors are counseled to linger and relish this vision of God's nature and his promises. God's "love in adoption, his truth in performing his promise, and his power in making good all of this" reveal that his nature, promise, and works are in service to mercy. The order of this sentence inverts the formula of Ames: here power follows from love and enacts God's essential benevolence.[51]

Faith in this benevolence leads the Cambridge Brethren to preach an alternative doctrine of the trinity. Time after time, they replace the distant covenantor favored by Ames with a near and dear counselor and friend. These preachers describe the human/divine relationship through a series of intimate family encounters. They focus on biblical passages that domesticate divinity—Canticles, the texts of John, and selections from Paul. In making these words of the Bible their own, the Sibbesians comfort rather than chastise their congregants. Moreover, they transform the *imitatio christi* from an anguished self-discipline to an effulgent expression of agape.

Contrary to scholarly consensus, then, God's sovereignty is not *the* defining attribute of orthodox theology. The sermons of the Cambridge Brethren refuse to enthrone an incomprehensible lord, but instead draw God down from heaven:

> Then as God's goodness is great and fit, so it is near us. It is not a goodness afar off, but God follows us with his goodness in whatsoever condition we be. He applies himself to us, and he hath taken upon him near relations, that he might be near us in goodness. He is a father, and everywhere to maintain us. He is a husband, and everywhere to help. He is a friend, and everywhere to comfort and counsel. So his love it is a near love. Therefore he hath taken upon him the nearest relations, that we may never want God and the testimonies of his love.[52]

Metaphors of kingship are never the most persuasive for the circle of Sibbes. In calculating the relation between God and humankind, they find a comforting equation: "There is a greater height and depth and breadth; there are greater dimensions in love and mercy in Christ than there is in our sins and miseries."[53] Unlike the disturbing balance struck by Hooker or Shepard, here benevolence answers human inadequacy.

Moreover, their doctrine of the trinity reflects this happy bias. The first person is imaged as the patient and solicitous father. Cotton declared that the Old Testament Jehovah served as a foil for the New Testament parent:

Under the Law they had but a dark draught of the Image of Christ found in them; but now the fulnesse of time being come, God sends forth a spirit of grace into their hearts and therefore they then called upon God, as God and Lord, and but seldome as Father . . . *Father in the old Testament is a rare expression;* but now scarce any of the poorest beleevers, but the name of Father is as ready with them, as if all were taught to say, Our Father, and Abba Father.[54]

It is Father, not Lord, that names Cotton's God. Rarely described as a harsh disciplinarian, this parent is gentle in his reproofs. As Davenport explains, chastisements are merely versions of care: "As a father, when he seeth his child doth but play with the candle which he afforded him to work by, takes it from him . . . for prevention of spiritual pride." The saint's anchorhold is the assurance that even in times of calamity God watches over his creatures, "God doth support their Spirits, and quicken their faith and hope in him."[55]

"For God so loved the world, that he gave his only begotten Son," was *the* proof text for the circle of Sibbes. Through Christ, the saint discovers a pledge of adoption to an indulgent father, who can no more deny his creature than he can deny himself.[56] The soul that is too broken to pray can count on God to supply the want. Cotton advises, "sweetly tell God thy mind . . ." If a "soule cannot speak, it can sigh, and mourne, and weep." And this is all that is necessary: for when "God hath given us a spirit of Prayer, then hath he in some measure enabled us to pray, whether we say much or little." To the doubting Christian, Cotton affirms, "if we have received the spirit of Prayer, we have received the spirit of Grace."[57]

Although the theological foundation for the doctrine of God's prevenience is better considered in light of covenant theology, it is sufficient here to say that God the father anticipates the saint's needs. Indeed, these preachers claim that God so "loves and delights in us" that it is "a fundamental mistake to think that God delights in slavish fears."[58] Celebration replaces self-loathing in this style of piety. The perseverance of the saints is guaranteed not by God's contractual obligation but by his unconditional devotion.

Similarly, the Cambridge preachers offer an alternative representation of the second person of the trinity. Christ's immediate, personal intercession replaces the pastorally mediated contract preached by the other orthodoxy. Christ, not covenant, restores hope: "To think of God alone, it swallows up our thoughts; but to think of God in Christ, of God 'manifest in the flesh,' is a comfortable consideration."[59] Even when these ministers occasionally adopt Paul's designation of Christ's lordship, they insist it is "a lordship with sweetness," "even as a husband is lord over his wife." Or again, "He is Lord as the Elder Brother, as the first begotten is over the rest." Rarely is this authority exercised from the distant heaven; this is a sovereign whose "government is with unspeakable, with unconceivable sweetness."[60]

These theologians stress neither the soteriological function nor the ascension of Christ. Rather, the incarnation elicits their wonder and thanksgiving. At the outset of the *Orthodox Evangelist*, Norton claims that his desire is identical to "Pauls desire to make known nothing but Christ unto the *Corinths*, his Travail until Christ was formed in the *Galatians*, with other like speeches, of him that breathed nothing but Christ." This breathing of nothing but Christ suffuses the writings of the Cambridge Brethren and inspired more radical followers like Anne Hutchinson and the Fifth Monarchists. To Norton, "the Incarnation is the miracle of miracles."[61] To Sibbes it is "a greater mystery than that of the creation." Christ's sacrifice bespeaks not power or glory but goodness and graciousness: "He hath taken our flesh upon him for that purpose, that he might have experimental knowledge of our infirmities and weaknesses, and from that he might be the more sweet, and kind and gentle to us."[62]

Far from counseling Christians not to lose themselves in this mystery, Sibbes urges that "we cannot too often meditate of these things. It is the life and soul of a Christian. It is the marrow of the gospel. It is the wonder of wonders. We need not wonder at anything after this."[63] In *The Way of Life*, Cotton urges his auditors to meditate on the wounds of Christ, on the manifest love and mercy measured in his sacrifice. The Cambridge ministers preached the gaze upward, not inward; the vision of Christ, not the true sight of sin. This was the marrow of their version of Puritan divinity.

Unlike the preparationists, for whom the riches of imagination were devoted to sin's exfoliation, John Cotton presses sermonic language to yield a poetry adequate to God's tenderness. Beginning with the biblical promise of John 16:26 that Christ "will pray in our behalves . . . making intercession for us," Cotton weaves this verse with a whispered subtext of Canticles: explaining that Christ "dresses and perfumes" our prayers, making them worthy by virtue his own sweetness sprinkled upon them. We are comely because he loves us and imputes his beauty to us. In a touching passage, Cotton offers an extended similitude of Christ's pledge:

> As if an elder brother should set a child one of his younger brethren
> to get his father a posie of flowers, and the child out of ignorance,
> should gather some weeds and put it in: And the elder brother gathers

out the weeds, and sprinkles the flowers, and then presents them in the childs name to the father. So doth Christ to us, while we gather up Petitions here and there, and as we thinke for the best, and some truth and work of grace there is in them, yet some weeds of sinfull folly, then Christ takes them out of our hands, and pulls out the weeds, and sprinkles them with the blood of his cross, and the merit of his sufferings, what he hath done and suffered for us.[64]

It is worth mentioning that this tenderness confirms the characterization of Cotton so remarked upon by his biographers—that his meekness and mildness were unsurpassed among the New England preachers. This is no theologian of the law, but a disciple of love. Implicit in this passage is a more sanguine representation of both human and divine nature than can be found in the sermons of the preparationist preachers. This God is not Hooker's sovereign who "by a holy kind of violence" "pluckes the soule from sinne."[65] Rather, Christ is a thoughtful brother who sees sins not as vile offenses but as the weeds of folly; who sees human beings not as rebellious subjects but as ignorant children. This homely and comforting vision of salvation, characteristic of the doctrine of the Cambridge Brethren, infused their pastoral practices as well as their pulpit oratory.

For Cotton, Sibbes, Preston, Davenport, and Norton, human sin is often presented as a lack, as an absence of good rather than an active principle of evil.[66] Compared with the spiritual deformities frequently described by the other orthodoxy, their conception of evil is mild indeed. Their backsliders are willful children, always already returning. The sottish murmurings of the flesh, the rebellious mutters of the doubting soul are the evils that occupy these theologians. This is not to say that they abandoned the reformed conviction of man's sinfulness, but that faith in God's diffusive goodness guaranteed their assurance of salvation. They preached not a reciprocal covenant based on human obligation, but an unconditional testament. In this context, human insufficiencies are made good solely by God.

Just as the Sibbesians have a more personal christology than the Amesians, so too their doctrine of the Holy Spirit is more personal and immediate. Their application of redemption more closely resembles a true marriage of hearts than the contractual arrangements of the Amesian covenant. Each person of the trinity has a distinct but inseparable role to play in the great work of salvation: "The Father in his wisdom decreed and laid the foundation how mercy and justice might be reconciled in the death of the Mediator. Christ wrought our salvation. The Holy Ghost assures us of it and knits us to Christ, and changeth and fits us to be members of so glorious a head, and so translates and transforms us more and more 'from glory to glory.'"[67] The metaphoric richness with which these offices are described again distinguishes Sibbes's treatment from that of Ames. Rather than the cool logic of contract, the indwelling of the spirit is known here by the warmth of God's breath in the believer's heart.[68]

Because of this domestication of the deity, the epistemological problems so keenly felt by the other orthodoxy did not seem as troublesome for the Cambridge Brethren. Unlike the mysterious God of Ames, the "I AM" to be tamed only by the covenant, Sibbes's deity "comes to spread his treasures . . . to empty his goodness into our hearts."[69] Moving from the Johannine round, "I in thee and thee in me," the Cambridge Brethren confidently urge every believer to take hold of this father personally: "The very life-blood of the gospel lies in a special application of particular mercy to ourselves . . . Take away *my* from *God,* and take away God himself in regard to comfort."[70] This transformation of thy God to my God is the central moment in the saint's life. When the imperial nominative is married to the humble dative, when the great God "undertakes to bee a God *to us,*" the application of redemption is complete.[71]

While the preparationists rarely described consummated union, the Cambridge Brethren frequently expressed confidence in adoption as a past event. It is not the stages before adoption, but the life of the regenerate Christian afterwards, that they preach. But precisely how this application of mercy, by which sinners are made children, is accomplished must be understood within the framework of covenantal doctrine. If theologians must calculate the equation of sin and love, God's covenantal promise is the term that mediates between them.

4

※

The Gospel-Covenant of Grace

> Behold, the days come, saith the Lord, that I will make a new
> covenant with the house of Israel . . . Not according to the
> covenant that I made with their fathers in the day that I took
> them by the hand to bring them out of the land of Egypt,
> which, my covenant, they broke, although I was an husband
> unto them, saith the Lord; But this shall be the covenant that
> I will make with the house of Israel: After those days, saith the
> Lord, I will put my law in their inward parts, and write it in
> their hearts, and will be their God, and they shall be my people.
>
> Jeremiah 31:31–33

Despite differences in imagined anthropologies, regardless of whether they constructed their auditors as wayward sinners or willful children, all Puritan preachers agreed with Augustine that humankind deserved God's damnation. That God elected a few saints to salvation, that he transformed their stony hearts to flesh and engraved them with his name was a wonder both of his mercy and his power. This miraculous reconciliation was effected by God's covenant with his creatures.

The Puritans diligently searched their Bibles for clues concerning the nature and history of this most important of agreements. Relying on such texts as Jeremiah, they drew distinctions between God's pact with Adam and his free promises vouchsafed by Christ. Originally Adam had been joined with God in a covenant of works in which God's blessing descended as a reward for merit and obedience. Quite simply, God granted eternal life in return for perfect obedience to his Law. Secured by a mutual pledge, this first covenant, then, was between consenting contractors, each of whom had obligations to fulfill. Yet the Puritans knew from reading their own hearts as well as their Bibles that this responsibility was beyond human strength to perform. Siding with St. Paul as well as Martin Luther, the Puritans argued that after the fall humankind stood indicted by the Law, worthy only of damnation.[1]

Reconciliation with God was made possible only by Christ's interces-

sion, by the imputation of his merit to the children of Adam.[2] This was
the covenant of grace. Originally made with Abraham in anticipation of
Christ's gift, this covenant united the Old Testament and the New into a
single history of salvation. Faith in the Son rather than obedience to the
Law of the Father secured the saint's place in heaven. And even that
reconciling faith descended from God. The new covenant, then, was based
not on human ability but on God's will; it did not demand obedience as
a condition but bestowed the ability to believe and to act as the fruit of
God's love.[3]

The work of a number of scholars has shown that this distinction
between the covenants of works and grace was elaborated over time and
that early reformers preached a single covenant, differing only in its administration from age to age. The elaboration of the distinction between
the covenant of works and the covenant of grace was in large measure the
invention of Elizabethan divines. The rhetorical advantage of a double
covenant, according to Michael McGiffert, was to sanction pastoral exhortations applicable to all auditors without tainting the unconditional
freeness of grace reserved only for God's elect. Therein a language of
contractual obligation was introduced into covenantal discourse, explicitly
associated with the Adamic bond but also at times attached to the condition of faith in the covenant of grace.[4]

Though all Puritans clearly distinguished the covenant of works from
the covenant of grace in precisely these terms, they did not fully concur
about the character of the covenant of grace itself. There were disagreements particularly over the status of conditionality within this gracious
dispensation. Differences in the representation of God's attributes were
echoed in subtle but important differences in the representation of his
promise. Puritans came to disagree over the normative characterization of
this bond as either a covenant or a testament—conditional and requiring
faith, or absolute and wholly of God's doing. In no small measure, the
battles of the 1630s were waged over questions of conditionality within the
covenant of grace.

When Increase Mather assessed the state of the covenant in 1682, he
noted the ambiguous relationship of absolute to conditional promises that
had troubled New Englanders' understandings of covenant. Enumerating
the various heresies of antinomianism, Arminianism, and Anabaptism,
Mather comes close to suggesting that at the center of a history of New
England churches lay questions concerning the nature of God's promise
to his plantation—his covenant with the saints and with New England.[5]
Another ambidextrous theologian who trod the line between the pietists

and preparationists, Mather spoke with the authority of one who had personally agonized over these questions. From the 1620s through the end of the century, Puritans debated the character of the covenant of grace, whether it was unilateral or reciprocal, absolute or conditional, most properly termed a covenant or a testament. By the 1660s the arguments of the antinomian decades had been reincarnated in the Half-Way Covenant quarrels, and Mather himself had changed his allegiance from the pure promise of Cotton's Testator to the conditional and tribal terms of Hooker's Covenanter.

Much discussed by recent scholars, the doctrine of the covenant is another index of the difference in temperament between the Cambridge theologians and their preparationist counterparts. Again, it was Miller who first identified the importance of the covenant in Puritan theology. Covenantal doctrine represented the very "Marrow of Puritan Divinity." It was the founders' ingenious invention to harness the remote power at the heart of the Godhead. Drawing primarily from Old Testament texts in which the omnipotent God voluntarily limits his own power, Miller's Puritans reconceived of God's dealings with humankind in terms of "a bargain, a contract, a mutual agreement, a document binding upon both signatories."[6] This contract mitigated the problem of assurance while providing for God's actions through secondary means in the world of time. Conditions of the covenant afforded a human sphere of action—if one could believe, he or she could lay claim to God's mercy.[7] By means of the covenant, then, the unknowable God was tamed and the saint was made in some measure responsible for his or her salvation. Voluntarism and the doctrine of preparationism were born. Miller took this position to be representative of the whole of the Puritan spectrum, joining Sibbes with Ames, Cotton with Hooker in a falsely monolithic wedding of sensibilities.[8]

Revision has come from a number of quarters, with some scholars arguing for an emotional dimension of covenant, in which affective response replaces rationalist bargaining as the individual's part.[9] Others, noting a persistent ambiguity in ways of speaking about the covenant, have accounted for these differences in terms of horologicals and chronometricals, of conditionality understood in terms of God's time or man's.[10] Still other scholars have argued that by the late sixteenth century two separate traditions of the covenant theology emerged within Reformed thought generally, each with a different genealogy and emphasis. They distinguish between Calvin's formulation of God's covenant as a wholly gratuitous testament or promise and the conditional or bilateral covenant of Bullinger and Zwingli. Essentially the argument hinges on the assertion that in Calvin's unilateral covenant the burden of fulfillment rests entirely with God himself and is effected through the agency of Christ. The Rhineland theologians, on the other hand, insist on a bilateral covenant in which the promise is conditional. God offers a contract of sorts, in which human beings retain some responsibility for fulfilling the condition—not of obedience as in the covenant of works, but of the condition of faith. The scholars first advancing this distinction did so as a corrective to Miller. They contended that Miller mistook the federalism of English covenant doctrine as a departure or declension from the high Calvinist tradition, while in fact the Puritans were influenced by this second tradition.[11] This argument, nonetheless, proposes a kind of uniformity of opinion among English Puritans with respect to the covenant; it insists that most Puritans were federalists but that their innovations were rooted in soil other than Calvin's Geneva.

It seems likely, however, that both senses of covenant existed side by side in the writings of all Reformed theologians of the period, as indeed they existed side by side in the Bible itself. Michael McGiffert, Lyle Bierma, and Charles Cohen have argued that all of the Reformed theologians "recognized both a unilateral and a bilateral dimension to the covenant of grace within the context of a monergistic soteriology."[12] Yet even within the context of a monergism, such rhetorical differences are important to track. As with the metaphoric preferences in anthropopathy, an emphasis on covenant over testament as characteristic of God's work is a telling one that again reveals partisan structures within the larger Puritan community.

Whether or not the differences between testament and covenant can be ascribed to distinctive traditions rooted in peculiar continental sources cannot be decided here, nor is this issue particularly relevant to my concerns. Given their shared culture, it would seem a mistake to argue that Cotton and Sibbes looked to Geneva while Ames and Hooker drew upon the Rhineland tradition, just as it would be wrong to argue that Hooker always spoke of the conditional or that Cotton only preached the free promise. Surely the entanglements of tradition and language are more complicated than a simple bifurcation or quest for origins would allow. I do not wish to dispute the simultaneous sounding of these two traditions in the writings of all the Puritan divines here considered. Indeed, Ames often hedged his presentation of covenant with assurances of God's prevenient grace, just as Sibbes and Cotton sometimes enjoined believers to act as if there were conditions.

Yet here as in all else, the issue is not doctrinal consistency but rhetorical emphasis. The Intellectual Fathers and Spiritual Brethren did not frame the question of human responsibility and divine prevenience in the same way. Though both groups spoke of the covenant, they came to different conclusions about the relative importance of absolute or conditional promises in that relationship. This difference was manifested in their lexical preferences for describing God's promise as either a covenant or testament.

Both the Cambridge theologians and their preparationist counterparts acknowledged that there was a difference between the terms *covenant* and *testament*. A covenant, according to the *Oxford English Dictionary* and the general usage of the period, was understood as "a mutual agreement," a "league" or a "contract." Hooker writes, "As in a covenant there are articles of agreement between party and party, so between God and his people."[13]

A testament, on the other hand, is unilateral; it directs the bequest of goods and property after death. As Richard Sibbes explained, a testament "indeed is a covenant, and something more." That something more was precisely the freeness of the gift. A testament "bequeatheth good things merely of love"—in this case Christ's free love made manifest by his sacrifice. As Sibbes goes on to explain the difference, "A covenant requireth something to be done. In a testament, there is nothing but receiving the legacies given."[14]

These terms were often used interchangeably, and, if pressed, Ames and Hooker would have agreed that though they used the term *covenant*, they meant the unconditional promise of the testament. Some scholars have dismissed this emergent rhetorical emphasis as merely strategic, in terms of pastoral expediency; others have claimed that linguistic ambiguity does not imply differences of meaning.[15]

Yet I would argue that far from being insignificant or merely strategic, such rhetorical patterning produces meaning. Just as the doctrinal formulation of attributes first reflected and then amplified significant differences, so preferred ways of speaking about the covenant emerged to define distinctive discursive communities. Over time, the Amesians spoke of the covenant as if there were an implied condition of faith, and they stressed the importance of preaching the law as a precursor to the gospel.[16] In the decades after the Antinomian Controversy, preachers such as Peter Bulkeley would eliminate the subjunctive to suggest that the covenant promise was indeed conditional.[17]

This manner of speech was rarely employed by the Cambridge Brethren, who either preached their preferred doctrine of testament or struggled to clarify the unconditional terms of the covenant bond. This preference, present in the early sermons, was gradually refined in the decades before migration and then dramatized in the public dialogues and ritual trials of the Antinomian Controversy. While the doctrine of the covenant developed its definition through historical permutations, as many critics have shown, the term acquired sharper delineation more immediately through that contestation.[18]

From the outset, but then more keenly in the midst of controversy, the Cambridge theologians argued that the proper articulation of God's essential mercy was to speak of the covenant as a free gift. So too for the Amesians, a more consistent stress on covenant as contract bespoke the power of God and the responsibility of believers, describing a relation based on mutual obligation.

❦

William Ames was careful to maintain the distinction between covenant as contract and as free testament; he argued that the first sense properly applied only to Adam's bond. The fall of Adam made necessary the death of Christ and the testament of his free grace. The first covenant was between friends and implied mutual responsibilities; the second was a "reconciliation between enemies" made possible only by divine intercession.[19]

Yet Ames's discourse, like that of his famous teacher William Perkins, seems consistently caught in the undertow of legalism.[20] His admirers argue that "theologically and propositionally Ames preached the omnipotence of God," yet admit that for Ames "on the practical level man was responsible." Detractors like R. T. Kendall claim that Ames's theology "is 'Arminian' in every way but in the theoretical explanation that lies behind the actual practice of the believer."[21]

In terms of the covenant, this emphasis meant that despite strong reminders of God's prevenience, Ames exhorts auditors *as if* faith were a condition of the covenant, contingent on human action. Practically speaking, the doctrine of the covenant became an exhortation to the saint to work out his or her salvation with fear and trembling; it offered a means of assurance but also enjoined the saint to make that assurance secure. In one sense, it was a doctrine of great comfort, motivated by a humane desire to provide a place for human initiative. In another sense, however, it bound men and women to unremitting self-scrutiny and anxiety.

The stress on conditionality evolved with the elaboration of English covenant theology; it entered into the formulation not only by the avenue of antecedent faith but from the other direction, by a consequent moralism.

Once elected, God's saints manifested their gratitude by observing the moral law. Since Ames de-emphasized the doctrine of perseverance, keeping within the covenant also became tinged with the conditional. Even theologians who were adamant about the absolute freeness of grace might admit conditionality in this second sense.[22] Flexibility with respect to perseverance of the saints, then, allowed conditionality even where God's prevenience was insisted upon. Covenant-keeping became the province of human beings, and the engine for communal as well as individual exhortation. It was by this means that the tribal identification with Israel was effected, and the jeremiad as a rhetorical strategy for social control was born.[23]

Ames first introduces the covenant as a part of God's providence, his special government of intelligent creatures: "the revealed will of God, which is the rule for the moral life, applies to the rational creature" and requires obedience. God's governance demands that he "give to everyone according to his ways and according to the fruit of his action." From this sense of justice and reasonable recompense, "from this special way of governing rational creatures there arises a covenant between God and them."[24] Resting on justice and its conditions, "this covenant is, as it were, a kind of transaction of God with the creature whereby God commands, promises, threatens, fulfills; and the creature binds itself in obedience to God so demanding." This description properly applies to the governance of creatures under the covenant of works.[25]

In this context, Ames seems to advocate the kind of contractualism with which he has been so widely associated. He argues that moral deeds done under the rubric of the covenant "lead either to happiness as a reward or to unhappiness as a punishment." In theory, however, he protects God's sovereignty by adding that "the latter is deserved, the former not." Men and women are fallen creatures who deserve only reprobation; grace is wholly gratuitous. The terms of the covenant of works are satisfied only by the sacrifice of Christ. Accordingly, at one point Ames declares that the new dispensation is termed a testament as well as a covenant. Yet, this is a designation and a meaning he does not pursue.[26]

Indeed, though Ames repeatedly reminds his readers that God fulfills all of these conditions under the covenant of grace, in practice he begins to exhort them, to stress the necessity of an active faith. Just as he argues that the two covenants are parts of the single work of redemption, differing only in application from age to age, so too Ames discovers conditions in both covenants. Christ performs obedience to God's decrees, but human beings must accept Christ's offer of righteousness. Drawing on biblical injunctions to believe and live, Ames and his followers argued that the covenant of grace depends "upon condition of faith and obedience." Even though God himself provides faith as the fruit of his favor, human beings must actively hope in Christ. To the Amesians, the very term *covenant* implies this reciprocal relation.[27] In contrast to the unilateral testament of the Sibbesians, Ames asserts that this is a covenant in which faith defines human obligation.[28]

The original relation of the sinner and God, based on such vast disproportions of sin and power, now issues in a relation suggesting greater mutuality. Emphasis on the condition of faith focuses Ames's theology on practical divinity.[29] Indeed, though his rhetoric takes him further in the direction of human voluntarism than he would wish, it might be argued that the central concern of the *Marrow* is to map the *ordo salutis* as a series of predictable and practical increments.[30] The first step on Ames's path involves not only passive receiving of the habit of faith but also active believing, in which the individual turns to Christ. For Ames, both of these steps precede justification.[31]

Faith is that virtue whereby "we lean upon [God], so that we may obtain what he gives to us." Ames uses active verbs to describe the life of faith: "by faith we first cleave to God and then fasten on to those things which are made available by God." Faith is "our duty towards God," the condition by which we enter his covenant and secure his promises for ourselves.[32] Ames is not afraid to spell out the "divers duties . . . which both ought and are wont ordinarily to be performed before the certainty of this grace can be gotten."[33] As with Perkins, there is an implied condition or contract whereby human beings deal with God. The activism implied in the constructions "to cleave," "to labor," "to fasten on to" become more pronounced in Ames's followers, as does the appeal to self-interest in laying hold of the covenant.

Conditionality is admitted into an otherwise predestinarian schema by way of the distinction between chronometricals and horologicals—God's time and ours. This distinction allows for the simultaneous understanding of God's promise as absolute and conditional, and therein underwrites an emphasis on preparationism. Ames argues that justification is a twofold change, "relative and absolute." In real terms, "the change, of course, has no degrees and is completed at one moment and in only one act." This absolute change, however, is according to God's reckoning. As Ames goes on to say, "yet in manifestation, consciousness, and effects, it has many degrees; therein lie justification and adoption."[34] This space between the relative and absolute allows preparationism to thrive, and with it the pragmatism closely associated with American religious expression. By focusing on the relative change, men like Ames and Hooker could map the steps to the altar and enjoin their auditors to make their salvation sure. Their antinomian critics, however, would argue that even when deployed in the interests of a pastoral pragmatism, preaching the conditionality of faith invests doctrine with a legalistic aura.

❧

Thomas Hooker was no Arminian, nor did he preach a doctrine of works as Anne Hutchinson claimed.[35] From first to last, Hooker made clear the differences between the covenant of works and the covenant of grace, between conditional and absolute promises. The covenant of works was "a covenant between God and Adam only, Adam in his innocency." This was a bond of true and strict contractuality, in which blessing was dependent upon obedience. Adam's rebellion proved human frailty, that we have "no power of our own."[36]

Under the new dispensation the second sense of covenant prevails; one in which God fulfills the terms and in which "according to the measure of grace received," we learn to "walk in this obedience."[37] On the face of it, this formulation is not unlike that which might be found in the writings of Sibbes or Cotton. Hooker, however, does not focus on God's prevenience. Like Ames, he shifts his attention instead to the issue of right walking, the issue of human obligation in the covenant. Moreover, when Hooker casts the drama of salvation into the world of time, he leaves behind the past-tense verbs denoting "grace received," which tell of God's gift, and emphasizes active verbs denoting human initiative in the present world—the walk in obedience. The insistence on action as a fruit of grace seems to be a consequent condition in the above doctrine, a clause which suggests Hooker's ambivalence concerning perseverance. But Hooker sometimes transformed obedience into the antecedent condition of faith as well.

This transformation is evident in Hooker's sermon series on the application of redemption. Hooker begins *The Soules Implantation*, for example, with the text Isaiah 57:15, where God proclaims, "I will dwell with him that is of a contrite and humble spirit." The subject of his sermon is the "two maine parts of the preparative work." Hooker makes clear the exegetical principle he will use in unfolding this scriptural text: "And I intend not to trade with every particular in the Verse, but so much in it as fitteth my intendment in hand."[38]

This editorial principle results not merely in trimming down the verse to the doctrinal truth "I dwell with him that is of a broken heart," but also in a subtle addition to the biblical text. When Hooker recasts text into doctrine the language of conditionality is added: "So the Doctrine in generall from hence is this: *The soule must bee broken and humbled, before the Lord Jesus Christ can, or will dwell therein, and before faith can be wrought therein.* There must be contrition, before there will bee an inhabitation of Christ in the soule."[39] Hooker's insertion of the word *before* into this text was not a neutral gesture—indeed the Antinomian Controversy was in some measure fought over the question of faith as a fruit or condition of grace.[40]

Cotton would argue that Christ makes the heart humble even as he enters; before union, no repentance is possible.[41] Just as the goodness of the world did not precede but rather came into being with God's proclamation, so for men like Sibbes and Cotton the heart is made fit *with* and not before indwelling. The distinction is a subtle one; for though Cotton would agree with Hooker that God infuses the *habit* of faith into the waiting heart coincident with union, he would also insist that the *act* of faith must be subsequent to it.[42]

Though not a position he would declare explicitly, Hooker seems implicitly to stress the act of faith as antecedent to union as well. Moreover, in distinguishing between the absolute and the conditional promise, Hooker argues that the language of contingency belongs to and is the proper expressive mode for a temporal, human world. Acting through second causes and with respect to the creature's intelligence, God relies on means and processes in the worldly execution of his absolute decree. It is in the instrumental operation of his will that the absolute and unconditional are made contingent in a world of time. The previous chapter argued that Hooker shifts the human gaze from Christ to the heart. The analogue is the shift from the absolute promise to its gradual application. Such a change was secured by the doctrine of covenant, in which God freely bound himself and the creature became an actor.[43]

In the preaching of doctrine, Hooker begins with a full acknowledgment of God's prevenience: "When we have received mercy and grace through the goodness of God in acceptation of our persons, in and through Christ, then the Lord requires that we should walk in new obedience before him, answerable to that grace bestowed." In unfolding the sermon, however, Hooker shifts his focus almost exclusively to this second sense of covenant, "a covenant of walking before or with God." This language of activism, argued from pastoral needs rather than scriptural promises, implicitly undermines prevenience in favor of consequent moralism.[44]

Hooker goes on to add, "this is the covenant of new obedience or of thankfulness, which the Lord reveals, requires, and exacts of all that have given their names unto him."[45] Note that rhetorically prevenience is replaced by God's exacting, by the consequent condition of obedience as an evidence of justification. Indeed, Hooker calls this a new covenant of obedience, in that God gives us power and we act. Now, it is the creature who gives his name to God, not God who calls. Again, this is a substitution of human potency for God's that Hooker would have denied, even abhorred. Yet, his manner of speaking, his continual exhortations, and his use of active verbs reveal the homocentric bent of his theology. This tendency opens the way for the substitution of labor for assurance—the substitution that Weber found so characteristic of the Puritan ethic.[46]

The emphasis on right walking is pervasive even in those sermons celebrating union with Christ. So strong is the dilation on human initiative in Hooker's sermons that reminders of God's prevenience sometimes seem afterthoughts.[47] After the first bow to unconditionality in "The Faithful Covenanter," for example, Hooker goes on to speak the language of contracts. To be sure, the ability to act is understood as following God's justification, but once the saint is made acceptable, "the Lord requires that we express the covenant and walk answerable unto it." The covenant is likened to a lease, for which the saint must "pay God his full rent." This payment is "an answering the means of grace with the measure of our uprightness and obedience."[48] The assurances that God will make such acts possible fade, while entreaties to labor, to fulfill one's obligations, proliferate.

Hooker often reminds his auditors of the subsequent conditionality rather than the initial freeness of covenant; of "the likeness between, and the resemblance of, a covenant that is made between two parties, and the law, which is the covenant which is given us of the Lord."[49] Indeed, under the pressure of fashioning an effectual word, Hooker sometimes transforms the language of contract into the language of bondage. First the individual is bound: "The world is naught, and one cannot tell who to trust; and therefore God must bind us, brethren, to keep our covenant." Man is "bound to keep covenant by virtue of his oath." Yet God is also bound: "Why, we have the Lord in bonds for the fulfilling [of] his part of the covenant. He hath taken a corporal oath of it, that he will do it."[50]

Replacing Sibbes's confidence in God's free and eternal effulgence, we find Hooker's anxiety at the danger of God's desertion, not simply of the nation but of the individual saint. This anxiety produces the language of unceasing labor, of keeping commandments, which Hutchinson condemned as crypto-Arminian. Yet, fulfilling these conditions of sanctification produced comforting assurance. "The Lord takes a corporal oath that if we will keep his commandments, he will not be God if he bless us not."[51]

Hooker's great contribution was to analyze the ways in which we fulfill this obligation—the ways in which human beings labor to prepare the heart. In these sermons the verbs denominate the creature to be an active agent. The believer *hammers* the heart, *gives up* sins, *lays hold* of the promise. Hooker's sermons are veritable handbooks for the labor of true Christians. And in this, as in the matter of conditionality, he spoke for his pastoral peers who became the American orthodoxy.

Shepard, too, condemns the preaching of too free a grace, stressing instead the necessity of the law and of labor. Hooker's active verbs find an even greater place in Shepard's formulations. To his mind "the gate is strait, and therefore a man must sweat and strive to enter . . . it is a tough work, a wonderful hard matter, to be saved." The language of prevenient grace loses its primacy amidst these vibrant and vigorous tropes of human action: "Hence the way to heaven is compared to a race, where a man must put forth all his strength, and stretch every limb, and all to get forward." "This way is further compared to fighting and wrestling; it is a strait gate of humiliation, faith, and repentance, which man must pass through." Consistently, Shepard likens the soul's preparations to a pilgrimage, and his pastoral role as revealing to the auditor "his journey's end and the way in general to it, but also the several stadia or towns he is orderly to pass through." By Shepard's lights, to presume regeneration without that incremental and orderly progress is to flirt with antinomianism; of less concern to him are the inroads made on the freeness of grace by a too-exacting doctrine of preparation. Shepard's pastoral mission was to "bring men unto the rule, and try men's estates herein."[52]

The very presentation of a way, a path, a pilgrimage, inserts salvation into the world of human time. This growth in grace emphasized process rather than the sudden remaking of the soul. For Shepard, only the diligent, the prepared virgins, are admitted into the covenant.[53] And while Cotton would argue that if we have Christ in the free covenant we have all, Shepard condemned such a repudiation of human obligations: "It is strange to see what a faith some men have that can close with Christ as their end, and comfort themselves there. It is not means, (say they,) but Christ; not duties, but Christ; and by this faith can comfort and quiet themselves in the neglect and contempt of Christ in means—as infallible a brand of God's eternal reprobation of such a soul as any I know." In the midst of controversy, Shepard was prepared to argue that "this is New England's sin."[54]

This passage inverts the emphasis on the freeness of grace that was so important to the Spiritual Brethren. Cotton instead declared, "In the Gospel the promise is made to Christ, so that, give me Christ and I claim my right to the promise and to all the comforts and blessings thereof." It was always Christ, not the means to Christ, that provided assurance. Cotton, of course, would join Shepard in deploring true antinomianism, which abjures the return of fruits for grace received. But he also argued that there was a good distance between fervent Christocentrism and the antinomian heresy—a distance Shepard collapses in the foregoing passage. While Cotton encouraged responsive preparation of the heart, he objected to the substitution of covenant for Christ and the insistence on covenant conditions.[55]

❦

The shading of conditionality into legalism is perhaps most visible in the writings of Peter Bulkeley. Preached during and in the immediate aftermath of the Antinomian Controversy, Bulkeley's *Gospel-Covenant* represents more fully than any other treatise the emergent orthodoxy's understanding of the nature and conditions of God's promises. Well into the 1640s Bulkeley defined his position against opponents like Cotton. Throughout these years, extant letters suggest that Bulkeley continued to quiz Cotton on his opinions regarding the nature of the covenant and its conditions. Like the letters exchanged in 1637, this correspondence is cordial in tone; it is hard to discern in these letters where the line between "brotherly instruction" and a less genial discipline fell.[56] Despite continued pressure, however, Cotton yielded little on the question of the conditional promise, holding to the positions he articulated in his earlier sermons on the covenant. Read together, Cotton's *New Covenant* and Bulkeley's treatise may be said to rehearse the disputes of the 1630s. Significantly, Increase Mather's 1682 reprisal of the covenant debates cites these texts by Cotton and Bulkeley as key examples of seemingly opposed but essentially reconcilable opinions regarding conditionality. Mather is silent about the fractious debates of the 1630s and about the preemptive measures whereby that reconciliation was legislated rather than freely embraced.[57]

Since Bulkeley's treatise has been the subject of several learned studies documenting his flirtation with legalism, my purpose here is not so much to offer a new reading, as to challenge the general sense that he alone pressed conditionality toward the *quid pro quo* of contract. As the foregoing readings suggest, there was a symmetry between his positions and those of the other Amesians.

Yet, more than any other preacher of the first American generation,

Bulkeley documents the strong undertow of conditionality implicit in Ames's rhetoric. Prefaced by none other than Thomas Shepard, *The Gospel-Covenant* methodically revisits key issues of the Antinomian Controversy, announcing the new orthodoxy's positions. As if answering the elders' 1636 interrogatories in Cotton's stead, Bulkeley declares that justification indeed may be evidenced by sanctification, that faith should be understood as an antecedent condition of the covenant of grace.[58]

Throughout the treatise Bulkeley privileges covenant over testament, capitalizing on common parlance and common sense to assert that a covenant is a contract "which doth require mutual stipulation or condition on both parties." Acknowledging that the "terme or name of Testament, is given to the Covenant," Bulkeley argues that this description is meant "not to exclude the condition, but to shew the firmnesse, and inviolable and unchangeable nature of it, being confirmed by the death of Christ the Testator." Contrary to spiritist opinion, Bulkeley zealously argued that "the Apostle had not intent (in so calling it) to exclude the condition."[59] Though he preaches that human ability to fulfill the condition of faith is contingent on God's prevenience, Bulkeley returns again and again to the language of contingency. The habit of faith may indeed be consequent to God's initial calling, but it is the act of faith prior to the final closing that interests Bulkeley.

To auditors hungry for assurance, this distinction provides space for human activity, self-scrutiny and finally satisfaction: "It is the act of faith which receives the promise . . . A man may have an hand and yet not have the gift which is offered him, unless he put forth his hand to receive it; faith is the hand of the soule, and the putting of it forth is the act by which we receive Christ offered."[60] The acts of faith, along with the daily practice of piety, offer security of conditions fulfilled. Bulkeley's is not an Arminian position, as Hutchinson and modern detractors might claim. However, his emphasis on subsequent human action rather than initial divine infusion shifts theology toward a pragmatic humanism the Sibbesians could not support, a view that could be misinterpreted by less theologically astute auditors. Just as Hutchinson popularized Cotton's doctrine of indwelling into a seeming libertinism, so conditionality in the hands of men like Winthrop could come perilously close to Arminianism, as Thomas Shepard himself discovered.[61]

Taking up the vexed question of conditional and absolute promises, Bulkeley performs this same homocentric turn. While the absolute promises guarantee God's benevolence to being in general, they "do not describe the persons to whome the blessings of the Covenant do belong." For personal assurance, the consuming concern of Bulkeley's auditors, one had to rely on the conditional promises of the covenant: "onely the conditionall promises do point out the persons to be saved, as the absolute do shew the cause of our salvation; if therefore we will try, and in a way of tryall have any knowledge of our personall interest in the salvation promised, we must either come to know it by the conditionall promises, or not have it from the word at all, &c."[62]

To be sure, Bulkeley allows the doctrinal necessity and the pastoral uses of God's promise absolute "as the foundation of our salvation," but his focus is on "the conditionall as the foundation of our assurance."[63] Cotton would argue that the foundation not just of salvation, but also of personal assurance, was more surely rooted in God's complete prevenience and in the absolute promise of his graciousness. Throughout his exchanges with the elders and in his treatises on the covenant, Cotton persisted in characterizing the conditional covenant as a misguided appeal to fallible human agency and as an uncertain foundation for human assurance. His more radical adherents viewed the conditional as the signature of emergent moralism at the cost of true religion.

Explicitly critiquing this spiritist position, Bulkeley insists "neither would I make the absolute promises uselesse, as some have gone about to do with those that are conditionall."[64] Yet implicitly he reverses what the Sibbesians took to be the proper valuation of conditional and absolute promises by flatly decreeing that "the Lord doth not absolutely promise life unto any." Even after his chastening in the 1630s, Cotton countered this position, insisting on God's unconditional mercy.[65]

Just as the enumeration of God's attributes functioned as a heuristic strategy, so high Calvinists understood the conditional covenant as something of a pastoral negotiation between God's eternal decrees and human conceptions of incremental time and personal history. For Cotton, Christ stood as the sole beneficiary of God's testament; all conditions were met by him, all promises were received through him. The rhetorical stresses of Bulkeley's *Gospel-Covenant* refigure the relationship between Christ and covenant, recasting the conditional promise as the center of soteriology.[66] Bulkeley asks "whether the covenant of grace be made at all betwixt God and us, or onely betwixt God the Father and Christ."[67] He answers that through Abraham, God makes a covenant directly with human beings.

With this assertion, Bulkeley shifts the focus from Christ to creature more fully than any of his contemporaries. Arguing that "if therefore any will maintaine, that God makes no promise or covenant with us, but only with Christ, then let them answer the Apostle . . . Let them tell us how the promises were made unto *Abraham,* if they are made onely to Christ."[68] Sibbes and Cotton were consistently anxious that the covenant should not replace Christ as the spiritual center of Puritan piety. Bulkeley's formulation prefigured legalism and the substitution of a proto-bureaucratic soteriology for the more personal faith. Bulkeley not only tends to replace Christ the Fountain with the Gospel Covenant, but then diminishes the Son's role as sole executor of the bond.[69] Christ's centrality is minimized and the human obligation to labor is assured in this assertion that "the same promise" made to Christ "is afterwards in time made to us also."[70] This is, of course, a doctrine which in its practice could bypass Christ's personal intercession altogether. The rise of sacerdotalism in the 1650s can be seen as one consequence of this emphasis on mediated process.[71] Given this fundamental difference of opinion, it is perhaps understandable that Cotton and Wheelwright refused to attend Bulkeley's ordination at Concord.[72]

By the fourth part of his treatise, Bulkeley is willing to highlight even more dramatically the centrality of covenant over Christ, of action over dependency. He does this by insisting on the absolute primacy of the conditional promise: "for the tryall of our interest in the salvation which the Covenant promiseth, there can be no more direct, evident and certaine way taken then by examining our selves concerning the condition of the Covenant, expressed in the conditionall promises." This is a "sure way of tryall" to determine our estates—this is the very assertion of sanctification as evidence of justification which Cotton descried as popish doctrine.[73]

Indeed, Bulkeley empowers human beings to a degree unprecedented in the literature of preparationism. In answer to the question of what one must do to be saved, Bulkeley enumerates human responsibility in a fashion that might be fairly described as providing a handbook for storming God's throne.[74] He advises, "Break your covenant with your old sins . . . Goe before the Lord as guilty of thy former rebellion . . . lay downe thy selfe and life before God . . . yeeld up thy selfe to the obedience of the will of God."[75] While such injunctions are to be found occasionally in the sermons of Preston or Sibbes, they form the core of Bulkeley's writings. They reveal the turn inward and earthward of a theology progressively focused on human agency.

Contrasting Cotton's insistence on the soul's passivity, Bulkeley says, "When you come to make a covenant with God, you must not come to *give lawes* unto God, but to *take lawes* from God; not to impose lawes upon him, that he shall save you so and so, but you must leave God free to make the conditions of the covenant after his own minde and will . . .

let him command and require what he will, he must be free, or else he will not make a covenant with you."[76] Though Bulkeley explicitly asserts God's prevenience as enabling these actions, the phrasing of this passage foregrounds human agency.[77] Taken to their furthest degree, Bulkeley's formulations could appeal to a self-interest that would qualify traditional Puritan anxiety about the dangers of self-love. In a secular context, this focus on the personal could become egocentric; emphasis on the conditional covenant and subsequently on human initiative could fuel not only self-empowerment but anxious and unending self-performance.

❧

In this language of reciprocity scholars like Weber and Miller thought they had unmasked the irony of Protestantism itself—thought they could explain how a theology committed to an implacable sovereign became so profoundly homocentric and how the spirit of Protestantism was transformed into an ethic of a spiritualized capitalism. In the course of less than a century, so it seemed to them, the *ordo salutis* was transformed into a secular "way to wealth."

Though this transformation exceeds the scope of this essay and its commitment to the specific case of early Puritanism, I would briefly suggest that it is in the history of preparationist rhetoric, understood as part of but not embracing the whole spectrum of Puritan thought, that speculations concerning the spiritualization of the work ethic might be best situated. The transformation of Protestant faith into the spirit of capitalism might be read as a history of preparationist rhetoric as it is translated into the secular world of eighteenth-century enlightenment. In that context, earlier injunctions to labor unceasingly (understood both as a consequent condition of the covenant and as the sure ground of assurance) may have contributed to the spirit of self-help and the ethic of deferred gratification that Weber marks as fundaments of the new economic order. Though Hooker and Bulkeley taught no covenant of works, their emphasis on conditional faith before justification and their anxiety about covenant-keeping afterward seem linguistically and philosophically compatible with the system of signs and rewards Weber identifies with emergent capitalism.

To be sure, when defined as a quest for spiritual goods, injunctions to labor infused preparationist rhetoric. These preachers were not only aware of this aspect of their language; they exploited it. Ames admits that "since our love is a desire of union with God it comes in part from what is called concupiscence or appetite. We desire God for ourselves, because we hope for benefits and eternal blessedness from him."[78] Without question, Ames's disciples rhapsodize over the beauty of the beloved, but they also appealed to more self-interested and material desires. Rather than reading Christ's joy in the saints, they read the individual's joy—not just in the beauty of Christ, but in the bounty of his gifts. The dowry characterizes their presentation of the spiritual marriage as often as does the ecstatic enjoyment of the bridegroom.

The Amesians often convert the affective union of Canticles into the contractual marriage bond of Protestant practice, a contract stipulating duties and rewards. As Hooker would urge: "now see your dowrie, and the point is this, that there is a conveyance of all spirituall grace from Christ to all faithfull beleevers in the world; well then, you see the point."[79] The point was to lay hold of that dowry. The riches to be had by entering into the nuptial contract are "fair indeed"; since "the Lord Jesus Christ is no bad match, you must not thinke you could have done better."[80]

When marriage is thus invoked as the trope of union, it is often as a legal contract. This not to say that images of lying in the arms of Christ do not appear in the writings of these preparationists, but rather that they are not central. The language of contract usually follows passages celebrating spiritual ecstasy and re-centers attention on human interests once more. In these writings, love is less often the free flow of agape or even a self-forgetful erotic desire; rather, it is a more substantial, a more self-regarding desire for consummation, as Ames observed.

For men like Bulkeley marriage was also a bond of submission. Consider for example this statement: "we must present our bodies as a living and acceptable sacrifice, consecrate and devote them to God, to live unto him, and to be our own no more: as it is in a marriage-covenant, when a man and woman make a covenant, they doe resigne up themselves one to another, not to be to themselves any more; it is a marriage-covenant that we make with God, *I will marry thee to my selfe,* saith the Lord, *Hos.* 2.19. therefore we must doe as the Spouse doth, resigne up our selves to be ruled and governed according to his will."[81]

Here marriage becomes a metaphor for submission to power—the bridal becomes a bridle both on God's power and human activity. This is a covenant of subservience: "wee must give the hand under God, submitting to him, to be ruled by him."[82] This language of dominance and submission is also to be found in the writings of the Sibbesians, but to a far less degree. More often, they stress reciprocal desire and mutual surrender that modify Christ's power.[83]

Though this subject will be treated at length below, for the purpose of comparison it is important to remark that Sibbes and Cotton worried about the all-too-human tendency to focus on the material benefits of marriage over the pleasures of spiritual desire. Cotton argues that we must love Christ before consideration of "any benefit or gift that we have from him." Sibbes characterizes such concupiscence as "no better than a harlot's love."[84] Rather, as the bride of Christ, the true Christian "regards first the person of her husband" and only "then looks to the enjoyment of his goods, and inheritance, and nobilities."[85]

For the preparationists, the appeal to self-interest is not limited to the trope of marriage. Hooker refers quite literally to other forms of appetite in *The Soules Preparation:* "When the dainties of salvation are distributing, you that are at the lower end of the Table, should thinke with your selves; will the dish never come to the lower end?" Those starving saints who want the dainties and sweetmeats of salvation should "labour to get something to thy owne particular."[86] Christ is "the shop from whence all grace is to bee had" and those who want spiritual goods must choose to enter.[87] The whole of this doctrine may be expressed in Hooker's pithy phrase: "endure all in hope of the harvest."[88]

Citing texts like these, some recent critics have renewed and extended Weber's speculations. As less sanguine readers of Puritan culture, they have claimed that the self-interestedness of covenant theology and the anxiety surrounding assurance led these saints to be zealous in labor if not love. Moreover, the application of the covenant to the tribal aggregate seemed to foster not just the egocentrism they associate with American exceptionalism but with American imperialism as well. To such readers, in its most extreme and secularized form, the language of conditional covenants provided a site where self-interest, anxiety, and hope for reward could be transformed into the the least appealing qualities associated with the "American Way."[89]

As others have argued, however, though this general genealogical history has validity as it applies to the dominant culture, the outlines of the story must be nuanced. First, for many, perhaps most, eighteenth-century Americans there was no crude translation of religious fervor into entrepreneurial zeal. The *ordo salutis* still guided their lives.[90] Challenging the Weber thesis from yet another direction, Charles Cohen has argued that for all Puritans a distinction between the two covenants insured that agape rather than anxiety sped the saints along their path: "The Covenant of Grace commands obedience like the Covenant of Works but encourages it through a motivational system that reverses the latter's imperatives." In this construction, "work and love reinforce each other. Evidence of God's love motivates the Saints to work, and the absence of evidence initiates efforts to regain it. The more the Saints love, the more duties they can perform, and through so doing, they feel, with more certainty, the inexpressible caress of *agape*."[91]

Yet, I would add that Cohen does not mark fundamental differences in rhetorical style between Sibbesians and Amesians that would qualify the general applicability of this formulation. While emphasis on sanctification may have prompted labors of love, the high preparationist insistence on both antecedent and consequent conditions may indeed have infused the covenant of grace with some anxiety as well as providing psychological comfort. Bulkeley's innovations introduced the potential for a new kind of anxiety into the doctrine of assurance. Reciprocity understood as unceasing spiritual labor may well have exacted as much anguish as Bulkeley attributed to the high Calvinist endorsement of unconditional election.

Finally, it is important to note that more recently another scholarly contingent has argued that the initial response of the first planters to England's changing economy should not be understood as entrepreneurial enthusiasm but rather as moral anguish.[92] My own speculation is that while preachers like Cotton and Davenport may have resisted the *quid pro quo* of the contractual model, in the aftermath of the Antinomian Controversy high preparationists came more fully to embrace the language of labor and exchange as describing God's covenant.

Indeed, Thomas Shepard's growing support for the discipline of the economic order as a check on enthusiasm is written in the unfolding not just of the *Parable of the Ten Virgins*, but more particularly in the *Theses Sabbaticai*. This treatise is directed toward "frothy, allegorizing wits" who in typologizing the Sabbath would also "allegorize all the commandments out of the world!" Although his intention was to protect the sanctity of the Sabbath, Shepard ended by limiting the spiritist piety that sought to embrace all aspects of everyday life.[93]

Shepard worried that making every day a celebration of spiritual enjoyment would undermine religious discipline; a cynical reading would suggest that Shepard worried that such daily devotions would interfere with the labor necessary for the founding of a new society. Resigning himself to planting churches in the world rather than preparing for the millennial dawn, Shepard cites "the eighth commandment, which would not have us steal, commands us therefore to labor for our families and comforts in all the seasons of labor. This fourth command, therefore, which not only permits but commands us to labor six days, must have another respect in commanding us to labor, and a higher end, which can be not any thing else but with respect to the Sabbath."[94]

In effect, Shepard abjures the utopian vision in which "holiness is to be writ upon our cups and pots, and horse bridles, and plows, and sickles" in favor of a separation of this world and the next.[95] In his injunctions to divide the week, Shepard established the separate claims of sacred and secular, yet he subjected each to the rigorous routine of zealous labor. In a reminder that budding entrepreneurs might later find useful, Shepard begins his thesis by declaring, "Time is one of the most precious blessings which worthless man in this world enjoys, a jewel of inestimable worth; a golden stream, dissolving, and as it were continually running down." To be sure it is a sea change, but also only a step from this statement to Franklin's motto that "Time is money."[96]

Whether or not the genealogy of capitalistic rhetoric might be traced to men like Bulkeley and Shepard is not finally my concern. What does concern me in light of the recent attempts to track that history, however, is the continued presumption of a monologic Puritan "spirit." In the end, Miller, Weber, and others may prove just in claiming that the stress on conditionality, as well as a substitution of the contractual covenant for the personal Christ, provided a way of conceiving of a system of spiritual labor and compensation that was ultimately compatible with and even conducive to the rise of capitalism. But whatever rhetorical resemblances and homologous patterning they may have noted between the *ordo salutis* and Franklin's way of wealth, such parallels are found with far less frequency in the writings of the Sibbesians.

Yet it should also be remembered that all the preachers here discussed, high preparationist and spiritist alike, held in principle to a covenant of free grace. The consequent condition of faith was never meant to supplant God's prevenient care. If preparationist rhetoric came to be inscribed in later definitions of community as tribe, covenant as contract, and saint as entrepreneur, that appropriation can only be understood as a sequel to the ambiguous, contradictory, and densely textured story of the founding generation of American Puritans.

5

The New Testament of Love

Henceforth I call you not servants: for the servant knoweth not
what his lord doeth: but I have called you friends . . . Ye have
not chosen me, but I have chosen you.

John 15:15–16

When the Cambridge Brethren preached the covenant, they described an unconditional promise: the personal Christ, not the covenant bond, secured spiritual adoption. Reversing the emphasis of the Intellectual Fathers, Sibbes and his disciples invented a language stressing divine activity and human passivity in the work of salvation. Consistently, they favored metaphors of God as effulgent, a fountain of goodness overflowing, or an abundant river of graces pouring forth. The Brethren carefully qualified legalist language that might restrict the freeness of this exuberant flow.

Just as these theologians resisted instrumentalizing Christ as the agent of God's contract, so they refused to make his ascension central. Rather, their wonder at Christ's incarnation produced a rhetoric of praise and thanksgiving. As if anticipating the inroads conditional faith could make on the freeness of grace, Sibbesians took up the question of human reciprocity primarily to dispense with it. Reversing the rhetorical order typical of Ames, Sibbes begins rather than concludes his discussions of covenant with a nod to God's requirements: "God will so in the covenant of grace entertain covenant and league with us, as that he will have his justice have full content, he will be satisfied." The last word, however, is reserved for Christ's primacy and sufficiency: "he that will be the foundation of intercourse between God and us, he must be God-man, perfectly able to satisfy divine justice; he must be a friend of God's and a friend to us. Hereupon the promise must come from God's love in Jesus Christ; and he must first receive all good for us, and we must have it at the second hand from him."[1]

Reformed dogma emphasized that "whatsoever we have, Christ must have it first for us; whatsoever is done to us, must be done first to Christ."[2] In principle, preparationists and spiritists alike would agree to this truth. Yet as the previous chapter argued, there is a difference between doctrine as stated and as developed. Ames began with the caveat that God does all only to develop a doctrine of eupraxia, in which human responsibilities take center stage and voluntarism is invigorated. Building upon this position, Shepard was soon to organize salvation into a normative soteriology, and Bulkeley to reinstate the efficacy of Abraham's covenant. But the Sibbesians emphasized the personal God over the transactional covenant. To them, men and women were redeemed only through Christ's indwelling. In 1636 Cotton mounted the pulpit in Salem to affirm this emphasis: "all the promises of this covenant are made directly to Jesus Christ; the old covenant was made to the people, but this is made to Christ. To Abraham and to his seed were promises made, He speaketh not of seed, as of many, but as of one even Christ."[3] Just a few miles up the road in Concord, Peter Bulkeley would soon preach *The Gospel-Covenant,* which was to diminish Christ as the sole agent of redemption by reinstating the exemplarity of Abraham.

Reformed dogma notwithstanding, many scholars have recognized that "Christ has become dim" for Puritan theologians as the seventeenth century progressed: "Neither the human person of Jesus nor the incarnate Logos nor the mystery of participation in the death and resurrection of Christ is a theme of lively interest in the Federal Theology."[4] John Coolidge, for example, claims that "by substituting the assurance of salvation for salvation itself as the object of the quest, and the conditions of the Covenant for Christ as the effective means for mediation between God and man," preparationist doctrines abandoned the faith of the magisterial reformers.[5] Yet these claims are insufficiently attentive to the multivocality within the Puritan community. In Coolidge's account, for example, John Cotton alone seemed to resist theological innovations; by implication, Sibbes and Preston countenanced contractual entailments on the freeness of grace.[6]

Among others, Norman Pettit and R. T. Kendall have argued a more extreme version of the case, casting Sibbes as a covenant theologian who, like Ames, authors a humanist theology: "Of all the preparationists Sibbes was by far the most extreme in terms of the abilities he assigned to natural man."[7] Moreover, they claim that Cotton exhibited Arminian tendencies in England, converting to a higher Calvinism in America and repudiating both Sibbes and his doctrine. Yet these critics seem to forget that the young Cotton resisted what he took to be Perkinsian compromises on the freeness of grace, only to be converted by Sibbes's rejection of the negative righteousness and his powerful articulation of God's prevenience.

My purpose in this chapter is twofold: first, to challenge the standard scholarly accounts of Sibbes as a preparationist preacher by proving that his covenantal doctrine was at odds with the Amesian contract; second, to demonstrate that this position should be understood as part of the larger discursive formation including the writings of Cotton, Davenport, Preston, and Norton. In America Cotton did not repudiate the opinions of Sibbes but brought them to consummation.[8] His understanding of the covenant was based upon the same assertion of God's prevenient grace and human desire as that found in the sermons of Sibbes. The remainder of this chapter will press these claims by foregrounding the shared rhetorical patterns and doctrinal symmetries that united this group.

Like all theologians of his age, Sibbes addressed the crucial distinction between absolute and conditional promises in the working of redemption. He argued:

> all the promises that God hath made to us, either (1.) they are *absolute,* without any condition. So was Christ . . . Some promises (2.) be *conditional* in the manner of propounding, but yet absolute in the real performance of them. As, for example, the promises of grace and glory to God's children. The promise of forgiveness of sins, if they believe, if they repent.[9]

Contrary to critics' assertions, Sibbes rarely allows the consideration of the human/divine relationship to rest with this conditional "if." He completes this particular passage with a characteristic rejection of chronometrical processes, asserting instead God's preemptive agency: "They [the promises] are propounded conditionally, but in the performance they are absolute, because God performs the covenant himself; he performs our part and his own too."[10] While Ames made such caveats, he did not rest with them; by contrast, Sibbes and his followers consistently focus on divine initiative rather than human response.

Indeed, a reading of Sibbes's corpus confounds the depiction of him as a preparationist. Consistently, he dramatizes God's loving prevenient care for weak-hearted Christians, teaches the primacy of the free testament over the conditional covenant, and rhapsodizes over the friendly reconciliation made good by Christ. Though he may sometime present God's dealing with his creature "by way of commerce," far more often Sibbes emphasizes the contingency of human agency: "We do all subordinately; we move as we are moved; we see as we are enlightened; we hear as we are made to hear; we are wise as far as he makes us wise. We do, but it is he that makes us do."[11] Faith is not antecedent to justification but a consequence of it.

How then can we account for those passages, focal points in Pettit's and Kendall's analyses, where Sibbes does seem to flirt with conditional promises, urging his auditors to help in softening their heart, or perfume their souls for the Lord? First, scattered in the body of Sibbes's writings there are sermons that are exhortatory, but these are neither representative nor unqualified.[12]

Furthermore, there is something to the witticism that a man is Calvinist when he prays and an Arminian when he preaches. Norton reports that Cotton himself was once accused of Arminianism for occasionally adopting exhortatory prose.[13] In *God's Mercy Mixed with his Justice* and the beginning sections of *The Way of Life*, Cotton does enjoin his auditors to lay hold of the covenant. However, these injunctions are not central and must be weighed against Cotton's English corpus, with its emphasis on the freeness of grace. Partial readings might support charges of Arminianism against any of the preachers here discussed, but only by emphasizing anomalous rather than representative utterances.

Moreover, since the Cambridge preachers constructed their auditors as already regenerate, their exhortations properly apply to the fruits of sanctification, not to the antecedent faith of the conditional covenant. As Preston says, "every good action proceedeth from Grace, and good actions intend grace." The latter is wholly contingent on the former. After grace, good men "bring forth good fruit." That good men labor is a description, not a prescription.[14]

To underscore this difference, Cambridge theologians routinely translated God's covenant as a loving testament. Overturning Ames's formulation of uneasy servitude, Sibbes persistently invokes Christ's covenant as an intimate union: "Henceforth I call you not servants . . . but I call you friends." Seeking adequate descriptions for this new relationship, Sibbes avoids contractual language with an appeal to affections: *the Spirit speaks to us by a secret kind of whispering and intimation,* that the soul feels better than I can express . . . There is, I say, as sweet joining, as sweet kiss givine to the soul. 'I am thine and thou art mine, Cant. vi.3.'"[15]

Even in his most hortatory sermons, Sibbes tempers his injunctions with frequent reminders that "a testament *bequeatheth good things merely of love.* It giveth gifts freely. A covenant requireth something to be done." By contrast, "in a testament, there is nothing but receiving the legacies given."[16] Sibbes insists that the term *testament* is more descriptive of the process whereby God "chooseth us, and then we choose him." This opinion is echoed by every member of his circle.[17]

Contrary to current critical opinion, Sibbes and his circle consistently emphasize the understanding of sin as privation of the good.[18] Originally, "there was planted in man by nature a desire of holiness, and a desire of happiness." But after the fall, "the desire of happiness is left still in us, but for holiness, which is the perfection of the image of God in us, is both lost, and the desire of it extinguished."[19] In this postlapsarian world "the light troubles man against his will."[20] Privation is remedied only by indwelling; sin is a void to be filled, not a stain to be removed: "The soul is the chamber, and the bed, and, as it were, the cabinet for God himself, and Christ to rest in only."[21]

Using a trope shared by all the Brethren, Cotton describes the saint as an "an empty vessell" that "receyveth oyle: but this receyving is not active, but passive." By the 1630s, Cotton understood that the difference between the Spiritual Brethren and the preparationists turned on this point, arguing: "An empty vessell actually receyveth oyle poured into it, when it self is passive"—so the Christian receives grace. He is not to be likened to "a child [who] actively receyveth milke out of his mothers breasts . . . by sucking it." This last simile would claim too much human agency.[22]

As if to resolve all doubt on the issue of human passivity, Sibbes turns to the language of the Bible itself, finding a text quite different from the one preparationists read. He argues that the verb tenses used by the prophets make the saint's patience and passivity manifest: "therefore it is here in the passive term, 'We are changed from glory to glory, as by the Spirit of the Lord.' So in the chain of salvation you have passive words in them all."[23] The prominence of passive verbs in Davenport's prose also illustrates Sibbes's claims of divine activity and human passivity: "by this gift of grace, which I call divine hope, that affection is sanctified, and lifted up unto God, and set upon him and heavenly things, and so quickened and made alive unto God."[24] Even a brief survey of sermons by Cotton and Preston would prove these rhetorical patterns representative.

Moreover, this assurance of God's complete agency frequently produces a prose-poetry dedicated not to exhortation but to celebrating the joys of passive reception: "Therefore we must open as that flower that opens and shuts as the sun shines on it. So must we as Christ shines on us; and we ebb and flow as he flows upon us . . . For we do what we do, but we are patients first to receive that power from the Spirit. We hear and do good works, but the activity and power and strength comes all from the Spirit of God."[25]

Rather than taxonomizing conversion, here is a melting, a flow in both the sound and the sense. The repeated open vowels of the first clause mirror the motion of the flower, and the concluding sibilants mimic the shutting. The communication of doctrine through rhythmic cadence rather than the logic of plot will be fully addressed in the following chapter. In brief, this passage suggests that Sibbesians often rely on incantation, repetition, and aural association as much as doctrinal content to convey meaning.

All of the Brethren turn to Canticles for inspiration; the garden is a favorite trope. Characteristically, when Hooker or Shepard invoke this image, they move to injunctions to clear the weedy heart of sin. Sibbes, on the other hand, imagines fruitfulness freely flowing from the breath of the Spirit: "that grace is increased in the exercise of it, not by virtue of the exercise itself, but as Christ by his Spirit floweth into the soul, and bringeth us nearer unto himself the fountain, and instilleth such comfort in the act, whereby the heart is further enlarged."[26]

It is Christ's action—his infusion into the soul, his drawing of our hearts—which proves the essential moment in the drama of salvation. Sibbes's doctrine of prevenience can be simply stated: "without blowing, no flowing." In its application, this truth yields images of great beauty and mystery: "The heart of a Christian is Christ's garden, and his graces are as so many sweet spices and flowers, which his Spirit blowing upon makes them to send forth a sweet savour."[27] How very unlike Hooker's pithy adage: "endure all in hope of the harvest."[28]

Both in England and in America, Cotton's understanding of the covenant harmonized with Sibbes's positions. In the early sermons that make up *Christ the Fountaine* (c. 1624), Cotton begins by describing the three ways scripture presents the covenant—as "between Prince and People," "Friend and Friend," and "Man and Wife." Not surprisingly, the first relation of sovereignty, essential to the preparationists, receives only brief treatment.[29]

Cotton moves quickly to the second sense of covenant—as friendship— to unfold the mutual love of God and his people in homey metaphors. This is a covenant of salt, for "salt eaten together expresses familiarity, and durableness, now God expresseth himselfe thus." The most common yet most essential seasoning, salt is the perfect trope for this familiar yet requisite union. Such reconciliation recalls George Herbert's enjoyment of the holy supper of "Love III" and starkly contrasts with Hooker's portrait of the suppliant exiled to the far end of the table, greedily awaiting his share.[30]

This covenant of salt was first undertaken with Abraham, whom God takes "as a friend for ever." Ames thought the bond of friendship was past, that now there could be only a "covenant of reconciliation between enemies."[31] But Cotton insists that this is a "league of friendship," and moreover one that "implyes not only preservation of affection, but it requires a kinde of secret communication one to another, and a doing one for another."[32] Anxiety is alleviated by the unadorned, flat declaration that there is perseverance of affection and adoption. This secret communion again inscribes the intimacy characteristic of Cotton's descriptions of God's nature: "God he grants our Petitions for us as a friend, and we doe his Commandments as a friend"—not out of obligation or self-interest, but "out of the integrity of our hearts." There is great sweetness in Cotton's description of the saint's life within this friendly embrace: God "wil play a friends part, he wil counsell us for the best, he wil tell us, this, and that, is the best course for us to take."[33]

The prevenience of God is never far from sight in Cotton's hortatory passages: "God should looke upon you, and consider your case, your just and due desert is everlasting destruction; and therefore you account your selves unworthy of any mercy from God, but yet notwithstanding if he wil be pleased to accept the death of Christ for you, and to be-sprinkle you with the blessing of his grace, you wil give up your selves to an acceptable service of him all your dayes."[34]

It is *God* who looks, who is pleased to accept Christ, who rebaptizes his creature with grace; God works all things in this covenant of grace. And though some may hear an echo of preparationist rhetoric in Cotton's prediction, "you wil give up your selves to an acceptable service," this phrase describes rather than prescribes the saint's response. There is no prerequisite to grace, but service afterward; no threat of deprivation, no promise of reward. God bestows and then the saint labors in loving return: "it is the spirit of God breathing in his grace"; it is "not he, nor any grace in him, but the grace of God *with him,* that wrought with him, and acted, and did all he did wherever he came."[35]

In rhetorical formulations that clearly link him to Davenport and Sibbes, Cotton persuades his auditors of human passivity through a variety of metaphors that counter Hooker's descriptions of saintly preparation: "Christ gave us our life, and he preserves it, wee cannot better explain it then thus; A wind-mill moves not onely by the wind, but in the wind; so a water-mill hath its motion, not onely from the water, but in the water; so a Christian lives, as having his life from Christ, and in Christ, and further then Christ breathes and assists, he stirs not."[36]

We are passive until we are moved, and even then our life is in Christ and no further.[37] The saint's ability is secured not by increated graces inhering in their nature, but by Christ's continued indwelling. As Davenport explained: "We act, but not in our strength, nor in the strength of grace received, but from the quickening, strengthening influence of the Spirit."[38]

This point is made most forcefully in Cotton's final understanding of God's covenant as marriage. Even more than the friendship initiated with Abraham, this conjugal union with and through Christ typifies the freeness of grace. Again Canticles proves to be the subtext for the Brethren's preaching of grace:

> And looke what affection is between Husband and Wife, hath there been the like affection in your soules towards the Lord Jesus Christ? Have you a strong and hearty desire to meet him in the bed of loves, when ever you come to the Congregation, and desire you to have the seeds of his grace shed abroad in your hearts, and bring forth the fruits of grace to him, and desire that you may be for him, and for none other, and you desire to acquaint him with all your counsels and secrets, and desire to doe nothing but as he shall counsell and direct you? And have you therefore been willing to give up your selves, you and yours to be ruled by Christ; and is it the griefe of your soules if any of your Children, and Servants shall not stoop to God . . . truly then you have Christ for your Christ, because you have him by way of covenant: When God gives us hearts thus to agree with him, he alwaies prevents us, he is ever before us, then Christ thou hast, and in him thou hast life.[39]

This passage contains in brief the whole of the Cambridge theology. It bears little resemblance to the conversion handbooks penned by the Amesians. Here, desire is the key, signifying God's outpouring love and the saint's returning flow. Desire produces desire. Cotton's sentence, with its rolling cadences and dynamic expansion by verbal addition, itself insists on the diffusive nature of this emotion. The word *desire* is sounded and re-sounded, as if its meaning could be apprehended by the mere act of repetition—and indeed it can, for those who have ears to hear, whose hearts have been melted. This is in marked contrast to the salvation plots of preparationist sermons, in which each step can be logically anticipated. Cotton's circular, repetitive structure refuses anticipation, relies on a remembered affection, a recalled experience of grace.

This experience is neither synonymous with the weak faith of first calling nor subject to the incremental increase preparationists describe.

One of the crucial differences between spiritists like Sibbes and Cotton and preparationists like Ames and Hooker was in this understanding of the heart and how it was changed. While Hooker anatomized the heart, Cotton rejected mechanical metaphors in favor of organic ones. Not a hammering or breaking of the heart, but melting is the way Cotton describes this transformation. Sibbesians and Amesians alike may have languished under periods of grief during the process of their conversions, but the spiritists did not rest with such tribulation. While Preston is reported to have been changed in an instant, we know that Cotton suffered protracted anguish. Yet, he did come to feel the full certainty of spiritual joy under Sibbes's ministry. The difference between the two groups is perhaps best understood in terms of their experience of closure and subsequent confidence in God's overwhelming love. To a person, the Brethren came to an assurance that was full, complete, and joyous. This experience underwrote their ecstatic faith in the perseverance of the saints.[40]

In *The Way of Life* Cotton explicitly draws a distinction between the pricking of the conscience and the piercing of the heart. This first action can be the fruit of preparation—it marks the effect of legal preaching on the understanding. Though Hooker agreed there was a distinction between these two operations, he accorded more efficacy to preaching law to the conscience. For Cotton, this pricking cannot be efficacious. The heart itself must be turned, for it "is the principall faculty of the soule, it rules all, it sets hand and tongue, all within, and all without a work."[41] When this change occurs it is a melting of stone, a warming of ice, a quickening of the paralyzed will.

In perhaps the most often quoted passage, Cotton likens spiritual baptism to a wading in grace: "First a Christian wades in the rivers of God his grace up to the ankles, with some good frame of spirit." Still afflicted with the dryness of his soul and overpowering thirst and desire, the saint wades further—to the knees, the loins, and further still till all is drenched. As Cotton joyously predicts: "then you shall swimme; there is such a measure of grace in which a man may swimme as fish in the water, with all readinesse and dexterity, gliding an-end, as if he had water enough to swimme in; such a Christian doth not creep or walk, but he runs . . . so every way drenched in grace . . . he is never drawn dry."[42]

While there is a progressive baptism in grace, there are no discrete steps here. Rather than measured units, there is a fluid motion, which culminates in the sudden change—"then shall you swimme." For the auditor the appeal is made to past experience and to the new affections. This is an experimental faith known only to initiates; this is a draught of holy water recalled only by those who have been so drenched.[43] Although such experimentalism is also found in the writings of Hooker and Shepard, with Sibbesians the emphasis stays on affectionate identification, while Shepard and Hooker more frequently allow the efficacy of historical faith in assessing one's spiritual estate.

In keeping with the doctrines of prevenience and infusion, the Sibbesians argued that justification produces a change that is immediate and complete. There is no incremental process of becoming; no growth in increated graces. The saint is not simply given a new ability to do or will, as the preparationists emphasize. Indeed Cotton declares "he that is borne of God to a Spirituall life, is become a *new Creature, and old things are past away,* 2 Cor 5, 17. He hath a new mind, and a new heart, new affections, new Language, and new employments that he was never wont to do before."[44] In good Pauline fashion, Cotton's God remakes human nature entire. Grace does not fill up uneven nature, or restore Christians to Adamic purity as Hooker and Shepard would have it.[45] Rather this is a new creation, and one manifested by regenerate sensibility.

For Sibbes and Cotton, Preston and Davenport alike, "grace altereth the relish" and restores the honey-taste of holy things: "There is a sweet relish in all divine truths, and suitable to the sweetness in them, there is a spiritual taste, which the Spirit of God puts into the soul of his children."[46] There is a "hungering and thirsting" for Christ answered by a new sense of "some sweetness and rellish" in the Word, in the ordinances and in prayers to God. The saint partakes of this spiritual food as the starving man does his meat, and for both it "is an evident signe of life, because you finde *sweetnesse* in it, its a signe of health to rellish a sweetnesse in our meat."[47] So essential a sign is this renewed sense that "none but a Christian can have spiritual taste answerable to a spiritual life . . . Yea, it is the very being of a Christian to have a taste of spiritual things."[48]

As he is inhabited by Christ, the saint *becomes* sweet: "His heart is as fine silver, everything is sweet that comes from him . . . grace in a Christian, it makes us sweet; it sweetens our person and our actions. It sweetens our persons to God. God delights in the smell of his own graces. It makes us delectable for Christ and his Holy Spirit to lodge in our souls as in a garden of spices."[49] This pleasurable litany contains no argument from point to point, no description of gradual or arduous self-renovation. It merely asserts and repeats the gracious change coincident with the Spirit's indwelling and explains the source of God's own pleasure in the covenant.

All injunctions to stir oneself to holy zeal must be understood as addressing the saint not before justification but after. In gratitude for these graces received, the saint responds with prayer and praise to God and love for other Christians. In the opening of "The Soul's Conflict," Sibbes celebrates the book of Psalms, which "may well be the heart" of scripture; "they are so full of sweet affections and passions." Sibbes reveres this book, because "in other portions of Scripture God speaks to us; but in the Psalms holy men speak to God and their own hearts."[50] David, then, becomes the exemplum for the regenerate saint, who pleases God with prayers and praise: "Praising of God may well be called incense, because as it is sweet in itself, and sweet to God, so it sweetens all that comes from us."[51] As psalmists, Christians become "like the box in the gospel, that when it was opened, all the house smelled of it."[52]

The Sibbesian injunction is clear: just as "God is glorified in making us happy," so "we enjoying happiness, must glorify God"—and praise is the central act.[53] And just as God flows in "rivers of grace," so the regenerate become effulgent. The "affections of the heart, or words of our lips, or ways of our whole man, they are all lively and spirituall." With "a borrowed speech"—a spiritual echo of God—the saint's "heart, it being the fountaine of our thoughts, and words, and waies, out of it well kept, flowes forth such things as have life in them; it is meant of spiritual life."[54] Like warm embers, the saint stirs and sends his heat back to God: "if there be any true life in the heart of a Christian soule, there is always some kind of warm breathing, there is some measure of warmth in his prayers." The zealous soul is remarkable for its "panting, and longing, and eager desire after God."[55] This is a theology of human desire and God's delight. Conditions and contracts have no place in this union of emanation and remanation.

Such returns counter the first sin of self-love. Unlike Hooker's sinner, the Sibbesian saint is taught not to look for spiritual harvest; his heart is "set upon Christ, more than upon the pardon of sinne, or salvation . . . [he] hath Christ in his eye and heart above all blessings."[56] Davenport always cautioned his auditors to take pleasure in the divine Testator alone: "not to trust in grace received, but in Christ; depending on him to quicken and actuate his own gifts of grace in you, waiting with fervent desires and prayers for the Sun of righteousness to arise upon you, with healing in his wings."[57]

These preachers expressed contempt for the appeal to self-interest the preparationists sometimes employ: it is a "spirit of harlotry" when a woman "hath a strong affection to match with such a man . . . that hee might pay her debts, and that she might be well provided for."[58] Only true and disinterested love, the human equivalent of God's agape, marks the saint in Cotton's version of the spiritual marriage.

The closest appeal to self-interest the Brethren make is to suggest that "when we return praises to him, he returns new favours to us, and so an everlasting, ever increasing intercourse betwixt God and the soul is maintained."[59] It is important to note that the saint—already sealed—makes *returns* to God. Moreover, this is not the concupiscence Ames acknowledged, but a more immediate yearning for personal union with God. And lest the auditor worry about his or her inadequacy, Sibbes assures that God will hear the most broken chants as mellifluous harmonies: "we cannot love and joy in God but he will delight in us."[60]

To the dismay of preparationist preachers, the sanctified saint is not to be recognized by right walking or visible progress along the path to salvation, but by spiritual liveliness, warmth, and relish. The life of sanctification is all motion, it "is growth, for that which lives, growes"; and the enlivened heart moves and stirs toward God as does all "naturall, vegitative, or sensitive life."[61] The new saint is alive in a way denied to the sinner. Union with the Spirit of grace "makes a man fervent, and warme." "Wheresoever there is warmth there is life, if no warmth, nor heat, there is no life." Note Cotton does not write a set of instructions on how to gather the embers or fan the flames as a preparationist preacher might, but rather describes the experience of grace received. The Cambridge Brethren preach not steps to the altar but signs of religious affections already received.[62]

Here there is less confidence that God is bound to honor his covenant than the certainty that by his very nature he *will delight* in us. This is a mild form of bondage indeed, one secured with true ligaments of love. When God becomes so *to us,* then we become sweet *to and for God:* love flows from God, through the saints, and to God in a closed circle of spiritual joy.

It is important to note that the Spiritual Brethren never conceived that this active dependence could endanger the doctrine of perseverance. Indeed, while Bulkeley's saint, with his increased graces, could fail the covenant, the Cambridge preachers rested in the assurance that in Christ we cannot fail or fall. There is no opening in their doctrine for the subsequent moralism inscribed in the conditional covenant. When Sibbesians anguished over their sins, it was not for fear of losing claim to God's blessings but for grief at their ingratitude. Cotton wonders: "How should I commit (saith the Soul) this great wickedness against the father of mercies, the God of all grace?" Making this wound all the more painful is the thought that "he hath abused so rich grace unto wantonness, and hath loved him so little, who hath so much, and so freely, and so unchangably loved him."[63]

This last emphasis on God's unchangeable love insures the perseverance of the momentarily wayward saint. Davenport assuages fears by likening the regenerate soul's constancy to that of Noah's dove returning to the Ark, or to the needle of a compass that points to the true spiritual north. Though "it may be forced, by Temptation, from its bent, for a time, yet it hath no rest, till it stand God-ward."[64]

The conditional covenant was invented in the hope of providing such assurance, through the process of preparation and the doctrine of means. Sibbesians were skeptical about its success. Throwing the creature back upon himself instead of upon the breast of God produced a different form of anxiety, one at odds with the tranquil confidence of the Cambridge theologians. As the New England elders argued, the freedom of the Christian was a hard faith—assurance was rare. But for those few saints convinced of God's abiding love, the doctrine of unconditional grace provided a greater and more joyous surety than all the works of preparation. Such was the difference between a testament of love and a covenant of conditions.

⚜

The Antinomian Controversy was fueled by the disparity between these two competing versions of God's promise to his plantation. The New England Puritans disputed these issues of conditionality, prevenience, and the perseverance of the saints, providing the terms by which they came to experience and express their opposed conceptions of God's nature and his covenant. Though by 1648 Cotton was forced to acknowledge efficacy in the conditional promise in order to assure that the new orthodoxy would concede some claims for the absolute, in the 1630s he repudiated conditional promises as popish doctrine.[65] In his exchanges with the elders, his sermon at Salem, and his treatise on *The New Covenant*, Cotton persisted in arguing that assurance cannot be had by virtue of any condition but only by "applying Gods free grace in an absolute Promise." Cotton took the Sibbesian high ground that faith is the fruit and never the cause of our union with Christ.[66]

The controversy made explicit what had been Sibbesian doctrine from the outset. The ritual confrontations of the 1630s brought differences into sharper focus, and perhaps produced greater militancy on both sides. Cotton's rejection of the conditional promise only became more vehement in the context of his interrogation: "I do conceive that God not only may and doth often, but even alwaies work that faith by his Spirit coming and breathing in absolute promises; or if in conditional, it is alwaies without respect to any such condition as pre existent in the soul, though by the promise the condition will be wrought in us."[67] What had been first taught in richly metaphorical sermons became the substance of a stark and more emphatic argumentative prose. Under the interrogatives of the elders and the court, Cotton perceived that his person, his opinions, and his church were under siege. While these threats did not alter his opinions, they radicalized his expressions.

Though many have pondered the extent of Cotton's commitment to the more extreme positions taken by Anne Hutchinson, there was no equivocation for him on the issue of conditionality. At the height of the confrontation, Cotton himself came close to indicting the preparationist elders of preaching works righteousness. To base assurance of justification upon evidences of sanctification, he declares flatly, is "to clothe unwholsome and Popish doctrin with Protestant and wholesome words."[68] Though he never went as far as Hutchinson, Cotton did suggest that, by inserting the conditional, the elders had returned Christians to Adam's first world of obligation. By stressing increated graces and a doctrine of assurance based on sanctification as evidence, the preparationists did then "indeed make our Sanctification the same with that of Adams."[69]

In words that closely resembled Hutchinson's own trial testimony, Cotton vehemently restated his faith in the centrality of Christ: "In the Gospel the promise is made to Christ, so that, give me Christ and I claim my right to the promise and to all the comforts and blessing thereof . . . all the promises are given to Christ, and all the conditions are fulfilled in Christ, and the revealing of both is by the revealing of Christ given of grace freely to the Soul."[70]

Cotton rejected the elders' use of Aristotelian distinctions between formal and efficient causes to explain the gap between God's deposings and human process. He labeled such ploys a mere "distinction between material and formal," declaring he would not be "put off" with such scholasticism.[71] It is essential to state that the reasons and explanations offered by the preparationists for the admission of conditionality were rejected outright by Cotton as improper human innovations and corruptions of the scriptural promise. There was no consensus on this issue at all. In fact, Cotton claims that preparationism undermines true Protestantism: "if we will speak as Protestants, we must not speak of good works as causes or waies of our first Assurance." In unmistakable language, he declares to the elders, "call you our good works what you please, whether Sanctification or gifts of Grace or saving graces (or any such like)"—it is a popish doctrine.[72]

Despite the claims of many historians, John Cotton understood that foundational disagreements were discovered in 1636. To his mind, he was a sacrificial lamb to the cabal of preparationist High Priests: "For an Answer unto your (Interrogatories, shall I call them?) or Questions. Though I might without Sinne referre you (as our Saviour did the *High-Priest* when his Doctrine was questioned) to what *I* have ever taught and spoken openly to the world, as having in secret said nothing else, *John* 18.20.21."[73] This is not the rhetoric of minor disagreement within a general consensus. Cotton obviously disputed that he and the elders held the same doctrine of grace. Rather, this was a declaration of war, in which both parties claimed God on their side. This battle was fought over issues that had always implicitly divided these Puritan preachers. Though the Brethren lost the battle for dominance in 1636, they were neither converted to preparationism nor were they silenced.[74]

Though Davenport left Boston and Cotton publicly yielded on some doctrinal formulations, neither abandoned commitment to Sibbesian theology. New Haven, modeled on Cotton's own prescriptions for a Bible commonwealth, became synonymous with high Calvinist practices. Rather than join this more congenial plantation, Cotton decided to remain in Boston. Throughout this period—in *The Way of Congregational Churches Cleared,* his apocalyptic tracts, his treatise on *The New Covenant* (collecting sermons probably delivered circa 1636), and his preface to Norton's *Orthodox Evangelist*—Cotton nonetheless continued to preach the freeness of grace and the efficacy of the absolute promise.[75]

In the aftermath of the controversy, it fell to John Norton to respond to Bulkeley's *Gospel-Covenant,* reasserting the claim of the absolute promise and defending the piety of the Cambridge Brethren. Norton took the compromised position necessary in 1654, yet beneath the straightened surface of *The Orthodox Evangelist* ran an ecstatic subtext of Sibbesian piety. The title of this treatise testifies to the marriage of opposites Norton proposed; but his pen was dedicated to more than simple reconciliation. He reinfused the evangelical warmth of the Sibbesians into the already cooling formalism of New England's orthodoxy.

Cotton's hand-picked successor to the Boston pulpit as well as his biographer, Norton was a divine of the Cambridge school, "the true follower of Dr. Sibs!"[76] Like Preston before him and like his student, Increase Mather, Norton was an "ambidextrous" theologian who was prepared to allow the utility of conditional promises, so long as the absolute decree was acknowledged as preeminent. He would not compromise, however, on the efficacy of Christ over the uses of the covenant or on the freeness of

grace. To be sure, John Norton modified the high spiritist position, allowing that "the Doctrine of absoluteness, and infallibleness of the Decree,
discourageth from the use of means."[77] Moreover, Norton acknowledged
the legitimacy of second causes to a greater degree than Cotton might
have allowed, admitting the usefulness of pastoral mediation in the daily
life of common faith. He also conceded that the doctrine of means and
the conditional covenant had their place as expressions of God's eternal
degree in the contingent world of time.

In doing so, Norton nonetheless rejected conditionality as it was articulated by Bulkeley. He remained unwilling to admit the necessity of the
temporal preparatory sequences insisted upon by the orthodox elders. In
good Cottonian fashion, he argued that faith was never to be understood
as a cause but always as the fruit of union, and that legal preparation was
not to be confused with saving grace.[78]

It is important to underscore the complex agenda of *The Orthodox
Evangelist* and the ambivalence of Norton's own character and disposition.
Like Shepard, Norton occupies an intermediate position between the two
groups that both reveals their differences and testifies to their shared
heritage. Consequently, some readers have seen Norton as a champion of
the most developed sort of preparationism, while others claim him as the
embodiment of the purest spiritism.[79] In his day, Norton wrote polemics
against theological liberals like William Pynchon as well as attacking the
Quaker radicals.[80] I would argue that Norton, like Shepard, was tempera-
mentally inclined to aspects of both styles of piety but that his greatest
allegiance was to the Cambridge faith. Just as the proliferation of sectaries
in England pressed Thomas Goodwin to restrain his zeal, so Norton
modified his pietism in the late 1650s, becoming a strong advocate of the
Half-Way Covenant practices in the face of First Church's spiritist opposition. Yet in his construction of the orthodox evangelist, Norton proposed
a theology laced through with the major tenets of Sibbes and Cotton.

This piety is witnessed from the outset, both in Norton's lengthy exfoliation of God's essence and in the warmth of his expression. Though
Norton includes three lengthy chapters on preparationism, he is careful to
establish the crucial distinction between "legal" and "evangelical" preparation that safeguarded the freeness of grace even while it restrained enthusiasm. Moreover, Norton follows these chapters with an equally long section on the saint's passivity, concluding with a celebration of the soul's
ecstatic union with Christ.

On the volatile issue of preparationism, Norton tries to carve a space
for Cottonian prevenience within the standing orthodoxy. Answering the

hypothetical, "Is a distinct Experience of the several Heads of Preparatory Work, necessary according to Gods ordinary Dispensation unto conversion," Norton treads a thin line between self-assertion and accommodation. His answer, "No: yet the more distinctness, the better," entertains the orthodoxy's counter-claims even while it asserts the discredited principle of God's absolute promise.[81]

Similarly, in asserting that "faith is a consequent condition, not an antecedent condition," Norton seems to hedge, deploying the language of preparationism to soften the doctrine of perseverance.[82] Yet in this textual strategy Norton practiced a brand of pragmatism the Cambridge Brethren had always countenanced: making the compromises necessary to gain a hearing. In this same passage, Norton converts the definition of the consequent condition into an opportunity to qualify Bulkeley's claims. Beginning with God's promise, *'I will give Eternal life unto the Elect, if they do believe,'* Norton declares this text "aequivolent" to one that insures God's absolute decree: *'I will out of my Absolute Will give unto the Elect Eternal life, because I will out of my Absolute Will give unto the Elect to believe.'*[83]

Faith is not the creature's turning but God's turning of him. "The Condition of Faith depends not upon the Will of the Elect; either to be or not to be; but upon the absolute and gracious Will of God."[84] In this statement, Norton not only insists on God's prevenience but applies it to the Elect. At every instance he subtly narrows the wide way of human agency that Bulkeley's rhetoric permitted.

Repeatedly, Norton takes back the concessions that he seems to proffer. In speaking of the decree of God, for example, he begins by conceding the difference between horologicals and chronometricals so essential to the preparationist case: "Though the Decree be absolute, yet the Dispensation of the Decree in the Gospel is conditional." He concludes this discussion, however, with an essential amendment, "Yet, here carefully observe, That by a condition we are always to understand not a condition properly so called, but a consequent condition . . . the performance whereof is not left unto the Elect, but is undertaken for by the Elector; and therefore is not only opposite unto, but is both an effect and argument of an absolute Decree; and also of an absolute Covenant of grace."[85] It will be recalled that Bulkeley chose to emphasize faith as a necessary condition and to harness personal assurance to the conditional promise. That Norton argues for over one hundred pages that the soul is "not only passive; yet so, as that it is passive before it is active," testifies to the direction of his own thought and to the orthodox party's slow drift toward Arminianism.[86]

The distance that had been traveled in the sixteen years since the first examination of Cotton can be measured by Cotton's preface to Norton's *Orthodox Evangelist* in 1652. In the 1630s the elders wanted to protect the possibility of gradual regeneration against what they saw as the exclusive claims of Cotton's anti-preparationism: thus they asserted "this we add, That Gods free grace may be reveiled and received as freely in a conditional (where the Condition is first wrought by Gods free grace and not trusted to, as we desire ever to be understood when we mention conditional promises) as in an absolute promise."[87]

But by 1652 Cotton recognized that the mantle or at least the power of sanctioned orthodoxy had passed to preachers like Bulkeley and Shepard. His hope seems to have been that Norton's treatise would provide a ground for the absolute to coexist with the conditional promise without compromising free grace. In his preface Cotton begs that "such Protestants as excell in holiness and knowledg, and yet seem (and but seem) to vary (though *Logically*, yet not *Theologically*) in some doctrines of Grace, may (through grace) either judg and speak all one thing, or at least condescend . . . mildely to bear with difference of judgment in such a case." This framing of fundamental disagreement as inessential variation, along with the plea for coexistence, eloquently witnesses the power of the preparationist regime and the precarious position Cotton felt himself to occupy.[88] The mannered style with which Cotton makes this plea suggests his reluctance and/or fear to speak plainly, but his sarcasm touches on a deeper bitterness.

It is no accident that the chastened, yet still radical, Boston Church chose Norton to replace the beloved Cotton (or that they would later seek out John Davenport). Norton deftly appeased the regnant orthodoxy and held the line against more radical sectaries, while nonetheless covertly disseminating the core of Sibbesian theology. This orthodox evangelist recalled the essential point of dispute in 1636: if faith were an antecedent condition, "there would soon be an end of the Covenant of grace: yea, the Covenant of grace, were indeed no covenant of grace."[89]

Norton always insists on the prevenience of grace; that God "seeks us before we seek him."[90] He most frequently appeals to the language of affect; though a Christian has a "soul-thirsty disposition after Christ," we cannot sincerely desire until such desire is given to us.[91] We are only empty vessels to be filled; our inability is matched by the ability of God to draw us upward.[92] The heart is fitted and framed not by human preparations, but by Christ's entrance. The heart is good because God declares it his own.[93] Such are Norton's tenets.

Softening Cotton's more radical positions, Norton always acknowledges the usefulness of preparatory work, but without admitting its necessity.[94]

He refuses to countenance faith before justification by carefully restricting his discussions of preparatory work to "the Elect." His consistent reference to elected saints subtly insists on prevenience without explicitly stating it. This is in contrast to Hooker's use of the more generic referent of "sinner," which does not at all imply prevenience but insists on saving labor before full justification.

And, like all of the Spiritual Brethren, Norton speaks not of covenant but of Christ. He wants his text to breathe with "nothing but Christ."[95] The incarnation is *the* mystery, and human hope rests solely in Christ's sacrifice as "the testimony of his love." The believer lies before Christ like wax before the seal: "As the impression upon the wax, answereth to the character of the seal: so faith answereth the truth of this testimony or promise. The promise is the mouth of Christ, faith is the mouth of the soul: by this act of faith upon the object of faith, Christ and the soul kiss one another."[96] The promise here is no contract but an amorous embrace, in which reciprocity is understood in terms of spiritualized eroticism.

Norton joins his Brethren in condemning qualifications of this pure desire; it is only a legalist who will "seek rather the benefits of Christ, then Christ." This is a self-love which is not to be confused with true Christian love.[97] Human labor is never the product of anxious questing for assurance; Christian love never seeks the covenant before Christ. Rather there is a return, a remanation of blessings received and still flowing though the heart of the saint.

In *The Orthodox Evangelist* it is clear that Norton agreed that anti-nomianism was a danger, but he was equally if not more concerned with curbing the erosions of grace implicit in the errors of the Pelagians and Arminians. While Shepard and Bulkeley raged against the antinomians throughout the late 1630s and early 1640s in such sermon series as *The Theses Sabbaticae, The Parable of the Ten Virgins,* and *The Gospel Covenant,* Norton directed his criticism elsewhere. While he admitted that "some erre on the one hand with the *Enthusiasts,* not giving them [that is, qualifications before faith] their due; by denying any preparatory use of them," this was not the most prevalent spiritual error. Norton worried that more of the faithful err "on the other side," by giving such qualifications too much value: "we all being prone, thereunto, by reason of that legal self, the remainders of which are yet dwelling in us."[98] These legal Christians, "whose differing tenets together with their gradual aberrations from the truth, and defections even unto the *Pelagian* heresie," are the ones most dangerous to the life of faith in New England. He lists the various opinionists to be condemned, beginning with Pelagius, adding the papists and Arminians, and concluding with a criticism which might have been applied to most of the ministers of the Bay: "Others (with whome the fore-mentioned are not to be named) reverend, learned, judicious, and pious (though they justly abhor the tenets of the fore-mentioned, yet) seem to teach, that there are some qualifications before faith that are saving, whereunto faith and salvation may be ascertained."[99]

This error, not to be confused with Arminianism yet nonetheless to be condemned, is the position taken by the high preparationists. Norton found himself in 1654 with the difficult task of delimiting conditional faith and preparatory work without encouraging the heresies of antinomianism. And he was compelled to do so in language that would not enrage the orthodox elders. Indeed, he had learned a great deal from Cotton's chastening twenty years before.

Norton was well aware of his dilemma and drew a subtle analogy between his own position and that of St. James. Though both James and St. Paul agreed on the nature of justification, Norton argues that they expressed themselves differently. The reason was that they were faced with different audiences and different enemies to the true faith. "Paul disputes against the Legalist, James both against the Legalists and Libertines."[100] In deference to his own double audience, Norton, like James, was in some measure forced to modify his objections to conditionality while still protecting the freeness of grace. Nonetheless his text makes it clear that Norton was more concerned with New England's flirtation with legalism than with Shepard's "golden dreams of grace."

Norton insisted once again to New England that it was love not labor, agape and not anxiety, that should be the saint's portion. He uses the word *ecstasy* to describe this closing circle wherein the Christian makes return to God: "Goodness so descends and cometh from God unto the creature, as that it stops not there, but ascends and returns again unto God." Benefits flowing to the saints remanate to God in human expressions of love and desire: "Hence love is said to be both extatical, that is, carrying the lover as it were out of himself unto the loved; as it is with the soul removed out of the body in a Trance: and circular, the beginning and the end of which Circle is God, that *Alpha* and *Omega:* from whom, and to whom are all things. Unto that infinite and increated Sea, whence all created rivers of goodness come, thither, they return again."[101]

❧

Jeremiah's God promised to be "an husband unto" the saints; Richard Sibbes created a universe around that promise. Safely locked in God's embrace, the Christian had only to express delight—nothing is required or lacking in this spiritual marriage. This was a universe that Preston,

Cotton, Davenport, and Norton inhabited with pleasure and praise. Throughout decades of struggle, first in England and then in America, the Cambridge preachers defended the freeness of grace and the abundance of God's love against the encroachments of contract and preparation.

Upon reflection it seems logical or at least aesthetically pleasing that God's sovereignty should be cast in the language of conditions, while his love was most often expressed by means of free testament. Though the covenant constrains power, it nonetheless recognizes its primacy in the form of human obligation and servitude. The testament that flows from God's unqualified love demands no terms yet stimulates an answering love in the grateful recipient. Thenceforth the saints themselves become flowing fountains, bringing forth fruits of answering love.

The antinomian years did not prove that this vision would produce heresy, as the orthodox elders claimed, but rather that it supported a heightened version of Christian liberty. Anne Hutchinson claimed the full freedom of a Christian to read her Bible without clerical mediation, and to witness her faith in private meetings and public gatherings. Having themselves renounced faith in the immediacy of the millennium and seeking social stability in the newly planted colony, preparationist clergy and magistrates may well have feared the self-confidence of Cotton, Hutchinson, and the Boston congregation. The Sibbesian piety did indeed seem to produce citizens more sure of their own authority than they were susceptible to discipline, in church or in court.

It would be crudely cynical as well as insupportable to suggest that the elders' conscious desire was to institute disciplinary mechanisms in the battle against the Cottonians. Worried about the potential despair in a doctrine so removed from human remediation and motivated by a humane sympathy for their sinful auditors, these preparationists hoped to preserve the freeness of grace while carving out a place for human agency. First by means of legal edict, and then by the subtler discipline of church and community practices, the normative faith in New England produced Christians eternally en route to salvation.

As a response to the bleakest formulation of preparationism as routinization or deferred consummation, it is perhaps easy to understand the nostalgia of some scholarly accounts of the Antinomian Controversy. The orthodox preachers neither experienced nor sympathized with the freedom written into the Cambridge theology. Sibbes and Cotton celebrated a pleasure and a knowledge that was perhaps denied them: God's testament produced saints all the more zealous in their spiritual labors precisely because they were freed from a system of obligation and reward.

6

❧

Charity and Its Fruits

Though I speak with the tongues of men and of angels, and
have not charity, I am become as sounding brass, or a tinkling
cymbal. And though I have the gift of prophecy, and understand all mysteries, and all knowledge; and though I have all
faith, so that I could remove mountains, and have not charity,
I am nothing.

I Corinthians xiii:1–2

Nearly one hundred years after the Antinomian Controversy was
abruptly terminated, New England ministers revived debate over
the *ordo salutis* and the duties of a Christian. Foremost among them was
Jonathan Edwards, the great revivalist of the eighteenth-century awaken-
ings. Noted for his antipathy to the Arminianism of his day, Edwards
articulated a doctrine of grace and a style of piety richly reminiscent of
the doctrines of the Spiritual Brethren.

St. Paul's ecstatic hymn to the Corinthians was a founding text for
Edwards's sermon series on *Christian Love, as Manifested in the Heart and
Life,* also known as *Charity and its Fruits.* As the two titles suggest,
love—to be *Christian* love—must bear fruit in the actions as well as in the
heart of the saint. Edwards rehearsed the ancient Christian dictum so
central to the Cambridge Brethren, that good trees bear fruit—by virtue
of an ontological change rather than by human design.

The Brethren understood that though charity has many branches "in
good words and behavior," it has only one root, and that root is love: "the
word properly signifies *love,* or *that disposition or affection whereby one is
dear to another;* and the original ('agape'), which is here translated '*charity*',
might better have been rendered '*love*.'"[1] Human charity, then, is a version
of divine agape; it is not self-centered, but diffusive: "If your heart is full
of love, it will find vent; you will find or make ways enough to express
your love in deeds." Love is the "summ of all true grace in the heart."[2]
This definition of sanctification as a life of Christian love suffused the
piety of Sibbes and his followers.

Just as God's agape extended freely and without condition, so by definition Christian love was to be diffusive, extending not just upward to God but outward to one's fellows. The real Christian labored not in anticipation of spiritual rewards but in a loving return for graces already received. As noted above, recent critics who have cast this relationship between love and labor as a challenge to Max Weber's work ethic mistake the general applicability of their observations.[3] Far more than the other orthodoxy, the Brethren substituted joy for anxiety, making consummation not anticipation the focus of their pastoralism. When the Cambridge preachers use the language of labor, they describe not works of preparation but sanctification—the fruits of charity.

Reading St. Paul's prescription that "knowledge puffeth up, but love edifieth," the Brethren took the injunction to edify in its most literal sense. Rather than private and egoistic pleasures of knowledge, love built their truer edifice: the spiritual church made from the lively stones of awakened hearts. They distinguished between mere knowledge of Christian things and the higher religious affection of desire. The Brethren's sermons, prayers, and deeds were inspired by a yearning for union with God, the communion of saints, and the advent of the Kingdom.

The argument advanced in the previous chapters is that the widely held assumption that Puritans agreed about the efficacy of preparationism based on a conditional covenant is inaccurate, that instead American Puritans were divided over the issue. Yet to identify Cotton and Sibbes as antipreparationists is also incorrect; they did not reject preparation of the heart but rather rejected its efficacy as a sign of election. Moreover, focusing on a single pair of opposing categories such as "preparationist" or "antipreparationist" oversimplifies the complex of ideas in question and improperly defines the Brethren in the negative. In positive terminology, it was sanctification that engaged their interest. Refusing a self-centered preparation before justification, they set their spiritual clocks to the moment of God's indwelling and the saint's remanations. This choice influenced their understanding not only of the course of the individual's life but of the history of God's church.

Presuming a regenerate audience who needed only to be recalled to the moment of faith and united in works of fellowship, they developed a preaching style designed to provoke that memory and therein to re-member the congregation. Moreover, personal confidence in election was answered by a faith in the coming of the Kingdom of God. Although the moment of transforming grace was in the past life of the saint, the Kingdom was still to be anticipated. The saints were enjoined to watch for its coming.

In contrast to the lonely pilgrimage on the path to individual salvation, the Sibbesians described the wider way of communal glory. Though men like Cotton refused to anatomize the heart, they scrutinized with painstaking care the progress of the church in the world. They sought to determine where they were along the path of a global and historical pilgrimage, one destined to fruition in a millennial season of glory. With respect to the estate of the church, they did recognize the claims of time and process; in this context they admitted the principle of incremental advancement that their counterparts had applied to the heart but that they applied to historical process. If the Brethren can in any sense be called preparationists, it is in this sense of making ready for the New Age. Internationalism and millennial optimism were the practical and political analogues to God's effulgence and produced a communal version of preparationism. Claims for a more general Puritan consensus are both supported and modified by this observation: their communal version of preparationism suggests an essential economy of ideational structures that were given alternative articulations within specific discursive fields.

Along with preparationism, millennialist fervor is usually regarded as a unifying mark of New English Puritanism.[4] The doctrine of the millennium is a complex theological matter, the subject of many monographs. The Puritans themselves struggled to sort out the implications of Revelation, debating over whether the Second Coming would be accomplished only after an apocalyptic judgment (what we now call a premillennial position) or whether it would unfold within history (now designated as postmillennial). The clergy at times held both opinions in a mixed and confused series of meditations on the last days.

Following Miller, Bercovitch has argued that while the Puritans were technically premillennialist, there was a strong postmillennial optimism in their articulation of their errand into the wilderness.[5] Recent revisionists of the Miller/Bercovitch formulation of the Puritan errand as generally postmillennialist argue that, quite to the contrary, most Puritans were biblical primitivists, that they were generally pre- or amillennial. Although readers like Delbanco and Bozeman have rejected the progressivist reading of the millennium, they do not challenge the monologic view of Puritan elites on this issue. Rather, they remark Cotton's excited anticipation of the last days and characterize it as somewhat unique.[6]

Yet as with so many aspects of doctrine, I would argue that the millennium was understood differently by the Amesians and their Sibbesian counterparts. The Cambridge preachers did indeed express enthusiasm for the coming of a period of spiritual joy and transformation within history. This yearning was countered, however, by the preparationists' anticipation of apocalypse and their desire for return to the purity of the primitive church. The preparationist stress on anticipation rather than consummation of spiritual marriage in the *ordo salutis* was refigured in their imagined millennium as probation rather than pleasure.

Generally speaking, the Sibbesians argued that the millenium would unfold in historical time, would be a transformation of the world in anticipation of the Second Coming. They believed there would be a reign of the saints on earth, while the preparationists argued that the church's resurrection could come only with a shattering of nature. In technical terms, the Cambridge group espoused a belief in what Bozeman has identified as the "Middle Advent," while the preparationists more often spoke as premillennialists.[7]

Given this contrast between predictions of utopia and cataclysm, it is not surprising that there were varying degrees of commitment to bringing forth the Kingdom. Since their vision of the millennium was far less optimistic in terms of this world and time, the Amesians were less eager for its arrival. They meditated on the redemption worked in each heart, not as it was unfolded in history. The Sibbesians, however, waited and watched eagerly, calibrating current events against the celestial calendar.

The Brethren's desire for the Kingdom was written in expansive metaphors of charity and in programs for universal Christian union. This vision contrasts with the localism generally associated with Ames and his disciples. The preparationists constrained their love to God, to family, to self. It was often the possessive pronoun—whether identified with the single heart, the local/familial congregation, or the national church—that characterized the Amesian position. For them, the language of contract was realized in a contraction of religious affections. As this chapter and the next will demonstrate, the difference between these two parties within mainstream Puritanism can be described by the contrasting vision of love as expansive or contracted, of the church as global or contained within local boundaries, of the millennium joyously imminent or anxiously deferred.

❧

Their faith that grace remakes the soul and that the fruit of this change is love led the Spiritual Brethren to speak of sanctification both as a new spiritual sense and a transformation of society into an affectionate union of saints. The Brethren easily moved from the knowledge that God is a fountain of love to the assumption that the saint receives an expanded knowledge and appreciation of divine things.

On the personal level this meant the sacralization of even the most common aspects of daily living. Grace provided a new basis for knowing and saying, sanctifying the world of nature and the language of the senses. Sibbes's dictum that "a sanctified fancy will make every creature a ladder to heaven" insured that the amorous songs of Solomon, the language of human love, and the colloquialisms of daily living became idioms of the divine.[8] The sealing of the spirit makes it possible to speak "of heavenly things after an earthly manner." Before justification human beings are so subject to "wantonness" that even the study of biblical texts like Canticles can tempt readers "to incontinency." But after gracious transformation, "as the light and heat of the sunne extinguisheth a kitchen fire, so doth heavenly love to Christ extinguish base kitchen lusts." For the saint the seductive discourses of taste and smell, of fragrances and perfumes, are made holy; the honey-phrases of earthly pleasure are washed clean in cadences of Solomon's song.[9] The joy of the Christian was a doctrine celebrated in the experience and the expression of the Brethren.

But grace not only sanctifies what the saint sees and feels, it dictates all that she or he says and does. To be true, sanctification must be turned outward, converted to labors of love. As always, the Brethren reminded that the temporal ordering of salvation is essential. First the saint is infused; then, goodness becomes diffusive: "We must first take in, and then send out; first be cisterns to contain, and then conduits to convey."[10] Remanation is always contingent upon God's emanation: God must be "an heape and fountaine of goodnesse . . . to us" before we can "offer ourselves back again to God."[11] Implicitly countering preparationists' in-junctions, the Cambridge Brethren discredit claims of human initiative: "We give nothing. The stream gives nothing to the fountain. The beam gives nothing to the sun, for it issues from the sun. Our very blessing of God is a blessing of his."[12]

The passion of justification must, of course, be transformed into the action of sanctification. Though works are never preparatory, redeemed saints must labor: this was not an injunction but a description. Preston, for example, argued that "whereas before there was nothing but self-love in [the saint]: which plant growes naturally in the garden of nature, when grace comes, it brings love with it, and that love makes us useful and serviceable both to God and man: So that whatsoever a man hath, what gifts, what knowledge, what authority he hath, he is ready to use it for the good of others."[13] Grace effects an ontological change: good actions grow in the heart "as naturally as fruit growes on the tree, that flows from the sap within."[14] The saints "finde an inward longing desire in your souls after the Lord Jesus Christ in the duties you goe about." Grace is motion: "that which lives, growes, till it comes to its full perfection," a perfection unrealized until the second advent.[15]

On one level, this faith in reciprocity emerges from the general sense that "the best things in nature are communicative and diffusive." The fertile tree is the favored emblem of the Christian, who "so soon as he finds any rooting in God, is of a spreading disposition."[16] Henceforth all actions are sanctified: "He prays in the Spirit, and sighs and groans to God in the Spirit. He doth all by the Spirit." The true test of faith is when "we do common ordinary things in a holy spiritual manner."[17]

On a deeper level, however, the Brethren's doctrine of remanation follows from their understanding of God's ontological nature: "He desires to open himself," his "goodness is a communicative, spreading goodness." God is a communicating being whose happiness is realized in dissemination. The Brethren argue that the fusion of being with communication informs God's glory both *ad intra* and *ad extra,* in the creation of the Trinity and of the world.

First, this principle of diffusion informs the Cambridge doctrine of the Trinity, in which the three-personed God testifies to the desire for union in holy society, with members actively loving and enjoying one another. The Brethren read the Trinity as an injunction to cultivate the union of saints. As Cotton argued, before the beginning of time, the persons of the Godhead took pleasure in their union; they "nourished, delighted and solaced each other."[18] Human love serves as a mere type for the pleasures of this transcendent relation: "If the Creature can fill and ravish us with servile delights, how much more can the Persons of the blessed Trinity one another."[19]

In a language of spiritual erotics, Cotton explained that the Father, as primary essence, created the Son in his image for the purpose of his own delight: "The Father from eternity considering and understanding himself, from this conceiving of the Father resulted the Image of himself, that was his son, from them both resulted the Holy Ghost."[20] The Holy Ghost was understood literally as the breath exchanged between and knitting Father to Son: "As the Holy Ghost hath communion in proceeding from the Father and the Son, and knows the secrets of both . . . [t]he love of God the Father, and the Son, and the communion of the Holy Ghost; so the Holy Ghost proceeds from the Son as well as from the Father; he is called here the Spirit of the Lord."[21] In order to enjoy communion, three separate yet inextricable beings are requisite. This understanding of the Trinity is God's communicative nature *ad intra.*

Joy in otherness was also manifested *ad extra*—in the creation of the world and the work of redemption. As Sibbes declares: "If God had not a communicative, spreading goodness, he would never have created the world. The Father, Son, and Holy Ghost were happy in themselves, and enjoyed one another before the world was. But that God delights to communicate and spread his goodness, there had never been a creation nor a redemption."[22] The texts of the Bible and of the world, then, are proofs of this diffusive desire.

The phenomenal world provides the emblems by which human beings may understand both this conjunction of being with communication in God's nature and secondarily in its outflowing to the creature. God's essence is typed not only by the fountain but by the sun, which "delights to spread his beams and his influence in inferior things." Being and energy are fused in this heavenly body; heat and light are then extended to and through secondary objects.[23] By means of such types, humankind is to learn that God's emanations are the free overflow of a goodness that is nonetheless completely self-sufficient: God can declare "I am good in myself, but I desire to shine on you, to impart my goodness to you."[24]

God's desire for communication models the life of sanctification. Their doctrine of the Trinity was reflected in the high value the Brethren placed on the communion of saints. Sibbes explained: "the Trinity should be the pattern of our unity. Because, I say, all good is in union, and all that comes from us that is accepted of God, it must be in peace and union."[25] Christ, being ours, is "the foundation of communion" and our model and injunction to love one another.[26] This great commandment of the heart generated the Brethren's sociology.

Against the logic of preparation, but in keeping with love, the human desire to communicate inspires works of sanctification. "Before regeneration," Preston explains, "when a man is a stranger to this goodnesse, he onely serves himself, he is full of self-love, all his ends are to look to himself, that he may be kept safe; he cares not what becomes of any thing else, so it be well with him." Self-love was the mark of depravity; regeneration was manifest in love to others: "but when once goodnesse comes into his heart . . . he goes about doing good." As a new principle of "love of God and man," grace makes the saint a social being: "whatsoever a man hath, what gifts, what knowledge, what authority he hath, he is ready to use it for the good of others."[27]

Love of God cannot be divorced from social affections: "to those that are led with the Spirit of God, that are like him; they have a communicative, diffusive goodness that loves to spread itself."[28] God is no longer spoken of in isolation; the conjunction *and* joins God to humanity in the life of sanctification: "So it may be said of all Saints, when once this goodness is put into them, now they are profitable to God and man, they do serve God and man with their fatness, and with their sweetness." Preston never tired of reminding his auditors that the true faith "is the common Faith, therefore every Man had interest in it."[29]

Therefore, though exercises of private prayer, thanksgiving, and meditation were to be performed, they did not satisfy the claims of God's desire or human yearning. Cotton declares that human happiness can only be realized in union: "Our joy cannot be full, except we enjoy union with him, and communion with his Children."[30] The saint is like a warm ember that needs kindling: "if you take but two or three of them things that are well kindled, and they will set all a fire that comes nigh them . . . the breath of such Christians, is like bellows, to blow up sparkes one in another, and so in the end they breathe forth many savoury and sweet expressions of the hearts, and edifie themselves by their mutuall fellowship one with another."[31]

The Brethren preached that God's pleasure, too, is directly increased as the union of saints grows ever larger, that he is in love with public meetings: "God loves to be praised by many joining together." The prayers of the gathered society of saints become a choral antitype to David's Psalms: "So, when any give God thanks, and every one hath a good heart set in tune, when they are good Christians all, it is wondrous acceptable most to God, it is sweet incense."[32] Or, as Sibbes declares, "If every star be beautiful, how beautiful are all in their lustre! When so many saints shall be gathered together, they shall be far more glorious than the sun in his majesty; and this glory is reserved till all be gathered together."[33] God's pleasure in the saints' lustre is proportionate to their ever-increasing magnitude. The extensions of grace bear fruit in anticipations of glory.

The obligation of the preacher is to facilitate this tendency to good union. Sibbes describes the inextricability of God's love to his saints and their subsequent love to each other:

> The Spirit works in us, but in us with you, and in you with us; that is, as all the spirits come from the head and heart to the several members of the body, so they must be united, they must be in the body . . . There must be an union with Christ the head and with the rest of the members before we can have the Spirit to strengthen and anoint us . . . This should be a bond to tie us to the communion of the saints. We have all that we have in the body; we all grow in the

body; we are all stones in one building, whereof Christ is the foundation; therefore as stones in an arch strengthen one another, so should we . . . As we are knit to Christ by faith, so we must be knit to the communion of saints by love. That which we have of the Spirit is had in the communion of saints.[34]

Psalms, Canticles, and John provide images which serve as types for the experience of communion in the Christian life. The family of saints becomes the embodiment of God's own excellency and the source of strength: "The communion of saints is chiefly ordained to comfort the feeble-minded and to strengthen the weak."[35]

The complaint that good Christians commit their worst sins against self and society through spiritual coldness and drowsiness is a commonplace of all Puritans, but it was especially emphasized by the Brethren. The communion of saints was a valuable counter to this torpor: "It is one of the best fruits of the communion of saints, and of our spiritual good acquaintance, to keep one another awake."[36] Preston goes so far as to suggest that the practice of Christian virtue and the expression of love to God is impossible outside of the bonds of fellowship. The saint's first qualification is that he "love the Brethren."[37]

Moreover, the saint's greatest pleasure derives from union: "there is a benevolence and a beneficence to all; but there is a kind of complacency, a sweet familiarity, and amity which should be reserved to a few, only to those in whom we see the evidences and signs of grace." This distinction between benevolence to being in general and the benevolence of complacency rests on love to all, but it nevertheless allows reservation of the greatest love to those "that we admit even into the closet of our hearts: and those are they with whom we hope to have communion for ever in heaven, the blessed people of God, termed here 'saints.'"[38]

In this way, anthropology is transformed into sociology—love of individuals is fused with love of the body of saints. This communalism does not violate the perception of the Spiritual Brethren as counselors to the weak-hearted Christian but merely expands it. Their care for individuals was never separate from a commitment to the body of saints; indeed it is always implied.

For example, as Sibbes's unfolding of Canticles reveals, the history of the heart and of the church are always interconnected, intertwined in each biblical passage and each Christian truth. The full title of the *Bowels Opened* makes this relationship clear: his exposition of the Song is *A Discovery of the Neere and deere Love, Union, and Communion betwixt Christ and the Church, and consequently betwixt Him and every beleeving Soul.* Although this sermon series focuses on the individual soul, it also insists on the identity of union with the communion of the saints. Indeed the sentence structure, with the essential placement of the word *consequently,* insists on the priority of the gathered saints.

Similarly when Cotton first preached on Canticles in the 1620s, he traced the work of redemption as it applied to the estate of the church. In the next cycle in the 1640s he did not exclude the communal but added practical observations on the application of redemption to the single heart.[39] The garden of the heart and church in the world were simultaneous temples for the Spirit. Yet the Brethren also preached that Christ comes to the single believer most efficaciously in the presence of others. Canticles, and indeed the whole of Scripture, provided a model whereby these preachers understood that redemption worked ontologically in the heart of each believer and redemption worked historically in the course of the world and time were one. The destiny of the single soul was inextricably wedded to the society of saints.[40] It was the preacher's job to bring home this truth to the heart of each auditor, to facilitate the spiritual marriage of the saints first to Christ and then one to another.

❧

The Brethren promoted the tendency to Christian union in their ecclesiology, conception of the ministry, and sermonic style. Community was perceived as so essential that they sometimes went so far as to cast private devotions as counterproductive: "Some do not find, because they seek in one means and not in another. They seek Christ in reading and not in the ordinance of hearing, in private meditation, but not in the communion of saints."[41] Again, the question turns on emphasis. The Brethren advocated meditation and prayer, of course; but they neither stressed private devotions as heavily as did the preparationists nor did they privilege them over communal exercises.

Cotton argues that God gives us Scripture so that we may "enjoy union with him, and communion with his Children." Scripture is for "filling our hearts with Joy," and the "purpose of hearing is fellowship."[42] Hearing the word in the company of others is always preferred to private reading: "*faith comes* not by reading, but by *hearing* . . . If ever God had intended that the reading of these writings had been effectual to the begetting of faith, surely he would have followed them with mighty works . . . but you shall not read in any Scripture that ever God so farre blessed the Word read to any man."[43]

For Sibbes, too, the word preached and heard in community is always more efficacious than the word read. Indeed, in response to the query, "Cannot I as well read privately at home?" Sibbes confirmed the primacy of the communal: "The truth read at home hath an efficacy, but the truth unfolded hath more efficacy."[44] In a statement harsher than is usual, Sibbes makes clear that while he advocates all forms of devotion, public acts of faith have primacy: "the use of private exercises, with contempt of the public, they have a curse upon them instead of a blessing."[45] The exclusive use of private forms of worship is forbidden, not only because they are insufficiently pleasurable to God but because they are ineffectual as means to comfort.

If the purpose of hearing is fellowship, so too the inspiration for preaching is union. As Paul Seaver has argued, the sermon had a greater effect on a larger number of auditors than almost any literary form in the Elizabethan world. And how much more true is this observation when applied to New England, where Sunday sermons were supplemented with weekly lectures, occasional sermons, and informal prayer groups. The sermon was not only God's ordinary means of pricking the heart but also the most important means of gathering the saints. As such, it was the linchpin of their piety.[46]

The role of the minister was conceived as so sacred that he is represented as a type of the Holy Spirit. Just as the Spirit is the "procurer of the marriage, between Christ and the soul," the preacher is to "procure the marriage between Christ and his church." Both minister and Holy Ghost are called *"paranymphi,* the friends of the bridegroom." Of course, this trope was not the exclusive property of the Brethren but was shared by almost all Puritans, including Shepard and Hooker. Such instances remind us of the common heritage and the values shared by these preachers. Yet it is also true that often the preparationist preachers represented themselves as agents of a contractual marriage, negotiating the dowry of salvation.[47]

The Brethren, on the other hand, represented themselves as bridesmen in an affective union. Ministers breathed God's word to the saints in a near imitation of the love breathed between the Father and Son. They were to preach often and amiably, to be "full as the honeycombe dropping out of itself, to preach sweet doctrine as honey and wholesome as milk, for the nourishments of Christs lambs."[48] The triad of living word, minister, and gathered saints was emblematic of the Trinity itself. With such value placed on preaching, it is not surprising that throughout the 1620s these ministers hedged on conformity to retain their pulpits.

Nor is it surprising that more than many other Puritans, they stressed the importance of a ministry sealed with the Spirit. In earlier decades of Anglican persecution, ministers were forced by circumstances to provide a rationale for believers to practice their faith within the corrupt structures of the church. Perkins, for example, sometimes downplayed the necessity of a converted ministry. He argued that in "the ruinous estate" of the church, when "by apostasy the foundations thereof are shaken and the clear light of the word is darkened," effectual words can be preached even by a corrupt clergy: "then this word read and repeated, yea the very sound thereof being but once heard, is by the assistance of God's Spirit extraordinarily effectual to them whom God will have called out of that great darkness into his exceeding lights." In thus reassuring parishioners that their prayers to God were received, even through the hands of an unregenerate clergy, Perkins declared that "it is very plain that the minister's impiety doth not make a nullity of the sacrament, neither doth it any whit hinder a worthy receiver, because all the efficacy in worthiness thereof dependeth only upon God's institution."[49]

This was a position Amesians and Sibbesians both rejected, but perhaps for slightly different reasons. Though preachers like Hooker could not abide the corrupted form of the church and insisted on the congregation's rights to ordination, they did not demand that ministers attest to their own full assurance of salvation. Hutchinson, it will be recalled, was condemned for "slightinge of Gods faythfull Ministers," primarily because she argued that they were not sealed with the Spirit.[50] Both Hooker and Shepard argued that many saints are uncertain of their closing in Christ and need not enjoy full assurance to enter full church membership. Their own tortured conversions and, to Hutchinson's ear at least, their waffling on the issue of assurance suggest that the preparationist clergy were less adamant about these qualifications in their definition of an able ministry.

Sibbesians, on the other hand, preached a religion of affections that required a regenerate ministry. The witness of the Spirit, not ordination even within a properly constituted congregation, made the minister: "none should take that office upon them to which they are not called of God, nor qualified by his Spirit, especially ministers, because Christ did not set upon his office, till the Spirit was put upon him. The Spirit must enable us and fit us for everything."[51] In keeping with this injunction, Sibbes argues for a warm-hearted piety manifested in the words and manner of the sermon. His plea, "Let us labour to be deeply affected with what we speak," "if we would kindle others, we must be warmed ourselves; if we would make others weep, we must weep ourselves," was to be echoed in America by John Cotton and his less orthodox followers, who urged that spiritual estate and not earthly calling justified the preaching clergy.[52]

Preaching was not limited to the ordained clergy, however. The Brethren enjoined all saints to evangelize. In keeping with the Spirit's diffusiveness, preacher and parishioner are "knit . . . by bonds of love" and common obligations.[53] Cautioning, "do not think it belongs only to the ministry" to evangelize, Sibbes provided the principles upon which lay participation could rest: "For when we are confident from spiritual experience, it is wonderful how we shall be instruments of God to gain upon others."[54] Spiritual confidence was the hallmark of this piety, as Anne Hutchinson's declarations in the General Court would prove. Her teacher, Cotton, also emphasized full assurance, arguing that this new creature with a new heart should work to gather other souls: "now he can read Gods Word, and conferre with Gods people about the things of God, and can instruct others."[55] Lay preaching, prayer groups, and conversion narratives were some of the means by which the saint was to ignite the affections of others. Though lay prophesying was outlawed in the aftermath of the Antinomian Controversy, the Cambridge Brethren sanctioned all such means of effecting the communion of saints.

Paradoxically, their concept of the preaching brotherhood was both more exalted and more egalitarian than that of their preparationist counterparts. By stressing the importance of a converted ministry, they elevated the status of the clergy.[56] Yet by adding that all saints participate in harvesting souls, they opened the way for a more democratic congregationalism, albeit one that was restricted to the elect. As Cotton declared, "minister and people maintain brotherly love" between them, a love bearing three fruits: "Unity, equality, and spiritual communion."[57] Posing the question, "What is the Office or duty which God calleth the Brethren unto in members of the Church?" Cotton answered: "To brotherly love (1) and the fruits thereof brotherly unity (2) brotherly equality (3) brotherly communion."[58]

This emphasis on the egalitarian community rather than on a clerical hierarchy is somewhat unique to the Brethren. The gathered saints were to be as one body in Christ, typified by the diffusive oil poured over the head of Aaron: "The oil that was poured on Aaron's head ran down to his beard, and to the skirts of his clothing . . . the meanest parts of his garment were bedewed with that oil: so the graces of God's Spirit poured upon our head Christ, our Aaron, our High Priest, run down upon us, upon all ranks of Christians, even upon the skirts, the weakest and lowest

Christians. Every one hath grace for grace; we all partake of the oil and anointing of our spiritual Aaron, our High Priest."⁵⁹ Cotton, too, borrowed this diffusive image of "the most precious oyntment" to describe "how comely a thing is it for brethren to live together in unity."⁶⁰ The oil poured upon "all ranks of Christians" suggests a flow of fellow feeling that dissolves the many into the one.

This bodily image of union recalls Winthrop's famous description of a society bound together by ligaments of love. The difference is that in *A Modell of Christian Charity*, Winthrop identifies the social body as constituted of discrete parts—some high, some low, all providentially positioned in stations roughly synonymous with places in the social hierarchy. Winthrop's sermon opens with the doctrine that "God Almighty in his most holy and wise providence hath so disposed of the condition of mankind, as in all times some must be rich, some poor, some high and eminent in power and dignity, others mean and in subjection."⁶¹

Members of Winthrop's model society are bound by charity into a single whole, but that charity is not diffusive but instead supports a static social order. I am not suggesting that Winthrop's vision is less utopian than Cotton's, but it is certainly less committed to a fluid reordering of this world in anticipation of a kingdom of saints in the next.

Cambridge optimism and emphasis on fellow feeling was reinforced by the very manner in which the Brethren addressed their auditors and in the structure of their sermons. Preparationist preachers favored the trope of pilgrimage, of discernible stadia and towns the wayfarer must traverse on the path to salvation. This trope is most fully realized in a plotted narrative whose orderly and predictable progression, like Winthrop's orderly arrangement of the body politic, implies the superior status of the speaker. To be sure, there may be a profoundly democratic aspect to this style of piety and expression. In *The Pilgrim's Progress*, for example, Bunyan constructs a narrative that enables his readers both to plot their position and to map their pathway to salvation. Yet it is also true that this tale is told from the privileged position of one who has completed the journey and is reconstructing it as a handbook for other Christians.

While Bunyan diminishes this privilege by casting himself as the everyman-wayfarer with whom readers are encouraged to identify, preachers like Hooker and Shepard characteristically resist identification with their auditors. Instead they stand in a didactic and hierarchic relation to their flock, a position marked even in their use of pronouns. Characteristically, Hooker and Shepard use an *I/thou* construction that separates and elevates them above their flock as prophets and judges. A typical passage from

Shepard's *Sincere Convert* serves to demonstrate this rhetoric of difference between preacher and congregant: "thou wilt ask me how it may be proved that there will be such a day [as the day of judgment] . . . I answer, God's justice calls for it." Shepard warns, "then all the sins that ever thou hast or shalt commit shall come fresh to thy mind."[62]

Sibbes and Cotton, on the other hand, identify themselves with their auditors (as did Bunyan); they seem to partake of their cycles of spiritual joy and despair. As a few examples will demonstrate, this identification is manifest in the persistent use of the plural pronoun:

> All treasure is hid in Christ for us . . . If we want particular graces, go the well-head Christ, consider of Christ now filled for us, as it was in Aaron.

> Is there such a store-house of comfort and grace every way in Christ? Why are we so weak and comfortless? Why are we so dejected as if we had not such a rich husband?[63]

> The spirit of God, wheresoever it is shed abroad in any member of Christ, it doth make us one with the Lord Jesus, it unites us into one fellowship of nature.[64]

As with their advocacy of a mutual interpretive community over private reading, this collapse of auditor and speaker might be read as arrogantly magisterial or even coercive, rhetorically eliminating all possibility of feeling oneself as "other." Yet neither their project, tone, nor effect on their flock supports such interpretation. Rather, an enabling intimacy results from the identification of spiritual guide with supplicant, one confirmed by the terms of endearment by which the preacher engages his auditors.[65] Calling them his "brethren" and his "beloved," Sibbes imitated the love Christ expressed toward his disciples and his church.

Similarly, their presentation of the classic dialogic mode suggests a more mutual exchange between equals than is found in preparationist catechisms. The interchanges between the Brethren and their self-doubting questioners are reminiscent of the loving exchange between the reluctant guest and the welcoming Christ of George Herbert's *Love III*. With the same brotherly patience he extols in the Saviour himself, Sibbes reassures and comforts shy and reluctant members of his flock:

> *Obj:* But I have often relapsed and fallen into the same sin again and again.

Ans: If Christ will have us pardon our brother seventy-seven times, can we think that he will enjoin us more than he will be ready to do himself . . . Where the work of grace is begun, sin loses strength by every new fall . . . That should not drive us from God, which God would have us make use of to fly the rather to him.[66]

Evident in this passage is not merely Sibbes's faith in the goodness of his "sinful" auditor, thereby confirming his membership in the society of saints, but also his willingness to take on the sorrows of his fellows in a personal way. Unlike Hooker, who often instructs from a position of superiority, Sibbes, in an act of kenosis, converts parishioners' doubts into his own and then assuages them. Always there is the transformation of the "I" to "we" which is the essence of fellow-feeling. If the possession of Christ himself is manifest in the saints' ability to turn the "thy" God of Scripture to the "my" God of the heart, then the community of saints is built upon this essential conversion of "I" to "we" which the Brethren so deftly execute in every instance.

Indeed, the shift from the third- to the first-person plural occurs throughout Cotton's corpus. Frequently, he begins a sentence in this impersonal mode: "When a man thus worships God, patiently submitting himselfe to him . . ." Yet Cotton concludes such sentences with the shift to the first-person plural: "if we can finde this in us, that in our hearts we thus worship the Lord Jesus, [and] so highly prize him," then we are certain of our election.[67] The doctrine supporting this linguistic transformation rests on John 17:21: "our Saviour prayes the Father, *that all those whome he had given him might bee one with him, as thou and I art one:* thou in me by thy spirit, and I in thee, by the same spirit: and this spirit is such, as makes not only mee, one with thee, but them also, one with mee . . . it makes us and Christ as it were one."[68]

Ministers, then, preach with and out of a shared knowledge and experience, enhancing their power to be heard.[69] This identification with one another implicitly confirms the communion bond. It must be stressed that the basis for this knitting together of souls was the presumed graciousness of both preacher and auditor—a tribalism of sorts, but one established by spiritual affinity rather than local allegiance or family heritage.

While they preached to a mixed multitude, the sermons of the Brethren were primarily addressed to a converted audience, one initiated in the mysteries of godliness. Like Scripture itself, God's truth can be fully accessible only to those that have the eyes to see and the ears to hear. Knowledge of God's love is experimental; it is "a certain divine expression of Christ to the soule, whereby a man is secretly assured *without* any argument or reason."[70]

As mentioned above, Cotton proposes the prophet as a model for the preacher, one whose words are intended for the inner circle of saintly auditors. He opens the twelfth sermon of *Christ the Fountaine* with a verse from one of his favorite biblical texts, I John: *"The things have I written unto you that beleeve on the name of the Son of God, that ye may know that ye have eternall life, and that ye may beleeve on the name of the Son of God."* Glossing the verse, Cotton derives the doctrine, *"This Epistle of John was written, or directed to beleevers on the name of Jesus Christ,"* from which he concludes, "he writes to such, who by reading this Epistle might attaine to *fulnesse of joy,* and those are only beleevers, who are capable of that mercy and blessing."[71]

Or again in his *Practical Commentary on I John* Cotton urges, "if you write to some, thinking to convert them, it will be a labour in vain." Of course, the Brethren did not at all disdain the doctrine of means or the importance of the ministry. Yet their faith in God's full prevenience meant that while the sermon could edify the saints, true understanding had to proceed from God's renovation of the spiritual senses. Cotton likened himself to the apostles who knew "they should never prosper in writing to men that believed not, but to such as believed, that they might have joy in believing."[72] Indeed Cotton claims that the scriptures "are all written to *Beleevers* . . . they are written sometimes to *Saints by calling,* sometimes to *faithfull brethren,* sometimes to the *Churches of Christ* . . . in a word, only to those that were *faithfull beleevers in Christ Jesus.*"[73] Just as Norton stipulated that his discussion of the covenant properly applied to the Elect, Cotton implicitly claimed that the experience of justifying faith is a prerequisite for the proper understanding of the word *delivered.*

This does not mean, however, that Cotton or Sibbes abandoned fainthearted Christians—they did not. In fact, they were justly famous as ministers to such "bruised reeds," generously constructing their audience as already redeemed. This presumption shapes the very structure and intent of their sermons. It is not the enlightened reason but only the regenerated sensibility which allows the saint to understand truths delivered from the pulpit. Cotton asserts that "all Christians know that unless the Spirit of God set in and clear up the truth and power and grace of God in all those reasonings, their souls will not be able to gather clear evidences of their estates from all they hear."[74] Not simply to know one's status, but even to hear with full understanding the words of the sermon requires regenerate senses. Without grace, the path from reason to will, the understanding to the heart, is impossible to traverse. With grace, it is a short distance indeed.

Hence Cotton and Sibbes try less to exhort and persuade than to recall the regenerate auditor to the moment of union. It is through sharing this memory of spiritual fulfillment that the ties between saints are consummated. In the Brethren's sermons narrative gives way to incantation, logic to affect. Rather than the forward movement of plot, these sermons dig deep; they hover over the words of Scripture rather than ride roughshod over its terrain. Lyrical, incantatory, threading thoughts together on a chain of repeated words, these sermons privilege rhetoric over logic, association over argument, sensibility over meaning, even sometimes sound over sense.

Abjuring strict adherence to the Ramean dichotomies, the sermons sometimes turned on a syllogistic strategy, but most often they unfolded by an organic ordering of associational logic—that is, by pursuing the ways in which biblical texts allude to and clarify each other. Text not application, metaphor not simile, are the foundations of this sermonic style, which many readers have characterized as fluid, organic, at times even illogical or, more accurately, antilogical.[75]

Of course, none of these preachers adopted the ornate language of a John Donne; they achieved their ecstatic cadences with plainness, recreating the music as much as the sense of sacred texts. Reveling in the allusive links to be traced between biblical passages, they felt little anxiety about corrupting their auditors precisely because they believed their audience was justified.

Though it is generally assumed that Perkins's *Arte of Prophesying* offered a normative structure for Puritan sermonizing, there was a good deal of latitude exercised with respect to that model. In the structure and style of their sermons, the Cambridge Brethren forged a form reflective of their particular theological beliefs. Their sermons were essentially exegetical rather than hortatory, unfolding in fluid associations rather than an orderly analysis of parts.[76] Leverenz says Cotton's "similes are often more extended than Hooker's, creating a flowing, circling effect rather than a sense of parts in order."[77] The same observation might be applied to the writings of his mentor, Richard Sibbes.

While the Amesians emphasized the didactic mode, the Sibbesians saw themselves as conduits for the Word; they refused to be taskmasters of the heart. In describing the office of the ministry, Sibbes refers to yet another constellation of metaphors. Ministers bring forth what is hidden; they "lay open the unsearchable riches," "unfold the hidden mysteries of Christ," the incarnated Word.[78] They are miners who "dig deep, and find out the treasure;" friends who "lay open the tapestry, the rich treasure of God's mercies;" servants who open "the box of sweet ointment, that the savour of it may be in the church, and spread far."[79] In all it is the hidden Christ who is to be preached, and "'to preach Christ' is to lay open all this, which is the inheritance of God's people."[80] Clearly the auditors are those already entitled to Christ's bequest of grace and able to embrace such holy mysteries.

The same principle informing Cotton's doctrine of things indifferent infused this understanding of scriptural exegesis. In *Some Treasure Fetched out of Rubbish,* he argued that nothing should be added to or subtracted from Scripture: "all signs of men's devising cannot teach or stir to true devotion, but delude and nourish superstition." But in Cotton's hands this meant not simply attending to God's dictation, but unfolding every letter of that communication: "we are forbidden to add ought to the Word written or to take ought from it."[81] For Cotton, this dictum had implications for literary theory. While Hooker edited the scriptural text to suit his own requirements of plot, Cotton insisted that every word of the verse be considered. He regarded himself as the medium, not as the editor of God's Word. In harmony with his general emphasis on passion rather than action, he assumed passivity before the Word.

It is not difficult to see how such a position would dictate a sermon form that would be associative and allusive rather than linear and plotted. Beginning with an assumption akin to George Herbert's sense of Scripture as a "box where sweets compacted lie" and his hermeneutics of collation, Sibbes and his followers unfold the wonders of such mysterious sweetness. The techniques they use—opening biblical texts word by word, meditating on single phrases and tropes, collating like texts, and privileging exegesis over applications—could make sense only to an audience endowed with eyes to see and ears to hear.[82] By almost hypnotically repeating single words of Scripture, Sibbes and the others find themselves becalmed in its phrases.[83] Communication in this mode relies on the spiritual literacy of the auditors and places them in a passive position before the Word, a position designed to recall them to their greatest moment of passivity—the infusion of grace. This is a technique that leads the auditors to trace the words of the Scripture in their own hearts. God's promise that he will write his love "not in tables of stone but in the fleshy tables of the heart" (2 Corinthians 3:3) is not a metaphor but a truth Cotton and Sibbes relied upon every sermon day.

Through the yearning of the regenerate heart, a single word of Scripture can open God's intent. Consider for example the way in which the text may thread through the many meanings of a single word such as *behold, wonderment, godliness,* or *mystery.* In "A Description of Christ," Sibbes begins with the verse from Matthew 12:18: "Behold my servant whom I have chosen." Ranging over such diverse texts as Revelation, Hebrews, and the Gospels, Sibbes unfolds the multiple significances of the seemingly neutral form of address: "*Behold!*—this word is as it were a beacon lighted up to all the rest." Collating the many occurrences of this word in the Bible, Sibbes declares "in all the evangelists you have this word often repeated, and the prophets likewise when they speak of Christ; there is no prophecy almost but there is this word, 'Behold.'"[84]

Behold is a call and a presentation; it "was to present Christ to the hearts of the people of God," just as Sibbes's own sermon was to set forth Christ. It was also "to call the people's minds from their miseries;" "to raise the mind from any vulgar, common, base contents;" to raise "up the minds of men to look on an object fit to be looked on." By its repetition, *Behold* is drained of literal content; the word becomes instead something of a spiritual mantra, recognized and repeated by the saints. It is a chant to arouse an already kindled heart, not an argument to persuade the mind of a hesitant sinner.

Sibbes said "the prophets mount up with the wing of prophecy, and in regard of the certainty of the things to come, they speak as if they were present, as if they had looked on Christ present, 'Behold my servant.'" As a preacher, Sibbes speaks with a certainty of things past as well as to come. His unfolding of the meanings of *Behold* serves as a summons to the saints to recall their own experience of looking on Christ present, in the moment of spiritual union.[85]

Sibbes concludes his chant by declaring, "'behold', it is a word of wonderment, and, indeed, in Christ there are a world of wonders, everything is wonderful in him. Things new and wonderful, and things rare, and things that are great, that transcend our capacity, are wonderful, that stop our understanding that it cannot go through them . . . Now whatsoever may make wonderment is in Jesus Christ, whose name is Wonderful . . . therefore the prophet saith, 'Behold.'" At last, by verbal association, *Behold* becomes identified with the very wonder of Christ himself. The word becomes a blank counter, finally transformed into a conduit to Christ. The repetition of words and phrases reaches the heart by means other than reason. As Sibbes says, "things that are great . . . transcend our capacity

. . . stop our understanding." But the incantation of things glorious conveys a sense of transcendent meaning, beyond rational understanding but accessible to the heart.[86]

Sibbes continues in this fashion to analyze every word of the scriptural text. This is a technique Cotton employs as well. His own treatment of the word *Behold* in *God's Mercie Mixed with His Justice* illustrates a similar method of exegesis. Most of Cotton's sermons are shaped by this painstaking analysis of the scriptural text—first word by word, and then phrase by phrase. As Teresa Toulouse argues, such incantation "reveals his pleasure in developing the different possibilities of meaning . . . He is clearly leaving a good deal to his listener's capacities." She adds that Cotton "obviously does not use such collation to prove an argument . . . this technique of expanding possible meanings continues throughout the entire sermon."[87] Amplification is perhaps a better description of this sermon style. A brief glance at *Christ the Fountaine,* for instance, reveals that Cotton takes Scripture as dictation, that he explores and amplifies every word and every verse in the course of his sermon. If God is communicating being, the preacher must be attentive to every syllable, every letter of His communiqué. The order of the biblical passage rather than the logic of a predetermined doctrinal message shapes the sermon. The appeal is to God's reason rather than to mechanical, human logic. The preacher makes himself a passive vessel through which the Spirit flows from Bible to saint—he is "a conduit to convey."

In this way Sibbes and Cotton place themselves in the very midst of the words of Scripture. By divorcing words from their context in a sentence and endowing them with this associative and affective function, these preachers wash words of their human meaning, giving them an almost mystical power to communicate the unutterable wonder of Christ. While Hooker and Ames move from illustration to concrete illustration, Sibbes and Cotton rest with the single word or verse.

For the regenerate ear, this repetition "engenders stasis; instead of pressing movement, rest; and instead of an appetite for ever more varying images, it appears to create a confidence and even a complacency that no further images are necessary."[88] This stasis or complacency is rooted in a confidence available only to the elected saint. The restless urge to explain and exhort that characterizes preparationist sermons gives way to this more tranquil and languid wonder.

In these passages it is not the sense only but also the music that melts the heart. Repetition has the effect of substituting connotation for denotation, sound for sense. There is an almost hypnotic effect to reiteration. Meaning is threaded on sound and on the incantatory power of single words. The ways in which verses echo one to another absorb the Brethren, as if merely hearing such resonances was sufficient edification for those with the proper sensibility.[89] The saints are not presented with a privileged narrator offering advice concerning the road marks of spiritual passage, but instead find themselves in the presence of a fellow singer—a conduit whereby they, too, are laved with the words of Scripture.

As conduits for the "divine kind of rhetoric," these preachers have "tongues that are as refined silver." Persuading with quiet whisperings rather than in thunder, the verbal performances of these preachers underscore the hypnotic effect of their sermons.[90] William Hubbard reported that Cotton had "an insinuating and melting way in his preaching."[91] Mather records that Cotton's delivery, unlike the "noisy and thundering" style of the day, "had in it a very awful *majesty;*" the cadences "set off with a natural and becoming motion of his *right hand,*" so that the auditors felt the Lord's presence in that *"still voice."* Not even John Wilson was immune to Cotton's charismatic presence, declaring that when "he preaches out of any prophet I hear not him; I hear the very prophet and apostle; yea, I hear the Lord Jesus Christ himself speaking in my heart."[92]

Davenport was also styled "a princely preacher," who gave up the "very fervent and vehement" style of his youth in order to imitate the affective style of Cotton, his "counterpart in gesture and in mien."[93] Sibbes, too, was said to have "had a peculiar gift in unfolding and applying the great mysteries of the gospel in a sweet and mellifluous way . . . sweet and heavenly distillations usually dropping from him with such a native elegance not easily to be imitated."[94]

The effect of such texts and performances is not to evangelize so much as to induce the same sense of passivity and high emotion that characterizes the experience of grace itself.[95] The appeal is to the heart, to kindle the relish for divine things. Theoreticians of language have long remarked on the effect of repetition as a compositional device. Reiteration without explanation or progression stops the plot, neutralizes rational cognition, and appeals to the senses: "When repetition converts the words of a narrative from a cognitive function to a musical presence and so discounts their signifying action, it may at the same time be said to insist on their 'quality.'"[96]

The use of repetition rests on a confidence that the word itself is sufficient, that the restless quest for variety is unnecessary. It is not multiple applications that instruct, but penetration and re-cognition of the single truth that are blessed. Repetition signals a shift from denotation to connotation, from logic to affect. It engenders stasis, not motion, so that the words of Scripture drench the parched soul. The Brethren and their flock wade into the words of Scripture up to the loins, until they are saturated with the expanding meanings.

This style must rely on a converted audience; it must presume a past infusion of grace. Repetition sets in motion the process of memory. The word re-sounded reaches backwards to its first utterance, just as the auditor is to recall the moment of grace. Moreover, incantation demands the same passivity on the part of the auditor as does the infusion of grace. The listener must "lend himself to the power of the music." There must be "an ultimate willingness in the listener to be moved and affected . . . in the sense of controlled . . . one's fundamental posture . . . entails the awareness that one is yielding to the music's terms and action."[97] Contrasting the logical or plotted structure in which the next step might be actively anticipated, the circular, repetitive structure refuses anticipation, relies on a pliant intellect. Thus, passive and waiting, the congregants recall together the essential spiritual truths, and therein the congregation is literally re-membered. Quite successfully, the preacher recreates that privileged moment in which "God's Spirit poured upon our head Christ, our Aaron, our High Priest, run[s] down upon us, upon all ranks of Christians."[98]

As critics have shown, the same principles of persuasion, association, and repetition inform the larger structure of these sermons. Collation of verses substitutes for logical order, and a focus on exegesis rather than applications keeps the auditors rooted together in the common ground of Scripture.[99] While the didactic mode of the preparationists would turn the auditor inward—to a rather lonely and sometimes agonized inspection of the heart—the Brethren's chants join the auditors together in a common celebration of Christ and Scripture.

It is quite likely that this desire to rekindle the moment of grace and to melt the congregation together also inspired Cotton to institute what is taken to be the hallmark of American Congregationalism—the testimony of conversion.[100] For Cotton, the value of the narrative was as a means to communal edification; he never regarded the testimony a method for policing admissions. The testimony, like the hearing of the word, was to draw the community together.

As Cotton explains, it is "publicly professing his faith before Christ and his fellow disciples in Christ's school" that marks the saint and makes the church. He goes on to add that "faith giveth a man fellowship in the invisible church, and in all the inward spiritual blessings of the church, but it is profession of faith that giveth a man fellowship in the visible church." Fellowship is intrinsic to this life of faith, then; it also is essential in constituting the congregation. Indeed Cotton remarks that the church is made not by its officers but only by the gathered saints: "the form is induced not by any formal act of the ministry . . . but by the voluntary stipulation or profession . . . of this society of believers." Elaborating on the trope of marriage, Cotton observes that "the church as it is the house of God so it is also the spouse of Christ." Though ministers serve as "friend of the bridegroom and of the bride," they are not essential to the marriage. The gathered saints constitute a church "whether ministers be present and assistant or no."[101]

This is a tenet the preparationists would agree to in principle; but in practice they assert the superior ontology of the preacher and the necessity of a ministry that breaks the sinner's heart. For Cotton, however, the conversion narratives wed the witness to the auditor, who is resealed in grace. The narrative ritual reenacts the moment of transformative grace, weaving the auditors into a single body.[102] Just as faith cometh by hearing, so fellowship cometh by the twin action of speaking and hearing, memory and identification. The narrative was not a test but a testimony to the wonders of God's love worked in the heart of the saint.

Since there are no remaining records from Cotton's church, we must surmise the quality of the Bostonians' narratives from their teacher's sermons. Cotton's piety of high emotion, his presumption of a regenerate audience, and his disavowal of preparationism suggest that testimonies offered in his church were joyous proclamations of grace received and the heart restored. For him, it is not the content but the cadence that identifies one saint to another. As Cotton says, it is "what Spirit breaths in such a speech" that marks the regenerate saint.[103] In the testimony of the elected "you shal as in a pattern discern, what the manner of the expression of a living soul is."[104] It is this manner of expression, as much as the content, that identifies the truly gracious heart. Cotton says that the saints are identified by "their sensible feeling of a lost estate," by a "breathing and panting after Christ." Again, the language of affect, the expression of feeling, and the sense of the heart entitle the faithful to join the glorious community of saints.[105]

By such methods and means the saints were gathered together in congregations to experience the pleasure and beauty of union. This communion was the greatest proof and fruit of God's agape. Valuable in itself, charity also elicited a greater outpouring of God's love, thus promoting the golden age of the New Jerusalem.

✻

Though gathering saints together was central to the Spiritual Brethren, enjoyment within their local congregations alone was insufficient to their expansive theology. Both in England and America, these preachers held to the utopian vision of a church international. If fellow feeling was the true exercise of grace, Sibbesians concluded that "nothing doth more characterize and is a better stamp of a true Christian than a public mind." This public mind was to be as expansive as God's own love. Sibbes ranges in his sermons from the more restrained formulation that "so soon as grace entereth into the heart, it frameth the heart to be in some measure public," to the assertion that "next to heaven itself, our meeting together here, it is a kind of paradise."[106] The gathering of saints was not only an emblem but a type of the new heaven and new earth.

These preachers went so far as to argue that the saint's life could be fully realized only in the company of others: "living Christians are loving Christians, so farre as living so farre loving, for the whole life of Christianity is but faith towards God, and love towards our brethren."[107] This was a dictum that the Brethren applied to the church international. Just as "it is an ill sign when any man will be a solitary Christian and will stand alone by himself," so the Brethren took it as an ill sign for any congregation to rest in its own purity without considering the world church. True Christians "must have and exercise publick Spirits in the communion of saints."[108] As Preston continually urged, "every Man hath an interest in it; doe not say therefore, what have I to doe, it belongs to these and these men to looke after it: it is the common Faith, and every Man hath part in it."[109]

The communion of true believers was to be desired not just in heaven but on earth; throughout the 1610s and 1620s it was hoped that sectarian agitation could result in a revolution of saints. Indeed, the gathering of saints was to be sought as a precursor to the coming of the Kingdom. Far more than their preparationist counterparts, the Brethren read the signs of the times, prayed for the millennial dawn, and worked on its behalf.[110] Rather than conceiving of the Kingdom as the product of cataclysm or the shattering of the natural world, they believed in the unfolding of the Kingdom on earth and in time. They attached communitarian desires to an optimistic providentialism, believing that their ecstatic theology of union had real consequences in the practical world of English politics.

Before the rise of Laud, in the days when irenic reform seemed plausible, Sibbesians preached that commitment to the union of saints meant devotion to the church international. Davenport, Preston, Sibbes, Cotton—all enjoined their flocks to consider not just the purity of their own churches but "the present state of all the Churches of Christ in Europe."[111] Sibbes counseled Englishmen to look beyond their own borders and consider the state of the church universal, for "God hath but one true church in the whole world, which spreads itself into divers nations and countries upon the face of the earth."[112] The true church was neither limited to the present age nor geographically defined—either in terms of the chosen tribe or the local congregation.

The self-absorbed had to be reminded that true saints, "although they should be scattered each from the other," must participate in "the preservation and enlarging of His *church mysticall.*" National boundaries did not avail; there was but one church, and all saints owed their love and labor to that church international.[113] As Sibbes described, "Christ's fulness is made up, when all the members of his mystical body are gathered and united together . . . Christ and the church are are but one mystical."[114] While many Puritans held this position before the Great Migration, it was a central tenet for the Brethren both in Old and in New England.[115]

During the turbulent decades of the 1620s and 1630s, the Brethren were especially concerned with the cause of Protestantism abroad. Their roll call of the troubled congregations in the Palatinate and Bohemia was to awaken English saints to their broader responsibilities:[116]

> And surely there is not a heart that was ever touched with the Spirit of God, but when he hears of any calamity of the church, whether it be in the Palatinate, in France, in the Low countries, or in any country in the world, if he hears that the church hath a blow, it strikes to the heart of any man that hath the Spirit of God in them, by a sympathetical suffering. It is one good sign to know whether a man be of the mystical body or no, to take to heart the grievance of the church.[117]

Mere intonations of doom, however, were insufficient responses to a crisis of international, indeed cosmic, proportions. Every member of the brotherhood agreed that the saints must be zealous on behalf of the church. In response to the "combustion" of the churches, Preston declared:

> Let every Man therefore stirre up himselfe to doe his dutie. In a word, we should strive and contend for the advancing of *Christs* kingdome, for the furtherance of the Gospell, for the good of mankinde, for the

flourishing of the Church, wherein our own good consisteth; and we should doe it earnestly, we should contend for it, contend with *God* in prayer, contend with our Superiors by intreaty, and with our Adversaries by resistance, with cold and lukewarme men by stirring them up by *provoking one another to good works.*[118]

Social station or national allegiance made no difference in this injunction: "it belongs to everie one to look to it, to us that are Preachers in our places, to Magistrates in their places, to everie man to contend for the common Faith." The moment of kairos was at hand, and the saints were warned not to neglect God's plan: "there are certaine opportunities which the *Lord* gives you, and you must take heede of neglecting them, it may bee to let a thing goe sometimes, it will never bee recovered againe." As it turned out, the rise of Laud and increased persecutions, Preston's death and the Puritan migration deferred the crisis for a decade or more, but from the early 1620s many of the Brethren anticipated a revolution of saints.[119]

This is not to suggest that the Cambridge preachers advocated violent reform, though many would support the Civil War. More characteristically, however, moderates like Sibbes and Cotton advocated contention by means of spiritual weapons. Their activism on behalf of Protestantism abroad—the feoffees, the circular letter and collection of funds to support Protestant ministers in the Palatinate, and the endorsement of the irenic program of John Dury—evidenced the reforming zeal of the Brethren.[120]

Most reflective of their commitment to peaceful reform was union in prayer: Sibbes argued, "we should do more good with our prayers at home than they shall do by fighting abroad." Though only God can dictate the course of history, human prayers are ordained helps against evil: "The prayers of others joining all together, is a mighty prevailing means for the conveying of all good."[121] Union in prayer was Sibbes's irenic version of a holy war: "Everyone, the poorest man, may contend with his prayers . . . If he pray in faith, he desires that God would pull down all opposite kingdoms to the kingdom of his Son Christ; that the kingdom of Christ may come, more and more in the hearts of his people; that he may reign everywhere more freely and largely than he doth. Every one may help forward the kingdom of Christ; he may help forward Jerusalem and pull down Jericho; everyone that hath a fervent devotion of prayer."[122]

Moreover, mutual prayer had the added benefit of joining the saints at home: "There is an article of our faith, which, I think, is little believed . . . 'I believe in the communion of saints.' Is there a communion of saints?

wherein doth this communion stand? Among many other things, in this, that one saint prays for another." Therefore, Sibbes concluded, "those that truly believe in the communion of saints do truly practice the duties belonging to that blessed society, that is they pray for one another. I mean here on earth."[123]

It is far from my intention to suggest that the Brethren were alone in viewing the Catholic invasions of Bohemia as the work of the Anti-Christ. This was a position held by almost all members of Ames's circle as well. The danger of God's desertion of England should good Protestants fail to act was, of course, the subject of one of Thomas Hooker's last English sermons. But Hooker's primary concern was for the preservation of the English church against God's abandonment. There is little in this sermon that anticipates a millennial period of glory; Hooker's version of kairos contains all of the anxiety but none of the promise of Preston's formulation:

> Look to it, for God is going, and if he do go, then our glory goes also . . . *The glory is departed from Israel.* So glory is departed from England; for England hath seen her best days, and the reward of sin is coming on apace; for God is packing up of his Gospel, because none will buy his wares (not come to his price) . . . Oh, therefore my brethren, lay hold on God, and let him not go out of your coasts. (He is going!) Look about you, I say and stop him at the town's end, and let not thy God depart! Oh, England, lay siege about him by humble and hearty closing with him.[124]

While this passage has much in common with the injunctions of the Brethren, it is less committed to the larger concerns of international Protestantism than to the cares of England; therein, it reiterates the theme of self-reproach and the appeal to self-interest that pervade Hooker's sermonics. In the end, it was not God but Hooker himself who departed England. In one sense migration for Sibbesians and Amesians alike was a response to crisis on an international scale, but while their ultimate destination was the same, their paths to the decision were slightly different.

Migration was not the first alternative but a last resort for the Sibbesians.[125] Though they allowed the lawfulness of "fly[ing] for our own safeties," Sibbesians also argued that since "the common good is to be preferred before private good," the minister had a special obligation to stay with his endangered flock as long as possible.[126] In fact, Sibbes reminded his auditors that suffering for the truth was a privilege, that the persecuted were "as the three children in the fiery furnace" witnessing for the truth of the gospel.[127] Sibbes died in 1635, before Laudianism made this position impossible.

What ultimately led some Puritans to America while others stayed closer to home remains somewhat mysterious. Moreover, the fact of migration itself complicates and challenges the partisan structures I have here delineated, both suggesting sympathies that cross party lines and reminding of the shared heritage that subsumed such divisions. At least on this issue, John Cotton found greater affinity with a preacher like Hooker than he did with Goodwin or Sibbes.[128] Without falsifying these complexities, there are some differences to be remarked on this issue of migration.

First, as I argue in Chapter 2, the Amesians tended to choose exile earlier than Sibbesians. Hooker, for example, first retreated to Holland before joining Cotton for the voyage to America in 1633. Second, the casuistry around removal has a slightly different tone for each group. Cotton, it will be recalled, was taken to task by Davenport, Goodwin, and Nye for his decision to leave England. Defending his actions, Cotton argued that he preferred exile to silencing: since God had "shut a door . . . from ministering to him and his people," New England offered a way to hold a pulpit and preach the gospel.[129]

Though I would not claim fundamental difference, Cotton's "Reasons for Removal," framed in terms of continued ministry, do vary from Hooker's view of migration as refuge against England's destruction. Cotton's decision was made only after agonized self-scrutiny and extended consultation. The guilt and anxiety of this determination is revisited in Cotton's defense of the 1640s: "It is a serious misrepresentation, unworthy of the spirit of Christian truth, to say that our brethren, either those returned from the Netherlands or those exiled in New England, fled from England like mice from a crumbling house, anticipating its ruin, prudently looking to their own safety, and treacherously giving up the defence of the common cause of the Reformation."[130]

Though this passage must be contextualized in terms of the heightened political stakes of the mid-1640s, still this anxious tone of self-reproach and self-defense offers a somewhat stark comparison with Winthrop's earlier sanguine speculation that though "all other churches of Europe are brought to desolation, and our sins, for which the Lord begins already to frown upon us, do threaten us fearfully . . . who knows but that God hath provided this place to be a refuge for many whom he means to save out of the general calamity."[131] Though these differences of tone and expression—the vision of a "common cause" versus that of a "general calamity"—may seem less important than the shared act of migration, they nonetheless must be registered. Moreover, it makes logical sense that their commitment to the "common cause of the Reformation" would make migration an especially vexed question and deferred action for the Cambridge preachers.

❧

On the doctrine of the millennium, however, partisan differences remained as evident in New England as in Old. Though they refused to anatomize the heart or measure degrees of grace, the Spiritual Brethren actively calibrated the millennium, calculated the fate of the churches in anticipation of a kingdom to unfold within historical time. Throughout his career Cotton, for example, measured his own times against the biblical accounts of Canticles and Revelation: in his reading reformers like John Huss or Luther became fulfillments of Old and New Testament prophets. Cotton and Davenport, along with most of the Brethren, read the world against Scripture, finding typological fulfillments in the events of the day.

It is not my intention in the remaining pages to rehearse the vast and complex body of scholarship on Puritan millennialism. However, I would suggest that current debates over American primitivism versus progressivism, as well as disputes over the pre- or postmillennialism of the first generation of New World Puritans, might be usefully clarified by acknowledging differences between Amesians and Sibbesians on this issue. As the next chapter will show in greater detail, preachers like Hooker and Shepard were less interested in historical prophecy. Theirs was the voice of Puritan primitivism: their utopia was adamic; when they thought of the last days, it was as probation.[132]

Yet, both in England and America, Cotton and Davenport, following Sibbes and Preston, preached the coming of a middle kingdom, a period before the final judgment in which the saints would enjoy the pleasures of communion. These men were cosmic optimists, predicting the unfolding of the Kingdom in human time; at one point Cotton prophesied that 1655 would mark the opening of the new era.[133] With respect to current academic debates, it must be noted that Cotton's millennialism was not born in the 1640s but was present in his first sermons on Canticles and the Johannine epistles. This does not mean, however, that he promoted the parochial vision associated with an errand into the wilderness.

Sacvan Bercovitch, among others, has argued that Cotton conflated "the heavenly Canaan with New England." This identification of the spiritual Israel with America was supposedly made possible by the typological practices of American Puritans, which allowed them to read their national fate in terms of Old Testament history. Neither Cotton nor Davenport, however, restricted the definition of the church to the New England Way. They often reminded their New World congregants that though the American churches may have served as one point of origin for the new age, they were not necessarily its consummation.[134]

In fact, Cotton routinely resisted the exclusive identification of the Kingdom of God with the local habitation called New England. One of the causes and the chief benefit of the advent would be the glorious union and rule of a universal body of saints on earth. In the darkest days of persecution and in the period of prospective optimism, Cotton recalled that the saints are scattered like sands on the shores of the world. It is true that in the 1630s Cotton celebrated the special quality of the New England Way, writing to Davenport that "the order of the churches and the commonwealth was now so settled in New England, by common consent, that it brought into his mind the new heaven and the new earth."[135] Moreover, Cotton did read history through the lens of scriptural typology, and he remarked America's special role as one of God's plantations.

Yet, he never asserted America was *the* plantation, *the* New Jerusalem. Though the title of his sermon to the departing Winthrop fleet is often misquoted in the singular, Cotton preached on "God's Promise to his *Plantations*." Just as God's pledge was to all godly communities, so his care was not to single congregations alone but the church international. In the first instance the plural, "plantations," expands the meaning of promise beyond the American shore. In the second instance, the singular, "church," establishes the essential unity of all Christian gatherings. In both cases, internationalism modifies American exceptionalism.

On the eve of the Great Migration, Cotton's anxiety was that New World saints might rest in their enjoyment of pure ordinances and forget the cause of the church at home and abroad. Even as he blessed the fleet, Cotton cautioned the departing pilgrims, "forget not the womb that bare you and the breast that gave you suck." Rather than celebrating an exceptional status, Cotton reminded the departing saints of their essential tie to the English church. The communion of saints was not determined by geographic proximity: "As God continueth his presence with us (blessed by his name), so be ye present in spirit with us; though absent in body."[136] Though dispersed to many shores, the saints were members of a single family. Just as "ducklings hatched under an hen, though they take the water, yet will still have recourse to the wing that hatched them," so the

New World voyagers were not to sever the bonds joining the body of saints.[137]

This was not an injunction Cotton forgot, even after his own migration. Along with Davenport, he kept a regular correspondence with the Brethren in Old England, and in his millennial sermons of the 1640s he condemned the growing tribalism he observed among his New World companions. In *The Churches Resurrection* Cotton cautioned the churches of New England not to rest in their own purity, because *all* of God's churches must be aroused before the Kingdom can be established on earth: "Therefore let it be a serious warning to everyone not to rest in Reformation and formes of it, and to blesse your selves in Church Membership, because to this day, this first Resurrection hath not taken its place, nor will not take place till Antichrist be ruinated."[138] This ruination required the prayers and deeds of all saints, required their commitment to the church catholic. What distressed Cotton as he surveyed New England was the growing complacency and self-interestedness of New Englanders.

Cotton condemns those "private Christians" who live "always in a private State," who know "not the order of Gods house, nor addresseth himselfe to it."[139] He worries about the rise of prosperity and business interests in New England that divert attention from the true enterprise of the New Jerusalem: "if our spirits be such, we cannot be busie in our calling but wee lose Christ. I meane as much as in us lies, not that we can lose him altogether, but many that make profession of him lose him wholly, they have such business to doe in the World, that so many yeeres agoe they saw him as they thought, but now they see him not."[140] Even at his most exhoratory, Cotton protects the perseverance of the saints, arguing that Christ can neither be gained or lost by human actions. Yet, Cotton does wish to recall New England from what he sees as its misguided self-interest. Rather than being a spokesman for the emergent capitalism so often associated with Puritan progressivism, Cotton was profoundly critical of the materialism of his congregants. It was not the business of this world but the worldwide advent of the Kingdom that inspired him.

Modifying his earlier praise of New England's church order, in 1640 Cotton warned, "Therefore let not *New England* be secure, and blesse ourselves in our Resurrection, because we have our part in this Reformation."[141] Indeed, against claims of America's chosen status, Cotton argued, "no promise there is to any Church in the world."[142] He chastised those New World believers who contentedly forgot that a "Plantation of Churches" was "not a Resurrection of Churches."[143] New England was to know that the inward turn to complacency was blameworthy: "It is not enough for your blessed Estate to have your parts in the Reformation of Churches, nor does your holinesse stand in it."[144]

As Davenport, too, observed the growing complacency and self-satisfaction of New Englanders, he rejected the hebraizing of the covenant and the growing tribalism of the preparationists. He condemned those New England saints who,

> if their garners may be full, their sheep multiply, their oxen be strong to labour, their sons be as plants grown up, and their daughters polished and set forth with ornaments, and there be no complaining in the streets; think themselves happy, and regard not what becomes of religion, and of Christs cause and interest in the Churches; take not to heart the afflictions of God's people, if their trading increase; one good bargain will more comfort them than all the calamities of the Church can grieve them; they can hear and speak of the breaches and ruines of Sion . . . without remorse or regard.[145]

These auditors, having heard Davenport's account of the sad state of the world church a few passages before, must have registered the depths of his disapproval. New Englanders, absorbed in their own prosperity, had turned away from Europe. The last of his circle, Davenport could only deplore this spiritual decline.

In the aftermath of the Restoration, Davenport still voiced faith in "the Majesty and glory of the Church," and in a promised thousand-year reign, despite the strain events placed on his optimism.[146] This hope was the root and flower of his faith and joy in Christian union. The true distinguishing mark of the saint remained the desire for union with Christ and with one's fellows.

This faith, enunciated in the Sibbesian certainty that the bride's deepest "desires are the breathings and motions of the Spirit in the world, tending to further union," sustained Davenport in the dark decade of the 1660s.[147] Such communion is the perfection not only of the saints but of God himself:

> Christ is in some sort imperfect till the latter day, till his 'second coming'. For the mystical body of Christ is his fulness. Christ is our fulness, and we are his fulness. Now Christ's fulness is made up, when all the members of his mystical body are gathered and united together . . . Hence it is that the saints are called 'the glory of Christ' . . . Christ in this sense is not fully glorious therefore till that time. The

church desires therefore that Christ may be glorious in himself, and glorious in them, that he may come to be 'glorious in his saints.'[148]

This glory, brought to fullness with the golden age of the millennium, is the fruit of Christian union. Sibbesians preached that God's love flowing to the saints, and spreading through the saints, would be the consummation of both human and divine, in this world and the next.

7

❧

The Heart of New England Rent

> *How* happy would be the condition of Gods people in this
> world? *How* sweet and amiable would their conversing together
> be? *How* honourable to God and Christ, and to the Gospel of
> Truth and Peace in the sight of All? if their love to every Divine
> truth, and mutually among themselves, in the truth, and for the
> truths sake, did so shine forth, that it might be said of them,
> as it was observed and said in former times by Heathen Perse-
> cutors; *See how these Christians love one another?*
>
> John Davenport

In 1670 Giles Firmin published his treatise on *The Real Christian*, publicly challenging the preparationist practices of the New England orthodoxy. Author of such texts as *Separation Examined* and *Stablishing
against Shaking*, Firmin was certainly no friend to sectaries. Indeed, this
former New Englander and deacon of Cotton's Boston congregation had
joined ranks with English Presbyterians by the time he wrote *The Real
Christian*. Though criticizing New English orthodoxy from a position of
churchly conservativism rather than from separatist enthusiasm, Firmin
ironically articulated many of the same complaints of New England's
spiritists.

Firmin's purpose in writing was twofold: to describe "the work of God
in drawing the Soul to Christ," and to remedy some of the "Trouble to
serious Christians" arising from doctrines recently promulgated by certain
"late Divines." Leveling criticism at some of the descriptions of "the
Preparation of the Soul for Christ," Firmin charged that this doctrine
produced spiritual despair. Although Firmin criticizes a number of enemies
to his version of the true faith, he singles out for special mention the New
England luminaries, Thomas Shepard and Thomas Hooker, whose insistence on "some Things . . . as necessary to a right Preparation for Christ
. . . have caused, and do still cause much Trouble to some serious Christians." Firmin adds Perkins's name to theirs, as one whose "Description of
Faith" has troubled the devout. Firmin observes that "thro' the high Re-

spects [Christians] bear to the Persons of these Men, being holy and eminent," the faithful have unfortunately "believed what they write must needs be the Truth of God in every Particular."[1]

Reporting the story of "a Maid-servant who was very godly," Firmin narrates her spiritual depression after reading "in Mr. Shepard's Book," a text which Firmin confesses, "I opposed." Having studied Shepard's brand of piety, the maid "was so cast down, and fell into such Troubles, that all the Christians that came to her could not quiet her Spirit." Rehearsing the biographies of other anxious supplicants, Firmin deplored the preparationist discipline of self-doubt.[2]

Firmin was not alone in questioning the piety and practices of the New England orthodoxy. In 1656 Thomas Goodwin and Philip Nye, both associated with the Cambridge circle, included an important caveat in their otherwise laudatory preface to Thomas Hooker's *Application of Redemption*. In the aftermath of the war, Goodwin and Nye found themselves in a position not unlike that of John Norton, deploring enthusiasm and proto-Arminianism alike. Enthusiasm was on the rise and needed to be restrained; yet these men also worried that the religious ideals for which they fought could be undermined by a growing legalism.

In this context Goodwin and Nye endorsed *The Application of Redemption* as a check on radical spiritists—Ranters, Quakers, and the like—who had "slipt into Profession, and Leapt over all both *true* and *deep Humiliation* for sin, and *sense of their natural Condition*." Their preface bespeaks a good deal of sympathy with Hooker's position. Yet, even in the context of what they deemed a too-radical spiritism, a time when men spend too little time on "the *great things of Regeneration*"—humiliation and contrition—Goodwin and Nye withhold wholehearted approval of Hooker's doctrine.

While reckoning the need for a John the Baptist, "to bring back and correct the Errors of the spirits of these times," they also assert that Hooker's doctrine errs "perhaps by urging too far, and insisting too much upon that as *Preparatory*, which includes indeed the beginning of true *Faith*." Even when loose professors abound, these two leaders at Westminster, both converts and students of John Cotton, conclude that "a man may be held too long *under John* Baptists *water*."[3]

While some readers argue that Goodwin and Nye merely lament Hooker's failure to treat "the other *Great Points*, as *Union with Christ, Justification, Adoption, Sanctification*, and *Glory*," I would argue that they are also critical of a religious imagination that accords so little importance to these crucial stages in spiritual life.[4] Moreover, it could not have escaped their notice that in those few sermons where Hooker does treat union, there is a noticeable decline in rhetorical invention, a failure of experience and expression. Compared with the metaphoric richness of the sermons on humiliation and contrition, texts describing consummation and spiritual joy are curiously dry and abstract. Hooker now resorts to citing authorities, as if his access to the experience of unmediated union is primarily by means of second-hand accounts.

Sargent Bush, one of Hooker's biographers, observes, "Ironically, though Hooker's description of the soul's journey had now brought him and his congregation to the part of the journey which had seemed the ultimately desirable end, he now reveals a seemingly diminished level of enthusiasm for the task that remains."[5] Perhaps this tepid engagement is not ironic, however, but predictable. It was always preparation not justification, anticipation not consummation, that engaged preachers like Hooker. Theirs was an anxious and a strenuous faith, one that evidenced little of the joyous confidence in union that was the hallmark of the Cambridge Brethren.

Though the saints of Old England and New divided over a variety of issues, including church polity and tolerationism, the observations made by Firmin, Goodwin, and Nye suggest the English audience's growing awareness of the dominance of preparationism in the New World colony— and a criticism of that conservative shift. Even though they had once issued invitations to attend and advise the Westminister divines, the Independents were now voicing some concern that New Englanders were privileging the forms of religion over the spirit.[6] Significantly, these criticisms came from men closely tied to Cotton; their anxieties may be read in part as a defense of the Cambridge spiritism.

To their detractors, Hooker and Shepard placed too great an emphasis on personal faith and too little on the larger gathering of saints. As both modern and seventeenth-century observers have remarked, a growing tribalism among the New England divines emerged in tandem with the rhetoric of preparationism. Their original devotion to pure church ordinances prompted these men to focus first on reform of their own hearts and then on the New England churches. Little energy or interest was left over for the millennial dreams that absorbed English radicals, to whom the preparationist emphasis on local purity may have seemed self-absorbed. With the inauguration of the Half-Way Covenant in 1662, this inward turn was made manifest. Enjoyment of church ordinances became a matter of family heritage as well as spiritual election. The truths of faith now became the secrets of the tribe.

Moreover, just as their migration was fueled by a pessimism about the possibilities of reform in England, so pessimism was relived in the preparationists' eschatology; in general, they subscribed to a premillennialist reading of history, modeling their utopian ecclesiology on Old Testament precedent. While countering arguments for the importance of a general millennial fervor, this primitivist pattern supports claims of increasing tribalism based on congregational localism and preparationist individualism.

Sacvan Bercovitch, it will be recalled, argues that the Puritans read the migration as a key point in the history of redemption, the American saints as latter-day Israelites. The Puritans, he claims, understood the meaning of America typologically, as the New Jerusalem, the capital of God's coming Kingdom. Preparationism was a "personal analogue to the tribal concept of the errand," and the Half-Way Covenant was "the doctrinal counterpart of the concept of errand."[7]

Preparationism, tribalism, and American exceptionalism were indeed constitutive parts of the orthodox platform. These tenets, however, did not promote the same kind of utopian communalism or millennial optimism espoused by the Cambridge Brethren; nor did they provide an origin for an American faith in progress. Instead, the local congregation and the national church became the singular concern of religionists who viewed themselves as living through Old Testament plots. Attendant upon this view of New England's special role was the biblical primitivism that redefined the church as tribal rather than global.[8]

The "genetics of salvation" substituted descent for consent, family genealogy for personal conversion as the prerequisite for church affiliation.[9] This inward turn is predicted early on in the Amesians' understanding of charity, in their eschatology, and even in their sermon style. The hegemony of the preparationists in New England meant that the expansive vision of the Cambridge circle became constricted and contracted into a narrowed view of the self, the church, and the world.

✳

William Ames's description of "charity or love" is a different affection than the diffusive caritas of the Spiritual Brethren. Like them, Ames at times preached that love was benevolence to being and that humans desired a self-forgetful union with God. Often, however, he recognized that love was also egocentric; that human yearning for God was self-regarding: "desire of union with God . . . comes in part from what is called concupiscence or appetite. We desire God for ourselves, because we hope for benefit and eternal blessedness from him." Though Ames goes on to add that "the highest end of this love should be God himself," he was sufficiently practical to allow for less than the highest ends.[10]

Ames's understanding of human weakness marks him both as shrewd and empathic. While he did not confidently assume the best of his audience, he allowed for a frailty that the Brethren, because they spoke only to the regenerate, did not admit. Similarly, Ames records the imperative to love one's neighbor but recognizes certain limitations of that emotion: "Our neighbor is to be loved in a certain respect, but with another objective and without such esteem or intensity" as our love of God.[11]

While the Sibbesians would agree that God is to be loved first and foremost, they deferred the conclusion that saints love each other less. They never express themselves in the language of qualification or decrease, but rather urge greater and greater love for God so that love of others may intensify. Ames and his followers seem frightened by such unrestrained emotion; just as the excesses of sin are to be curbed, so the aroused heart is to be constrained as well.

Indeed, Ames's chapter on "Justice and Charity toward Our Neighbor" is a handbook for regulating affections rather than igniting them. Charity means being "rightly ordered towards God and towards his neighbor;" it is a duty to be exercised, rather than a desire to be actively stimulated. Ames uses static, passive verbs in describing charity: "The love toward God contained in religion of its own nature produces love toward men, for they are in some sort partakers of the image of God." Love is *contained* in religion, it *produces* love to others; never does the language suggest that it is the spontaneous overflow of the heart, diffusive as the oil of Aaron.[12]

Ames categorizes and orders this love into ever-narrowing confines:

This is the order of love: God is first and chiefly to be loved and is, as it were, the formal reason of love towards our neighbor. After God, we are bound to love ourselves with the love of true blessedness, for loving God with love of union, we love ourselves directly with that greatest love which looks toward our spiritual blessedness. Secondarily, as it were, we ought to love others whom we would have to be partakers of the same good with us. For others may be deprived of blessedness without our fault, but we cannot be. Thus we are more bound to desire and seek it for ourselves than for others.[13]

This ordering of love in terms of formal causes would be a foreign concept to Sibbes, but not as alien as the language of bondage. Ames tells us whom we are "bound" or "ought" to love, rather than describing our joy in unbounded charity. Moreover, the love of self as the second most proper object, ahead of love of others, is an ordering absent in the Brethren's work; it is one, however, in perfect harmony with the preparationists' self-directedness.[14]

In a somewhat surprising turn, Ames uses Christ's new commandment not as an injunction to an ever-increasing fellow feeling but as a near justification of self-love: "Hence it is that the love of ourselves has the force of a rule or of measure for the love of others, *You shall love your neighbor as yourself*." This is not to say that love is not a central tenet for Ames. Rather, such images suggest that Ames saw love as governed by a principle of measure, not as the spontaneous flow of emotion.[15]

This discourse hinges on the force of rule and the trope of measuring. Just as their sermons unfold in measured units, and just as the *ordo salutis* insists on a measured progression, so too love is quite literally to be divided and weighed. Ames sets out rules for those times "when we cannot exercise our love actively towards all," a contingency that Sibbes and Cotton prefer not to consider. Ames, however, spends his energy on precisely this circumstance and declares: "First, that our blood kin, other things being equal, are to be given more love than strangers." "Second, a special friend is to be given more love than an ordinary blood kinsman." Parents are to be loved more than friends; children more than parents, wives more than children, etc. The whole reads as though there were a limited quantity of agape, to be measured and conserved and rightly applied lest the storehouse be emptied. Nothing could be more contrary to the image of the overflowing, inexhaustible fountain of Sibbes.

As his biographers have noted, there is a certain "shrewdness" in Ames's Christian love, a principle of calculation that abjures "any insistence on the absolute, impossible-to-be-fulfilled character of the second great commandment."[16] In Ames's defense it should be said that he recognized and allowed for human frailty in religious life. He knew sinners would always fall short of the highest expectations, and so he established modest goals and provided steps and helps along the way.

Though Hooker and Shepard are not so explicit in their discussion of the limits of charity, the self-reflexivity implicit in preparationism produces modified expectations of human benevolence. Since they dilated so completely on the individual heart prior to justification, there was little time to consider the communion of saints, sanctification, or the diffusive love that was the fruit of union. As one biographer has noted, "apart from recommending the companionship of the saints, [Hooker] does not explore the implications of this observation."[17] Conceiving of their auditors as unregenerate, men like Hooker had little hope or faith in the possibility of expansive fellow feeling. Hence, they spoke less of the public spirit that absorbed the Brethren. When they did consider matters of public good, their response was more often to control and regulate the populace than to stir them. It will be recalled that both Shepard and Bulkeley openly expressed disgust with the "heady multitude."

Rather than teaching effulgent love, these preachers narrowed their focus to the impending wrath that might be visited on the saints. In response to Firmin's criticisms of his doctrine, Shepard wrote: "Let my love end in breathing out this desire: Preach humiliation. Labor to possess men with a sense of wrath to come, and misery." Love here results in pastoral reproof; diligent introspection, not joyous effulgence, provides a surer path to salvation.[18]

This narrowing of interests manifested itself in numerous ways. As argued above, though the Amesians believed in the importance of the word preached, they were willing to cede their pulpits rather than compromise on matters of purity. Cotton's query—"why do men stand so much upon visible Churches, and their purity?"—might have been directed at them. For Cotton the true church is a matter of fellowship and the "holy Ghost breathing amongst them" rather than a formal purity.[19] For the Amesians, ecclesiology was the fundamental concern, for which fellowship was sometimes sacrificed. For this reason, they were more often silenced, more often than their brethren forced to resort to the written rather than the preached word. Moreover, their treatises often contain a defense of that writerly mode.

Whether regarded as a means of conversion or as a mode of edification, the word preached formed the locus of Puritan spiritual life. Hooker as well as Cotton, Ames as well as Sibbes, would agree with Paul's declaration that faith cometh by hearing. The Brethren took this injunction quite literally. In a preface to one of his own works Chaderton argued, "Let no man think that the reading of this can be half so effectual and profitable to him as the hearing was or might be." In imagery close to Cotton's description of the saints as warm embers, Chaderton argues that the written text "wanteth the zeal of the speaker, the attention of the hearer . . . the mighty and inward working of his holy spirit." These benefits result primarily from the word preached. Chaderton warns that they "are not to be hoped for by reading the written sermons of [God's] ministers."[20] Similarly, when the Sibbesians insisted that faith comes only by hearing they were not being merely literal-minded. Rather, they were insisting on the importance of the gathered community of saints. Like the enjoyment of church ordinances, sermons stirred the affections.[21]

The preparationist, of course, valued the preached word as well. Yet when he writes of the efficacy of the word, Ames modifies this fundamental principle by expanding the definition of "hearing": "Hearing . . . means any receiving of the word of God whether it be communicated to us by preaching, reading, or any other way . . . The word *hearing* ought not to be taken so literally and strictly as to mean always necessarily the outward sense of hearing; it denotes any perceiving of the will of God, and especially inward receiving and submission."[22]

Initially, the isolation of exile forced men like Ames to resort to the written word more often than they might otherwise have wished. Such circumstances may have encouraged as well as reinforced the introspection implicit in preparationism itself. If reading "shatters the unity of the audience," as Walter Ong suggests, it also allows for the introspection that preparationists desired. It is no wonder then that Ames saw little difference between reading and hearing, since both were to produce "inward receiving" though not necessarily shared edification.[23] In keeping with this focus, private exercises are acceptable to Ames and his followers to a far greater degree than they would be to Sibbesians, on either side of the Atlantic. In addition to reading the word and private prayer, preparationists encouraged the practice of private meditation, a position that emerges from and reinforces the isolation of a solitary pilgrimage. Again, the issue is one of emphasis; all preachers valued both private exercises and communal worship. Preparationists preached most warmly, however, about the discipline of personal piety.[24]

Not surprisingly, this interest in the personal application of religion had an influence on the way the preparationists conceived of the preacher's role, his relation to his flock, and the content, structure and style of his sermons. Ames argued that study of the law as much as sealing of the spirit answered the qualifications for the converted ministry: "a man cannot be a fit preacher unless he has *Set his heart to study the law of the Lord and to do it, and to teach his statutes and ordinances in Israel.*"[25]

The preparationist mode of instruction is generally characterized by a harsher tone than is found in the preaching of the Cambridge Brethren. Shepard makes clear that he speaks to an unregenerate audience in need of this austerity: "The gospel consolations and grace, which some would have dished out as the dainties of the times, and set upon the ministry's table, may possibly tickle and ravish some, and do some good to them that are humbled and converted already. But if axes and wedges, withal, be not used to hew and break this rough, uneven, bold, yet professing age, I am confident the work and fruit of those men's ministry will be at best mere hypocrisy; and they shall find it, and see, if they live a few years more."[26]

Clearly Shepard numbers few in his congregation as "humbled and converted already;" his tone reflects a skepticism concerning those few who might make that claim. In this context, the language of ravishment takes on an unsavory, almost prurient quality of "tickling" the soul. Shepard is uninterested in Cotton's notion of a ministry that melts the heart; it is hewing and hacking that these sermons must undertake. It is not the role of elder brother but a didactic father that Shepard's preacher must assume.

Hooker, too, conceives of himself as a superior parent, who may not spare the rod lest he spoil the child. Having flailed the Dedham congregants, he explains, "you may think I deal something harshly with you, but I deal for the best for you. Is it not better to hear of this now, in time, than hereafter, when the Lord hath arrested you, and you are locked up in close prison forever?"[27]

As noted in the previous chapter, the distance between preacher and auditor is made explicit not just by the didactic intent; the preparationists almost always abjure the common pronoun of *we* and insist on the distance of an *I/thou* relation. Hooker and Shepard often greet their auditors as "close-hearted hypocrites," "filthy toads," "fooles," "covenant breakers," and "Wretches."[28] Rejecting a dialogic mode in which identification and response assuage the auditor's doubts, Hooker accuses his listener and magnifies their differences: "My hand is on your heart, brethren, for I fear many of you have some one back door which you mean to keep . . . Is this honest: to scrape out what you please and leave what you please still? There is no honesty in this, brethren. But you will say, 'Who can lay anything to my charge?' I say, thou art a covenant-breaker."[29]

This exchange is not without human sympathy, yet Hooker also assumes an interrogative that trades on the minister's wisdom and the sinner's weakness.[30] "My hand is on your heart"—could there be a more powerful evangelical sympathy and yet a more explicit statement of superior power? This is less an egalitarian union of preacher with congregant than a battle for souls. To Hooker, the Word was an engine to "humble the heart and soul"; an effective ministry was "a powerful ministery."[31]

In this pastoral project Hooker seems to expect resistance—his preacher must have courage to chastise. In England, deprived of their pulpits, preparationists expressed anxiety about lay rebellion. Yet in America, even after the Antinomian Controversy, these preachers chafed under what they read as disrespect for the clergy. While Cotton's dying words concerned the danger of spiritual coldness, John Wilson warned of the dangers of rebellion.[32]

Whether as a source of lay discipline or a clerical response to existing intransigence, these sermons demand a submissive posture. Echoing almost verbatim Shepard's decree, Hooker declares to his flock, "the Minister must hew your hearts, and hack them, he must frame and fashion your soules before they can be prepared." He adds, "Give up your soules therefore to the word, and come unto it with holy dispositions: let the Ministers of God cut and hew you, let them doe anything that may do you good." Rather than a healing balm applied by the physician of the soul, Hooker's Word is "a sword" and its application is to "strike a blow."[33] Similarly, in his New England ministry, Thomas Shepard abjured the style and aspiration of the Spiritual Brethren. Though once sympathetic to spiritist tendencies, Shepard increasingly insisted that sinners need "humbling ministries" and "law sermons."[34] It must be stressed, however, that while this preparationist instruction began with assumptions of human depravity, it placed hope in the perfectibility of the saint. Sermons were constructed with an unregenerate but educable audience in mind.

It will be recalled that Sibbes and Cotton focus on exegesis not applications, converting the applications into a second opportunity for collation and meditation on scriptural texts. Such a method relies on an audience that has transcended the need for instruction. Sibbes declared, "I intended not a treatise, but opening of the text." Preparationists, on the other hand, rejected this conception of exegesis. They criticize the "mealy-mouthed preachers, who come with soft, and smooth and toothless words."[35]

Of this method of collation, Hooker voiced the objection: "A common kind of teaching when the Minister doth speake only hoveringly, and in the generall, and never applies the word of God particularly, may be compared to the confused noise that was in the ship wherin Ionah was, when the winds blew, and the sea raged, and a great storm began to arise." Without practical application, such mariners drown: "little good will they doe if they doe only explicate, if they doe onely draw out the sword of the Spirit: for unlesse they apply it unto the peoples hearts particularly, little good may the people expect, little good shall the Minister doe."[36]

This didactic purpose inspires a sermonic style quite different from that of the Sibbesians. Far more than the Brethren, preachers of Ames's circle adhered to the standard sermon form set forth by William Perkins in *The Arte of Prophesying*. Perkins divided the sermon into identifiable parts: biblical text; statement of doctrine; collation of proof texts (identified by Perkins as the "reasons"); and the practical applications.[37] While the Brethren focused on the gathering of texts, Ames simplified Perkins's system to argue that only "two things are necessary: First, the things contained in the text must be stated; second, they must be applied to the consciences of the hearers."[38] Bypassing the additive method of collation of texts, preparationists most often insisted on the logic of dichotomy and practical application.[39]

If edification rests on composition by collation and incantation, instruction trades on the principles of argument and application. It is most effectively realized in the plotted narrative.[40] To this end, the minister is enjoined to edit and shape the words of Scripture to his own purpose—he is required neither to exhaust the text nor to suggest all of the meanings of any part of it.[41]

As Hooker argued, the preacher was to employ rather than to unfold biblical texts. He always places Scripture in the service of his own narrative of the soul's pilgrimage.[42] In *The Application of Redemption,* he asserts, "We shall chuse such Texts, in which all those divine truths contained in the descriptions are expressed; that so we may go no further than we have the Oracles of God (his good Word) to go before us; Neither shall we meddle with every particular which the several Texts will offer to our consideration, but only handle such as concern our purpose."[43]

Hooker unfolds only those biblical passages that illuminate or exhort the saint in his journey. Scripture serves as illustration rather than inspiration in such sermons. Nor was scripture the only source of sermonic material; unlike their Cambridge counterparts, who mined treasure from the Bible, the preparationists also scoured the world for images and lessons. They allowed that "Illustrations may be drawn from almost anywhere they may be found."[44]

For Hooker and for Ames, then, the dictations of reason and the plot of salvation—the *ordo salutis*—inform structure. These are programmatic and narrative sermons, composed of the manageable and discrete units of text. They offer portable lessons and truths that the saint may extract and apply. Just as the sermon as a whole was divided into Perkins's orderly parts, so in each section points were divided and enumerated. Moreover, within these smaller sections, ideas and arguments, images and phrases are further divided and ordered. This is most obvious in treatises like the *Marrow,* where parts are easily discerned; but even in sermons, one finds a division of ideas into balanced, short phrases that insured intelligibility.

Hooker, for example, unfolds the general truth that "all things are become new, all old things are passed away," by setting up a series of short, pithy explanations:

There must be a new frame of the heart, and a new course of life and conversation. Now for the soule to approve of its condition, and, yet desire to goe out of it, these two cannot stand together in reason;

and there know, that while people please themselves in this condition, and, let the Minister say, what he will, and let God reveale what he will, still they thinke they cannot be in a better estate: I say it is impossible, that ever, upon these termes, faith should come into the heart: for faith will bring a change. Therefore when the Lord will doe good to a soule, hee will make him see his sinnes, and make him weary of them, and tire him with the sense of his condition, and shew him the necessity of faith, and that he must be a new man.[45]

Short phrases, set off by commas, extend and modify the doctrine, suggesting a logical order to the lessons of faith.[46] This subdivision of the surface of the text divides the massive surface of Scripture into units of a human scale. Similarly, Hooker often selects memorable and discrete emblems for the workings of redemption: watchworks, shop inventories, orderly households are but a few of the concrete metaphors that serve him as portable truths.[47] Complex truths are attached to tangible, exact visual signs, so that they can be taken away as practical knowledge—faith delivered as eupraxia.

Illustration after concrete illustration compose these sermons. It has been said that there was no man with uses like Hooker, and even a cursory glance at the sermons reveals this to be the case. Hooker moves quickly from those parts of the sermon devoted to Scripture (the text, the doctrine, and the reasons) to the section on applications. He says, "application is that special part of our recovery from our lost condition whereby all that spiritual good which Christ hath purchased for us is made ours or for his is made theirs." This focus on uses rather than reasons is the pastoral analogue to Ames's dilation on the *operati* rather than the *esse* of God.[48]

The primary purpose of scriptural application was to pull down the individual will: "When a man hath taught men what they should doe, he is but come to the walls of the Castle; the fort is in the heart, the greatest worke of the Ministery is to pull downe the wills of men."[49] To be sure, this purpose worked against atomic individualism by a logic of submission, but it did not therefore refocus attention on the community of saints. Rather, this self-consuming theology defined a new dependency on clerical leadership, underscored by the institutionalization of conversion narratives. Though conversion narratives were insisted upon by some of the preparationist party, this practice was inspired less by a Cottonian desire for communal edification than as a mechanism of group discipline. Hooker, for example, seems to have set little stock in the narrative. Though he apparently allowed the importance of private interrogation by the minister, he objected to the public testimonies that Cotton valued so highly as a means to promote fellowship.

Since Hooker argued that there are cases in which the saints "never knew the time and manner of their conversion, and therefore cannot relate it unto others," he objected to a form of narrative pledged to a past moment of conversion rather than to the ongoing process of preparation.[50] Given the agonized and sometimes unconsummated conversions of many of the preparationist ministers and their conception of growth in grace as incremental, it is perhaps not surprising that they did not insist on narratives of full assurance.

Most preparationists accepted testimony of struggle, rather than of consummated joy, as a proof of faith. Hooker judged his congregants on the basis of what Sibbes might have called "negative righteousness": "if a person live *not in the commission of any known sin,* nor *in the neglect of any known duty,* and *can give a reason of his hope towards God,* this casts the cause, with judicious charity, to hope and beleeve there is something *of God and grace in the soul,* and therefore fit for Church-society."[51] The absence of sin here substitutes for Cotton's ecstatic celebrations of God's love.

More essentially, Hooker objected to the narratives because they seem to "disturb the peace" of the church and "prejudice the progresse of God's Ordinances."[52] Distrustful of the congregation's ability to judge, and relying on the signs of righteous living rather than the warmth of expression, Hooker dismissed public narratives as proof of election and as a means of communal fellowship.[53]

Thomas Shepard warmly supported the public testimony of the saint as a prerequisite for church admission, but arguably as much from a motive of surveillance as of edification. In Shepard's hands, the conversion narrative acted as a means of ecclesiastical control as well as a force knitting the congregation. Within his own church Shepard used the narrative "to pick forth fit stones." While Cotton hoped the testimonies would unite members and recall to them their own moment of conversion, Shepard employed them to scrutinize applicants and to normalize the process of preparationism. Readers of Shepard's *Journal* may find this assessment too harsh. To be sure, in his private notebooks Shepard blissfully rehearsed the sweetness of grace and the beauty of God, yet I propose that after the Antinomian Controversy that ecstasy was increasingly exiled to private utterances. Publicly, Shepard preached and enforced spiritual discipline. It should come as no surprise, then, that few of Shepard's congregants could testify to a complete conversion or that their narratives were filled with anxiety.[54]

Just as his own sermons frequently traded on the anxiety of living this side of justification with the joy of union continually deferred, so anxiety characterized the testimonies of Shepard's congregants. Such uncertain witnesses might well have provoked the kind of debate and division over admission that Hooker feared. Nonetheless, these narratives also provided the occasion for the minister to examine their flocks and expunge unacceptable doctrines.

Thomas Shepard's biographer reports that throughout the 1640s Shepard was "zealous in the public vindication of the true doctrines of grace against the abominable errors of the Antinomians." In such sermons as *The Parable of the Ten Virgins* and *Wine for Gospel Wantons* Shepard cautioned against the "spiritual drunkenness" he attached to spiritist opinions. Warning auditors against "being deceived by meer colours and pretences of things; as now upon the colour of Free-Grace they bringe in free-vice," Shepard set the terms of the normative conversion experience. Since his "advice and assistance were often sought in the organization of new churches in the colony," Shepard was able to transform the conversion testimony into an instrument furthering the policies of the emerging orthodoxy. This regulatory rather than evangelical deployment of the narrative is revealed most fully in the case of the Dorchester church.[55]

Early in March 1636, on the eve of the antinomian unrest, the General Court expressed its growing anxiety by formulating new restrictions on the gathering of churches. Henceforth, in order to enjoy official status, including the privileges of freemanship for its members, congregations would have to satisfy the requirements of a visiting council of clergy and magistrates. A few weeks later, on April 1, this new statute was put to the test, when the people of Dorchester, along with their minister Richard Mather, submitted their conversion narratives for scrutiny by a committee led by Shepard. Shepard's panel of orthodox clergy found the testimonies unsatisfactory and refused to sanction the church. Winthrop reports they discovered many errors—antinomianism was present in those who based their testimony on "dreams, and ravishes of the spirit by fits"; Arminianism in those who relied on "external reformation" and "upon their duties and performances."[56]

In a letter to Richard Mather, Shepard instructed him that "it is not faith but a visible faith, that must make a visible church." In these opening months of the Antinomian Controversy, then, Shepard was claiming the right to define the terms of "visible faith." Criticizing ministers who had been lax in accepting "blurred evidences" of grace, Shepard sought ground from which to launch his attack on Cottonian piety:

> For believe it, brother, we have been generally mistaken in most men and in great professors; these times have lately shown, and this place hath discovered, more false hearts than ever we saw before. And it will be your comfort to be very wary and very sharp in looking to the hearts and spirits of those you sign yourself unto, especially at first, lest you meet with those sad breaches which other churches have had, and all by want of care and skill to pick forth fit stones for so glorious a foundation as posterity to come may build upon and bless the Lord.[57]

The solution to these errors was to prepare the heart with greater diligence before presenting it to the assembly. Shepard hoped that denying the right hand of fellowship to the Dorchester group would spur such holy activity: "it may be some of your virgins have been sleeping, and this may awaken them." He counsels them to submit to scrutiny again but "with your lamps trimmed, your lamps burning, your wedding garments on to meet the bridegroom."[58] Only when the Dorchester congregation revised their testimonies in August 1636 were they allowed to assemble. Just as Anne Hutchinson's trial would subject her religious experience to regulation, so at Dorchester the conversion narrative proved an arm of orthodoxy, another means to script the religious life of the colony.[59] In keeping with preparationist discipline, the eschatological optimism of the parable of the virgins was reduced to monitoring the polity of local congregations.

This aesthetic of constriction informs not just the preparationists' view of the narrative ritual, sermon style, and definition of caritas and community, but also their more general sense of the world and time. To round out this discussion of their piety, I will briefly return to the issue of primitivism versus postmillennialism taken up in the previous chapter.

❦

As noted there, contrary to the received wisdom, preparationist preachers were not optimists anticipating the glory days of the coming kingdom. Just as they anticipated but never enjoyed spiritual marriage, so they rarely anticipated the millennium, but when they did, it was often as an unrealized probation rather than pleasure. Perhaps preachers like Hooker and Ames were so engaged with questions of personal salvation that they could take little notice of redemption as it was worked throughout history.

Predictably, Shepard occupied a rather more complex position. He did preach on eschatological themes, but he read the end time as premillennial cataclysm. Understandably, he was less eager for its arrival.

While the Cottonians optimistically furthered the coming of latter age, preparationists turned a practical eye to the less transcendent society of the current day. They settled for pure local congregations, acknowledging a waste world beyond those parameters. Only in the modestly local congregation, not the glorious church international, could human sin be contained and controlled. Only there could pure ordinances be guaranteed. The preparationists did not expect that holiness would soon be writ on everything or that knowledge of divine things would be ever increasing. It was the image of Adam restored rather than Christ in glory that suffused the millennial mind of New England's orthodoxy.[60]

To retrace the preparationist line is to discover the near absence of any active faith in the millennium. As Keith Sprunger has observed, "absent from all of Ames's outlines of the church was any place for the millennium."[61] To a slightly less degree, the same is true of Thomas Hooker. Sargent Bush's observation, that Hooker "recommended the companionship of the saints, but did not explore the implications of this observation," could also apply to Hooker's millennialism. While Hooker participated in the general millennial fervor of the period, he did not dilate on such prophetic anticipations. Bush observes that "for all his urgency, however, Hooker was not a part of the millenarian school of Puritan preachers." Of the many extant sermons, in only two does Hooker take his inspiration from Revelation.

Hooker's description of Christ's garden as the modest habitation of the heart rather than the world church was reflected in his version of apocalypse as personal rather than historical, "coming to every man at the moment of death."[62] Hooker paints with frightening hues the terrors of the deathbed and of God's fearful judgment, but he never tallies the account books of the final Judgment Day. Unlike Cotton, who calibrated the world and time, Hooker is as vague about the millennium as he is about the soul's exaltation.[63] Accordingly, his most prophetic utterances are general rehearsals of doom and fear of destruction. As argued above, in the "Danger of Desertion" Hooker is more concerned with avoiding destruction than with bringing forth the Kingdom.[64] His advice to his auditors is reform to avoid perdition; wholly absent is any postmillennial anticipation of glory.

Similarly, the American *Survey of Church Discipline*, generally regarded as Hooker's most prophetic utterance, is only vaguely millenarian. He

declares, "these are the times drawing on, wherein Prophecies are to attain
their performances." Yet he does not offer a timetable as Cotton does, or
single out meaningful events as did Sibbes or Preston or Davenport.
Rather he says, "it is a received rule, and I suppose most safe, when
Prophecies are fulfilled they are best interpreted, the accomplishment of
them is the best commentary." Though Hooker goes on to declare "these
are times when prophecies are fulfilled," he manifests none of the care and
calibration of Cotton or Joseph Mede, Davenport, or Increase Mather.[65]
Similarly, Peter Bulkeley includes an intimation of apocalyptic doom in
his prefatory letter to the first edition of the *Gospel-Covenant* in 1646. Even
this general sense of historical crisis is supplanted, however, by Bulkeley's
interest in the "Covenant of life." In the second edition of the treatise in
1653, Bulkeley's brief mention of Revelation is omitted.[66]

This disregard for the Final Days is understandable in light of the
general temperament informing preparationism itself. Hooker was not a
preacher of fulfillment but of deferred gratification—a position that was
perhaps less conducive to postmillennial optimism. His extreme individualism was an uncomfortable fit with study of global prophecies. Indeed,
when Peter Toon, John Wilson, or Theodore Dwight Bozeman survey the
seventeenth-century for proponents of postmillennialism, it is to Cotton
and his Sibbesian compatriots Gouge, Goodwin, and Owen that they turn.
Hooker and Bulkeley are invisible figures in their accounts.[67]

As in other regards, Thomas Shepard presents a more complicated and
self-divided version of the preparationist line. His millennialism was a
blend of Sibbesian anticipation and preparationist pessimism. He was a
true premillennialist who anticipated a cataclysmic end to the world and
time. Like Hooker, he constantly warned New Englanders about the
dangers of apostasy. It is appropriate to recall Shepard's purpose in preaching his two great sermon series of the period, *The Parable of the Ten Virgins*
and *The Theses Sabbaticai*. The *Parable*, according to the preface by
Jonathan Mitchell, was preached between June 1636 and May 1640, as a
response to the "leaven of Antinomian and Familistical opinions stirring
in the country." Like Norton's *Orthodox Evangelist*, Shepard's treatise was
"to teach others the true middle way of the gospel, between the Legalist,
on the one hand, and the Antinomian, or loose gospeler, on the other."[68]
Just as Norton slanted his *via media* toward Sibbesian piety, Shepard
inclined increasingly to the rhetoric of preparationism in the years between
1636 and 1640.

Indeed, the *Parable* might be read as a record of the changes wrought
upon Shepard by the controversy. Originally Shepard chastised New Eng-

landers for a lack of spiritual fervor: they had "come over hither for
ordinances" but now "neglect them." At moments Shepard comes close to
sounding the honeyed tones of Sibbes; he asserts the freeness of grace and
praises of the "Tender-heartedness" of Christ. Beginning with the invitation to his auditors to "consider" that Christ "makes love to thee," Shepard
focuses on the nature and scope of God's love.[69] By the conclusion of the
Parable, however, Shepard diagnoses the ills of the colony in a quite
different way—it is not torpor but false enthusiasm, the danger of evangelical hypocrisy that poses the threat to New England.

Though the sermons were seemingly utopian in choice of subject matter,
in Shepard's hands "discovering the state of the times towards and about
the days of [Christ's] coming" supports a doctrine and practice of anxious
"watchfulness" instead of joy. Rather than describing the pleasures of the
Middle Advent, Shepard predicts premillennial probation: "there shall be
lamentable and sad times, and that when they are at their worst, that the
sun and the moon, through the horrors of men's hearts, and the universal
confusions in the world, shall seem to be darkened, &c., that then it is
time for [Christ] to come and set all in order again." Shepard's purpose in
writing the treatise is to "speak of the preparation made by the church to
meet with Christ Jesus."[70]

As the sermons unfold, Shepard becomes progressively strict about the
necessity of preparation and worried about the possibility of punishment.
In a series of questions to his auditors, he enumerates the sins of New
England: "Let me come to every man's bedside, and ask your consciences
. . . Have you not forgot your god, and forgot your work also . . . Have
we not shaken off all fear almost of sin and misery . . . Is not the spirit
of prayer, that lamp, going out in the church of God?" He ends with an
indictment aimed at the hearts of Hutchinson, Cotton, and the Boston
spiritists: "Have we not fallen a-dreaming here?: what meaneth else the
delusion of men's brains?" To Shepard these gospel-wantons are dreaming,
"first, drunken dreams of the world. Secondly, golden dreams of grace." To
his mind, only repudiation of free grace as preached by the pastors of
Boston Church could once again place New England within the comforting fold of the saving remnant. Significantly, and perhaps in response to
his own early enthusiasm, Shepard became more vituperative in his condemnation of antinomianism than any other preacher.[71]

The Theses Sabbaticae, preached in the 1640s at the behest of "some
students in the college," continued this rhetorical war against "familistic"
spirits. Shepard's tract repudiated the opinions of postmillennial optimists,
who "under pretense of more spiritualness, in making every day a Sabbath

(which is utterly unlawful and impossible, unless it be lawful to neglect our work all the week long)," would have every day infused with godliness.[72]

Shepard argued that the expansion of holiness advocated by spiritists would bear fruit in a realized eschatology destructive of stable social order. He warned that this false doctrine would authorize individual freedom bordering on anarchy, a freedom at odds with any principle of orthodoxy. Abandoning allegiance to ceremonial laws and persuaded that the Kingdom was reinstituted in the heart of each believer, advocates of this position would allegorize history, human society, and even the incarnation and New Jerusalem.

A doctrine to be espoused in the 1650s by Quakers and Ranters, this opinion was held by neither Cotton nor any of his followers. Yet, Shepard maligned them as "frothy, allegorizing wits" who would typologize all the commandments out of the world and urge that "every day then should be our Christian Sabbath."[73] To his mind, the Antinomian Controversy had demonstrated the danger of such unrestrained piety—daily prayer meetings had proven nurseries for radicalism, diverting colonists from their worldly occupations.

Although Shepard's professed intention in this treatise was to accord the Sabbath greater holiness than other days, a covert motive was to routinize the spiritual life of the colony by restricting religious exercises to a single day, a single context. Although he conceded "we are to take some time for converse with God . . . every day of the week," Shepard reminds his auditors that "our worldly occasions soon call us off." The inevitable return to the business of the world is not only "lawful," but desirable.[74]

Originally the expansion of the Sabbath's holiness to all days was the espoused hope of Protestants. Sibbes celebrated the day when the sanctified imagination would make this world a ladder to heaven. To Shepard's mind such sacralization of the commonplace was synonymous with the antinomian spirit. While he admits that "every day was a Sabbath" to Adam's soul, Shepard denies that a coming glory may reinstitute such a condition for the saints.[75] Declaring that such spiritualizing would "make every man a king," Shepard warned that there would "be the introduction of confusion . . . the destruction of a civil government." He feared precisely what Sibbes most hoped—that the time was approaching when "life on earth would be as it is in heaven."[76]

By the 1640s he had abandoned the hope that "holiness is to be writ upon our cups, and pots, and horse bridles, and plows and sickles."[77] Instead, he argues that the extension of piety to the commonplace cheapens it; that sacralization is achieved by limiting holiness to a single day. There is perhaps no more poignant moment in the aftermath of the controversy than Shepard's abandonment of the utopian dream of the Kingdom, his acceptance of the compromises of life in this world.

In preaching to the boys at Harvard College of the importance of restricting piety to the Sabbath and the necessity of being in and of the world the other six days of the week, Shepard defers his hope in the imminence of the New Jerusalem. While Cotton was reading the signs of the times in anticipation of the Second Coming, Shepard was settling for an only slightly improved Old England in the New—settling for a Christian commonwealth planted in an irredeemably fallen world.

By the 1640s Shepard was prepared to argue that the churches of New England were not destined to participate in that expansion of the holiness that signaled the advent of the Second Coming.[78] Convinced that the fate of these churches was ever to remain rooted in the corrupt world, Shepard not only rejects radical typologizing, but also repudiates the orthodox practice of Cotton that was dependent on a progressive reading of history. Shepard chastises men like Cotton who, "mistaking the meaning of the 20th ch. of the *Revelation*," imagine "an earthly kingdom here for a thousand years."[79]

In harmony with his insistence that the Dorchester conversions exhibit anxious incompletion, Shepard's millennial timetable bore the marks of deferred culmination.[80] Rather than a season of glorious union, there would be a shattering of the natural order: Christ would not return "in the churches spiritually, but 'in the clouds of heaven.'"[81] His Coming would not bring a thousand-year rule of the saints but initiate a "burning and consuming of the world."[82] Differing from Cotton and Davenport, Shepard calculated that the slaying of the witnesses was still at hand. Therefore, he earnestly prayed for the Kingdom's postponement rather than its advent.[83]

To this end, Shepard cautioned the churches of New England to reform, to trim their lamps and avoid damnation. His sermons were to be an "exhortation to these churches in New England. O, be watchful."[84] Yet this vigilance was not that of a watchman at the furthest outpost, straining for the first sight of the millennial dawn. Rather, the horizon of Shepard's sentry was the boundary of his own and his tribe's sinfulness. *Reform* and *doom* were his passwords.

Throughout Shepard's writings, interests of self and tribe replace those of the communion of saints and the church international. His pleas are specifically to New Englanders, who are "by the terror of God to be dreadfully awakened."[85] The sins of local congregations—neglect of ordinances, the "strange security" bred by "New England's peace and plenty," the "contempt of Christ in means"—are his topics. Shepard preaches local reform in order to avoid tribal perdition.[86] He thinks less of the advent than of the judgment, less of the reign of saints than of the destruction of the tribe.[87] In these sermons, there is less attention to the coming of the Kingdom and more emphasis on making one's own estate sure against that dreadful day.[88] Christ's coming is "the entrance and passage into eternity, and into an eternal state of weal or woe." It does not represent the threshold of an earthly rule of saints; it is not a vision to inspire the rhetoric of revolution.[89] Far from being an ecstatic postmillennialist, Shepard ends his career as a rather anxious Jeremiah.

❧

It seems fitting to end this study by looking at the final days of the last American survivor of the Cambridge Brethren, John Davenport. At the end of his life, Davenport found himself embroiled in another colony-wide controversy over the nature of grace and the constitution of the true church. From the first days of foundation, New Englanders had debated the qualifications for church membership. Was the church to be composed only of visible saints who could testify to their conversion, or would it include the larger populace—was it to be a walled garden reserved for the tribe of New England, or was it to open out as a universal gathering of souls? Involved in these issues were questions about the saints' qualifications. Did evidence of preparation, historical faith, and moral living entitle one to membership in the church; or was the melted heart the only distinguishing mark of God's elect? From the controversies involving Roger Williams and Anne Hutchinson in the 1630s, through the covenant debates of the next two decades, and finally in struggles over qualifications for baptism in the late 1650s, these issues dogged New Englanders.

In 1662 the adoption of the measure known as the Half-Way Covenant answered these questions by affirming the claims of the tribe. To the aging John Davenport, the last American member of Sibbes's original circle, the synod formalized the drift away from a millennial utopia and toward the pragmatic vision of community implicit in Ames's definition of charity.[90] Briefly, the new measures provided baptism for the grandchildren of saints, those members of the third generation whose parents were unable to testify to a saving conversion. As early as 1648 some orthodox ministers had supported "halfway" measures that would extend the privilege of baptism—and not insignificantly extend ministerial discipline as well—to these children who would otherwise pass out of the covenant.[91] Testimony of conversion was still required for full membership, but Davenport and his followers complained that this measure broadened eligibility for baptism to the offspring of those church members who could exhibit only a negative righteousness: "understanding the doctrines of faith and publicly professing their assent thereto, not scandalous in life, and solemnly owning the covenant."[92] Though they could not testify that their hearts had been changed, these morally diligent congregants would henceforth be able to present their children for baptism into the church.

Though the measure may seem innocuous, necessary, and humane, to Davenport such hereditary privilege violated all the Brethren held dear. He flatly declared, "A members childs historical faith and blameless life are not sufficient . . . to fit him for membership." From his early challenges to John Paget's baptismal practices in the 1630s, Davenport had been fighting to preserve the pure communion of saints against what he saw as these "popish" encroachments.[93] First in England, then Amsterdam, and finally in New England, he insisted that only a remade heart could entitle one to membership in the communion of saints.[94]

When Davenport reiterated this position in 1662, Charles Chauncy, Eleazer and Increase Mather, many of the deputies of the General Court, and a large portion of the laity sided with him. Against him stood the "orthodox" ministers and magistrates of New England. In large measure, this configuration replayed the alignments first dramatized in the Antinomian Controversy nearly three decades before and reiterated in the subsequent polemics of Shepard and Bulkeley. These events framed issues of ontology and history similar to the ones that had separated Amesians and Sibbesians as early as 1620.[95]

Characterized as the most significant conflict of the latter half of the century, the Half-Way Covenant, like the Antinomian Controversy, has become something of a litmus test for historical and moral assessments of American Puritanism. The 1662 innovation has been viewed by some historians as a humane embrace of family values, a practical recognition of the claims of daily living.[96] To others, it marks a moral decline from "originary" Puritan ideals.[97] To still others, the measure symbolizes a "genetics of salvation" in which the Puritan errand is sealed as tribal nationalism and bourgeois subjectivity.[98]

There are dangers in tracking such historical and ideological continuities over three decades. The density and specificity of cultural, political, and religious formations in the 1660's must complicate any simple claim for intellectual tradition and coherence. Moreover, a rich understanding of these events must position them within the context of events in Old England.[99] In light of these qualifications, my interest in these last few pages does not lie in negotiating between competing interpretations by means of an alternative narrative of historical development, but rather in reading this seemingly belated controversy over church membership through the eyes of John Davenport and in view of the shared ideology of the Cambridge Brethren. Both his actions and speeches during the last years of his life suggest that Davenport, at least, felt himself to be battling old wars, reliving earlier controversies.

To John Davenport, the 1660s witnessed the failure of the Christian Commonwealth in England, the outrage of Restoration and the reinstatement of the episcopacy, the persecution and death of friends, the loss of the New Haven Charter, and what he read as the apostasy of the New England churches. These events provided the immediate context for his understanding of the Half-Way Covenant measures as a betrayal of the values of pure religion.

Sociologists of religion from Max Weber to Reinhold Niebuhr have observed that a shift from charismatic to institutional, sectarian to churchly organization is requisite for the survival of religious groups. This shift was incarnated in the Half-Way Covenant. But mere survival was not of transcendent value to a Cambridge preacher like Davenport, who persisted in imagining a millennial world church. To him, there was a logical path from the Half-Way Covenant to tribalism, and with it the abandonment of the kingdom of saints. He read the new measures as evidence of a self-love and self-interest, individualism and isolationism that directly opposed his theology of infusion and communion.

Characterizing the Half-Way Covenant as mere "humane invention," Davenport and his supporters argued that once New England embarked on this path there would be no return—the church would become of this world. The act seemed of a piece with Shepard's chastened millennialism and Bulkeley's conditional promises—concessions to life on earth and in the world of time. Davenport argued that such measures were motivated by a desire as much to thwart lay resentment and extend ministerial discipline as to expand church membership. He instructed fellow clergy, "we have no warrant to exercise church discipline toward [children]" out of the covenant; he had no interest in either controlling or evangelizing the unwashed children of the tribe. The church was to be a temple, not a schoolroom.[100]

In 1662 it seemed to Davenport that human genealogy was being substituted for a spiritual heritage, biological descent for spiritual consent. In keeping with Bulkeley's sense of the covenant but in violation of Cotton's, the blessings of eternity were being promised to the seeds of Abraham and not to the saints of Christ. An indignant Davenport wrote to the orthodox ministers of the Bay, "I demande to know how many generations shall the right of the infant seed of such parents be extended else it may proceed *ad infinitum.*" Chauncy and the Mathers echoed this fear that "thus the covenant and baptism are entailed to a thousand generations," by definition destroying the covenant of free grace.[101]

Rather than establishing its claim to an exceptional status, these Anti-Synodists argued that by such measures New England sank back into the common waste world: "If the members of orthodox churches may upon the terms expressed . . . claim Baptism for their children," then "New England Christians are of all Christians in the world most miserable and foolish." Therein, they argued, New Englanders sacrificed transcendence for survival: "we have suffered many things in vaine in leaving such a countrye for this: our estates, friends, comforts there, to enjoy God and Christ and our consciences in the Congregational way in a low, afflicted condition in the wilderness for so many years together and now we must loose those things which wee have wrought, and may returne to our former state." In the aftermath of Restoration, when so many sacrifices seemed betrayed, New England's apostasy must have seemed especially grievous to Davenport and his sympathizers.[102]

Preachers like Richard Mather celebrated the innovation; modern critics like Bercovitch describe the empowerment of Puritan ideology in this collapsing of church into the world.[103] But the remaining supporters of the Cambridge theology saw this measure as a final and terrible decline. They always argued that men "must distinguish betwixt the covenant of grace, and the church covenant, which differ very much, for the covenant of grace belongs only to the elect and true believers." To confuse God's free covenant of grace with a church covenant based on human agreements was both improper and impious.[104] It signaled the final compromise of heaven with earth.

Espousing their own version of Puritan primitivism by claiming the mantle of the "founders," these dissenters argued that they were the only true heirs to that "burning and shining light, which was sometimes amongst us, wee meane blessed Mr. Cotton." With all the intellectual power and prestige of that tradition supporting them, they declared that the Half-Way Covenant "exposeth the blood of Christ to contempt, and baptism to profanation, the Church to pollution and the commonwealth to confusion."[105]

And indeed in 1670 the commonwealth was pitched into violent controversy. Throughout the 1660s Davenport had expressed his opposition to the synod in frequent communiqués from his pulpit in New Haven. Though he counseled over and over that "the peace of the Churches is to be highly prised," nonetheless he contended that peace should not be purchased by compromise. By asking "who are to be accounted the disturbers of this peace?" Davenport preempted criticism, accusing the synodists of initiating schism.[106]

In 1667, Davenport abandoned his long-distance quarrel to "contend for the faith" in a more active way. In that year John Wilson died, leaving free the pulpit of Boston's First Church. The still radical church now repudiated the Half-Way measures urged upon them by Wilson and their beloved Norton. Loyal to the Cambridge spiritism, they called John Davenport to fill the office of pastor.[107] It must have seemed to this aged dissident that the stage was set for a final battle against apostasy and on behalf of the glorious union of saints. In 1668 he mounted his new pulpit with courage and determination.

Since he has come under censure from admirers and critics alike for his behavior during the Half-Way Covenant controversy, it is important to contextualize Davenport's decision to accept the offer of the First Church. Davenport had first been called to a Boston pulpit in 1651, by the newly formed Second Church.[108] At that time he preferred to remain with his New Haven congregation. Governed by the biblical code drafted by Cotton himself and a favored colony of English Independents, including Oliver Cromwell, New Haven was said to be the most utopian of the New World settlements.[109] There, away from the turmoil of controversy and the interference of the Massachusetts orthodoxy, Davenport established his model of true fellowship.

Idealistic about the church international yet more stringent than any other New World minister on church admissions, Davenport incarnated in his own church the paradoxical relationship between purity and tribalism. On the one hand, Davenport's church was more exclusive—purer—than any other; membership was restricted to those saints alone who were sealed with the spirit. Neither local residence nor family heritage secured New Haven colonists a place. Yet, the pathway to this community was also broad; church doors opened out to saints across time and national boundaries.

Neither Amesians who first privileged the purity of ordinances in local congregations, nor Half-Way synodists who later modified those ordinances to insure congregational survival, could satisfy Davenport. His version of purity—every bit as exclusive—was spiritual, not to be identified with local institutions. One might criticize this rejection of local communities and family loyalty as austere, but for the Spiritual Brethren such carnal alliances were never primary.

In America, Davenport maintained loyalty to the world church. As early as 1651 he contemplated re-migration; only the objections of his New Haven congregation kept him in America.[110] Though remaining in New Haven, he maintained his commitment to the cause of the church international and gave continuous support to English radicals, including sheltering regicides Edward Whalley and William Goffe after Massachusetts leaders had expelled them.[111]

Given this commitment to the global church, the events of the 1660s must have been especially devastating for John Davenport. Few critics have taken this factor into account in evaluating his actions. Throughout the dark period of the Restoration, Davenport received regular letters from English correspondents apprising him of the terrible end of the Christian Commonwealth and the return of conditions "as bad as in Queene Maries dayes."[112] In 1663 William Hooke wrote of the plight of Protestants under the Act of Uniformity: "God's people have mett with very hard measures by means herof. Multitudes of ministers have bin ejected out of their habitations and employments." Hooke estimates that some 1,500 or 1,600 ministers had been silenced. Moreover, he reports that "Popery and popish worship is openly sett up at Somerset House."[113] To the man who had braved the reprimand of the Star Chamber to organize the feofees in the 1620s, this news must have been devastating.

Davenport had the sad task of reporting to John Winthrop, Jr., that "Dr. Goodwin, Mr. Nie, and Mr. Peters are in prison, and likely to lose theyre lives, and that there is a consultacion to settle church discipline, in a way of joyning Episcopacy and presbytery."[114] It is hard for those of us who live in a world without transcendence to imagine the depth of despair this failure must have engendered in a man like Davenport. He spent his life watching and waiting and laboring for Christ's Kingdom, and what he now witnessed must have seemed like utter devastation.

Of course, Davenport was not alone in his despair. Conservatives like John Hull also mourned the news from Old England and lamented the plight of "poor suffering saints." To the distressed observers it seemed that the clock had been turned back to the darkest days of persecution: Bishops back in power, "and with them the old formalities of surplice, &c. were begun to be practised again in our native land,—which had been now twenty years expunged,—and many good ministers put out of place."[115]

Many New Englanders were grieved by these events, and many found cause to number the blessings of New England in being spared such upheaval. But the Brethren's greater commitment to the church international left them among the most despairing of New England's flock; they took little solace in such parochial good fortune.

Instead, they feared more widespread catastrophe.[116] Davenport worried that the whole of Protestant Europe might be in danger; that there were "greater things feared: Spain like to make peace: France like to differ." He prayed, "the good Lord prepare his people in old Eng[land] and New, for what they and we may expect, and, in the meane time, give us hearts to sympathize with afflicted Joseph!" Davenport's solace was the faith that had always sustained the Brethren: "our comfort is that the Lord reigneth."[117]

Yet this was not the last of the calamities Davenport would witness. In 1660 he wrote, "We, at Newhaven, are stil under Gods afflicting hand." Added to the failure of the Puritan revolution, the restoration of the episcopacy, and the executions of friends like Henry Vane, was the terrible failure of the Kingdom in New England. In 1662 the Half-Way measures were passed; soon after, Davenport's beloved New Haven was forcibly consolidated with Connecticut Colony. Through manipulations that Davenport characterized as "unChristian" and "unrighteous," Connecticut seized jurisdiction of its neighbor colony. Davenport despaired: "I perceive that the powers of darknes which have prevailed in other parts of the world are at worke here also, to subvert the kingdom of Christ in these ends of the earth."[118]

These events shattered Davenport's utopian dreams, producing in him an intensely local focus that hitherto had been absent but that characterized the more conservative jeremiads of Shepard and Bulkeley. His only hope was that there was time for New England, despite this apostasy, to repent: "But God hath not yet said that this is theire hour in reference to N.E. though our unthankfulnes for the gospel, unfruitfulness under it, disobedience to it, declensions from the simplicity that is in Christ, and sinful compliances, etc. have deserved that our hedge should be broken down."[119]

In this spirit, reeling under the terrible losses and disappointments of the decades, Davenport accepted the invitation of Boston Church. He desperately hoped to recall the New England saints to the aspirations that had inspired the Cambridge Brethren nearly a half-century before. In accepting the Boston pulpit, Davenport revived the strategies he had learned so long ago from Sibbes and Preston—the strategies of expedient dissembling in service to the Kingdom. No doubt, his methods in securing the pulpit were scandalous; and, indeed, they divided the colony. Violating the principles of congregational polity, Davenport left his New Haven congregation without permission and against their expressed wishes.[120] Moreover, Davenport willfully conspired with Boston's ruling elders to conceal this fact and suppressed letters from New Haven objecting to his removal.[121]

Historians have been as shocked by this subterfuge as they were by Cotton's dissembling in 1636. Thomas Hutchinson judged that "neither the church of New-Haven nor the elders of the church of Boston can be wholly justified. There does not seem to have been that fairness and simplicity in their proceeding which the gospel requires." Perry Miller states the case more strongly: "there is nowhere in the annals of New England a more sordid story than that of the fission of the First Church in 1669."[122] Yet, in all fairness, it must be said that though his methods may have been sordid, Davenport's motives were not. To some degree, perhaps, he was self-aggrandizing and arrogant, exercising his will over the saints of the Bay. But more important, he saw himself as the last prophet of the Cambridge Brethren and was determined to fight the good fight— and against all odds of success.

From his new pulpit, Davenport posed old questions about New England's purpose. His arrival set in motion a series of events that divided the colony as violently as it had been in the 1630s. Refusing Davenport's ministry, Half-Way supporters formed the new Third Church, using the doctored letters of dismissal as justification for their actions.[123] For his part, Davenport declared the dissenters in rebellion against the true faith and refused them permission to form a church. The two groups battled for more than a decade; Mather recorded "these two particular Churches in Boston, like the two distinguish'd rivers, not mixing, tho' running between the same banks, held not communion with one another at the table of the Lord."[124]

A council of orthodox ministers was formed to resolve the dispute, but Davenport disregarded their authority and ignored their injunctions to release the dissenters. He became so wayward in his resistance that he refused to acknowledge any communications from the council. In a head-to-head dispute between the two most powerful first-generation patriarchs, Davenport even rebuked the efforts of Richard Mather to resolve the controversy: "the church of Boston would not let [Mather] into the doors, when he, with sundry others, waited with a letter from the council to them."[125] There is no question that Davenport was needlessly and self-destructively reckless. The locking out of Richard Mather was seen by many to be the cause of his death a week later. Whether or not this tragedy alone succeeded in converting Mather's son, Increase, from opposition to support of the halfway measures cannot be known, but it certainly contributed to that change of heart and to Davenport's ultimate defeat. These acts of resistance were as dramatic as any in New England's history, including Cotton's boycott of Bulkeley's ordination in the 1630s.[126]

As in those earlier disputes, the deputies of the Court once again formed themselves in support of the actions of the Boston Church and against the standing order of ministers and magistrates. Once again controversy nearly sundered the colony, as challenges concerning the constitution of the church and the definition of grace were lodged against the reigning orthodoxy. Along with Governor Bellingham, the deputies not only sided with Davenport to resist the foundation of Third Church, but they also repudiated the earlier Court's approval of the tenets of the 1662 synod. Thomas Hutchinson observed that "two parties" were produced "not in the other churches only but in the state also." "The strict union, which had been from the beginning between the civil and ecclesiastical parts of the constitution, was about this time in danger of being broke, or greatly weakned."[127]

As in the 1630s, disputes within the churches spilled over into political contests. In a passage reminiscent of Winthrop's history of the antinomian disputes, Cotton Mather observed that "the whole people of God throughout the colony were too much distinguished into such as favored the old church, and such as favored the new church; whereof the former were against the synod, and the latter were for it."[128] In this fevered context, Davenport delivered his incendiary election sermon of 1669. Preached at the request of the deputies, this sermon broadened the attack from the dissenting members of First Church to include all supporters of the Half-Way synod measures. Wheelwright found a worthy successor in Davenport, whose 1669 election sermon did as much to inflame the Bay congregations as the Fast Day sermon of 1637. On this day in May, John Davenport cast himself as a wilderness prophet, exposing the apostasy of New England. He chose for his text 2 Samuel 23, the scriptural echo of Cotton's 1645 sermon on *God's Free Grace*.[129]

This text records the last prophetic words of David, enjoining his people to respect the covenant and cautioning civil rulers to be just. Similarly, Davenport warned his auditors to avoid human invention and "cleave to the truth of the Precepts, and live by the truth of the Promises." To the magistrates who were interfering with his own governance of the First Church, he warned "Take heed and beware that you deprive not any instituted Christian church, walking according to Gospel Rules, of the Power and Privileges which Christ hath purchased for them with his precious blood."[130] His concluding evocation "of the first beginning of this Colony of *Massachusetts,* which I have the better advantage and more special engagement to do; being one of them, by whom the Patent, which you enjoy, was procured," asserts Davenport's originary claim as the founder in whom New England's purpose was more surely sealed than in all the second-generation magistrates and ministers currently urging innovation. Davenport's appeal is to the faith as it was first delivered to the saints, a faith for which he was prepared to contend with all of his remaining strength.[131]

To Davenport the sins of New England were many. First, he worried that in adopting the Half-Way measures the saints "have transgressed the Laws, changed the Ordinance, and broken the everlasting Covenant." He scourged those "sinful children" who thought to say along with Peter Bulkeley, "we have Abraham to our father" and therefore have the covenant by everlasting descent. Davenport recalled that *"Jesus saith unto them, If ye were Abrahams children, you would do the works of Abraham."*[132] Repudiating the human covenant of Bulkeley, Davenport reasserts the claims of Christ and of a pure church of professing saints.

Though the Half-Way measures filled his thoughts, they were not his only concern. Despite his own growing obsession with New England, Davenport condemned the saints' complacency: New England was guilty of "a Sinful remisseness to neglect the public service of God, and to be too intent upon their own private concernments."[133] He and his disiples condemned the typological readings of tribal privilege: "to build so much upon the largeness of Jewish practices, is as great a sin, seeing it is a stretching and enlarging of the narrow way that leadeth unto life, to bee as wide as the broad way that leadeth most unto destruction."[134] Not all New Englanders, then, approved the typologizing of America's mission.

Moreover, as noted earlier, Davenport deplored the self-interested quest for material prosperity that distracted saints from their proper Christian duties. He observed, if "their trading increase one good bargain will more comfort them than all the calamities of the Church can grieve them." This complacency seemed of a piece with the tribal nationalism he linked to the issue of church membership. Like Jeremiah "labouring to convince the Jews of their sin . . . to bring them to repentance," Davenport harangued, cajoled, and tyrannized over the New England saints to abandon their self-love in favor of his definition of a more public-spirited and diffusive affection of charity.[135]

Yet, like his mentor Richard Sibbes, Davenport also offered words of comfort, should the cause be truly lost. In gentler tones he always added that God will comfort his saint in the darkest hour, that he will be an anchorhold in times of distress, and never abandon the faithful. This was a comfort the saints would need in the dark days ahead.

In 1668, then, Davenport hoped to provide the leadership and theological arguments with which the laity and the deputies could battle the policies of another new orthodoxy. Even his sudden death in March 1670 did not end the controversy. The deputies, who both supported the cause of the First Church and opposed the Half-Way measures, continued to express public approbation of Davenport's position. In a report to the court in 1670 they enumerated the judgments of God against New England, including the ruin of Harvard, the "obstruction to the trade," the presence of sickness and other "prodigious signs, such as comets, earthquakes." The causes for these disasters were "contentions, unbrotherly distances," faults clearly to be laid at the doorstep of the 1662 synod and the "woeful declining from our primitive and foundation work."[136]

The deputies criticized the "innovation threatening the ruin of our foundations, and the extirpation of those old principles of the congregational way, laid down by so many of the Lord's worthies who are now at rest." This new version of primitivism invoked by second- and third-generation dissenters appealed to the millennialist prospect of the first Cambridge preachers. Borrowing the incendiary complaints of this earlier generation, the deputies condemned the new orthodoxy for the an "invasion of the rights, liberties, and privileges of churches, an usurpation of a lordly and prelatical power over god's heritage, a subversion of gospel order, and all this with a dangerous tendency to the utter devastation of these churches."[137]

These charges were expressed in a rhetoric as inflammatory as any to be discovered in the Antinomian Controversy. Accusing the dissenters of "turning the pleasant gardens of Christ into a wilderness; and the inevitable and total extirpation of the principles and pillars of the congregational way," the deputies characterize the events as "the corrupting gangrene, the infecting spreading plague, the provoking images of jealousy set up before the lord, the accursed thing which hath provoked divine wrath, and doth further threaten destruction."[138]

The strife was so fever-pitched that Deputy Governor Willoughby feared it would be "published to the world that the Government of New England is broken, and that your animosities are such that tis Impossible for you to agree in anything that may tend to the Saving the whole." In language that echoes Winthrop's narration of thirty years before, this official assessment does much to confirm the thesis that orthodoxy was as hotly contested and the Bay Colony in as great a danger of explosion in the 1660s and 1670s as ever it was.[139]

Not surprisingly, the magistrates refused to approve the deputies' report, thus exacerbating the divisions between the upper and lower body of the legislature.[140] Declaring "greiffe and dissatisfaction" with the deputies' report, the magistrates charged them with misrepresenting and abusing the orthodox ministers of the Bay.[141] Incensed, the magistrates declared a de facto war on their counterparts in the lower house, and a two-year political battle ensued.[142] Hamilton Hill has said that the next election "turned chiefly on the question, Who are for the old Church and who for the new? . . . so strong was the popular feeling against the conservatives that a majority of the members of the House of Deputies of 1670 lost their seats, and more enlightened men were chosen to succeed them."[143]

Miller speaks with less glowing tones of the shift, observing that there was a good deal of electioneering on the part of the orthodox party to reestablish their hegemony in the Court. As with many of the events of the Antimonian Controversy, the means whereby radicalism was thwarted remain obscure. As Miller says: "However the clergy managed it, in the winter of 1670–71 they went to work upon the country." One of the factors in their success was, no doubt, the death of the great opposition leader in 1670. With John Davenport's passing and Increase Mather's conversion to the standing orthodoxy, the flames of controversy gradually subsided. The dominant clergy and magistrates managed to oust their opponents in what Miller concludes "to have been the first organized campaign in America to elect an entire ticket."[144] It might be argued that the Newtown election of 1637 was the first organized campaign and that the events of 1671 merely reconfirmed the dominance of the orthodox, preparationist party.[145]

Yet it must also be remarked that the strong support for Davenport can be read as a testament to the continued appeal of the piety of the Cambridge Brethren. It has been observed that "as late as 1690 . . . a few earnest believers even yet hankered after Cotton's rarified doctrine."[146] The events of the 1670s prove that more than a few of New England's faithful chose to pledge allegiance to the Brethren's aspirations for a pure church and a holy communion of saints. When Davenport arrived in Boston he found a gathering of this saving remnant praying for a leader to guide through what they saw as New England's apostasy. Davenport stirred these drowsy yet faithful disciples, and they embraced him and his doctrine.

Miller has judged that Davenport "had no business to accept" the call to Boston. "Not only was he old, but his people in New Haven, having stood by him, did not want to lose him . . . Davenport's motive was obvious: he wanted to mount the throne of Cotton and from it condemn the Synod of 1662."[147] No doubt, a good measure of arrogance and self-righteousness motivated him. Clearly, he believed that his vision alone was the proper one for New England.

Yet surely Davenport deserves a more generous judgment than Miller has offered. His dreams of the kingdom and of the communion of saints were rightly called golden dreams of grace. It would take a hardened heart not to sympathize with the feelings of loss and disappointment that filled Davenport in the aftermath of the Restoration. With his beloved Cotton and Sibbes long since dead, the English saints mounting the scaffold or flying for their lives; with pulpits shut against the true word and New England resting snugly in the blessing of the tribe, Davenport must have felt fathomless grief. That he raged and connived and cajoled is not evidence of his villainy, but testament to his undying determination to contend earnestly for the faith once delivered to the saints. That the Boston Church rallied to his holy cause must have comforted him; must have assured him that, though deferred, the Kingdom would arrive, and someday the saints would enjoy the beauty and good tendency of union.

The visitor to King's Chapel, Boston, will find only one tomb marked for John Davenport and John Cotton. Members of First Church thought it fitting that they should rest together.

✻

This study has tried to demonstrate the volatility and mutability of rhetorical constructions in the context of the first period of New English settlement. My interest in the morphological patterning of Cambridge spiritism is balanced by a commitment both to the specific circumstances of its enunciation and to the particularity of individual speakers. The first American decades were spent in constant testing of beliefs and refinement of their expression. This moment was shaped by a complex series of events, motives, aspirations, and utterances. Words like *covenant, grace,* and *charity* were posited, contested, and redefined in a highly charged, mobile process of dialogic exchange. Public debates, private exchanges, informal interrogations, and, in the most extreme instance, the ritual of public trial gave these rhetorical structures a density and specificity that asks to be respected.

Throughout I have argued against the notion of a univocal American orthodoxy, desiring instead to be attentive to the multivocal strains of a hybrid Puritanism, both English and American. An orthodoxy may well have been produced in these first decades; my intent is to expose the constructedness of that category, to restore some sense of the volatility of this early social history. The magistrates and ministers who emerged victorious in the aftermath of the controversies of the 1630s were not successful in redefining all opposition as heresy; nor were they able to contain or co-opt all expressions of dissent. Compromise and negotiation were not simply the means whereby the dominant group consolidated its position; equally, these were sources of empowerment for others who felt themselves in opposition.

Indeed, the exercise of power *within* the mainstream was far more fluid than has been supposed; authority was far more diffuse. Laying claim to and manipulating the codes of "orthodox" discourse, dissenting preachers like Cotton and Davenport effectively remained both in and out of the game—by subterfuge, they retained positions of influence in order to challenge or modify the policies of the ruling orthodoxy. In Old England these preachers remained in power long enough to educate a generation of revolutionaries. In New England, Cotton's ability to compromise allowed him to retain his pulpit, exert leverage against the standing order from within, and provide a haven for spiritist followers. Davenport's return in 1668 was enabled by these tactics of survival. Repeated eruptions of resistance in the General Court and in prominent congregations throughout New England over the course of the century suggest the effectiveness of such strategies.

Epilogue

His goodness is a communicative, diffusive goodness. [Christ] comes to spread his treasures, to enrich the heart with all grace and strength . . . he comes, indeed, to make our hearts, as it were, a heaven . . . to empty his goodness into our hearts. As a breast that desires to empty itself when it is full; so this fountain hath the fulness of a fountain, which strives to empty his goodness into our souls. He comes out of love to us.

Richard Sibbes

Whatsoever is good, that is in God, and it is but a drop, but a sparke of the well-spring of life in him, all the goodnesse that is dispersed in the creature, flowes from him . . . God is an heape and fountaine of goodnesse, and he undertakes so to be to us.

John Cotton

Love is always a sweet principle; and especially divine love. This, even on earth, is a spring of sweetness; but in heaven, it shall become a stream, a river, an ocean! All shall stand about the God of glory, who is the great fountain of love, opening, as it were, their very souls to be filled with those effusions of love that are poured forth from his fulness, just as the flowers on the earth, in the bright and joyous days of spring, open their bosoms to the sun to be filled with his light and warmth, and to flourish in beauty and fragrancy under his cheering rays.

Jonathan Edwards

Having just buried Davenport along with Cotton, I am aware that it may appear unseemly to exhume them in the next chapter. Yet, it is not only conventional, but almost obligatory at the conclusion of a study such as this to make claims for the importance of one's subjects for subsequent generations of Americans. This trio of epigraphs implicitly suggests how such an argument for continuity from Sibbes to Edwards might unfold.

Indeed, my warrant for making that journey is guaranteed by some of our most luminous critics. Perry Miller's inspirational mapping of the transformations from colony to province and thence from Edwards to Emerson has been recapitulated often, at times with brilliance. Andrew Delbanco and Sacvan Bercovitch, for example, make powerful recent cases for Puritan foundationalism. Though they read that legacy in quite different registers, both argue for a persistent Puritan symbolic that constructs and explains the American self from the first landfall through the jeremiads of the present day. Revisionists seeking to expand definitions of Puritan identity to include feminized and other "marginalized" selves often sustain their own versions of the claim (often a pejorative one) for the immediacy of the Puritan legacy as well.

Similarly, tracking the secret voice of antinomianism as a countertext to our national literature has become a staple of literary studies, and it is easy to imagine how the history of the Cambridge Brethren could fruitfully be brought to bear on such narratives. In that spirit, I can envisage reclaiming the "great" American authors for a Sibbesian canon. Emerson's conversion on Cambridge Common makes sense as the romantic embodiment of the Brethren's notion of privative sin and divine effulgence. Whitman's chant of the body politic is easily construed as a secularist incarnation of their Christian community, his song of Democratic Vistas an evocation of their postmillennial optimism. Rather than discovering the embryonic voice of American imperialism or the prefiguration of bourgeois subjectivity, an appreciative reading of the Brethren might uncover a utopian alternative within Puritanism itself.

How much more relevant is the case that might be made for the great preacher of the Awakening—Jonathan Edwards—who remained a citizen of a theocentric universe only teetering on the brink of Enlightenment. Treating the pietism of Cotton Mather as a historical bridge, one might argue that on almost every important issue Edwards gave new voice to the principles of the Cambridge faith.[1] For in repudiating the Half-Way Covenant measures, he, too, positioned himself against what he saw as a mechanical faith of a preparationism without the Spirit.[2] His redefinition of grace as passive infusion, producing a new relish for divine things and a diffusive love toward one's fellows springs out of an affectionate piety tonally similar to that of the Spiritual Brethren. Moreover, Edwards deplored what he saw as New England's tribalism with a fervor equal to Davenport's own—he argued that the province of the church was the world. Like the Brethren, Edwards urged men and women to labor zealously on behalf of the universal communion of saints. As Alan Heimert has shown, his postmillennial optimism led toward a second revolution of saints—this time in the American eighteenth century.[3]

Nor are these echoes of the Cambridge rhetoric merely subjective connections; we know that Edwards read and cited both Sibbes and Cotton in his notebooks and annotations.[4] Though Edwardsean scholars neither trace the instances nor consider the implications, they often remark his indebtedness to Sibbes.[5] Countering more remote theories of the influence of Newton and Locke, a familiarity with the writings of the Sibbesians suggests that Edwards struck roots deep in seventeenth-century soil. Indeed, it is plausible to argue that Edwards's theology significantly rehearsed the rhetorical and doctrinal affinities of the Cambridge group.[6]

Yet, the vast body of scholarship that easily assumes the transmission of symbolic constructions held together by the single denominator, "America," obliges me to point out that rhetorical echoes and ideological similarities per se cannot prove a continuity of symbolic structures. As this study has tried to show, identical words take on variant meanings for different groups and in particular periods and contexts.

The milieu in which Edwards framed his objections to the corpse-cold religion of his age presents a unique set of historical, personal, and literary densities. His articulation of spiritist pietism may well be read in relation to an earlier tradition, but it must also be understood as saturated by more immediate circumstances. For example, any assessment of Edwards's doctrinal formulations must reckon with his agonistic relation to Solomon Stoddard, the grandfather in whose church Edwards overturned the practices of that earlier generation. In addition, careful scrutiny is required to calculate the degrees to which Edwards positioned himself and was positioned by the war of words waged between conservatives like Charles Chauncy and radicals like James Davenport (both descendants of the Puritan patriarchy). Moreover, the social sources for Edwards's brand of spiritism—local class divisions and larger issues of status anxiety—enrich our understanding of Edwards by complicating claims for his indebtedness to intellectual precursors. Finally, the collision of Enlightenment philosophy with Edwards's theist universe requires judicious reading.

By way of rhetorical and ideational homologies, the distance between Cotton and Edwards seems short. However, the presumption of meaningful continuity of symbolic structures based on such identities is problematic—even counter to the spirit of this study. And, if the bridge to Edwards strains the limits of its credibility, investigating the persistence of these ideas and structures of feeling in a secular world exceeds those boundaries.

Yet, the astonishing resemblances—both ideational and rhetorical—

between Edwards and the Brethren also begs notice, though they cannot command explanation. The discovery of compelling similarities cannot and should not be dismissed: they confront us with the insistent issues of influence and authorship, tradition and cultural context. As a way to give these meditations flesh and to affirm the pleasure of recognition that readers of Edwards have perhaps already experienced in the foregoing text, the remaining pages will present what I take to be the most intriguing and significant correspondences between Edwards and the Cambridge preachers. However, these observations are offered with a proviso: while the resemblances are striking, similarities of vocabulary and ideological position do not in themselves constitute an argument for meaningful continuity, despite the regularity and conviction with which such claims are made. Rather than proving the case, these seeming identities raise the question instead of the assumption of symbolic transformations and intellectual traditions.

❧

In articulating a Christian theology and sociology both Edwards and the Brethren seem to begin with the same first principle: "the essence of all true religion lies in holy love" and its free dissemination.[7] God is a being whose "infinite virtue or holiness, and his infinite joy and happiness," is in "communicating the love of himself" to his creature.[8] Countering the orthodoxy of his own day, Edwards, too, denied that there could be any qualifications or conditions on this exuberant overflow of divine benevolence.[9]

When Edwards articulated his version of the doctrine of attributes, it was not sovereignty but charity that claimed ontological primacy. Edwards's deity is not essentially an omnipotent sovereign or a benevolent judge; nor can excellency or beauty, characteristics privileged by some scholars, be considered God's primary attributes. The first and essential attribute—the impetus in God's self-generation and his generation of the world—is love and its diffusion, being and its communication.

Though part of God's infinite being, power and will are understood by Edwards as attributes displayed "according to our way of conceiving of God."[10] Neither God's natural perfections (consisting of "his power, his knowledge whereby he knows all things, and his being eternal, from everlasting to everlasting, his omnipresence, and his awful and terrible majesty") nor his moral perfections (consisting in his "holiness . . . his purity and beauty as a moral agent . . . his righteousness, faithfulness and goodness") are perceived as primary in Edwards's description of divine essence.[11]

Instead, these are aspects of God's being, exhibited in proportion to the believer's disposition either to love God's holiness or to fear his power: "Like the two opposite scales of a balance," "God has wisely ordained, that these two opposite principles of love and fear, should rise and fall," and with them God's nature is manifested as either "terrible majesty" or "amiable" holiness.[12]

As was true for Sibbes, so for Edwards this apparent multiplicity of God's essence emerges as part of God's creation and governance of the world. As part of his loving care and desire to be understood, God reveals himself as each believer requires. As Edwards explained, God delights in displaying his various attributes of power and prudence, wisdom and love; "If the world had not been created, these attributes never would have had any exercise."[13] Indeed, the chief end for which God created the world and in which his primary nature consists is the "disposition to communicate himself, or diffuse his own *fullness*," so that "there might be a glorious and abundant emanation of his infinite fullness of good *ad extra*, or without himself."[14] The proper image of the deity is not merely the "living water" of scripture, but the fountain streaming forth and overflowing. As the opening epigraphs suggest, this depiction was written in the pages of every member of the Cambridge circle and informs every aspect of Edwards's doctrine.

For example, in explaining the phenomenal universe Edwards contended that "we must conceive of God's determination to glorify and communicate Himself as prior to the method that His wisdom pitches upon as tending best to effect this"—either through the works of creation or redemption. God's impulse to communicate his being precedes the genesis of the world and writes the history of salvation. Edwards defined being and its communication together as God's glory, signifying what is "internal . . . inherent in the subject"—God—but also standing for the "emanation, exhibition or communication of this internal glory." Edwards derived this meaning of glory from his translation of the Hebrew word *kavod*, which he rendered as "heaviness, greatness, and abundance."[15]

Following a logic similar to the Brethren's, Edwards argued that the same disposition to communicate his abundance not only moved God to create the world *ad extra*, but also inspired the creation of the Trinity *ad intra*. Though in its deepest sense the Trinity remained a sacred mystery to him, one "infinitely above us to conceive how it should be," much less express, Edwards nonetheless did try to describe the process by which God the Father, as "the deity subsisting in the prime, unoriginated and most absolute manner, or the deity in its direct existence," becomes three-in-one.[16] Furthermore, his version of the generation of the Trinity bears striking resemblance to the theories of the Brethren.

Edwards began "An Essay on the Trinity" by declaring that the happiness of the Father consists in displaying and observing himself, in "beholding and infinitely loving, and rejoicing in, His own essence."[17] The present participals underscore the immediacy of this self-articulation: "that God perpetually and eternally has a most perfect idea of Himself." God must become his own "eternal and necessary object." Edwards makes explicit what Cotton and Sibbes implied: perception requires an other— "there must be a duplicity." In the act of thinking and therein projecting an image of himself, the Father begets his Son. One God becomes two: "There is God and the idea of God."[18]

But this first emanation does not satisfy God's desire for effulgence or society; from the two a third entity overflows, born of the attractive force between them: "so the Holy Spirit does in some ineffable and inconceivable manner proceed, and is breathed forth both from the Father and the Son, by the Divine essence being wholly poured and flowing out in that infinitely intense, holy and pure love and delight that continually and unchangeably breathes forth from the Father and the Son."[19] As with Cotton's and Sibbes's prose, the dynamic and expansive cadences of Edwards's sentences perform the effulgent nature of being itself.

Edwards's Godhead is most properly described, then, as a holy society, produced not only from but for "the great design of glorifying the deity and communicating its fullness." The ineffable source of the Trinity is the inherent disposition of being in its "prime, unoriginated and most absolute manner" to be effulgent, to flow out even within itself. It is this quality, not Amesian sovereignty, that is essential to God's nature: "the divine essence it self flows out and is as it were breathed forth in Love and Joy."[20] This dissemination is properly called the glory of God manifested *ad intra*, within the deity.[21] This doctrine recalls Cotton's faith that desire for community transformed one God into three. Before the beginning of time or the framing of the world, Cotton wrote, persons of the Trinity "nourished, delighted and solaced each other" in a holy fellowship.[22]

It is harmonious for Edwards that God's effulgence *ad intra* is "agreeable" to "that which proceeds from *ad extra*": the works of creation and redemption.[23] *Esse* and *Operati* have a single source in the doctrine of divine effulgence. Emanating from the Trinity according to the order of subsistence and the economy of action, each of these works is identified primarily with a single person of the Godhead. First, Edwards described the work of creation as the emanation of God the Father, who intended "that his works should exhibit an image of himself their author, that it might brightly appear by his works what manner of being he is."[24] Just as Christ reflects God's idea of himself, the created world corresponds to God's projection of his own original being. Following creation in the economy of the Trinity is the work of salvation performed by the Son and the Spirit, first as it was purchased virtually by Christ in historical time, and then it is made actual by the Holy Ghost in the heart of each believer and in the unfolding of the Kingdom.

From such godly arrangements, Cotton and Sibbes had concluded that union with Christ was inextricably tied to the communion of the saints. Similarly, Edwards argued that the work of redemption is at once communal and individual, identifying these two parts of salvation with the historical work of redemption and the ontological transformation of grace. Like the persons of the Trinity, the two aspects are distinct but not separate; while they are "by no means to be confounded one with another," they do necessarily suppose each other.[25] Personal union with God, then, can no more be divorced from communion with the saints than the Spirit can be separated from the person of Christ. Both aspects of salvation magnify God's glory, and this understanding underwrites a pastoralism emphasizing the community as well as the individual believer.

Glory as this communication of being provides the foundation for Edwards's understanding of human nature as well. As he translates *kavod*, glory is also "the knowledge or sense, or effect of [emanation or communication of internal glory] in those who behold it; to whom the exhibition or communication is made."[26] The creature's "natural delight" in and disposition to receive impression find a complement in God's inclination to "glorify and communicate Himself."[27] God lovingly instructs "the minds that He ha[d] made," "to enlighten and illustrate, and to convey instruction with impression, conviction, and pleasure."[28] Anthropology as well as sociology is implicated in this theology, as the creature perceives God's fullness and participates in his glory.

Happily, the proportion between the divine and human nature here is not one of power and dependence, nor one of justice and responsibility. Recalling George Herbert's balance of sin and love, we might say that charity as the measure of God's nature is answered by the saint's returns of that love: "here is both an *emanation* and *remanation*."[29] As Communicating Being, God not only "loves to see Himself, His own excellencies and glory," but also "loves his creatures so, that He really loves the being honored by them."[30] Reciprocity is inherent in the notion of communication. Not only has God "exhibited himself, in his being, his infinite greatness and excellency," but he "has given us faculties, whereby we are capable of plainly discovering [his] immense superiority to all other beings." "In the creature's knowing, esteeming, loving, rejoicing in, and praising God, the glory of God is both exhibited and acknowledged; his fulness is received and returned."[31]

This configuration of communication and reception threads throughout Edwards's writings. The saint's role as perceiver of the divine is evidenced, for example, in Edwards's explication of the Fall and its effects. In *The Doctrine of Original Sin* he described prelapsarian nature, in which "two kinds of principles" existed—the "*inferior* kind . . . being the principles of mere human nature," and the "*superior* principles . . . wherein consisted the spiritual image of God."[32] Superior principles are described in the terminology of glory: they "immediately depend on man's union and communion with God, or divine communications and influences of God's Spirit."[33] Human disobedience forfeited spiritual principle and severed communion with the divine; God withdrew the creature's capacity to perceive or to act in terms of moral excellence. As it was for the Brethren, for Edwards sin was the privation of good.

But the infusion of grace, which is the "Holy Ghost dwelling in the soul and acting there as a vital principle," restores the ability to perceive "the true beauty and loveliness" and the "moral excellency" of divine things.[34] The regenerate saint receives nothing less than "a principle of a new kind of perception or spiritual sensation," one in which he or she is given "eyes to see and ears to hear" and a taste to relish the "glory and beauty of God's nature."[35]

A comparison of exemplary passages reveals the striking rhetorical and doctrinal similarities between Sibbes, Cotton, and Edwards on this issue:

> For the holy heart . . . there is a sweet relish in all divine truths, and suitable to the sweetness in them, there is a spiritual taste, which the Spirit of God puts into the soul of his children. Though there be never so much sweetness in things, if there be not a suitable taste, there is no relish in them. Therefore, the Spirit of God, in his children, works a taste of the sweetness that is in the word of God.[36]

> Have you then found some sweet rellish in the Ordinances, *the Gospell is a sweet savour to them that are saved* . . . and so for savor to smell, so, as a sweet savour to the taste; doe you therefore finde some kinde of *sweetnesse*, as spirituall *sweetness* in the Word you heare . . . it is a signe of health to rellish a sweetnesse in our meat . . . he that is

borne of God to a Spirituall life, is become *a new Creature* . . .
He hath a new mind, and a new heart, new affections, new Language . . .[37]

The mind has an entirely new kind of perception or sensation; and
here is, as it were, a new spiritual sense that the mind has, or a
principle of new kind of perception or spiritual sensation, which is in
its whole nature different from any former kinds of sensation of the
mind as tasting is diverse from any of the other senses . . . as the
sweet taste of honey is diverse from the ideas men get of honey by
only looking on it . . . Hence the work of the Spirit of God in
regeneration is often in Scripture compared to the giving a new sense,
giving eyes to see, and ears to hear . . .[38]

As it was for the Brethren, so for Edwards grace is experimental—it alters
the relish and implants yearning for God. Now there is "love, desire, and
delight."[39]

Edwards's understanding of the *ordo salutis* was similar to the model of
salvation preached by the Brethren as well. Countering the regnant doctrines of his day, Edwards argued that God requires no conditional preparation but supplies prevenient love; there was no contract, no increated
graces, but the new sense immediately bestowed and passively received.
Grace was to be understood as the indwelling of a personal Christ:

So the saints are said to live by Christ living in them . . . Christ by
his Spirit not only is in them, but lives in them . . . The Spirit of
God so dwells in the hearts of the saints, that he there, as a seed or
spring of life, exerts and communicates himself, in this his sweet and
divine nature, making the soul a partaker of God's beauty and Christ's
joy, so that the saint has truly fellowship with the Father, and with
his Son Jesus Christ, in thus having communion or participation of
the Holy Ghost.[40]

Moreover, like the Brethren before him, Edwards's understanding of the
sacramental ordinances, of prayer, and even of the singing of hymns was
rooted in the twin process of divine exhibition and human apprehension.[41]
This is a position wholly consonant with Sibbes's assertion that "the
sacraments . . . help our souls by our senses, our faith by imagination."[42]

Extending this understanding of holy communion, Edwards developed a new epistemology of nature. One of the most controversial aspects
of his thought is the extension of typology from Scripture to nature, an

innovation that has been widely credited to Enlightenment influences. Critics like Miller have argued that Edwards's reading of nature violated traditional Puritan views of divinity—that is, if God's essence is read as transcendent sovereignty.[43] The extension of typology to nature makes sense, however, in the context of Edwards's representation of God as a communicator and the saint as recipient of spiritual knowledge.

Describing typology as a "certain sort of Language, as it were, in which God is wont to speak to us," Edwards argued that God's voice still sounded in nature, in human history, and in the flow of contemporary events.[44] Natural types allow that "wherever we are, and whatever we are about, we may see divine things excellently represented and held forth."[45] Edwards's saint was created to perceive God's glory, revealed in the lessons of nature as in the words of the prophets. For Edwards, this expanded perception was part of the explosion of spiritual knowledge accompanying the advent of the millennium. Such a view is consonant with the Sibbesian faith that the saint was made a new creature and given a sanctified fancy.

So, too, Edwards preached that charity inevitably bears its fruits. Having been filled with the Spirit, the saint by this new nature exhibits a diffusive, spreading love: expressions of charity become the joy and duty of the Christian. Edwards finds a poetry in nature to describe this emanation: "the soul of a saint receives light from the Sun of Righteousness, in such a manner, that its nature is changed, and it becomes properly a luminous thing: not only does the sun shine in the saints, but they also become little suns, partaking of the nature of the fountain of their light . . . which though they were lit up by fire from heaven, yet thereby became, themselves burning shining things." Thence they are enjoined and of their own desire to send back God's love in prayer, and praise, and labor on behalf of Christ's church.[46] Moreover, Edwards understood these fruits as inextricably wed to promoting a union of saints.

Like the Brethren, Edwards argued that private returns are incommensurate with God's own effulgence. Defining the *imitatio Christi* in large measure as desire for Christian society, Edwards preached that saints fulfill their duty in fellowship. He understood the relationship between the ontology of conversion and the life of sanctification in terms that Sibbes and Cotton would have admired: "it is from the same Spirit that true Christian love arises, both toward God and man. The Spirit of God is a Spirit of love, and when the former enters the soul, love also enters it."[47]

Contrary to Ames's modest expectations of human benevolence, Edwards argued that grace "disposes a person to be public-spirited," that saints do not hesitate to "part with private interests for the good of our neighbors." Indeed the definition of sin is self-love, whereby "the mind of man shrank from its primitive greatness and expandedness, to an exceeding smallness and contractedness." The contracted circles of caritas that Amesians permitted were to Edwards signs of degeneracy: "sin, like some powerful astringent, contracted [the] soul to the very small dimensions of selfishness." Charity, by contrast, is expansive: "by love, a man's self is so extended and enlarged that others, so far as they are beloved, do, as it were, becomes parts of himself, so that wherein their interest is promoted, he believes his own is promoted."[48]

For Edwards the love of God must always produce an equally effulgent love to the saints, else it cannot be a mark of true grace: "Christian love both to God and man, is wrought in the heart by the same work of the Spirit. There are not two works of the Spirit of God, one to infuse a spirit of love to God, and the other to infuse a spirit of love to men, but in producing one the Spirit produces the other also . . . it is one and the same divine temper thus wrought in the heart, that flows out in love both to God and man."[49]

The link Cambridge preachers forged between the work of sanctification and a millennial kingdom, then, was articulated as a full-blown post-millennialism by Edwards. Just as God must be understood as a holy society, so human beings cannot be considered as unitary; each saint is part of the dynamic community of believers, a society to be enlarged over time and most particularly by seasons of awakening. Just as "the *degree* of the *amiableness* or *valuableness* . . . is not in the *simple* proportion of the degree of benevolent affection seen, but in a proportion *compounded* . . . of the degree of *being* and the degree of *benevolence*," so the beauty of the single regenerate soul is not as pleasing to God, who "esteems, values and has respect to things according to their nature and proportions," as a community of saints "consisting of many millions."[50] The reader is recalled to Sibbes's ecstatic observation that "If every star be beautiful, how beautiful are all in their lustre! when so many saints shall be gathered together, they shall be far more glorious than the sun in his majesty!"[51]

Like the Cambridge Brethren, Edwards watched and worked for the advent of the Kingdom. He believed that increasing the numbers of the faithful was instrumental in bringing forth those glorious days. Exhortations to the saints, unions in prayer, and efforts at international alliances with other churches were some of the ways Edwards labored to knit the churches and bring forth the Kingdom. Refusing all excuses for lukewarm passivity, Edwards repeated the Prestonian injunction to contend for the faith: "Do not make excuse that you have not opportunities to do anything for the glory of God, for the interest of the Redeemers Kingdom, and for the spiritual benefit of your neighbors. If your heart is full of love, it will find vent . . . when a fountain abound in water, it will send forth streams."[52] This commitment to the communion of saints, sealed with a fervent millenarian doctrine, produced a rhetoric of revolution as dynamic as that forged by Preston and Sibbes in the 1620s.[53]

Like the Cambridge preachers, Edwards had faith that the millennium was immanent, that revelations of God's purpose were accelerating.[54] As with the first coming of Christ, so with the "approaching glorious times of the Christian church" there would be a great increase in the knowledge of heavenly things; an increase to include revelation through nature.[55] In a statement that would horrify Thomas Shepard, Edwards declared that expressions of the divine will multiply until "holiness should be as it were inscribed on everything, on all men's common business and employments, and the common utensils of life, all shall be dedicated to God;" it will be a time "when little children should in spiritual attainments, be as though they were 'a hundred years old.'"[56]

In these last days the company of saints itself will expand until "the whole earth shall be united as one holy city, one heavenly family, men of all nations shall as it were dwell together, and sweetly correspond one with another as brethren and children of the same father."[57] Edwards spent his greatest imaginative energies describing those glorious days. His understanding of the final joy of Christians is reminiscent of the ecstatic anticipations of the Cambridge preachers, for whom desire for consummation is as "the breathings and motions of the Spirit in the soul, tending to further union."[58]

In his millennial writings Sibbes described this fulfillment of history in terms of mutual desire: Christ "is in some sort imperfect till the latter day, till his 'second coming.' For the mystical body of Christ is his fulness. Christ is our fulness and we are his fulness." His church mystical knows no local habitation: "If the communion of saints here be so sweet, even an heaven upon earth . . . what will it be when all the blessed souls that have been from the beginning of the world unto the end shall be all together!" In the great days coming "then we shall be near, not in soul only, but also in body and soul, and in both we shall be for ever joined to the fountain of all good. It is that which the Church desires here."[59]

Though America might occupy a special place as a source of pious activity, Edwards, too, privileged the universal gathering saints across time and national boundaries. He argued that the advent would be directly linked, indeed brought forth by the increased gathering of the elect. At one point in the *Nature of True Virtue* Edwards used the metaphor of gold to show that the degree of preciousness is directly related to the increasing quantity or mass of the body of believers.[60] Though the saints draw ever nearer to Christ, Edwards proposed that "there never will be any particular time" when union with God will be perfectly consummated. Indeed, how can there be, when the very principle of communication requires both subject and object? Yet, the last of days of history will be enjoyed as an anticipation of ever-approaching union: "the eternally increasing union of the saints with God" is represented "by something that is ascending constantly towards that infinite height, moving upwards with a given velocity; and that is to continue thus to move to all eternity."[61]

In place of consummation, then, Edwards posited an eternal dynamic, of effulgence and reflection, emanation and remanation. Borrowing from the science of Newton, Edwards explained that in the last days the bond of attraction between the two entities—God and creature, or more properly the society of the Godhead and the community of saints—grows ever stronger as the mass increases and the distance diminishes. As those glorious days of the earthly church approach, "wherein the whole earth shall be united as one holy city," God will perforce be drawn down from his heaven, even as the saints ascend. In the amorous equation of emanation and remanation—not in any contract or covenant—the saints are wedded to God. Simply stated, this theory of the millennium rests on a faith in copious love as the foundation of divinity; a conviction that charity could establish God's kingdom on earth as it is in heaven.[62]

❧

Despite the compelling quality of these similarities, this rehearsal of correspondences does not prove the case of symbolic continuity. It does not answer but instead raises questions about influence, authority, tradition, and symbolic transformations. Though explanation is the instinct of scholarship, in this instance that desire will be deferred in favor of sketching prospects for other readings.

First, consideration of an alternative pietist genealogy can deepen and enrich academic debates about Edwards and traditionalism. Many scholars propose that a bridge be built between the pietism of Cotton and that of Edwards; these homologies provide some materials for prospective constructions. A full consideration of Edwards in light of the Cambridge theism might usefully challenge the routine practice of positioning him within the English Enlightenment tradition.[63] Attention to his Sibbesian rhetoric, for example, affords an alternative context in which to read controversial aspects of Edwards's theology. Rather than the *forma ab extra* of Lockean epistemology invoked by Perry Miller, God's essential effulgence could provide a foundation for understanding Edwards's seemingly radical definition of grace as a new sense.

Similarly, Edwards's conviction that God is a communicating being suggests a less tortured explanation for his controversial typologizing of nature, challenging the usual appeal that is made to the new science as his primary inspiration. While many scholars have claimed that Edwards's understanding of God's dynamism is indebted to the philosophy of Enlightenment, far fewer have traced his primitivist borrowings from seventeenth-century theology.[64] For Edwards, God's disposition to communicate himself inspired and sanctified all human idioms, so that even the vocabulary of science became theologically resonant. Just as Edwards baptized Lockean language into traditional pietist discourse, so too he converted Newton's tropes of mass and force into types of God's glory.[65]

I must not be misunderstood as saying that Edwards's deployment of Enlightenment discourse is to be dismissed, however. Though I object to representations of Edwards as a thinker divided against himself, reconstructing a falsely unified "mind"—albeit theist rather than modernist—is not my intent.[66] Edwards articulated his theology at the intersection of a number of competing discourses. His negotiation among these positions is of great interest, but the multivocality of his corpus calls for assessment in light of his indebtedness to more traditional Christian sources.

Rereading Edwards in light of Sibbesian piety also revises regnant genealogical models, modifying our understanding of his postmillennialism and his commitment to religious nationalism. Rather than elaborating and extending the opinions of the orthodox Puritan patriarchs as Sacvan Bercovitch has argued, Edwards's postmillennialism reverses their tribalist mentality by evoking the universalizing aspirations last sounded in the Brethren's summons to the church international.[67] Moreover, recognition of his opposition to preparationism, as well as his repudiation of church admissions based on any standard other than a melted heart, challenges interpretive models that position Edwards in a direct and homogeneous trajectory from Winthrop to Emerson and beyond. An alternative and less cynical genealogy may substantiate a connection from Edwards to Sibbes, temporarily reversing the direction of our gaze away from the present and back to a more complex Puritan past. This realignment will have whiggish consequences as well, changing the position of Emerson and Whitman in relation to more nuanced Puritan origins.

There are many other ways to reread Edwards's pietism. One might abandon such genealogical projects altogether in favor of an intensely local analysis. Edwards's advocacy of affectionate religion is meaningfully constituted within and against the horizon of his contemporaries' rationalism and his own family dynamic. A local study might embed Edwards's utterances in these immediate cultural and discursive contexts while still deploying a variety of explanatory models.[68] Given that the orthodoxy of his day tilted toward the rationalist side, Edwards may have discovered pietism as a way to individuate himself within that larger religious culture. As suggested above, a density of specific local contexts—personal, psychological, social and political—inflected his articulation of pietism.

Neither local nor genealogical, yet another analytic might divorce Edwards from his American context altogether, to read him in light of the larger history of Christian theology. His quarrel with rationalist religion could be cast as part of a trans-historical cycle within Christian thought generally—one involving recurrent oscillations between spiritism and rationalism, grace and effort, love and calculation, piety and discipline. Such philosophical and ethical interpretations occupy a large place in Edwards scholarship; the inclusion of the Sibbesian piety would enrich that conversation by providing an additional instance that would specify and historicize Edwards's articulation of these categories.[69]

In raising these alternative possibilities, I do not want to force choices between diachronic and synchronic readings, general and local knowledge—indeed, my aspiration throughout this study has been to describe local discursivities while also exposing myths of origin. Accordingly, the provisional notes of these concluding reflections on Edwards's relation to a Sibbesian tradition serve to remind that adjudicating these claims is a matter of greater delicacy than is often supposed. My desire is to open the discussion out to other possible readings and approaches.

Besides enriching academic debates, however, these questions might have another relevance. There is a pleasure in naming these homologies and entertaining these possibilities—the intense pleasure of recognition that not only constitutes part of our enjoyment and purpose in studying the past, but also inclines us in the specific, embodied instance to be self-reflexive, to ask more general as well as more personal questions about how we understand the formation of selves and subjects, the relationship between self-conscious articulations and the currents of discourse that precede such constructions. One may find a pleasure in the possibility of mutual transformations as well as in the recognition of incommensurable differences in the imagined articulation of other voices with our own. Borrowing from poet Charles Olson, I propose the author and subject Jonathan Edwards as a "complex of occasions," a self experienced and articulated in relation to voices long dead but also saturated by his own immediate present.[70] As such, Edwards resides as epilogue, an integral part of this study of the Cambridge piety but also beyond its proper boundaries.

Notes

Introduction

1. Cotton Mather, *Magnalia Christi Americana; or, the Ecclesiastical History of New England,* 2 vols., ed. Thomas Robbins (London, 1702; rpt., Hartford: Silas Andrus and Son, 1855), 1:25, 23.

2. Perry Miller, *Errand into the Wilderness* (Cambridge: Harvard University Press, 1956), pp. vii–ix. Miller experienced this now famous vision while "seeking adventure" on the banks of the Congo. To modern readers the unconscious imperialism of his self-imagining as a latter-day Gibbon and of his vision of America as "vacant wilderness" is painfully clear.

3. Miller is not alone in personalizing his own critical errand into the meaning of Puritanism for later American culture. Sacvan Bercovitch foregrounds his identity as a Canadian "outsider" and a son of political radicals to provide the context for his resistance to a Puritan ideology that he reads as "a mode of consensus designed to fill the needs of a certain social order," by means of which Puritans "managed more effectively to explain away their greed" and to provide a script for bourgeois subjectivity; *The Rites of Assent: Transformations in the Symbolic Construction of America* (New York: Routledge, 1993), pp. 1–29, 32. Drawing on his experience as a scholar who came to maturity in post Vietnam America, Andrew Delbanco poignantly depicts a Puritanism conflicted within itself and agonized over the corruptions of power; "The Puritan Errand Re-Viewed," *Journal of American Studies,* 18:3 (1984), 343–360. By historicizing their own critical errands, they provide a ground for understanding all readings as partial, multiple, and supplementary. For an excellent review of these positions, see Donald Weber, "Historicizing the Errand," *American Literary History,* 2:1 (1990), 101–118. Of my own investment in the Puritans, I would observe that I find a less readable continuity with the orthodox patriarchs, though obviously I do identify with those ministers

who preached a different sort of piety and who learned to coexist within the standing order.

4. I borrow these terms from William Haller, who makes a distinction in passing between the "intellectual fathers of independency" and the larger Spiritual Brotherhood of dissenting Puritans. He does not argue, however, for the partisan divisions here described; *The Rise of Puritanism* (New York: Columbia University Press, 1938), p. 79.

5. For a description of this style of piety, see Perry Miller, *The New England Mind: The Seventeenth Century* (Cambridge: Harvard University Press, 1939), chap. 1.

6. *The Complete Works of Richard Sibbes*, 7 vols., ed. Alexander Grosart (Edinburgh, 1862–1864), 6:4.

7. Sibbes, *Works*, 1:60; John Cotton, *Christ the Fountaine of Life* (London, 1651), pp. 134–135.

8. Sibbes, *Works*, 3:11.

9. See Pierre Bourdieu, *Outline of a Theory of Practice*, trans. Richard Nice (Cambridge: Cambridge University Press, 1977), chap. 4, for a helpful discussion of orthodoxy within a social field. Bourdieu defines *orthodoxy* as "straight, or rather *straightened*, opinion." It is the "necessarily imperfect substitute" for doxa, the structures of thought and practice that appear "as self-evident." *Doxa* is distinguished from *orthodoxy* in that the latter implies "awareness and recognition of the possibility of different or antagonist beliefs" (pp. 169, 164).

10. Some scholars do argue for significant differences between individual ministers, but none trace the configuration of party allegiance here advanced. See Darrett Rutman, *American Puritanism: Faith and Practice* (Philadelphia: Lippincott, 1970); R. T. Kendall, *Calvin and English Calvinism to 1649* (Oxford: Oxford University Press, 1979); William Stoever, *"A Faire and Easie Way to Heaven": Covenant Theology and Antinomianism in Early Massachusetts* (Middletown, Conn.: Wesleyan University Press, 1978). Recent work compatible with aspects of my argument include Michael Schuldiner, *Gifts and Works: The Post-Conversion Paradigm and Spiritual Controversy in Seventeenth-Century Massachusetts* (Macon, Ga.: Mercer University Press, 1991), and Andrew Delbanco's beautiful account of *The Puritan Ordeal* (Cambridge: Harvard University Press, 1989). I will make my differences and agreements with these studies clear as this book unfolds.

11. For a brief but useful analysis of hegemony, counter-hegemony, alternative and residual cultural formations, see Raymond Williams, *Marxism and Literature* (Oxford: Oxford University Press, 1977), pp. 108–127.

12. Perry Miller, *Orthodoxy in Massachusetts, 1630–1650* (1933; rpt., Gloucester, Mass.: Peter Smith, 1965), pp. 22, 105; *New England Mind: Seventeenth Century*, p. vii. Miller's suspension of interest in individual authorship gains new life, however, in the context of contemporary discourse theory. For general assessments and criticisms of Miller's work, consult James Hoopes, "Art as History: Perry Miller's *New England Mind*: A Symposium," *American Quarterly*, 34 (1982), 3–25; Michael McGiffert, "American Puritan Studies in the 1960's," *William and Mary*

Quarterly, 3d ser., 27 (1970), 37–67; and David Hall, "On Common Ground: The Coherence of American Puritan Studies," *William and Mary Quarterly,* 3d ser., 44 (1987), 193–229.

13. This is not to suggest that Miller did not see differences within the mainstream culture—indeed he more than anyone appreciated the distinctiveness of the spiritist piety of Cotton and Davenport. But most often his definition of orthodoxy in terms of church polity and the evolution of federal theology led him to emphasize consensus. In this account not just Perkins and Ames but Preston, Sibbes, and Cotton participate equally in converting the free promise of salvation into the covenant "arrangement between equals," the "bargain between two persons with duties on both sides." Miller was in fact in sympathy with the anti-preparationists; he critiqued the crypto-Arminianism implicit in federal theology, observing that "it is one of the ironic dramas of the human intellect" that the idiom of covenant subverted the Augustinianism of the theologians; Miller, "The Marrow of Puritan Divinity," in *Errand into the Wilderness,* pp. 61, 49. Yet this was the drama he traced.

14. See Philip Gura et al., "Forum: The Study of Colonial American Literature, 1966–1987: A Vade Mecum," *William and Mary Quarterly,* 3d ser., 45:2 (1988), 305–353, for a recent discussion of scholarly issues in the field.

15. Though scholars interested in doctrinal issues have identified important areas of difference among Puritans, they regard these conflicts as less significant than consensus within the broad Reformed tradition. See Hall, "On Common Ground," for a summary of the work of these "seminary historians." Other seminary scholars, such as Stoever, Kendall, McGiffert, and John Coolidge, *The Pauline Renaissance in England: Puritanism and the Bible* (Oxford: Clarendon, 1970), have cogently argued for a dialectical and multivocal Puritan tradition on the basis of single doctrinal issues, but they have not been successful in undermining the overall power of Miller's argument.

16. For a review of the work of social historians, see James A. Henretta, "The Morphology of New England Society in the Colonial Period," *Journal of Interdisciplinary History* 11 (1971–72), 379–398. On popular religion see David Hall, *Worlds of Wonder, Days of Judgment: Popular Religious Belief in Early New England* (New York: Knopf, 1989), especially pp. 3–20, 239–246; Charles Hambrick-Stowe, *The Practice of Piety* (Chapel Hill: University of North Carolina Press, 1982); and Charles Cohen, *God's Caress: The Psychology of Puritan Religious Experience* (New York: Oxford, 1986). These studies discover a general consensus of belief and practice among the clerical elite.

17. Most notable among feminist readings are Ann Kibbey, *The Interpretation of Material Shapes in Puritanism: A Study of Rhetoric, Prejudice, and Violence* (Cambridge: Cambridge University Press, 1986); Ivy Schweitzer, *The Work of Self-Representation: Lyric Poetry in Colonial New England* (Chapel Hill: University of North Carolina Press, 1991); and Amanda Porterfield, *Female Piety in Puritan New England: The Emergence of Religious Humanism* (New York: Oxford University Press, 1992).

18. For examples, see William Cronon, *Changes in the Land: Indians, Colonists,*

and the Ecology of New England (New York: Hill and Wang, 1983); James Axtell, *The European and the Indian: Essays in the Ethnohistory of Colonial North America* (Oxford: Oxford University Press, 1981); Francis Jennings, *The Invasion of America: Indians, Colonialism, and the Cant of Conquest* (New York: Norton, 1975).

19. Sacvan Bercovitch, *The Puritan Origins of the American Self* (New Haven: Yale University Press, 1975), p. 46. Two recent books have set out to revise Bercovitch's revision of Miller's Puritan errand. Theodore Bozeman and Andrew Delbanco have challenged Bercovitch's representation of the Puritan errand as prospective, to be transformed into America's manifest destiny. Their Puritans are less ebullient about progress and more nostalgic for an earlier pre-capitalist order. Rather than projecting the millennial dawn, they are interested in living ancient lives, lives based on a primitive purity. In general, I agree with their conclusion as it applies to the preparationist orthodoxy. Surprisingly, however, they leave the assumption of consensus in the first generation relatively untouched, substituting one version of a univocal culture for another. While they interestingly redefine the character and tone of Puritan self-conceptions and American exceptionalism, with some qualifications both scholars argue that the experience of migration produces a shared set of behaviors and identities among members of the first generation. It is important to note that while Delbanco successfully identifies essential oppositional elements of the Cottonian tradition, he nonetheless chronicles the emergence of an American voice that inevitably must neutralize these differences or demote them to the status of a residual formation. Continuities of ideas and associations in the transatlantic context lose to Delbanco's own sense of American exceptionalism, one based on remorse rather than anticipation. Focus on the "experience of becoming American" inevitably underwrites an exceptionalist model. Delbanco, *Puritan Ordeal,* p. 1; Bozeman, *To Live Ancient Lives: The Primitivist Dimension in Puritanism* (Chapel Hill: University of North Carolina Press, 1988).

20. Sacvan Bercovitch, *The American Jeremiad* (Madison: University of Wisconsin Press, 1978), pp. 49, 37, 42, 64. Indeed, in this construction preparationism, as the "personal analogue to the tribal concept of errand," literally becomes "the doctrinal counterpart" of the secular mission. Bercovitch also revised Miller's conception of the jeremiad tradition, arguing that the Puritans came to read all events as part of a redemptive history in which each affliction or national failure confirmed the presence of God's corrective hand and the continuance of his promise (pp. 49, 55). Bercovitch has argued that what is uniquely American about the jeremiad, unlike the Hosead tradition of Old England, is this conversion of God's chastening into a confirmation of ultimate success.

21. Bercovitch, *Rites of Assent,* p. 32.

22. Bercovitch, *American Jeremiad,* p. xii. In Bercovitch's broad context, oppositional views are seen as minor fluctuations in a homogeneous mainstream; they do not interrupt "the overall consistency of rhetoric and approach" that he claims is intrinsic to American Puritanism. Allowing in a general way that Cotton did

have doctrinal differences with the other ministers, Bercovitch is uninterested in the specific character of these differences. To his mind, Cotton's anti-preparationism, along with his rejection of covenant as contract, are less important than his agreements with the orthodoxy. In this context, the Antinomian Controversy as well as later conflicts retain little significance as moments of rupture or volatility in which alternatives within the dominant culture were formulated; *American Jeremiad*, p. 62; *Puritan Origins*, p. 144. The centerpieces of this argument are John Cotton's "God's Promise to his Plantations" and John Winthrop's "A Modell of Christian Charity," which Bercovitch treats as harmonious utterances. Although Winthrop and Cotton were occasionally aligned, as this book will show, they were deeply antagonistic in the 1630s—Winthrop charged Cotton with responsibility for shattering the peace of the commonwealth.

In a more recent formulation, Bercovitch describes America as "a symbolic *field*," spawning "varieties of co-optation, varieties of dissent, and above all varieties of co-optation/dissent." In this formulation of later American culture, adversarial forms reaffirm the culture by their very opposition. Interestingly, however, his depiction of Puritan culture does not admit of even this limited version of variety but remains univocal; *Rites of Assent*, p. 20.

23. Williams, *Marxism and Literature*, p. 114. These "varying formations," Williams asserts, "resist any simple reduction to some generalized hegemonic function" (p. 119). Referring to Williams's formulations, Bercovitch observes, "My assumption is that oppositional forms, like those of cohesion, co-optation, and incorporation, are fundamentally and variously forms of culture. 'Emergent,' 'residual,' 'anti-hegemonic,' 'utopian'—all such definitions of the subversive are useful insofar as we de-mystify their claims to transcendence, universality and the Real"; *Rites of Assent*, pp. 345–346. It is not my intention to challenge Bercovitch's own a priori assumptions or to defend Williams, but instead to argue that in this specific, concrete historical instance an alternative to the orthodox culture was expressed in Puritan New England.

24. For discussion of sectarian groups as proving the orthodoxy's powers of assimilation, see Stephen Foster, "New England and the Challenge of Heresy, 1630–1660: The Puritan Crisis in a Transatlantic Perspective," *William and Mary Quarterly*, 3d ser., 38 (1981), 624–660, and his impressive elaboration of that case in *The Long Argument: English Puritanism and the Shaping of New England Culture, 1570–1700* (Chapel Hill: University of North Carolina Press, 1991); and Philip Gura, *A Glimpse of Sion's Glory: Puritan Radicalism in New England, 1620–1660* (Middletown: Wesleyan University Press, 1984). Gura's "Prologue" is a useful essay on the new literature of sectarianism. Focusing on more radical groups, these scholars argue that the peculiar genius of American Puritanism rested in its ability to absorb dissent and to convert it to the uses of social cohesion. In general, they presume unanimity on the part of the Massachusetts Bay leadership, one which obviates the wrenching internal struggles over doctrine discussed here. In Gura's story, for example, radicals are ranged against "moderate Puritans," who are per-

ceived as a united front. By Gura's lights, Cotton was as much a master in co-opting radicals as any member of the orthodoxy, a "crafty pragmatist" who spoke from within the standing order (p. 160). Cotton is seen at times as an anomaly and at others as a representative of mainstream doctrine; but never as a spokesman for an alternative tradition, one neither sectarian nor preparationist.

25. Gura, *Glimpse of Sion's Glory*, p. 7.

26. While these scholars stop short of explicitly arguing that deviance was the necessary creation and confirmation of orthodoxy, their analysis retains an implicit conception of power as producing and containing its own subversion as its very "condition" of existence. For a similar view of the containment of subversion, see Stephen Greenblatt, "Invisible Bullets: Renaissance Authority and Its Subversion," in Jonathan Dollimore and Alan Sinfield, eds., *Political Shakespeare: New Essays in Cultural Materialism* (Ithaca: Cornell University Press, 1985), pp. 18–47.

27. My debt to these scholars it substantial. See Delbanco, *Puritan Ordeal;* Jesper Rosenmeier, "New England's Perfection: The Image of Adam and the Image of Christ in the Antinomian Crisis, 1634 to 1638," *William and Mary Quarterly*, 3d ser., 27 (1970), 435–459; Norman Grabo, "John Cotton's Aesthetic: A Sketch," *Early American Literature*, 3 (Spring 1968), 4–10; Teresa Toulouse, "The Arte of Prophesying: John Cotton and the Rhetoric of Election," *Early American Literature*, 19 (1985), 279–299; Coolidge, *Pauline Renaissance in England.*

28. See Geoffrey Nuttall, *The Holy Spirit in Puritan Faith and Experience* (Oxford: Basil Blackwell, 1946); James Maclear has written several articles on this topic, including "'The Heart of New England Rent': The Mystical Element in Early Puritan History," *Mississippi Historical Review*, 42 (1956), 621–652. See Heimert's running narrative in *The Puritans in America: A Narrative Anthology*, ed. Alan Heimert and Andrew Delbanco (Cambridge, Mass.: Harvard University Press, 1985). All of these scholars cite the importance of Sibbes in the genealogy of Cotton's thought and have been invaluable sources for my own work. Recently, Schuldiner's *Gifts and Works* picks up their clue. I concur with some of Schuldiner's claims: we both agree that Sibbes and Perkins constitute two schools within early Puritanism. Elaborating and extending the work of William Stoever's *"Faire and Easie Way,"* Schuldiner, however, focuses his discussion on points of doctrine (primarily soteriology) exclusively, without considering either processual definitions of orthodoxy or the social and political contexts and implications of religious ideology. He identifies "orthodoxy" as a stable category—roughly synonymous with a Calvinist definition of faith—and claims that Ames articulated a compromised position that allowed both Cotton and Hooker to operate comfortably within that predetermined category. Naming the antinomian dispute as the "Hutchinsonian Controversy," he reinscribes the preparationist orthodoxy's own preferred version of the episode as a dispute between a clearly marginal group and a more or less stable and centered "orthodoxy."

29. Samuel Clarke, himself a student of Thomas Hooker, barely mentions Hooker or Ames in his *Lives* of the leading Caroline divines. See *A general*

martyrologie . . . Whereunto are added the lives of sundry modern divines (London, 1651) and *A collection of the lives of ten eminent divines . . .* (London, 1662). These men are liminal figures in Haller's genealogy of leadership in the Caroline church as well; *Rise of Puritanism*, p. 79. Haller focuses on more prominent actors of the British historical stage.

30. Miller, "Preparation for Salvation in Seventeenth-Century New England," in *Nature's Nation* (Cambridge: Harvard University Press, 1967), p. 60.

I. NEW ENGLAND WAYS

1. The classic expositions of errand are Perry Miller, "Errand into the Wilderness," in *Errand into the Wilderness* (Cambridge, Mass.: Harvard University Press, 1956); and Sacvan Bercovitch, *The American Jeremiad* (Madison: University of Wisconsin Press, 1978). Revisions include Theodore Dwight Bozeman, "The Puritan's 'Errand into the Wilderness' Reconsidered," *New England Quarterly,* 59 (June 1986), 231–251, and *To Live Ancient Lives: The Primitivist Dimension in Puritanism* (Chapel Hill: University of North Carolina Press, 1988); Andrew Delbanco, "The Puritan Errand Re-Viewed," *Journal of American Studies,* 28 (1984): 343–360; see also Delbanco's *The Puritan Ordeal* (Cambridge, Mass.: Harvard University Press, 1989); Stephen Foster, *The Long Argument: English Puritanism and the Shaping of New England Culture, 1570–1700* (Chapel Hill: University of North Carolina Press, 1991). See also Virginia DeJohn Anderson, "Migrants and Motives: Religion and the Settlements of New England, 1630–1640," *New England Quarterly,* 56 (September 1985): 339–383, and *New England's Generation: The Great Migration and the Formation of Society and Culture in the Seventeenth Century* (Cambridge: Cambridge University Press, 1991); David Cressy, *Coming Over: Migration and Communication between England and New England in the Seventeenth Century* (Cambridge: Cambridge University Press, 1987).

2. John Winthrop, *The History of New England from 1630 to 1649,* ed. James Savage (1853; rpt., New York: Arno Press, 1972), p. 213. In reconstructing the sequence of events in this chapter I have relied on Winthrop's *History,* though with full awareness of the partisanship of his account. Even a cursory examination of the manuscript of the *History* reveals the bias of Winthrop's record. Large blanks, additions, and deletions at key points in the original manuscript suggest Winthrop's intention to "rewrite" history in the original. Marginal additions, only some of which Savage includes in the body of his transcription, also testify to Winthrop's ongoing process of self-revision. Tragically, the manuscript of the second volume—the text chronicling October 1636 to December 8, 1644, and detailing the Antinomian Controversy—was accidentally destroyed by fire in 1825. For commentary on the manuscript of the *History* see Richard S. Dunn, "John Winthrop Writes His Journal," *William and Mary Quarterly,* 3d ser., 41:2 (1984), 185–212; also Mary Jane Lewis, "A Sweet Sacrifice: Civil War in New England" (Ph.D. thesis, State University of New York, Binghamton, 1986). In my reconstruction of events, dates conform to the "old style" of the Puritans' calendar, except

that the new year is considered to begin January 1, not March 25. I have not double-dated for the months between these two dates. In transcribing passages, I have followed as closely as possible the spelling and punctuation of the actual manuscripts or editions consulted.

3. Winthrop, "A Short Story of the Rise, reign, and ruine of the Antinomians, Familists, & Libertines, that infected the Churches of New-England," in *The Antinomian Controversy, 1636–1638: A Documentary History,* ed. David Hall (Middletown, Conn.: Wesleyan University Press, 1968), pp. 253, 201.

4. Studies of the Antinomian Controversy are numerous. An informative bibliography is supplied by David Hall in *The Antinomian Controversy.* See also Amy Lang, *Prophetic Woman: Anne Hutchinson and the Problem of Dissent in the Literature of New England* (Berkeley: University of California Press, 1987); and Emery Battis, *Saints and Sectaries: Anne Hutchinson and the Antinomian Controversy in the Massachusetts Bay Colony* (Chapel Hill: University of North Carolina Press, 1962). Seventeenth-century sources include [Edward] *Johnson's Wonder-Working Providence, 1628–1651,* ed. J. Franklin Jameson (1654; rpt., New York: Charles Scribner's Sons, 1910); William Hubbard's *A General History of New England, From the Discovery to 1680* (Cambridge, Mass.: Massachusetts Historical Society, 1815); Cotton Mather's *Magnalia Christi Americana; or, the Ecclesiastical History of New England,* 2 vols., ed. Thomas Robbins (London, 1702; rpt., Hartford: Silas Andrus and Son, 1855).

5. Johnson, *Wonder-Working Providence,* pp. 152, 131, 133.

6. Thomas Shepard, *The Parable of the Ten Virgins,* in *The Works of Thomas Shepard . . . with a Memoir of his Life and Character,* 3 vols., ed. John Albro (Boston, 1853; rpt., New York: AMS Press, 1967), 2:197.

7. Mather, *Magnalia,* 1:266.

8. Winthrop, *History,* p. 213.

9. Winthrop, "Short Story," p. 254. For a counterargument, see James F. Cooper, Jr., "Anne Hutchinson and the 'Lay Rebellion' Against the Clergy," *New England Quarterly,* 61 (1988), 381–397.

10. Giles Firmin, *A Brief Review of Mr. Davis's Vindication* (London, 1693).

11. Winthrop, *History,* p. 220.

12. Winthrop, "Short Story," pp. 200, 254. This same desire to project a vision of harmony may have prompted Winthrop to "save" Cotton from the aggression of the other preachers in the course of Hutchinson's civil trial. See Hall, *Antinomian Controversy,* p. 343. Winthrop's motive may have been to protect the charter at a time when the colony was under scrutiny. For the probable dating of the original compilation of the "Short Story" as 1638, see Dunn, "John Winthrop Writes His Journal," pp. 202–203. The "Short Story" was first published anonymously in 1644. Thomas Weld edited this first edition, producing the version now published in Hall, *Antinomian Controversy.*

13. See Hall, *Antinomian Controversy,* pp. 210–212; also Winthrop, *History,* pp. 177–179.

14. Winthrop, *History*, pp. 209–211.

15. The full passage, quoted from Winthrop, *History*, p. 213, reads: "The differences in the said points of religion increased more and more, and the ministers of both sides (there being only Mr. Cotton of one party) did publickly declare their judgments in some of them, so as all men's mouths were full of them. And there being, 12 mo. 3, [1636] a ship ready to go for England, and many passengers in it, Mr. Cotton took occasion to speak to them about the differences, &c. and willed them to tell our countrymen, that all the strife amongst us was about magnifying the grace of God; one party seeking to advance the grace of God within us, and the other to advance the grace of God towards us, (meaning by the one justification, and by the other sanctification;) and so bade them tell them, that, if there were any among them that would strive for grace, they should come hither; and so declared some particulars. Mr. Wilson spake after him, and declared, that he knew none of the elders or brethren of the churches, but did labour to advance the free grace of God in justification, so far as the word of God requireth; and spake also about the doctrine of sanctification, and the use and necessity, &c. of it; by occasion whereof no man could tell (except some few, who knew the bottom of the matter) where any difference was: which speech, though it offended those of Mr. Cotton's party, yet it was very seasonable to clear the rest, who otherwise would have been reputed to have opposed free grace. Thus every occasion increased the contention, and caused great alienation of minds; and the members of Boston (frequenting the lectures of other ministers) did make such disturbance by publick questions, and by objections to their doctrines, which did any way disagree from their opinions; and it began to be as common here to distinguish between men, by being under a covenant of grace or a covenant of works, as in other countries between Protestants and Papists." For an alternative interpretation, see Philip Gura, *A Glimpse of Sion's Glory: Puritan Radicalism in New England, 1620–1660* (Middletown, Conn.: Wesleyan University Press, 1984), pp. 172, 249. Gura offers a more sanguine reading of Cotton's speech as an attempt to "make the best of a highly serious situation."

16. Both Stephen Foster and Philip Gura claim that the introduction of conversion narratives and congregational ordination were mechanisms for establishing uniformity, but also exercises "in accommodating the enemy's strongest emotional appeals without sacrificing the essential commitment to a disciplined and orderly godliness"; Stephen Foster, "New England and the Challenge of Heresy, 1630–1660: The Puritan Crisis in Transatlantic Perspective," *William and Mary Quarterly*, 3d ser., 38 (1981), 654–657, and *Long Argument*, pp. 160–163. Gura observes that "Cotton and his fellow ministers buttressed in yet another way the New England Way against flank attacks by colonists who held more radical notions of church reformation . . . Beginning in 1637, with Bulkeley's installation in the Concord church, it became the rule for ministers to renounce their episcopal ordination and to assume the prerogatives of their new positions only after their election by the visible saints in their new church"; Gura, *Glimpse of Sion's Glory*, p. 179. Yet to

assume that Cotton sanctioned this new institutional control as a check on radicalism is to neglect the key fact that he refused to attend. I argue that these two ecclesiastical innovations were not in any measure concessions to spiritism, but attempts to control and extinguish it. They served as normalizing rituals as well as sites of surveillance. As a result of them, conversion narratives were routinized and ordination was placed under the supervision of a council of appointed "orthodox" ministers.

17. Winthrop, *History*, pp. 210, 217–218.

18. Winthrop, *History*, p. 189. The Concord church was first gathered on July 5, 1636; the ordination of the ministers took place in a separate ceremony on April 6, 1637. On the procedures for forming new churches, see J. William T. Youngs, Jr., "Congregational Clericalism: New England Ordinations before the Great Awakening," *William and Mary Quarterly*, 3d ser., 31:3 (1974), 481–490.

19. The transcription of this letter is included in Lawrance Thompson's unpublished M.A. thesis (Columbia University, 1932), pp. 115–116 (hereafter cited as "Letters of Cotton"). Thompson established the date of the letter as July 5, 1636. Sargent Bush, Jr., who is currently working on a modern edition of the Bulkeley–Cotton correspondence, seems to concur with this date. See Bush's "John Cotton's Correspondence: A Census," *Early American Literature*, 24 (1989), 91–111. His edition of the letters will greatly enhance our understanding of Cotton's career.

20. Manuscript letter, Prince Collection, Boston Public Library, Ms. Am. 1506, pt. 2, no. 7. Cited by courtesy of the Trustees of the Boston Public Library. I am indebted to Sargent Bush for kindly sharing his transcription of this very challenging manuscript. Copy within raised caret marks (^) was inserted between lines in the original.

21. Ibid. In May 1637, Winthrop provided a succinct version of Bulkeley's quarrel in his *History*, pp. 221–222: "The difference was, whether the first assurance be by an absolute promise always, and not by a conditional also, and whether a man could have any true assurance, without sight of some such work in his soul as no hypocrite could attain unto." By May 27, 1638, Cotton wrote Samuel Stone, pleading for unity and disavowing what he described as the extremes of Hutchinson's opinions. See Thompson, "Letters of Cotton," pp. 144–146, for a transcription of this document.

22. Hall, *Antinomian Controversy*, pp. 210, 209, 254.

23. John Wheelwright, "Fast Day Sermon," in Hall, *Antinomian Controversy*, pp. 158, 160, 165.

24. See Hall, *Antinomian Controversy*, pp. 152–153, 294.

25. Roger Williams as quoted in *The Puritans in America: A Narrative Anthology*, ed. Alan Heimert and Andrew Delbanco (Cambridge, Mass.: Harvard University Press, 1985), p. 209.

26. For a summary of the relevant scholarship, see Hall's review article, "On Common Ground: The Coherence of American Puritan Studies," *WMQ*, 3d ser., 44 (1987), 193–229. For scholars arguing for Cotton's unique theological position, see William Stoever, *"A Faire and Easie Way to Heaven": Covenant Theology and*

Antinomianism in Early Massachusetts (Middletown, Conn.: Wesleyan University Press, 1978); R. T. Kendall, *Calvin and English Calvinism to 1649* (Oxford: Oxford University Press, 1979); Perry Miller, *The New England Mind: The Seventeenth Century* (Cambridge, Mass.: Harvard University Press, 1939); Perry Miller, "'Preparation for Salvation' in Seventeenth-Century New England," in *Nature's Nation* (Cambridge, Mass.: Harvard University Press, 1967), pp. 50–77; John Coolidge, *The Pauline Renaissance in England: Puritanism and the Bible* (Oxford: Clarendon Press, 1970); Michael Schuldiner, *Gifts and Works: The Post-Conversion Paradigm and Spiritual Controversy in Seventeenth-Century Massachusetts* (Macon, Ga.: Mercer Press, 1991); and Delbanco, *Puritan Ordeal*. For Cotton as representative of the Puritan mainstream, see Ann Kibbey, *The Interpretation of Material Shapes of Puritanism: A Study of Rhetoric, Prejudice, and Violence* (Cambridge: Cambridge University Press, 1986); Charles Lloyd Cohen, *God's Caress: The Psychology of Puritan Religious Experience* (New York: Oxford University Press, 1986); and Sacvan Bercovitch, *The Puritan Origins of the American Self* (New Haven: Yale University Press, 1975), and *American Jeremiad*.

27. See Winthrop's "Short Story," pp. 202–203, for a list of the charges leveled at the dissenters.

28. "Sixteene Questions of Serious and Necessary Consequence," in Hall's *Antinomian Controversy*, pp. 43–60, articulates these differences. In addition to texts cited above, Jesper Rosenmeier, "New England's Perfection: The Image of Adam and the Image of Christ in the Antinomian Crisis, 1634–1638," *WMQ*, 3d ser., 27 (1970), 435–459, provides an excellent gloss on the issues. See also Stoever, *"Faire and Easie Way,"* pp. 192–199, for a helpful discussion of preparationism.

29. Shepard, *Works*, 1:32. Delbanco, in *The Puritan Ordeal*, argues a different case. In his reading, while in England Hooker as well as Cotton viewed sin as privative; migration and settlement precipitated a shift in their conception to a view of sin as positive (*passim*, especially pp. 53–56). I believe their conceptions of sin as privative or positive had less to do with the experience of the wilderness than with the larger constellations of thought and temperament here described. Cotton, along with Sibbes and Davenport, conceived of sin as privative before and after the Great Migration, just as Hooker and Shepard regarded sin as positive long before their transplantation to America.

30. Cotton, *Christ the Fountaine of Life* (London, 1651), p. 36. These gendered images—Hooker's image of the heart as menstrual cloth (*The Soules Preparation* [London, 1632], p. 31) or Cotton's favored image of the soul as waiting vessel—call out for comment. Among others, Ivy Schweitzer, *The Work of Self-Representation: Lyric Poetry in Colonial New England* (Chapel Hill: University of North Carolina Press, 1991), addresses the feminization of piety in Puritan discourse, arguing that figuration of the saint's conversion as subjection to a masculine God produces a gendering of conversion—what she describes as gynesis in Puritan discourse. Again, I would wish to qualify the general applicability of her argument with the observation that not all Puritans preached the same doctrine. Hooker may have preached a morphology of conversion that demanded a "feminized" subjection

followed by a reconversion to "masculinity" as a son of God, as Schweitzer argues. On the other hand, he often depicts the saint as masculine throughout the process, as hammering the heart, storming the throne of God, or enjoying a *husband's* privilege, with Christ figured as the submissive bride: "the soule is satisfied with Christ, and the riches of his grace . . . that which makes the love of a husband increase towards his wife, is this, *Hee is satisfied with her breasts at all times, and then hee comes to bee ravished with her love* . . . so hope hath an expectation of mercy, and is satisfied therewith; desire longs for mercy, and is satisfied therewith; the will closeth Christ, and it is fully satisfied with him"; Thomas Hooker, *The Soules Exaltation* (London, 1638), pp. 5–6. Cotton, however, almost always begins and ends with what Schweitzer would call a "feminized" piety; the saint does not relinquish passivity and is not, as Schweitzer claims, reconverted to masculinity. Cotton's rhetorical style, with its emphasis on incantatory repetition over linear argument, might be interestingly glossed as a version of "feminized writing." In this context, Sibbes's observation that women have greater natural piety than men may have more to do with their ready identification with his feminized language; see, for example, *The Complete Works of Richard Sibbes,* 7 vols., ed. Alexander Grosart (Edinburgh, 1862–64), 3:143. Similarly, Cotton's appeal to Anne Hutchinson and Mary Dyer may perhaps be related to his pietistic style. The eighteenth-century commentator Charles Chauncy suggests that feminized religion, hysteria, and antinomianism were of a piece with Cottonian piety. See Chauncy, "Preface," *Seasonable Thoughts on the State of Religion in New England* (Boston, 1743). These are not my questions in this book, but asking them might prove an interesting way to complicate the current tendency to homogenize Puritan discourse in relation to questions of gender.

31. See Cotton's *The Way of Life* (London, 1641), pp. 175–184.

32. Cotton, *Way of Life,* pp. 174–175. Cotton never repented this position. See *The Way of Congregational Churches Cleared* in Hall, *Antinomian Controversy,* p. 405.

33. [Thomas Shepard], *God's Plot: The Paradoxes of Puritan Piety: Being the Autobiography & Journal of Thomas Shepard,* ed. Michael McGiffert (Amherst: University of Massachusetts Press, 1972), p. 74 (hereafter cited as Shepard, *Journal*).

34. See Schuldiner, *Gifts and Works,* for a reading of these two groups in terms of this stable, theological reading of "orthodoxy." Many sociologists of religion discuss orthodoxy in terms of social process: see Kai Erikson, *Wayward Puritans: A Study of the Sociology of Deviance* (New York: John Wiley and Sons, 1966). See also Pierre Bourdieu's *Outline of a Theory of Practice,* trans. Richard Nice (Cambridge: Cambridge University Press, 1977), pp. 159–170.

35. For one defense of Cotton's high Calvinism, see Kendall, *Calvin and English Calvinism.* Kendall has argued that among the Puritan divines he studied, "John Cotton is the only major figure . . . to take Calvin seriously" (p. 211). Discounting his deep roots in English Puritanism in general and in the thought of Richard Sibbes specifically, and casting the whole of the New England clergy as essentially Arminian, Kendall makes the same claim for Cotton's theological purity and

isolation that Perry Miller was to repent having made on behalf of Jonathan Edwards.

36. Some historians characterized preparationism as proto-Arminian; most do not. Stoever, *"Faire and Easie Way,"* shows how the doctrine evolved within a traditional theological frame; see also Norman Pettit, *The Heart Prepared: Grace and Conversion in Puritan Spiritual Life* (New Haven: Yale University Press, 1966); Patrick Collinson, "Towards a Broader Understanding of the Early Dissenting Tradition," in *Godly People: Essays on English Protestantism and Puritanism* (London: Hambledon Press, 1983), p. 539.

37. See Winthrop, *History,* pp. 82–89, 177–179; Darrett B. Rutman, *Winthrop's Boston: Portrait of a Puritan Town, 1630–1649* (New York: Norton, 1965), pp. 27–32; also, Perry Miller, "Thomas Hooker and the Democracy of Connecticut," in *Errand into the Wilderness,* p. 25. These early conflicts reveal the shifting "alliances" as participants worked out their vested interests. Opposition to Winthrop temporarily allied Vane, Haynes, Hooker, and Dudley. Later, Dudley and Hooker sided with Winthrop against Cotton, Hutchinson, and Vane. The point is that loose political alliances emerged and then transformed in a climate of oppositional politics. By 1636 the lines of division had come clear.

38. Winthrop, *History,* pp. 177, 178. See also Rutman's account in *Winthrop's Boston,* pp. 27–32; and Edmund S. Morgan, *The Puritan Dilemma: The Story of John Winthrop* (Boston: Little, Brown, 1958), pp. 104–107.

39. Winthrop, *History,* pp. 177–178.

40. This personal competition between Cotton and Hooker is noted in Mather's *Magnalia* and in Thomas Hutchinson's *The History of the Colony of Massachusetts Bay,* vol. 1 (rpt., New York: Arno Press, 1972), p. 43. Perry Miller argued that the theo-political dispute between Hooker and Haynes on the one side and Cotton, Vane, and Winthrop on the other was the motive force behind the Hooker migration; see "Thomas Hooker and the Democracy of Connecticut." See also Norman Pettit, "Lydia's Conversion: An Issue in Hooker's Departure," *Cambridge Historical Society, Proceedings 1964–1966,* vol. 40, pp. 59–83. In one of those moments that reveals the folly of insisting on absolute partisan difference, Hooker invited Cotton to be his co-pastor. Cotton's refusal may have fueled Hooker's resentment.

41. *Letters of John Davenport, Puritan Divine,* ed. Isabel Calder (New Haven: Yale University Press, 1937), p. 191; Cotton, *Way of Congregational Churches,* p. 241. See Gura, *Glimpse of Sion's Glory,* for the founding of these various radical colonies. On the fate of Whalley and Goffe, see Douglas C. Wilson, "Web of Secrecy: Goffe, Whalley, and the Legend of Hadley," *New England Quarterly,* 60 (1987), 515–548. For Cotton's defense of them, see Francis J. Bremer, "In Defense of Regicide: John Cotton on the Execution of Charles I," *William and Mary Quarterly,* 3d ser., 37:1 (1980), 103–124.

42. Many scholars have noted the prominence of the mercantile gentry among Cotton's supporters. See Rutman, *Winthrop's Boston,* p. 73; also, Bernard Bailyn,

The New England Merchants of the Seventeenth Century (Cambridge, Mass.: Harvard University Press, 1956), and Emery Battis, *Saints and Sectaries.*

43. Winthrop, *History,* p. 214.

44. Winthrop, *History,* pp. 214–216, 249.

45. Winthrop, *History,* p. 214.

46. The many strikeouts, obliterations, and revisions in all of the antinomian documents, including but not limited to Winthrop's accounts, suggest editing in favor of an "orthodox" version. In representing these events to an English public after 1640, the participants of the controversy were anxious that the colonial experiment seem harmonious and successful. Moreover, the archive is incomplete; there are losses, omission, and silences. Papers have been edited, lost, or destroyed, including many of Cotton's letters, papers relating to the Hutchinson controversy, and the biography of Cotton written by Davenport. See Calder, *Letters of John Davenport,* pp. 9, 212; also, Lewis, "A Sweet Sacrifice," for an equally suspicious reading of the archive.

47. Samuel Eliot Morison, *The Founding of Harvard College* (Cambridge, Mass.: Harvard University Press, 1935), p. 177.

48. Winthrop, *History,* p. 220.

49. Winthrop, *History,* p. 220.

50. See Hall, *Antinomian Controversy,* pp. 251–252; Winthrop, *History,* pp. 220, 245–246.

51. Winthrop, *History,* p. 224.

52. For Wheelwright's objections see *Mercurius Americanus* (1645; reprinted in Volume 9 of the publications of the Prince Society, Boston, 1876). [Wheelwright's authorship of this document in now in question. See Sargent Bush, "John Wheelwright's Forgotten *Apology:* The Last Word in the Antinomian Controversy," *New England Quarterly,* 64 (1991), 22–45.] Vane's objections to Winthrop's new law are recorded in his *A Brief Answer,* in Thomas Hutchinson's *A Collection of Papers Relating to the History Of Massachusetts Bay* (Boston: Thomas and John Fleet Publishers, 1769), pp. 67–71. These passages are taken from the transcription in Heimert and Delbanco, *Puritans in America,* pp. 164–167. It is interesting to note that at the trial the first query posed to Anne Hutchinson concerned her association with Wheelwright (see Hall, *Antinomian Controversy,* p. 312).

53. Winthrop, *History,* pp. 239–240.

54. See Winthrop, *History,* p. 245; Hall, *Antinomian Controversy,* pp. 278–280.

55. John Cotton, "The Way of the Congregational Churches Cleared," in *John Cotton on the Churches of New England,* ed. Larzer Ziff (Cambridge, Mass.: Harvard University Press, 1968), p. 241.

56. Sargent Bush, "'Revising what we have done amisse': John Cotton and John Wheelwright, 1640," *WMQ,* 3d ser., 45 (1988), 733–750; and Bush, "John Wheelwright's Forgotten *Apology.*"

57. "Examination of Mrs. Anne Hutchinson," in Hall, *Antinomian Controversy,* p. 314. To Winthrop's credit he later repented his harshness. Thomas Hutchinson

reports that on his deathbed Winthrop refused to banish a dissenter at Dudley's urging, saying "he had done too much of that work already." Hutchinson concludes that in the years in which Winthrop "pursued with great vehemence Mr. Vane's adherents . . . he might have some political views mixed with this instance of his zeal" (*History*, p. 151). This is an understatement!

58. [Shepard], "Thomas Shepard's Election Sermon, in 1638," in *New England Historical and Genealogical Register*, 24:4 (October 1870), 316, 363; Bulkeley, "Letter to Cotton, April 4, 1650," in Lemuel Shattuck, *A History of the Town of Concord* (Boston: Russell, Odiorne, and Company, 1835), p. 156.

59. As some historians have noted, the founding of Harvard College is deeply enmeshed in these disputes. Morison claimed that "one outcome of the contest was to fix the location of the College" (*Founding of Harvard College*, p. 172). Indeed, tracing the origins of Harvard in relation to the Antinomian Controversy confirms the orthodoxy's determination to control the college. Though Vane presided over the October 1636 session of the General Court in which the first financial provisions were made, final decision on the location of the College was delayed until November 15, 1637. By then the Cottonians had been deposed and Harvard was placed under Shepard's watchful gaze. Shepard himself writes, "because this town (then called Newtown) was through God's great care and goodness kept spotless from the contagion of the opinions, therefore at the desire of some of our town . . . the Court for that and sundry other reasons determined to erect the college here" (Shepard, *Journal*, p. 68). During the controversy, Winthrop frequently expressed anxiety about Wheelwright's influence on "Scholars," arguing that "the next generation, which shall bee trained up under such doctrines, will bee in great danger to prove plain Familists and Schismaticks" ("Short Story," p. 279). Just as the Puritans in Old England recognized the importance of controlling Emmanuel, so Winthrop knew that the power of the political orthodoxy relied on the production of "orthodox" clerics (for an "official" expression of this position, see "New England's First Fruits" in Morison, *Founding of Harvard College*, p. 432). As Harry Stout has observed, "Harvard College played an indispensable role in supplying cultural cohesion and hierarchical control"; *The New England Soul: Preaching and Religious Culture in Colonial New England* (New York: Oxford University Press, 1986), p. 57. See also Bernard Bailyn, "Foundations," in *Glimpses of the Harvard Past*, ed. Bailyn et al. (Cambridge: Harvard University Press, 1986), pp. 1–18; and especially Alan Heimert, "Let Us Now Praise Famous Men," *Cambridge Review* (1985).

60. See Robert G. Pope, *The Half-Way Covenant: Church Membership in Puritan New England* (Princeton: Princeton University Press, 1969).

61. The careers of Hooker and Davenport in Holland illustrate the blurring that is possible in a context of more substantive division. When the Amsterdam congregation called Davenport they were expecting "Mr. Hooker under another name." See Keith L. Sprunger, *Dutch Puritanism: A History of English and Scottish Churches of the Netherlands in the Sixteenth and Seventeenth Centuries* (Leiden: Brill,

1982), pp. 112, 146. Debate over the importance of religion in the prewar period is a staple of English historiography. Nicholas Tyacke, for one, has argued that general consensus reigned in the English Church until the advent of Laud; "Puritanism, Arminianism and Counter-Revolution," in *The Origins of the English Civil War,* ed. Conrad Russell (London: Macmillan, 1973), pp. 119–43. For a general review of the literature, see Andrew Foster, "Church Policies of the 1630s," in *Conflict in Early Stuart England: Studies in Religion and Politics, 1603–1642,* ed. Richard Cust and Ann Hughes (London: Longman, 1989), pp. 193–223; and Peter Lake's *Moderate Puritans and the Elizabethan Church* (Cambridge, New York: Cambridge University Press, 1982).

62. Indeed the very process of debate forced refinement of the terms of difference. During her trial Anne Hutchinson frequently suggested that the dynamic of interrogation exaggerated and perhaps even produced difference where it had not existed before; Hall, *Antinomian Controversy,* pp. 325, 331. For commentary, see Patricia Caldwell, "The Antinomian Language Controversy," *Harvard Theological Review,* 69 (1969), 345–367. Frank Shuffleton has observed that "it was Cotton's ultimate refusal to accept the preparationist theory of conversion which in many ways led to a subsequent passion for elaborately systematized descriptions of religious experience upon the part of the orthodox ministers"; *Thomas Hooker 1586–1647* (Princeton: Princeton University Press, 1977), p. 252. See also Delbanco, *Puritan Ordeal,* p. 176.

63. Erikson, *Wayward Puritans,* p. 21.

64. The battles of the 1630s might be seen as attempts to seize and determine the meaning of such terms as *justification, covenant,* and *faith.* The regulation of such words is, after all, the purpose of an established orthodoxy. Bakhtin argues that canonization of texts "is that process that blurs heteroglossia, that is, that facilitates a naive, single-voiced reading"; *The Dialogic Imagination,* trans. Caryl Emerson and Michael Holquist (Austin: University of Texas Press, 1981), pp. 417–418, 425. Canonization might be seen as a literary analogue to the establishment of an orthodoxy in religion. It is in this sense that the Antinomian Controversy might properly be called a language controversy. Patricia Caldwell also sees the antinomian problem as a language controversy, although her argument concerns the complexities of an oral versus a written tradition and the ambiguity of fixing meaning between these two modes. See "The Antinomian Language Controversy," *Harvard Theological Review,* 69 (1976), 345–367.

65. See Erikson, *Wayward Puritans;* Gura, *Glimpse of Sion's Glory,* for the consolidating effect of sectarian groups. See Raymond Williams, *Marxism and Literature* (Oxford: Oxford University Press, 1977), pp. 112–114, 120–127, for a discussion of alternative forms within hegemony.

66. Emily Dickinson, "There's a certain Slant of light," in *The Poems of Emily Dickinson,* ed. Thomas H. Johnson (Cambridge, Mass.: Harvard University Press, 1951), vol. 1, p. 185.

2. Societies of Saints

1. Those who tarried in England during the first years of William Laud's reign—men like Davenport, Shepard, and Norton—were undoubtedly marked by their exposure to the tactics of his regime. See Stephen Foster, *The Long Argument: English Puritanism and the Shaping of New England Culture, 1570–1700* (Chapel Hill: University of North Carolina Press, 1991), chap. 4, for the importance of timing of migration. Alternative genealogies are also suggested in Francis Bremer, "Increase Mather's Friends: The Trans-Atlantic Congregational Network of the Seventeenth Century," *Proceedings of the American Antiquarian Society*, 94:1 (1984), 59–96.

2. One need only recall that in the 1620s Roger Williams, Hooker, Cotton, and Davenport consulted together regarding the practice of nonconformity and the decision to emigrate. Though they were destined to engage in heated struggles with one another less than five years after their arrival in Massachusetts, in the 1620s they found ample common ground. One can multiply the instances of collaboration across the boundaries: In old England, they sometimes shared the same patrons—notably Warwick and Vere. Preston stipulated in his will that Sibbes, Cotton, Dod, Davenport, but also Hooker and Bulkeley should choose a book from his library; Irvonwy Morgan, *Prince Charles's Puritan Chaplain* (London: Allen and Unwin, 1957), p. 43. Hooker is said to have invited Cotton to share his New World pulpit, though Cotton wisely refused. Bulkeley wept at Cotton's grave and Cotton wrote an elegy for Hooker. So, too, when true antinomians emerged in the 1650s, Goodwin, Nye, and Norton were in some measure drawn back from their own spiritist leanings. Despite his allegiance to Cottonian piety, by the end of the 1650s Norton became a staunch defender of the Half-Way Covenant and an opponent of Davenport. These examples testify to the mutability of boundaries under the external pressures of persecution by prelates and challenges by ranters and other sectaries. They also evidence a general agreement on key issues that must be remembered. They do not, however, diminish the existence or importance of the partisan allegiances that the Antinomian Controversy made all too palpable.

3. See Perry Miller, *The New England Mind: The Seventeenth Century* (Cambridge, Mass.: Harvard University Press, 1939), chap. 1; Peter Lake, *Moderate Puritans and the Elizabethan Church* (Cambridge, New York: Cambridge University Press, 1982), pp. 3–4, 46–54.

4. Describing an earlier generation, Lake observes that the radicals, "driven on by the considerations of ideological and polemical consistency, almost welcomed the confrontation with the conformists, and instead of seeking to limit and turn aside the conformist case tried rather to up the stakes and press for a final showdown with the bishops" (Lake, *Moderate Puritans*, p. 48). This would overstate the case for Hooker and Shepard, but the spirit of doctrinal consistency on formal aspects of the faith did produce a similar intransigence.

5. Cotton Mather, *Magnalia Christi Americana; or, the Ecclesiastical History of*

New England, 2 vols. ed. Thomas Robbins (London, 1702; rpt., Hartford: Silas Andrus and Son, 1855), 1:255; John Norton, *Abel Being Dead Yet Speaketh* (London, 1658), p. 13; see also Samuel Clarke, *A Collection of the Lives of Ten Eminent Divines* (London, 1662), p. 58. Modern biographies of Cotton include Larzer Ziff, *The Career of John Cotton: Puritanism and the American Experience* (Princeton: Princeton University Press, 1962); and Everett Emerson, *John Cotton* (New York: Twayne Publishers, 1965). I have relied on these sources for details of Cotton's life.

6. Mather, *Magnalia*, 1:255; Norton, *Abel Being Dead*, pp. 12–13.

7. Norton, *Abel Being Dead*, p. 12; Mather, *Magnalia*, 1:255. Many scholars mistake the role of Sibbes in Cotton's religious biography, attributing his conversion to Perkins's preaching.

8. Mather, *Magnalia*, 1:255. Michael McGiffert in "Grace and Works: The Rise and Division of Covenant Divinity in Elizabethan Puritanism," *Harvard Theological Review*, 75 (1982), 463–502, charts the beginnings of preparationism in the distinction between the two covenants.

9. James Maclear, "'The Heart of New England Rent': The Mystical Element in Early Puritan History," *Mississippi Valley Historical Review*, 42 (1956), 621–652, argues that Sibbes is the most important theologian of the 1630s.

10. Dod, "To the Christian Reader," a preface to Sibbes's *Bowels Opened*, 2:4, in *The Complete Works of Richard Sibbes*, 7 vols., ed. Alexander Grosart (Edinburgh: James Nichol, 1862); for Firmin's comment, see Sibbes, *Works*, 5:455.

11. Mather, *Magnalia*, 1:255.

12. Sibbes, *Works*, 6:541.

13. Mather, *Magnalia*, 1:255.

14. Norton, *Abel Being Dead*, p. 14; Mather, *Magnalia*, 1:256. For details of the life of Preston, I have relied on Thomas Ball's "Life of Dr. John Preston" in Samuel Clarke, *A generall martyrologie . . . Whereunto are added the lives of sundry modern divines* (London, 1651); Morgan, *Prince Charles's Puritan Chaplain;* and Irvonwy Morgan, *The Godly Preachers of the Elizabethan Church* (London: Epworth Press, 1965). Also essential is Christopher Hill, *Puritanism and Revolution: Studies in Interpretation of the English Revolution of the Seventeenth Century* (1958; rpt., New York: Schocken, 1964).

15. Mather, *Magnalia*, 1:256.

16. Grosart, "Memoir of Richard Sibbes, D.D.," in Sibbes, *Works*, 1:1.

17. It is important to note that my use of this language of spiritual birth rehearses the Puritans' own appropriation of images of generativity, usurping female prerogatives by claiming male reproductive power alone. To their flocks they were to be dispensers of "spiritual milk" for babes, as the title of Cotton's catechism claims. For commentary on this issue of gender and Puritan language, see Ivy Schweitzer, *The Work of Self-Representation: Lyric Poetry in Colonial New England* (Chapel Hill: University of North Carolina Press, 1991).

18. Sibbes, *Works*, 1:xxxviii, xxi.

19. Sibbes, *Works*, 1:lxxv. See also J. T. Cliffe, *The Puritan Gentry: The Great*

Puritan Families of Early Stuart England (London: Routledge and Kegan Paul, 1984), p. 38.

20. A small measure of Sibbes's influence is the wide admiration he enjoyed. On his deathbed, John Wilson testified to the force of Richard Sibbes's eloquence. Anglicans as well as Puritans found much to value in him. It is said that George Herbert may have been one of his auditors, and there is a congruity of sentiment and expression between the two which supports this claim. Richard Baxter, one of the key pietists of the next generation, credits a reading of the "Bruised Reed" with his conversion. See Grosart, "Memoir," for these many links.

21. See Samuel Eliot Morison, *The Founding of Harvard College* (Cambridge, Mass.: Harvard University Press, 1935), p. 362, for a list of graduates of Emmanuel and the other Cambridge colleges. See also Sargent Bush, Jr., and Carl Rasmussen, *The Library of Emmanuel College, Cambridge, 1584–1637* (New York: Cambridge University Press, 1986), pp. 1–33, for the importance of Emmanuel. Again, I am not arguing for an exclusive network of affiliations; rather my goal is to trace lines of allegiance within the larger Puritan counterculture.

22. Morgan, *Prince Charles's Puritan Chaplain*, p. 18.

23. Norton, *Abel Being Dead*, pp. 32–33. See also Mather, *Magnalia*, 1:264. Similarly, Cotton's powerful articulation of his reasons for migrating persuaded Davenport to leave England; Alexander Young, *Chronicles of the First Planters of the Colony of Massachusetts Bay from 1623 to 1636* (Boston: Charles C. Little and James Brown, 1846), pp. 438–444. During the antinomian crisis, Davenport played counselor to both Cotton and Hutchinson. And when Goodwin and the dissenting Brethren were preparing the case for independency, they relied on Cotton and Davenport, along with Hooker, for advice. All three were invited to Westminster. Perhaps skeptical that their cause could prevail, Hooker declined. Reluctant to abandon Boston to the emergent orthodoxy, Cotton also refused. Only Davenport was anxious to attend, but prefiguring his troubles of 1669, the New Haven congregation refused him permission to leave.

24. Grosart, "Memoir," in Sibbes, *Works*, 1:li. For Arminianism at Cambridge, see Nicholas Tyacke, *Anti-Calvinism: The Rise of English Arminianism* (Oxford: Clarendon Press, 1987), chap. 2.

25. Grosart, "Memoir," in Sibbes, *Works*, 1:li.

26. Mather, *Magnalia*, 1:260.

27. Morgan, *Prince Charles's Puritan Chaplain*, p. 33.

28. See Sibbes and Davenport's "Preface" to Preston's *New Covenant or the Saintes Portion* (London, 1630) for the history of this literary enterprise.

29. Of course there are counter examples that once again remind that drawing distinctions must be tempered by an awareness of the shared Puritan project. When they felt imperiled by the onslaught of radical spiritism in the 1650s, for example, Goodwin and Nye sponsored the publication of Hooker's *Application of Redemption*. However, in the prewar decades the Brethren most often discovered common cause among themselves.

30. A few examples will serve: Just as Preston visited Cotton in old Boston, so Davenport and Vane were sheltered by Cotton on their arrival in New England. In the dark days of the Antinomian Controversy, it was to Davenport's New Haven that Cotton considered removal. Tracing the successive teachers invited to fill Cotton's Boston pulpit, for example, provides a moving and persuasive case for recognized partisan difference. John Owen, Cotton's convert, was the first choice of the Boston congregants. Cotton himself nominated his biographer and advocate, John Norton; and after Norton's death John Davenport was invited to fill the pulpit. Mather, *Magnalia*, 1:245.

31. For this reading of Sibbes's life, I have depended upon the following works: Alexander Grosart's "Memoir," in volume one of his edition of Sibbes's *Works;* Clarke's *Martyrologie;* William Haller, *The Rise of Puritanism* (New York: Columbia University Press, 1938); the various articles of James Fulton Maclear; Sidney Rooy's chapter on Sibbes in his *The Theology of Missions in the Puritan Tradition* (Grand Rapids: William Eerdmans Co., 1965); also important are the works of Geoffrey Nuttall, *The Holy Spirit in Puritan Faith and Experience* (Oxford: Basil Blackwell, 1946) and *Visible Saints: The Congregational Way, 1640–1660* (Oxford: Basil Blackwell, 1957); Norman Pettit, *The Heart Prepared: Grace and Conversion in Puritan Spiritual Life* (New Haven: Yale University Press, 1966); Richard Strier's *Love Known: Theology and Experience in George Herbert's Poetry* (Chicago: University of Chicago Press, 1983); John R. Knott, Jr., *The Sword of the Spirit: Puritan Responses to the Bible* (Chicago: University of Chicago Press, 1971); and two unpublished doctoral dissertations: Bert Affleck, "The Theology of Richard Sibbes, 1577–1635," diss., Drew University, 1969; Harold P. Shelley, "Richard Sibbes: Early Stuart Preacher of Piety," diss., Temple University, 1972.

32. Sibbes, *Works*, 1:xxiii and 5:491.

33. Sibbes, *Works*, 1:xxxvi. Most biographers agree that Sibbes was suspended from Trinity for nonconformity. Mark E. Dever's recent article, "Moderation and Deprivation: A Reappraisal of Richard Sibbes," *Journal of Ecclesiastical History*, 43:3 (July 1992), 396–413, confirms my claim that Sibbes's success was due to his moderate stance on conformity, but discounts most biographers' claims that Sibbes was ever suspended for nonconformity. Drawing from contemporary accounts, Grosart's nineteenth-century biography argues that Sibbes was ousted and that his return in 1633 followed immediately on the heels of the dissolution of the feoffees (Sibbes, *Works*, 1:cxi), suggesting that Laud was unable to thwart his patrons. According to Grosart, Laud's determination to rid the church of Puritan divines did not prevent Sibbes's reinstatement at Trinity.

34. This post was secured through the offices of Sir Henry Yelverton, among others; Grosart, in Sibbes, *Works*, 1:xxxix; Dever, "Moderation and Deprivation," p. 399.

35. Grosart speculates that, in addition to George Herbert, Francis Bacon, Jeremy Taylor, John Milton, along with the Veres, Egertons, Cromwells, Drakes,

and others, may have been in Sibbes's audience. See Sibbes, *Works,* 1:xli. See also Haller, *Rise of Puritanism,* p. 66.

36. Sibbes, *Works,* 1:xlii. Not surprisingly, when Sibbes refused, Preston became Ussher's next candidate.

37. Morgan, *Prince Charles's Puritan Chaplain,* p. 44; Cliffe, *Puritan Gentry,* pp. 100–101.

38. Cliffe, *Puritan Gentry,* p. 101.

39. Morison, *Founding of Harvard College,* p. 101; Morgan, *Prince Charles's Puritan Chaplain,* pp. 18–20, 34.

40. Ball, "Life of Preston," in Clarke's *Martyrologie,* pp. 478–480.

41. See William Hunt, *The Puritan Moment: The Coming of Revolution in an English Country* (Cambridge: Harvard University Press, 1983), pp. 177–179; Morgan, *Prince Charles's Puritan Chaplain,* pp. 85–91.

42. Morgan, *Prince Charles's Puritan Chaplain,* p. 26. For a less sanguine reading of Preston's influence, see Derek Hirst, "Court, Country, and Politics before 1629," in *Faction and Parliament: Essays on Early Stuart History,* ed. Kevin Sharpe (Oxford: Clarendon Press, 1978), pp. 112–113. In the same volume, S. L. Adams argues that modern assessments of Preston's influence rely too heavily on such hagiographies as Thomas Ball's "Life of Preston." While I agree that "the prominence they assign to Preston should not be accepted uncritically" as an indication of his palpable influence in the complex political world of the 1620s, the fact that his contemporaries regarded Preston as central to their cause does confirm his preeminence among Puritans themselves. Given the disappointments to the Puritan cause in the 1620s and early 1630s, including the York House conference, the Forced Loan, the dissolution of the feoffees, and the rise of Laud, it is arguable that Preston's power was somewhat illusory. However, I would counter that Sibbes and Preston cultivated the influence that was to be had, and along the way they inspired their followers with visions of internal reform; Adams, "Foreign Policy and the Parliaments of 1621 and 1624," in Sharpe, *Faction and Parliament,* pp. 145–146.

43. Paul Seaver, *The Puritan Lectureship: The Politics of Religious Dissent, 1560–1662* (Stanford: Stanford University Press, 1970), pp. 5, 135, 138, 200, 235, 289, discusses the importance and the efficacy of these networks of clergical patronage. See also Barbara Donagan, "The Clerical Patronage of Robert Rich, Second Earl of Warwick, 1619–1642," *Proceedings of the American Philosophical Society,* 120:5 (1976), 388–419, for discussion of the network of lectureships in Essex.

44. Ball, "Life of Preston," p. 483; Morgan, *Prince Charles's Puritan Chaplain,* pp. 19–20.

45. Cliffe, *Puritan Gentry,* p. 81.

46. Ball, "Life of Preston," p. 495; Morgan, *Prince Charles's Puritan Chaplain,* pp. 112–115.

47. Mather, *Magnalia,* 1:254.

48. Morison, *Founding of Harvard College,* pp. 92–94.

49. Norton, *Abel Being Dead,* pp. 16–17.

50. See Ziff, *Career of John Cotton,* pp. 52–70.

51. Stephen Foster makes a similar argument about the existence of an inner congregation in "English Puritanism and New England Institutions," in *Saints and Revolutionaries,* ed. David Hall et al. (New York: Norton, 1984), p. 10.

52. Indeed, Richard Cust suggests that Cotton was at the center of local opposition to the forced loan, among his other activities. See *The Forced Loan and English Politics, 1626–1628* (New York: Clarendon Press, 1987), pp. 131, 172. Freedom from episcopal scrutiny supported activist oppositional politics.

53. For details of Davenport's life I have relied on Franklin B. Dexter, "Sketch of the Life and Writings of John Davenport," *Papers of the New Haven Colonial Society,* 2 (1877), 205–238; Isabel Calder, *Letters of John Davenport, Puritan Divine* (New Haven: Yale University Press, 1937); Calder, *The New Haven Colony* (New Haven: Yale University Press, 1934); also A. W. M'Clure, *Lives of the Chief Fathers of New England* (Boston, 1846), vol 2.

54. When Davenport fled, it was first to Paget's church in Amsterdam, and then to become Hugh Peter's assistant in Rotterdam. See Calder, *New Haven Colony,* pp. 19–31.

55. Calder, *New Haven Colony,* p. 27.

56. Haller, *Rise of Puritanism,* pp. 75–79, 67–69; Morgan, *Prince Charles's Puritan Chaplain,* p. 45. See Calder, *Letters of John Davenport,* pp. 26–27, for Gouge's participation in the Palatinate campaign. As late as 1632, when the Puritans of Colchester sought Gouge's advice before selecting a new lecturer, Laud angrily rejected him, complaining, "When you want one, you must go first to Dr. Gouge and to Dr. Sibbes, and then you come to me: I scorn to be so used. I'll never have him to lecture in my diocese." Laud's response to Gouge is cited in Seaver, *Puritan Lectureship,* p. 256; and Donagan, "Clerical Patronage," p. 399.

57. At least as early as Hawthorne's sketch of Mistress Hutchinson, Cotton has been accused of cowardice in events of the Antinomian Controversy. Philip Gura, for example, characterizes Cotton's sermon at Salem as a crafty strategy designed to co-opt radicalism, rather than as a display of flexibility of mind; *A Glimpse of Sion's Glory: Puritan Radicalism in New England, 1620–1660* (Middletown: Wesleyan University Press, 1984). In fact, Cotton was both open to reconsideration of his ideas and also always willing to hedge, neither of which is inherently amoral.

58. Cotton, *Some Treasure Fetched out of Rubbish* (London, 1660), p. 8.

59. Cotton, *Christ the Fountaine* (London, 1651), p. 35.

60. "Cotton's Reasons for His Removal to New England," in Young, *Chronicles,* p. 443; Cotton, *God's Mercie Mixed with his Justice* (London, 1641), pp. 81–85.

61. Calder, *Letters of John Davenport,* p. 24.

62. Calder, *Letters of John Davenport,* pp. 33–38; for Cotton's defense of his sacramental practices, see *New England Historical and Genealogical Register,* 28 (1874), 137–139.

63. Young, *Chronicles*, p. 443; Norton, *Abel Being Dead*, pp. 16–20, esp. pp. 18–20, for this history of Williams and Dorchester; Young, *Chronicles*, p. 427.

64. Young, *Chronicles*, p. 427.

65. For treatment of this idea with respect to antinomianism, see Ross Pudaloff, "Antinomianism in Massachusetts Bay," *Semiotica*, 54:1/2 (1985), 157.

66. The importance of maintaining the pulpit is everywhere in Sibbes's sermons. In response to the question *"Whether a minister ought to leave his congregation in the time of pestilence, or not?"* Sibbes maintained, "he ought not; for he is not, in regard of the work of God, to esteem his own life"; *Works*, 5:52. By analogy, we might presume that Sibbes would have advocated covert resistance throughout Laud's reign. Sibbes maintained that "the way to hinder [popery] . . . from being built again, is to lay open divine truths, and to plant the ministry." Consequently, Sibbes both remained in his own pulpit and organized the feoffees to support the establishment of an able ministry; *Works*, 7:470–471. For Sibbes's attitude on "things indifferent," see *Works*, 1:290–291.

67. Young, *Chronicles*, p. 439.

68. Ball, "Life of Preston," p. 512.

69. Morgan, *Prince Charles's Puritan Chaplain*, pp. 174–183. See also Hunt, *Puritan Moment*, p. 196.

70. Puritan disgust with James is the subject of many histories. Christopher Hill's *The Century of Revolution, 1603–1714* (New York: Norton, 1961) and *Puritanism and Revolution* (1958) are good introductions to the subject.

71. Sibbes, *Works*, 1:99; 3:187. For other relevant passages, see 1:100, 125, 135; 3:198, 219; 4:215, 428; 5:235, 532; 6:235; 7:307.

72. Ibid., 7:307.

73. Bozeman distinguishes between millennialist sermons that look forward to the unfolding kingdom and those he calls "the traditional Deuteronomic patterns" that predict doom. Hooker's sermon seems to fall in the latter category. Theodore Bozeman, *To Live Ancient Lives: The Primitivist Dimension in Puritanism* (Chapel Hill: University of North Carolina Press, 1988), pp. 107, 195.

74. See, for example, Preston, *The Breast-plate of Faith and Love* (London, 1632), pp. 211–216.

75. J. Minton Batten, *John Dury: Advocate of Christian Reunion* (London, 1944), pp. 26, 52. See also Frances Yates, *The Rosicrucian Enlightenment* (London, Boston: Routledge and Kegan Paul, 1972). Dury later sent petitions to New England, where they were also endorsed. See John Norton, "Letter to John Dury from Ministers in New England" (London, 1664).

76. Sibbes, *Works*, 1:lviii. For accounts of this letter, see also Calder, *Letters of John Davenport*, pp. 26–27.

77. Sibbes, *Works*, 7:470.

78. Extant manuscripts relating to the feoffees are collected by Isabel Calder in *Activities of the Puritan Faction of the Church of England, 1633–1635* (London: SPCK,

1957); see p. iii. Mather, *Magnalia*, 1:322. Important accounts of these activities are to be found in the works cited above: Seaver, *Puritan Lectureship;* Haller, *Rise of Puritanism;* Morgan, *Prince Charles's Puritan Chaplain,* and Calder, *Letters of John Davenport* and *New Haven Colony.*

79. Preston and Sibbes had long since proved that independent posts like those at the Inns could be a safe haven against the reach of the Churchmen. Preston found in Lincoln's Inn a haven against anti-Puritan scrutiny. See Morgan, *Prince Charles's Puritan Chaplain,* p. 47. As Thomas Ball tells us of Preston, "for he saw when that holy blessed Dr. Sibbs was outed both of Fellowship and Lecture in the University, yet by the goodnesse and prudence of Sir Henry Yelverton, he was received and retained at Grays Inne"; "Life of Preston," p. 512. The feoffees were to replicate those conditions of safety and liberty. For a counterargument about Sibbes's suspension, see Dever, "Moderation and Deprivation."

80. Morgan, *Prince Charles's Puritan Chaplain,* pp. 174–183; Calder, *Activities of the Puritan Faction;* Seaver, *Puritan Lectureship,* pp. 88–92, 235–238, 251–255, 333–336. For structures of lay patronage, see Donagan, "Clerical Patronage."

81. Calder, *Activities of the Puritan Faction,* pp. 112–114, 79; Cliffe, *Puritan Gentry,* p. 81.

82. Laud, *Works,* III:253, as cited in Calder, *Activities of the Puritan Faction,* p. xxii.

83. Calder, *Activities of the Puritan Faction,* p. 100.

84. Many historians have agreed that Laud's fears were justified. See Haller, *Rise of Puritanism,* p. 81; Seaver, *Puritan Lectureship,* p. 88.

85. Calder, *Activities of the Puritan Faction,* pp. xiii, 76.

86. Laud also established new restrictions on the licensing of ministers and exacting standards of enforcement that made peaceful reformation nearly impossible; Seaver, *Puritan Lectureship,* chap. 8, esp. p. 253. Sibbes and Gouge remained loyal to subversion from within the church and were effective in garnering support, much to Laud's distress; ibid., 241.

87. In addition to Perry Miller's titles, see R. T. Kendall's *Calvin and English Calvinism to 1649* (London: Oxford University Press, 1979). For details of Ames's life I have relied on Keith L. Sprunger, *The Learned Doctor William Ames: Dutch Backgrounds of English and American Puritanism* (Chicago: University of Illinois Press, 1972); Sprunger, *Dutch Puritanism: A History of English and Scottish Churches of the Sixteenth and Seventeenth Centuries* (Leiden: E. J. Brill, 1982); *William Ames by Matthew Nethenus, Hugo Visscher, and Karl Reuter,* trans. Douglas Horton (Cambridge: Harvard Divinity School Library, 1965); and John D. Eusden, "Introduction," in William Ames, *The Marrow of Theology: William Ames 1576–1633,* trans. John D. Eusden (Boston: Pilgrim Press, 1968).

88. See Morison, *Founding of Harvard College,* pp. 330–333; Sprunger, *Learned Doctor Ames,* p. 77.

89. This warning, issued on the eve of Ames's exile to Holland, came from none

other than Paul Baynes, the preacher who converted Sibbes (see Mather, *Magnalia*, 1:245).

90. Mather, *Magnalia*, 1:236.

91. Sprunger, *Learned Doctor Ames*, pp. 129, 14–15, 112–113; see also Lee W. Gibbs, "Introduction," *William Ames: Technometry*, trans. Gibbs (n.p.: University of Pennsylvania Press, 1979), pp. 28–29. Cotton Mather commented that Hooker was "most Richarsonian." See Sargent Bush, Jr., *The Writings of Thomas Hooker: Spiritual Adventure in Two Worlds* (Madison: University of Wisconsin Press, 1980), pp. 238–239. I am indebted to Stephen Foster for pointing out the "Richarsonian" connection between many of the Amesians.

92. See Cotton's poem, "On my Reverend and dear Brother, Mr. Thomas Hooker," in Hooker's *A Survey of the Summe of Church Discipline* (London, 1648).

93. Hooker's conversion focused on "such a sense of his being exposed unto the just *wrath* of Heaven, as filled him with most unusual degrees of horror and anguish." He continued in this desperate state for quite some time; Mather, *Magnalia*, 1:333–334. For Hooker's biography I rely on Mather, *Magnalia;* Frank Shuffleton, *Thomas Hooker: 1586–1647* (Princeton: Princeton University Press, 1977); Bush, *Writings of Thomas Hooker; Thomas Hooker: Writings in England and Holland, 1626–1633,* ed. George H. Williams et al. (Cambridge, Mass.: Harvard University Press, 1975) (hereafter cited as *English Writings*); and Edward W. Hooker, *The Life of Thomas Hooker* (Boston, 1849).

94. Mather, *Magnalia*, 1:339. Mather reports that Hooker was the pastoral assistant in Rotterdam, a claim modern historians have come to doubt. See Bush, *Writings of Thomas Hooker,* pp. 64–65; Hooker, *English Writings,* "Essay 1" (by George Williams), pp. 1–36, and especially p. 306. The paucity of clear biographical data about this period of Hooker's life is curious, perhaps suggesting an element of obscurity in his English career, or at least a failure to preserve the details of his early biography.

95. Mather, *Magnalia*, 1:339–340.

96. Ibid., 1:340. See also Sprunger, *Learned Doctor Ames,* pp. 251–252.

97. I am indebted to Keith Sprunger's detailed portrait of these allegiances in *The Learned Doctor William Ames.*

98. M'Clure, *Lives of the Chief Fathers,* 2:13. Also Mather, *Magnalia,* 1:304; Sprunger, *Learned Doctor Ames,* p. 254.

99. Mather, *Magnalia*, 1:310.

100. Sprunger, *Learned Doctor Ames,* pp. 248–251.

101. Ibid., p. 254. See also Morison, *Founding of Harvard College,* p. 143.

102. John Albro, "Life of Shepard," in his edition of *The Works of Thomas Shepard . . . with a Memoir of his Life and Character* (Boston, 1853; rpt., New York: AMS Press, 1967), 1:lxix, lxxi; Morison, *Founding of Harvard College,* pp. 303–314.

103. Many scholars, including Harry Stout and David Hall, portray Shepard as a representative figure. His deep ambivalence problematizes this status. See Stout,

The New England Soul: Preaching and Religious Culture in Colonial New England (New York: Oxford University Press, 1986), pp. 21–22, 35–38, 46–47. Also useful are Andrew Delbanco, "Thomas Shepard's America: The Biography of an Idea," in *Studies in Biography,* ed. Daniel Aaron (Cambridge, Mass.: Harvard University Press, 1978), pp. 159–82; Thomas Werge, *Thomas Shepard* (Boston: Twayne Publishers, 1987); and Michael McGiffert, "Introduction," in Shepard, *God's Plot: The Paradoxes of Puritan Piety: Being the Autobiography and Journal of Thomas Shepard,* ed. Michael McGiffert (Amherst: University of Massachusetts Press, 1972) (hereafter cited as *Journal*).

104. Shepard, *Journal,* pp. 41, 47; Mather, *Magnalia,* 1:381; Albro, "Life of Shepard," pp. xxvi–xxix.

105. Shepard, *Journal,* p. 47.

106. Albro, "Life of Shepard," in *Works,* pp. xxx, lxix–lxxx. Werge, *Thomas Shepard,* pp. 6–9; Shepard, *Journal,* pp. 46–47. As a matter of speculation, one might wonder why, given their control of so many lectureships, the Cambridge Brethren do not seem to have helped Shepard secure a pulpit after graduation. Shepard reports that before he entered the house of Thomas Weld he was anxious about his future: "But before I came there I was very solicitous what would become of me when I was Master of Arts, for then my time and portion would be spent, but when I came thither . . . Dr. Wilson had purposed to set up a lecture and give me £30 per annum"; Shepard, *Journal,* p. 46.

107. Shepard, *Journal,* p. 122.

108. Lucius Paige, *History of Cambridge, Massachusetts, 1630–1877* (Boston, 1877), pp. 51–53. Shepard listed among the reasons for removal "Mr. Vane will be upon our skirts."

109. See Shepard, *Journal,* pp. 42–48. For commentary on Shepard's ambivalence, see Delbanco, *The Puritan Ordeal* (Cambridge, Mass.: Harvard University Press, 1989), p. 160.

110. Shepard, *Journal,* p. 45.

111. Cotton, *The Way of the Congregational Churches Cleared,* in *John Cotton on the Churches of New England,* ed. Larzer Ziff (Cambridge, Mass.: Harvard University Press, 1968), p. 240.

112. Peter Bulkeley is something of an anomaly in this group. His ties to the preparationists seem ideological rather than biographical. As noted above, he was mentioned in Preston's will and was acquainted with Cotton in Old England. Certainly he was affluent and well connected. He too enjoyed the benevolent neglect of Williams's term as bishop of Lincoln, remaining in the family parish at Odell for over twenty years, until 1635.

Despite a personal history that would seem to group him with the Sibbesians, Bulkeley proved as staunch an enemy to Cotton's faith as any of the combatants. Bulkeley joined Shepard in launching the first attacks against Cotton in 1636 and was a central figure in the synod. His *Gospel-Covenant of Grace* was the summa of preparationist doctrine, receiving Shepard's endorsement. Though his correspondence with Cotton continued long after the Antinomian Controversy, as I note, the cordial tone of his letters is undercut by his persistent interrogation of Cotton's doctrines.

Every generalization has its exceptions, and Bulkeley stands as the anomalous case that usefully challenges my speculative prosopography. Such complexities must be granted without searching for a reductive and false consistency. Yet, I would also add that just as the Essex elites may have found preparationist preachers "prophets of the culture of discipline, at a time when the economic crisis made a reformation of manners more than ever imperative," perhaps Bulkeley (as a chief proprietor as well as preacher of Concord) discovered a sympathy with the secular as well as spiritual dimensions of preparationism. For Bulkeley's family history, see James M. Poteet, "A Homecoming: the Bulkeley Family in New England," *New England Quarterly*, 47 (1974), pp. 30–50. On Warwick, see Hunt, *Puritan Moment*, p. 198. The links between capitalism and preparationism are well-worn; see, for example, Michael Walzer, *The Revolution of the Saints: A Study in the Origins of Radical Politics* (Cambridge: Harvard University Press, 1965), chap. 6.

113. Sprunger, *Learned Doctor Ames*, p. 9.

114. *Winthrop Papers* (Boston: Massachusetts Historical Society, 1929–1947), 2:180; see also Sprunger, *Learned Doctor Ames*, p. 92; Morison, *Founding of Harvard College*, p. 143.

115. A. W. M'Clure, *The Lives of John Wilson, John Norton, and John Davenport* (Boston, 1846), p. 62.

116. Sprunger, *Learned Doctor Ames*, pp. 17, 254; Mather, *Magnalia*, 1:304.

117. Mather, *Magnalia*, 1:336.

118. When Shepard's first term at Earles-Colne expired after three years, his support was assumed by the congregation. In consultation with Shepard and Hooker, Wilson consented to moving the lectureship to Towcester. Albro, "Life of Shepard," pp. lxix, lxxiv.

119. Frank Shuffleton suggests that there was "a sort of shadow synod in that part of the country which held regular monthly meetings, and in these assemblies [Hooker's] voice was heard with respect"; *Thomas Hooker*, p. 74. See also Mather, *Magnalia*, 1:336. For the Essex confreres, see Hunt, *Puritan Moment*, chaps. 4 and 8; and Donagan, "Clerical Patronage."

120. For the publication history of the *Medulla* see John D. Eusden, "Preface," in Ames, *Marrow of Theology*, pp. 1–3; also Sprunger, *Learned Doctor Ames*, p. 77.

121. David Hall (ed.), *The Antinomian Controversy, 1636–1638: A Documentary History* (Middletown, Conn.: Wesleyan University Press, 1968), p. 104. However, there may be some difference between the way Hooker and Cotton use Ames. It may well be that citing Ames against his own disciples was Cotton's way of fighting fire with fire—a demonstration that they had exceeded their master in flirting with Arminianism.

122. Eusden, "Introduction," p. 65.

123. Sprunger, *Learned Doctor Ames*, p. 54.

124. Horton, *William Ames*, p. 30; Sprunger, *Learned Doctor Ames*, p. 24.

125. Sprunger, *Learned Doctor Ames*, p. 24.

126. On Abbot's liberality see Cliffe, *Puritan Gentry*, pp. 146–148.

127. Sprunger, *Learned Doctor Ames*, pp. 25, 33, 70.

128. Ibid, pp. 33, 63.; Horton, *William Ames*, p. 6. Nethenus insisted that Ames was not the author of the antiprelatical tract that precipitated his downfall; whether he was guilty or not, Ames's reputation for intransigence sealed his fate.

129. See Sprunger, *Learned Doctor Ames*, p. 70.

130. If Mark Dever ("Moderation and Deprivation," pp. 396–413) is correct in suggesting that Sibbes was never "outed," it is even more remarkable that he was maintained in his offices, since Sibbes was officially reprimanded for the 1627 circular on behalf of the Palatinate and brought to trial as one of the feoffees.

131. Seaver, *Puritan Lectureship*, p. 235.

132. Sprunger, *Learned Doctor Ames*, pp. 71–95.

133. Ibid., pp. 65, 70.

134. Donagan, "Clerical Patronage," pp. 390, 395. See Hunt, *Puritan Moment*, pp. 196–202. I have relied on these two sources for details of Rich's patronage.

135. Donagan, "Clerical Patronage," pp. 399–401, 407–408.

136. Ibid., pp. 405, 412–413.

137. Mather, *Magnalia*, 1:345.

138. Mather, *Magnalia*, 1:338. Bush, *Writings of Thomas Hooker*, p. 33; Morison, *Founding of Harvard College*, pp. 100–101.

139. Hunt, *Puritan Moment*, p. 196; see pp. 192–202 for Hooker's English career. Mather, *Magnalia*, 1:334.

140. Mather, *Magnalia*, 1:332 and 335; Bush, *Writings of Thomas Hooker*, pp. 3–4; Shuffleton, *Thomas Hooker*, pp. 12, 71–73. Hunt, *Puritan Moment*, pp. 196–197. Hooker's growing fame was such that Plymouth colony supporters chose the "Reverend Mr. Hooker" as an advocate in their quarrel over John Lyford. [William Bradford], *Of Plymouth Plantation, 1620–1647*, ed. Samuel Eliot Morison (New York: Alfred A. Knopf, 1979), pp. 167–168.

141. Bush, *Writings of Thomas Hooker*, p. 32.

142. Mather, *Magnalia*, 1:345 and 276. Hooker, *English Writings*, p. 211. For Hooker's peripatetic course, see the map of "The Travels of Thomas Hooker," ibid., p. ix.

143. See George H. Williams, "The Life of Thomas Hooker in England and Holland, 1586–1633," in Hooker, *English Writings*, p. 18, for the circumstances of Hooker's Dedham sermon.

144. Ibid., p. 213.

145. Mather, *Magnalia*, 1:336. Williams, "Life of Hooker," p. 20. Donager, "Clerical Patronage," pp. 395, 407–408. Hunt, *Puritan Moment*, p. 256.

146. As Donager observes ("Clerical Patronage," p. 408), Warwick "could do little beyond exerting the influence of his position, and by argument and interview obtaining some mitigation of punishment for his proteges. He could not modify

basic ecclesiastical policy, and Hooker, Peter, and Wilson all ended as refugees from England." To be sure, the harshness of Laud's policies meant that Warwick's influence was minimal in these cases. And yet, the unwillingness of these preachers to compromise sealed their fates.

147. Mather, *Magnalia*, 1:334, 340.

148. Morgan, *Prince Charles's Puritan Chaplain*, p. 17; Sprunger, *Learned Doctor Ames*, pp. 17,254–256.

149. Seaver, *Puritan Lectureship*, p. 241, records Laud's displeasure at learning of Davenport's conversion to nonconformity. In 1633 Laud complained to King Charles that Davenport—"whom I used with all moderation, and about two years since thought I had settled his judgment, having him then at advantage enough to have put extremity upon him, but forbore it"—had betrayed his kindness. Gouge and Sibbes, however, continued in their course of visible compliance and covert opposition, also to Laud's irritation; ibid., pp. 255–256.

150. Morgan, *Prince Charles's Puritan Chaplain*, chap. 6; Cliffe, *Puritan Gentry*, chap. 9. Similarly, one might consider the elements that allowed Davenport to outlast Hooker under Laud's regime. Surely, Davenport's compliance was a factor; yet it is also true that he commanded a cadre of loyal patrons. His flexibility enabled Warwick, Conway, and others to lobby effectively on his behalf. The devotion of the Puritan gentry to their "eminent friends" among the clergy may well have been enhanced by this willingness of preachers to present themselves as conformable.

151. Cliffe, *Puritan Gentry*, pp. 28, 201.

152. Cliffe, *Puritan Gentry*, pp. 28–30.

153. Mather, *Magnalia*, 1:305–306.

154. Morgan, *Prince Charles's Puritan Chaplain*, p. 17.

155. Cliffe, *Puritan Gentry*, p. 38.

156. Jesper Rosenmeier, "John Cotton on Usury," *William and Mary Quarterly*, 3d ser., 47:4 (1990), 548–565, persuasively argues that Cotton opposed usury, in contrast to Winthrop's careful articulation of the circumstances in which the practice is allowable. The strong presence of prominent merchants among Cotton's followers, however, suggests that his position on usury did not challenge the economy of their mercantile network. It may be that their inner fellowship allowed cooperative effort and a flow of resources that enhanced their activities.

157. I am indebted to Cliffe, *Puritan Gentry*, chap. 6, for some of these observations.

158. Bernard Bailyn, *New England Merchants of the Seventeenth Century* (Cambridge, Mass.: Harvard University Press, 1956), p. 40. Darrett Rutman, in *Winthrop's Boston: A Portrait of a Puritan Town* (New York: Norton, 1972), p. 72, observes that the already stratified classes in Boston were further divided with the arrival of Cotton's congregants: "But in Boston the distinction was exaggerated after 1633 by the arrival of John Cotton's well-to-do friends and parishioners from Boston . . . families which had the desire and wherewithal to follow their beloved minister

to the New World—the Haughs, Leveretts, and Hutchinsons." Bailyn, in *New England Merchants,* p. 40, remarks the merchant support of Hutchinson, claiming the schism "uprooted some of the most flourishing merchants of Boston and prepared the soil of Rhode Island for the growth of a commercial community." Again, the lines of dispute are rife with coincidences that suggest this to be a battle of "ins" versus "outs" for control of the economy as well as an ideological dispute. Robert Keane, Wilson's brother-in-law, experienced a rise in fortune after the exile of Cotton's flourishing merchant-disciples.

159. For a useful study of the nineteenth-century marriage of evangelical piety and the work ethic, see Paul Johnson, *A Shopkeeper's Millennium: Society and Revivals in Rochester, New York, 1815–1837* (New York: Hill and Wang, 1978). The dynamic he traces between economics and religion may have application to seventeenth-century preparationists. Finney's desire to instill piety while insuring the sanctity of the work week mirrors Shepard's concerns on this issue. Hunt, *Puritan Moment,* pp. 197–198, makes a similar argument: "Puritan preachers like Hooker and Shepard were invaluable to local elites during the crisis of the 1620s and 1630s. For one thing, they were good for business." Not only bringing in visitors to the market towns, these "prophets of the culture of discipline" preached a routinized piety congenial to the structures of emergent capitalism. Again, I do not mean to suggest that clerical patronage is reducible to economic motivation or that preparationism is a "culture of discipline." Rather, these psychological and economic "fits" are at best subliminal and inchoate. On the conscious level, spiritual economy was the fundamental concern of Puritan gentry and preachers.

160. See Sacvan Bercovitch, *The American Jeremiad* (Madison: University of Wisconsin Press, 1978), the most persuasive framing of the marriage of preparationist and capitalist rhetorics. For a brief summary of Bercovitch's reading of the issue, see *The Rites of Assent* (New York: Routledge, 1993), pp. 30–32.

161. Rutman, *Winthrop's Boston,* pp. 61–77.

162. Hutchinson, *History of the Colony of Massachusetts Bay,* vol. 1 (rpt., New York: Arno Press, 1972), p. 43; Mather, *Magnalia,* 1:342; William Hubbard, *A General History of New England, from the Discovery to 1680,* in *Collections of the Massachusetts Historical Society,* 2d ser., 5 (1848), p. 173. The classic exposition of this conflict is Perry Miller, "Thomas Hooker and the Democracy of Connecticut," in *Errand into the Wilderness* (Cambridge, Mass.: Harvard University Press, 1956). See also Alan Heimert, "Let us Now Praise Famous Men," *The Cambridge Review,* November 1985.

3. Measuring Sin and Love

1. *The Complete Works of Richard Sibbes,* 7 vols., ed. Alexander Grosart (Edinburgh: James Nichol, 1862), 4:270.

2. William Ames, *The Marrow of Theology: William Ames, 1576–1633,* trans. John D. Eusden (Boston: Pilgrim Press, 1968), pp. 83–84.

3. Ibid., p. 84. See also John Norton, *The Orthodox Evangelist* (London, 1654), pp. 1–3.

4. Perry Miller, *The New England Mind: The Seventeenth Century* (Cambridge, Mass.: Harvard University Press, 1939), p. 14. See also R. T. Kendall, *Calvin and English Calvinism to 1649* (Oxford: Oxford University Press, 1979).

5. Among the many fine studies of covenant theology, see William Stoever, *"A Faire and Easie Way to Heaven": Covenant Theology and Antinomianism in Early Massachusetts* (Middletown, Conn.: Wesleyan University Press, 1978), pp. 81–119; and Michael McGiffert, "From Moses to Adam: The Making of the Covenant of Works," *Sixteenth Century Journal*, 19 (1988), 131–155.

6. Mary Cappello, "The Authority of Self-Definition in Thomas Shepard's Autobiography and Journal," *Early American Literature*, 24:1 (1989), 35–51, and Michael McGiffert, "Introduction," in Thomas Shepard, *God's Plot: The Paradoxes of Puritan Piety: Being the Autobiography and Journal of Thomas Shepard*, ed. Michael McGiffert (Amherst: University of Massachusetts Press, 1972), are among those who have discussed Shepard's ecstatic imagery. The early sections of Shepard's *Parable of the Ten Virgins* amply demonstrates his mystical strain. Hooker's modern biographers, Frank Shuffleton and Sargent Bush, have performed similar compelling readings of his works, citing such sermons as *The Soules Exaltation* or *The Paterne of Perfection*. I do not dispute the presence of poetic and even mystical elements in these preparationist preachers. Indeed, Hooker and Shepard at times wrote quite movingly of spiritual joy; so, too, they spoke of sin as privation of the good. Even while they urged sinners to prepare hearts, these preachers also held that Christ must first enter the hearts. Yet, I would also claim that on balance Hooker and Shepard stressed human cooperation over divine prevenience, that they were more ambivalent in their descriptions of spiritual union than in their rehearsals of humiliation and contrition. Even Andrew Delbanco, *The Puritan Ordeal* (Cambridge: Harvard University Press, 1989), pp. 173–174, allows for a reading of Hooker as an ecstatic preacher. Counter to Delbanco's claim of fundamental change in Hooker's spiritual economy after the migration, however, I would argue that while examples of ecstatic piety are on balance rarer in *all* of Hooker's writing than in Cotton's, such emotion is expressed in America as well as in England.

7. As noted above, some scholars do consider the issue of difference, but not along the party lines here argued. For a psychodynamic reading of individual ministers, see David Leverenz, *The Language of Puritan Feeling: An Exploration in Literature, Psychology, and Social History* (New Brunswick, N.J.: Rutgers University Press, 1980). For a generational reading, see Emory Elliott, *Power and the Pulpit in Puritan New England* (Princeton, N.J.: Princeton University Press, 1975). Another reader sensitive to these questions is Charles Cohen, who notes differences in the language of Cotton and Hooker but sees "the variation in nomenclature" not as substantive but as "a difference in treatment, one more tactical than dogmatic"; *God's Caress: The Psychology of Puritan Religious Experience* (New York: Oxford University Press, 1986), p. 85.

8. Ames, *Marrow of Theology*, pp. 92–3; Cotton, *The Way of Life* (London, 1642), p. 99.

9. Ames, *Marrow of Theology*, p. 92.

10. See Ames, *Marrow of Theology*, chaps. 4, 5, and 6. John Eusden offers an illuminating discussion of these modes in his Introduction to the text, pp. 22–24.

11. Ibid., pp. 84, 91.

12. Ibid., p. 84.

13. Compare the nine short pages devoted to essence and subsistence in the *Marrow of Theology* (pp. 83–91) with the lengthy exposition in Norton's *Orthodox Evangelist* (pp. 1–50).

14. In *The Soules Exaltation* (London, 1638), Hooker expresses a similar sense of inadequacy: "This is our misery, we content our selves with termes in the generall, and never cracke the shell that wee may see the kernell: wee never dive into the truth, that we may see the intent of the Spirit therein." This misery is attributable not merely to a failure of energy but to the limitations of human understanding. Hooker humbly concludes, regarding the "manner how the soule coms so to be knit to Christ . . . wee will open it so far as our light serves us" (p. 26).

15. Ames, *Marrow of Theology*, p. 86.

16. Norton, *Orthodox Evangelist*, p. 13.

17. Ames, *Marrow of Theology*, p. 92 and chap. 23.

18. "Introduction," *Marrow of Theology*, p. 20. Similarly, Luther's attraction to the gospels and focus on communion are seen as outside normative English experience. Such was not the case for the circle of Sibbes. This is not to suggest that the Sibbesians engaged in the mystical devotion characteristic of Catholic christology, but rather that they had a greater appreciation for this style of piety than is allowed by most scholars. For an insightful reading on the importance of Luther for the Sibbesians, see Richard Strier, *Love Known: Theology and Experience in George Herbert's Poetry* (Chicago: University of Chicago Press, 1983).

19. Miller, *New England Mind: Seventeenth Century*, p. 45.

20. Consider for example Ames's description of the death of Christ: "The consummation of his spiritual punishment as loss was the forsaking of him by his Father, as a result of which he was deprived of all sense of consolation . . . This death of Christ was true and not feigned. It was natural or from causes naturally working to bring it about, and not supernatural. It was voluntary and not at all compelled; yet it was violent and not from internal principle. It was also in a certain way supernatural and miraculous, because Christ kept his life and strength as long as he would and when he desired he laid it down" (*Marrow of Theology*, p. 144). This passage unfolds as a series of rational propositions and qualifications—a structure that, along with the spareness of diction, restrains the emotionalism usually accompanying meditation on Christ's sacrifice.

21. See for example Ames, *Marrow of Theology*, pp. 128, 135.

22. Ibid., p. 91. As John Eusden has pointed out, God's efficiency "is the major unifying theme throughout the *Marrow*, the *Conscience*, and his commentaries" ("Introduction," *Marrow of Theology*, p. 23).

23. Ames, *Marrow of Theology*, pp. 91–92.

24. Thomas Hooker, *Writings in England and Holland, 1626–1633*, ed. George H. Williams et al. (Cambridge, Mass.: Harvard University Press, 1975), pp. 201, 216. It is important to note that the domestication of power is achieved only by means of covenantal obligation.

25. *The Works of Thomas Shepard . . . with a memoir of his Life and Character*, 3 vols., ed. John Albro (1853; rpt., New York: AMS Press, 1967), 3:25; 1:32, 33, 42.

26. Ibid., 1:33.

27. Ibid., 1:45. Shepard never tires of warning "men [who] think God to be all mercy and no justice; all honey and no sting" (ibid., p. 39). In *The Soules Preparation* (London, 1632), Hooker offers the same cautions: "You must not thinke God is so gentle; No, hee will set all your sinnes in order before you, if not here for your humiliation, yet hereafter for your everlasting confusion" (p. 48).

28. In fact, Kendall declares that Sibbes comes close to suggesting universal atonement. This is not in fact the case, although it is true that he does not focus on sin or wrath. See Kendall, *Calvin and English Calvinism*, chap. 7.

29. Hooker, *The Soules Implantation* (London, 1637), p. 2; Shepard, *Works*, 1:32.

30. Hooker, *Soules Implantation*, p. 15.

31. Ibid., p. 91.

32. See for example Cotton, *Way of Life*, p. 40.

33. Shepard, *Journal*, p. 44. See also Leverenz, *Language of Puritan Feeling*, p. 126. For Shepard's "secret" mysticism, see Capello, "Authority of Self-Definition."

34. Hooker, *Soules Preparation*, p. 5.

35. Ibid., pp. 5–6.

36. Ibid., p. 6.

37. Shepard, *Works*, 1:28, 1:32.

38. For discussion of the general use of the marriage trope, see Edmund S. Morgan, *The Puritan Family: Religion and Domestic Relations in Seventeenth-Century New England* (New York: Harper and Row, 1944), pp. 160–164; and Ivy Schweitzer, *The Work of Self-Representation: Lyric Poetry in Colonial New England* (Chapel Hill: University of North Carolina Press, 1991), chap. 1. The question again turns on emphasis—all preachers spoke of spiritual marriage, but the Amesians less often and with less affect. Frequently they converted discussion away from the person of Christ to the dowry of personal salvation. See for example Hooker, *Soules Exaltation*, p. 133.

39. Hooker, *Soules Exaltation*, p. 59.

40. Hooker, *Soules Preparation*, pp. 9–10.

41. Legalism is a curious phenomenon. Though on the surface it seems to rest on reason, it actually begins with a profound conviction of irrationality, one which must be constrained by social, legal, and moral means, as Miller quite elegantly argues in his discussions of covenant theology.

42. Emerson, "Introduction" in Thomas Hooker, *Redemption: Three Sermons*, ed. Everett Emerson (Gainesville, Fla.: Scholars Facsimiles and Reprints, 1956), p. xi.

43. Hooker, *Soules Preparation*, p. 19.

44. Sibbes, *Works,* 4:241.

45. John Davenport, *The Saints Anchor-hold . . . Preached in Sundry Sermons* (London, 1682), p. 4; Cotton, *Way of Life,* p. 432.

46. Sibbes, *Works,* 1:73.

47. Ibid., 1:12–13. Davenport also describes Satan as distorting the mercy of God: "He presents all things unto them in false glasses; the comforts of God, in a diminishing glasse, that God may seem to them lesse merciful, lesse gracious than he is, and the promises of God lesse free, lesse general than they are; that all the consolations of God may seem small things to them"; *Saints Anchor-hold,* p. 6.

48. Cotton, *Way of Life,* pp. 112, 114.

49. Sibbes, *Works,* 3:35. Preston also marvels at the benevolence with which God establishes "a kind of equality between us," when nature would insist on gross disparity; *The New Covenant or the Saintes Portion* (London, 1630), p. 331.

50. Sibbes, *Works,* 3:149.

51. Ibid., 3:149; see also 1:12, 72, 95; 4:33; 5:180.

52. Ibid., 4:196.

53. Ibid., 4:241.

54. Cotton, *Way of Life,* p. 99.

55. Davenport, *Saints Anchor-hold,* pp. 3–5. Goodwin, too, says that "before great revelations and comforts to make them more sweet, and more welcome, God useth to withdraw himselfe then most, thereby preparing the heart for them"; *A Child of Light Walking in Darkness* (London, 1636), p. 128. Faith in God's goodness means that deprivation is understood as a prelude to blessings.

56. Sibbes, *Works,* 3:38.

57. Cotton, *Way of Life,* pp. 11, 8–9.

58. Sibbes, *Works,* 1:12.

59. Ibid., 5:484.

60. Ibid., 5:330; Cotton, *Christ the Fountaine of Life* (London, 1651), p. 36.

61. Norton, *Orthodox Evangelist,* "Preface," p. 38. See also Cotton's pledge that it is Christ, not the covenant promise, that remakes the heart, in *The Antinomian Controversy, 1636–1638: A Documentary History,* ed. David Hall (Middletown, Conn.: Wesleyan University Press, 1968), p. 99.

62. Sibbes, *Works,* 5:482, 480.

63. Ibid., 5:485.

64. Cotton, *Christ the Fountaine,* pp. 223–224.

65. Hooker, *Soules Exaltation,* pp. 30–31. This passage counters Hutchinson's claim that Hooker preached a doctrine of works, offering another instance of the rhetorical ambiguities found in Hooker's writings. Here, the soul is passive in regeneration; indeed, this sermon series frequently seems positively "Cottonian." However, spiritual transformation is worked by plucking and tearing the soul from sin. Moreover, in this sermon series devoted to the soul's exaltation, celebrating the pleasures of union with Christ is still deferred in favor of describing an unconsummated, painful process.

66. For an alternative interpretation of the place of sin as privation in Puritan thought, see Delbanco's *Puritan Ordeal.*

67. Sibbes, *Works,* 4:294.

68. See Cotton, *Christ the Fountaine,* pp. 144–145.

69. Sibbes, *Works,* 2:67.

70. Ibid., 1:264.

71. Cotton, *Christ the Fountaine,* p. 33 (emphasis mine).

4. THE GOSPEL-COVENANT OF GRACE

1. See Romans 3:20: "Therefore, by the deeds of the law there shall no flesh be justified in his sight; for by the law is the knowledge of sin." Luther, of course, turned this passage into a foundation text for the doctrine of justification by faith alone. "The whole nature and design of the law is to give knowledge, and that of nothing else save of sin, and not to discover or communicate any power whatever. This knowledge is not power, nor does it bring power, but it teaches and shows that there is no power here, but great weakness." See Martin Luther, "The Bondage of the Will," in *Erasmus-Luther: Discourse on Free Will,* trans. Ernest Winter (New York: Frederick Ungar, 1972), p. 126.

2. The essential differences between the two covenants of work and grace hinge on the issue of human cooperation and on the extension of the covenant beyond the tribe of Israel to the elect. See *The Marrow of Theology: William Ames, 1576–1633,* trans. John D. Eusden (Boston: Pilgrim Press, 1968), pp. 202–210; Perkins, "The Golden Chaine," chaps. 29–33, in *The Work of William Perkins,* ed. Ian Breward (Abingdon: The Sutton Courtenay Press, 1970); John Preston, *The New Covenant or the Saintes Portion* (London, 1630), pp. 365–388; and John Cotton, *The Covenant of Gods Free Grace* (London, 1641), pp. 2–11, for a discussion of these differences. Also, see Keith Sprunger, *The Learned Doctor William Ames* (Chicago: University of Illinois Press, 1972), pp. 150–152; William Stoever, *"A Faire and Easie Way to Heaven": Covenant Theology and Antinomianism in Early Massachusetts* (Middletown, Conn.: Wesleyan University Press, 1978), pp. 81–119; Charles Cohen, *God's Caress: The Psychology of Puritan Religious Experience* (New York: Oxford University Press, 1986), pp. 47–74; and Norman Pettit, *The Heart Prepared: Grace and Conversion in Puritan Spiritual Life* (New Haven: Yale University Press, 1966).

3. See Ames, *Marrow of Theology,* chap. 24, for a full delineation of differences between the old and new covenants.

4. For an introduction to the lively debates over covenant theology, see Michael McGiffert: "Grace and Works: The Rise and Division of Covenant Divinity in Elizabethan Puritanism," *Harvard Theological Review,* 75 (1982), 463–502; "From Moses to Adam: The Making of the Covenant of Works," *Sixteenth Century Journal,* 19:2 (Summer 1988), 131–155; and "Federal Theology: The Perkinsian Moment" (unpublished). See also Leonard Trinterud, "The Origins of Puritanism," *Church History,* 20 (1951), 37–57; Richard L. Greaves, "The Origins and Early Development of English Covenant Thought," *The Historian,* 31 (1968), 21–35; and

Charles Cohen, *God's Caress,* pp. 47–74, 283–284, for a summary of recent arguments and literature on covenantal thought.

5. Increase Mather, "Preface" to Samuel Willard's *Covenant Keeping: The Way to Blessedness* (London, 1682). For commentary, see Emory Elliott, *Power and the Pulpit in Puritan New England* (Princeton: Princeton University Press, 1975), p. 165. Mather here conflates the personal application of redemption with the communal covenant with God.

6. Perry Miller, "The Marrow of Puritan Divinity," in *Errand into the Wilderness* (Cambridge, Mass.: Harvard University Press, 1956), p. 60.

7. As Miller saw it, "no grounds for moral obligation or individual assurance could be devised so long as God was held to act in ways that utterly disregarded human necessities or human logic"; *Errand into the Wilderness,* p. 55.

8. For a recent formulation of this monolithic portrait of Puritan voluntarism, see R. T. Kendall, *Calvin and English Calvinism to 1649* (Oxford: Oxford University Press, 1979).

9. Norman Pettit's *Heart Prepared* led the way for this substitution of affect for reason in the formulation of covenant doctrine.

10. Stoever, *"Faire and Easie Way,"* pp. 100–118.

11. There is a vast body of literature on the genealogy of the covenant. In 1951, Leonard Trinterud initiated the question of two traditions in "The Origins of Puritanism." Trinterud argued that Calvin's covenant was precisely the unconditional, unilateral bond in which God does all. In this construction, faith is passive and precedes repentance as God's free gift. Beza, Bullinger, Zwingli, along with other Rhineland theologians, were credited with conceiving of covenant as bilateral, in which men and women are charged with some responsibility in fulfilling terms, most notably of faith. Trinterud argued that this influence was formative for the English Puritans as they set about formulating the covenant theology Miller described—one in which sovereignty was bound, faith rationalized, and human sinners placed at the center. Calvin's high road of free grace was supposedly preserved by a very small saving remnant. Jens Møller in "The Beginnings of Puritan Covenant Theology," *Journal of Ecclesiastical History,* 14 (1963), 46–67; Greaves in "English Covenant Thought"; and to some degree Norman Pettit have subscribed to the argument of a double tradition.

12. Lyle Bierma, "Federal Theology in the Sixteenth Century: Two Traditions?" *Westminster Theological Journal,* 45 (1983), p. 321. See also John von Rohr, *The Covenant of Grace in Puritan Thought* (Atlanta: Scholars Press, 1986), and "Covenant and Assurance in English Puritanism," *Church History,* 34 (1965), 195–203, for a rejection of the double-tradition argument. Michael McGiffert shows that while Perkins and Bulkeley may have flirted with legalism, they always drew back, hedging notions of human responsibility with assertions of divine prevenience; the distinction between grace and works evolved slowly. See "The Problem of the Covenant in Puritan Thought: Peter Bulkeley's *Gospel-Covenant," New England*

Historical and Genealogical Register, 130 (1976), 125; and "Grace and Works," pp. 481, 498.

13. *Thomas Hooker: Writings in England and Holland, 1626–1633,* ed. George Williams et al. (Cambridge, Mass.: Harvard University Press, 1975), p. 198 (hereafter cited as *English Writings*). Insistence on mutual obligation threads throughout Bulkeley's *The Gospel-Covenant: or the Covenant of Grace Opened* (London, 1646). See, for example, pp. 312–321.

14. *The Complete Works of Richard Sibbes,* 7 vols., ed. Alexander Grosart (Edinburgh: James Nichol, 1862), 6:4.

15. Francis Lyall, in "Of Metaphors and Analogies: Legal Language and Covenant Theology," *Scottish Journal of Theology,* 32 (1979), 1–17, argues that the distinctions between covenant and testament are mere linguistic ambiguities rather than differences in intended meaning. Charles Cohen similarly observes that preachers spoke both of contractual and unilateral covenants, depending on homiletic needs, but he does not agree that these variations reflect fundamental differences within Puritanism: "there were different ways of talking about the Covenant of Grace, and Cotton's preaching of it emphasized God's absolute sovereignty more than Preston's did (which is not to say that Preston ignored or even subordinated the issue), but the structures of their theologies do not lead to such radically different casts of mind . . . For the period under discussion, it is questionable whether one can distinguish styles of Puritan religious mentality based on distinctive modes of preaching the Covenant"; *God's Caress,* p. 53. Obviously, I disagree with Cohen's conclusion, but I would also amend his description of Cotton as emphasizing sovereignty.

16. See the preface to Shepard's "Ineffectual Hearing of the Word," as quoted by Albro in *The Works of Thomas Shepard . . .,* ed. John Albro (Boston, 1853; rpt., New York: AMS Press, 1967), 1:clxxxvii: "Where there are no law sermons, there will be few gospel lives."

17. McGiffert points to the "high Calvinism" of Bulkeley, yet he also observes that "sometimes, disconcertingly, he adopts the conditional or contractual terminology of the *quid pro quo* in respect to salvation itself"; "Problem of the Covenant," pp. 107–129. McGiffert adds, "such injunctions . . . should not be discounted as mere homiletical rhetoric. They articulate a powerful underdrift of covenant theology toward the very ambiguity that provoked Hutchinson to charge Bulkeley and his colleagues with preaching a doctrine of works under the guise of grace" (p. 122).

18. Bakhtin's discussion of heteroglossia is helpful here. Both groups seized upon a word in common usage but struggled to cleanse it of alien associations, to baptize it into their own discursive formations. See Mikhail Bakhtin, *The Dialogic Imagination,* trans. Caryl Emerson and Michael Holquist (Austin: University of Texas Press, 1981), p. 282.

19. Ames, *Marrow of Theology,* p. 151.

20. Perkins frequently speaks in the legal language of contract. In "The Golden Chaine," p. 211, he says: "God's covenant is his contract with man concerning the obtaining of life eternal upon a certain condition. This covenant consists of two parts—God's promise to man, man's promise to God. God's promise to man is that whereby he bindeth himself to man to be his God, if he perform the condition. Man's promise to God is that whereby he voweth his allegiance unto his Lord and to perform the condition between them." Perkins stipulates that the only condition under the covenant of grace is faith, which God himself provides. Yet the rhetorical push in Perkins is toward an unfolding of the conditional in such a way that injunctions for human action gain greater resonance than reminders of God's prevenience. For a balanced reading of Perkins's flirtation with legalism, see McGiffert, "Grace and Works," p. 481. For a more critical view see Kendall, *English Calvinism*, chaps. 4 and 5. For partisan critique that links Perkins and Ames on the basis of their growing legalism and that compares them unfavorably to the evangelicalism of Luther (and implicitly the spiritism of Cotton or Sibbes), see Karl Barth, *Church Dogmatics* (Edinburgh: T. & T. Clark, 1961), vol. 3, pt. 4: 8. Barth's complaint was precisely the favoring of omnipotence over mercy, and legalism over free grace, noted in the previous chapter. Even the modern editor of Perkins's works, Ian Breward, observes that "the difference between Calvin and Perkins on predestination can be summed up neatly by the following contrast. Calvin insisted that Christ was the mirror in which man contemplated election. Perkins taught that predestination was a glass in which we beheld God's majesty . . . Hence Perkins stressed the omnipotence of God before speaking of his love and justice." Breward, "Introduction," in Perkins, *Work*, pp. 59–60, 86.

21. Sprunger, *Learned Doctor Ames*, p. 147; Kendall, *Calvin and English Calvinism*, pp. 151, 157.

22. McGiffert observes, "from the standpoint of high Calvinism, [Perkinsians] were solid on election but soft on perseverance"; "Grace and Works," p. 481.

23. Both Miller and Sacvan Bercovitch have shown that the hebraizing of the covenant coincided with the introduction of the jeremiad, the communal version of the preparationist exhortations. See Bercovitch's *The American Jeremiad* (Madison: University of Wisconsin Press, 1978), pp. 3–30. For revision of this argument, see Theodore Dwight Bozeman, *To Live Ancient Lives: The Primitivist Dimension in Puritanism* (Chapel Hill: University of North Carolina Press, 1988), pp. 298–343.

24. Ames, *Marrow of Theology*, pp. 110–111.

25. Ames, *Marrow of Theology*, p. 110. This covenant of obedience begins with Adam but still binds all people, who by its terms deserve damnation.

26. Ibid., pp. 111, 150.

27. Ibid., chap. 39; Stoever, *"Faire and Easie Way,"* pp. 96–100; Bulkeley, *Gospel-Covenant*, p. 76.

28. Ames, *Marrow of Theology*, pp. 150, 50.

29. Ibid., p. 159. On Ames's voluntarism, see Sprunger, *Learned Doctor Ames*, p. 146; Eusden, "Introduction," in Ames, *Marrow of Theology*, p. 50.

30. Kendall, in *Calvin and English Calvinism*, p. 151, argues that just such pragmatic (even Arminian) soteriology is the intended goal of *The Marrow of Theology*.

31. Stoever explains the difference between the habit and act of faith: "The habit of faith being defined as the principle or power of faith freely infused into the soul, the act of faith as the motion put forth from the habit. In receipt of the habit the soul is passive; in virtue of it the soul actively believes in Christ. Both were understood to be antecedent conditions of entry into the covenant and of justification"; *"Faire and Easie Way,"* p. 41. Sibbes and Cotton, on the other hand, argue that the habit and the act of faith are fruits of justification.

32. Ames, *Marrow of Theology*, pp. 240, 242.

33. Ames, *Conscience and the Power and Cases Thereof* (n.p., 1639), 2:8–9. Although God does all absolutely, Ames argues that we are actors: "yet we ought to forsake all unlawful things actually, and all externall and naturall goods also, in the purpose, and disposition of our minds, else we cannot obtaine the grace of God" (p. 8).

34. Ames, *Marrow of Theology*, p. 161. See Stoever, *"Faire and Easie Way,"* chap. 6, for an excellent discussion of these issues.

35. Critics such as Kendall, however, argue that Hooker drifted dangerously close to an "Arminian" position. See *Calvin and English Calvinism*, p. 138.

36. Hooker, *English Writings*, pp. 198–199.

37. Ibid., pp. 199, 197.

38. Hooker, *The Soules Implantation* (London, 1637), pp. 1–3.

39. Ibid., p. 3.

40. See *The Antinomian Controversy, 1636–1638: A Documentary History*, ed. David D. Hall (Middletown, Conn.: Wesleyan University Press, 1968), pp. 85, 93, 103.

41. Ibid., p. 36.

42. Stoever, *"Faire and Easie Way,"* pp. 41–42; Hall, *Antinomian Controversy*, pp. 37–38. As Stoever explains: "Crucial to this understanding was the scholastic distinction between 'habit' and 'act,' the habit of faith being defined as the principle or power of faith freely infused into the soul, the act of faith as the motion put forth from the habit. In receipt of the habit the soul is passive; in virtue of it the soul actively believes in Christ. Both were understood to be antecedent conditions of entry into the covenant and of justification . . . Cotton approached the understanding of justification rather differently. He excluded by definition the possibility of a gracious act prior to union with Christ and therefore reversed the relationship between faith and union, with the result that 'justifying faith' became equivalent to 'faith of assurance'" (pp. 41–42).

43. Stoever says that "the relationship between divine sovereignty and the liberty of second causes, as expressed in covenant doctrine was fraught with tension"; *"Faire and Easie Way,"* p. 115. In effect, the tension was resolved by the steady gaze inward, once God was secured in his chains of contract. Virtually every page of Hooker's sermons reveals this activist bent. See, for example, *The Soules Humiliation* (London, 1637), p. 61.

44. Hooker, *English Writings*, p. 197.

45. Ibid., p. 197.

46. Hooker, *English Writings*, pp. 197–199. See also *The Soules Preparation for Christ* (London, 1632), p. 30.

47. See for example Hooker's *The Soules Exaltation* (London, 1638), which begins with assertions of Christ's free covenant (p. 6) but in its unfolding dilates on the creature, who must actively cleave unto Christ (p. 16).

48. Hooker, *English Writings*, pp. 200–202.

49. Ibid., p. 202.

50. Ibid., pp. 203–205.

51. Ibid., pp. 202–203.

52. Shepard, *Works*, 1:64, 170. See *Works*, 1:139–140, for Shepard's discussion of Lydia's conversion as a model of gradual regeneration.

53. Ibid., 2:154.

54. Ibid., 2:171.

55. Compare this with Cotton's declaration: "And this I take to be one main difference between the promises of the Law and the Gospel: In the Law the promise is made to the Condition or qualification of the creature, though given him of God: so that, give me the condition and I claime my right to the promise." Cotton's insistence that the promise is made to Christ, "so that, give me Christ and I claim my right to the promise and to all the comforts and blessings thereof," summarizes the crux of difference between his reading of the covenant and that of Shepard and Bulkeley; Hall, *Antinomian Controversy*, pp. 98–99.

56. Much of the Bulkeley-Cotton correspondence is collected in the Cotton Papers, The Thomas Prince Collection, Boston Public Library, and transcribed by Lawrance Thompson. See also Sargent Bush, "John Cotton's Correspondence: A Census," *Early American Literature*, 24 (1989), 91–111.

57. Mather, "To the Reader," in Willard's *Covenant Keeping*, p. A6.

58. Bulkeley, *Gospel-Covenant*, p. 322: "The tryall of our interest in the blessings of the Covenant, is to be made by the conditionall promises." With respect to faith Bulkeley declares, "I lay downe this conclusion . . . That we are not actually justified nor in a state of grace and salvation, before faith, before we believe." Faith is "not a condition only consequent, but antecedent to our actuall justification" (p. 358).

59. Ibid., pp. 314, 317.

60. Ibid., p. 333.

61. Bulkeley's instructions "To the Reader" in the 1646 edition of *The Gospel-Covenant* admits the widespread confusion between the covenant of works and the covenant of grace, in large measure produced by misunderstandings of the preparationist rhetoric of conditionality. In the midst of the controversy in 1636, Thomas Shepard responded to some of Winthrop's theological writings. Recognizing the potentially explosive nature of Winthrop's misunderstandings, Shepard cautions him to refrain from publishing his opinions: ". . . it is a great scruple in

my thoughts . . . whether it will be most safe for yow to enter into the conflict with your pen . . . it being an easy thing for a subtill adversary to take aduantages at woords . . ."; *Winthrop Papers*, 5 vols., *Collections* (Massachusetts Historical Society: Boston, 1943), 3:327. Shepard warned Winthrop that "your adversary may take aduantages at, or your freinds, offence at" one of the answers that seemed to bear "a colour of Arminianism" (p. 328).

62. Bulkeley, *Gospel-Covenant*, p. 323.

63. Ibid., p. 324.

64. Ibid., p. 323.

65. Ibid., p. 313. See Stoever, *"Faire and Easie Way,"* pp. 70–72.

66. Stoever, *"Faire and Easie Way,"* pp. 71–72. For Cotton's position, see Hall, *Antinomian Controversy*, p. 99.

67. Bulkeley, *Gospel-Covenant*, pp. 31–45.

68. Ibid., p. 37.

69. Though the covenant "is to Christ onely," it is "yet to us also" as the spiritual seeds of Abraham. Ibid., p. 42.

70. Ibid., p. 43.

71. For a general discussion of sacerdotalism see David D. Hall, *The Faithful Shepherd: A History of the New England Ministry in the Seventeenth Century* (New York: Norton, 1972).

72. See Chapter 1 for discussion of this, and Winthrop's accusation that Vane, Cotton, Wheelwright, the two ruling elders, and the rest of Boston church "which were of any note" refused to attend. Winthrop writes, "The reason was conceived to be, because they accounted these as legal preachers, and therefore would not give approbation to their ordination." See John Winthrop, *The History of New England from 1630 to 1649*, ed. James Savage (rpt., New York: Arno Press, 1972), pp. 217–218.

73. Bulkeley, *Gospel-Covenant*, p. 322; Hall, *Antinomian Controversy*, p. 134. As stated above, Bulkeley argues that though the absolute promises "shew the cause of our salvation," "only the conditionall promises do point out the persons to be saved" (p. 323). It is really this need for assurance as well as a perceived need to contain radicalism that leads to a near doctrine of works.

74. McGiffert remarks that Bulkeley's "hortatory concern for evangelical praxis" is "evidenced not only in Bulkeley's emphasis on the 'uses' of doctrine but, less conventionally, by the subject index that enabled readers to employ the volume as a handbook of practical piety." See "The Problem of the Covenant," p. 113.

75. Bulkeley, *Gospel-Covenant*, pp. 48–49.

76. Ibid., p. 49.

77. Once enjoined, God is bound to keep his word. "The blessings promised in the covenant cannot faile them, God cannot break with them, if they breake not with him, he cannot lye; nor alter the thing which is gone out of his lips" (ibid., p. 52). The saint can now refuse grace, but God cannot withdraw. Bulkeley emphasized human activity more than other preachers did, as a few examples will illustrate: "grace may save the vilest, so they turn . . . flying to grace, finding mercy"

(p. 82). It is the sinner who turns and strives: "so long as we strive to doe the will of the Lord, and fly to grace for pardon and acceptance, we do fulfill the Covenant of grace. Therefore cast off that yoake which cannot be borne and take the yoake of Christ upon us, for that is easie and his burthen light" (p. 103). These attributions of power to the individual are singular, but they do show the Arminian drift implicit in Bulkeley's doctrine.

78. Ames, *Marrow of Theology*, p. 251.

79. Hooker, *Soules Exaltation*, p. 63.

80. Ibid., p. 59. Or again consider Hooker's remark: "when the wife is betrothed and married to a man, all her old debts are laid upon her husband, and the law meddles no more with her; and secondly, all his lands at least the third part of them are made over to her. What shee hath in point of debt is put over to him: so all our sinnes and debts of corruptions are laid upon Christ; and all the rich fefments of grace and mercy in Christ, are made over to a beleever" (ibid., p. 133). For a similar use of the metaphor of marriage, see also Bulkeley, *Gospel-Covenant*, p. 103.

81. Bulkeley, *Gospel-Covenant*, p. 50.

82. Ibid. The complicated psychology behind this theory of dominance and submission will go unremarked, except to say that this is very different from the relation of mutual affection in the Sibbesians' marriage trope. Bulkeley goes on to say "humble thy selfe before God, confesse thy treachery and rebellion, and look at God as having a golden scepter in his hand, and intreat him to enter into a Covenant with thee, and submit they selfe wholly to be at his command, plead the promise of his grace, touch the top of the scepter, and take hold of the Covenant" (p. 51). The Freudian implications of this passage are obvious. However, these theologians do not always take the submissive role. More frequently they storm the throne and compel God to submit to their entreaties. In either case dominance and submission define the dynamic of the relation.

83. See Ross J. Pudaloff, "Sign and Subject: Antinomianism in Massachusetts Bay," *Semiotica*, 54:1 (1985), 153; and David Leverenz, *The Language of Puritan Feeling: An Exploration in Literature, Psychology, and Social History* (New Brunswick, N.J.: Rutgers University Press, 1980), pp. 128–130, for a discussion of the marriage trope. Edmund Morgan, in *The Puritan Family: Religion and Domestic Relations in Seventeenth-Century New England* (New York: Harper and Row, 1944), pp. 161–168, argues for the omnipresence of this trope in the context of Puritan tribalism. Morgan claims that all Puritans used the trope of marriage in homage to the affective dimension of religion. He does not see the difference between the two parties in terms of this issue of contract.

84. Sibbes, *Works*, 5:516. Compare with Cotton's statement: "to omit to speak of the person of Christ and rather to speak of the benefits we receive by him" is harlotry, not the loving meditation on the glorious person of the bridegroom. See *A Practical Commentary . . . upon the First Epistle Generall of John* (London, 1656), p. 5.

85. Sibbes, *Works,* 5:516.

86. Hooker, *Soules Preparation,* p. 74.

87. Hooker, *Soules Exaltation,* p. 102. In this series, Hooker elaborates the trope of hunger as well as riches as an inducement to his auditors to engage in right walking: "this is thy miserie, thou poore creature, thou hast no part nor share therein, when a man that is hungrie shall see all dainties prepared, when a man that is almost starved, shall see abundance of provision, wardrobes of clothes to cover him, and abundance of meat to refresh him, and yet one starves, and the other famisheth; this is the greatest miserie of all, to see meat and not to eat it, to see clothes and not to put them on" (p. 83). This description of spiritual goods through materialist tropes not only foregrounds the self-interestedness of Hooker's appeal but also provides a bridge whereby metaphoric riches as signs of election become literal in the next century.

88. Hooker, *Soules Implantation,* p. 320.

89. This account is articulated most persuasively by Sacvan Bercovitch. Insofar as he traces "transitional stages in the growth of the dominant culture," I agree that "certain elements in Puritanism lent themselves powerfully to that conjunction [between Protestantism and capitalism], and precisely those elements came to the fore" in Massachusetts. Preparationism may well have been the counterpart to tribal nationalism, soon to be transformed into manifest destiny. But I would dissent on two counts. First, his argument that Puritan rhetoric functions to "explain away their greed" does not fully allow the supple and complex meaning of their religious beliefs to the Puritans themselves: the *ordo salutis* should not be understood to mask a "truer" reality of greed and expansionist designs. Second, this reading of Puritanism cannot encompass the piety of the Cambridge brethren. Bercovitch, The *Rites of Assent: Transformations in the Symbolic Construction of America* (New York: Routledge, 1993), p. 30–32.

90. For a fine study countering Miller's declension theory and Bercovitch's history of bourgeois selfhood, see Harry Stout, *The New England Soul: Preaching and Religious Culture in Colonial New England* (New York: Oxford University Press, 1986). Stout argues for the continued importance and vitality of religion throughout the period.

91. Cohen, *God's Caress,* p. 133. While I am in sympathy with Cohen's reading of the importance of sanctification rather than justification as a way to understand the zealous labor of saints, I would argue that this position is not equally applicable to Amesians and Sibbesians. Hooker and Shepard's stress on antecedent conditions does not seem as good a "fit" with Cohen's argument as does the Sibbesian stress on consequent fruits of grace received. See Cohen, *God's Caress,* chap. 4.

92. Two recent commentators on the relationship between Puritanism and capitalism are Andrew Delbanco, *The Puritan Ordeal* (Cambridge, Mass.: Harvard University Press, 1989); and Jesper Rosenmeier, "John Cotton on Usury," *William and Mary Quarterly,* 3d ser., 47:4 (1990), 548–565. Delbanco argues that the Puritans, as a group, feared the moral compromises implicit in the language of the new

economic order. Such anxiety seems to be most characteristic of the circle of Sibbes and Cotton. Rosenmeier's transcription of and comment upon Cotton's text on usury shows that Cotton, in particular, rejected the notions of credit and interest that fueled economic expansion.

93. Shepard, *Works,* 3:174, 370. Shepard apparently questioned Cotton about this issue of typologizing the Sabbath sometime during the 1640s. See Laurence Thompson's unpublished M.A. thesis (Columbia University, 1932), pp. 178–185, for transcriptions of this correspondence.

94. Shepard, *Works,* 3:254.

95. Ibid., 3:259.

96. Ibid., 3:25.

5. The New Testament of Love

1. *The Complete Works of Richard Sibbes,* 7 vols., ed. Alexander Grosart (Edinburgh: James Nichol, 1862–1864), 3:384–385. Compare with Preston, who also argues the centrality of Christ over the covenant. See *The New Covenant or the Saintes Portion* (London, 1630), pp. 202, 321–322, 325–327.

2. Sibbes, *Works,* 3:386.

3. "A Sermon Delivered at Salem, 1636," *John Cotton on the Churches of New England,* ed. Larzer Ziff (Cambridge, Mass.: Harvard University Press, 1968), p. 53. Preston also rejected arguments for the covenant through Abraham: "The Promises are made to the seed, that is to Christ . . . The Promises that are made to us, though they be of the same Covenant, yet they differ in this, the active part is committed to the *Messiah,* to the seed it self; but the passive part, those are the promises that are made to us"; *New Covenant,* pp. 328–329.

4. John Coolidge, *The Pauline Renaissance in England: Puritanism and the Bible* (Oxford: Clarendon Press, 1970), pp. 151, 129.

5. Ibid., p. 137.

6. Even the most astute scholar of the Antinomian Controversy, William Stoever, in *"A Faire and Easie Way to Heaven": Covenant Theology and Antinomianism in Early Massachusetts* (Middletown, Conn.: Wesleyan University Press, 1978), argues for the uniqueness of Cotton's position.

7. Norman Pettit, *The Heart Prepared: Grace and Conversion in Puritan Spiritual Life* (New Haven: Yale University Press, 1966), p. 73. Kendall and Pettit suggest that Cotton became a better Calvinist in America, disavowing what they take to be Sibbes's more liberal practices. However, Sibbes was never the preparationist they claim, nor was Cotton a theological liberal in Old England. See Norman Pettit, "Cotton's Dilemma: Another Look at the Antinomian Controversy," *Publications of the Colonial Society of Massachusetts,* 59 (1982), 401, and *Heart Prepared,* pp. 66–75; and R. T. Kendall, *Calvin and English Calvinism to 1649* (London: Oxford University Press, 1979), p. 113 and chap. 7.

8. Kendall, *Calvin and English Calvinism,* chaps. 7 and 8. Michael McGiffert has noted the difference between the two versions of covenant preached in the

1620s and 1630s, citing Preston, Sibbes, and Cotton as "antilegalist." While substantially complicating and enriching traditional accounts, McGiffert's characterization of this position as "Perkinsian" does not do full justice to the distinctiveness of their preaching; "Federal Theology: The Perkinsian Moment" (unpublished paper).

9. Sibbes, *Works*, 3:394.

10. Ibid., 3:394.

11. Ibid., 3:394, 3:286–287.

12. "The Faithful Covenanter," along with other sermons gathered in vol. 6 of the collected works, tends to be more preparatory. Pettit relies on such texts. One problem is that since we cannot date Sibbes's writings, it is not clear whether these represent occasional modes of expression or might perhaps reflect changes over time. However, these preparatory sermons constitute a small portion of Sibbes's corpus, not at all representative of the majority of the texts.

13. John Norton, *Abel Being Dead Yet Speaketh* (London, 1658), p. 31, says that Cotton did not escape "the imputation of Arminianism from some."

14. Preston, *New Covenant*, pp. 330, 436.

15. Sibbes, *Works*, 3:456.

16. This is in the context of Sibbes's most legal sermon, "The Faithful Covenanter"; *Works*, 6:4. See also 3:384, 394; 5:III, 342, for more examples.

17. Ibid., 6:19. Sibbes seasons all his sermons with discussion of prevenience. See *Works*, 1:72; 2:73, 10, 12, 404, 467, 104; 3:275, 283, 296, 434, 442; 5:III, 342, for a representative sample.

18. Sibbes's conception of sin as privation undermines the argument advanced by Andrew Delbanco in *The Puritan Ordeal* (Cambridge, Mass.: Harvard University Press, 1989). The Sibbesians, both in England and in America after the Great Migration, persisted in representing sin as lack.

19. Sibbes, *Works*, 5:413.

20. Ibid., 1:153.

21. Ibid., 3:143. Compare with Preston: "I confess, I am able to doe nothing of my self, but I bring my heart to thee as an empty caske, beseeching thee to fill it with grace"; *New Covenant*, p. 436, 476.

22. *The Antinomian Controversy, 1636–1638: A Documentary History*, ed. David D. Hall (Middletown, Conn.: Wesleyan University Press, 1968), p. 37. For Cotton, faith is no antecedent condition. In his "Rejoynder" to the "orthodox" elders of New England, he declared: "faith itself and our adherence to Christ by it, is a fruit of that union, or else we might be beleevers, i.e. good trees, and bring forth good fruit before union with Christ which the Gospel accounteth impossible"; ibid., p. 92.

23. Ibid., 4:293.

24. John Davenport, *Saints Anchor-hold . . . and Sundry Sermons* (London, 1682), p. 78.

25. Sibbes, *Works*, 4:298.

26. Ibid., 1:75.

27. Ibid., 1:75. Thomas Goodwin extends the sweet intimacy of this image of soul as garden, but with a more preparationist tone: "God *walkes* in this *garden* every day . . . he turns up all your leaves, sees what fruit is under"; *Tryall of a Christian's Growth . . .* (London, 1643), p. 10.

28. Thomas Hooker, *Soules Implantation* (London, 1637), p. 320.

29. John Cotton, *Christ the Fountaine of Life* (London, 1651), pp. 34–36. The trope of kingship is given one paragraph only in an entire sermon.

30. Ibid., p. 35. In Herbert's "Love III" the guest "guilty of dust and sin" refuses Christ's offer to sit in communion. After Love's imprecations, the hesitant soul is finally persuaded to sit together with Christ, and to taste his meat. For a compelling reading of this Herbert poem, see Chana Bloch, *Spelling Thy Word: George Herbert and the Bible* (Berkeley: University of California Press, 1985), pp. 99–112. Hooker, on the other hand, describes a laden table in which the sinner waits alone in hunger for the passing of the dish. See *Soules Preparation* (London, 1632), p. 74.

31. *The Marrow of Theology: William Ames, 1576–1633*, trans. John D. Eusden (Boston: Pilgrim Press, 1968), p. 151.

32. Cotton, *Christ the Fountaine*, p. 35.

33. Ibid., pp. 35–36.

34. Ibid., p. 36.

35. Cotton, *The Way of Life* (London, 1642), p. 276.

36. Ibid., p. 277.

37. For Cotton's formulations on indwelling during the Antinomian Controversy, see Hall, *Antinomian Controversy*, pp. 27–29, 32; also Stoever, *"Faire and Easie Way,"* pp. 68–80, 170–174.

38. Davenport, *Saints Anchor-hold*, pp. 67, 70, 74.

39. Cotton, *Christ the Fountaine*, pp. 36–37.

40. Compare with Preston's *New Covenant*, pp. 341, 356. Grace makes the "new Creature and melts the heart." In *The Way of Life*, p. 40, Cotton says, "The Spirit of Grace lets us see our sins as so many daggers pointing at the heart of Christ, it melts our hearts in regard of the kindnesse of God." The sight of sin, afforded only by the spirit, never results in the humbled shattering described by Hooker, but in this "melting of hearts." Just as Hooker and Ames divide and dichotomize doctrine and analyze the heart into constituent parts, so the critical moment for them is imagined through division and fragmentation. For Cotton, on the other hand, the image of flow characterizes everything from God's motion to man's melted heart, to the organic flow of the sections and parts of his own sermons.

41. Cotton, *Way of Life*, pp. 131–133.

42. Ibid., pp. 104–105.

43. Ibid. Similarly underscoring the difference between historical and gracious faith, Sibbes (*Works*, 2:463) distinguishes between notional and true knowledge: "a blind man can talk of colours, if he be a scholar, and describe them better than

he that hath his eyes, he being not a scholar. But he that hath his eyes can judge of colours a great deal better."

44. Cotton, *Christ the Fountaine*, pp. 98–99. Preston argues that regeneration makes men "new Creatures," filled with the same motion, heat, and "quickness" that Cotton describes. See *Breast-plate of Faith and Love* (London, 1632), pp. 205, 209.

45. Cotton declares it is "the spirit of God's grace in the heart of man, that makes him of another spirit, he is not the same man, that he was before his spirit was changed, his inclination and disposition is changed"; *Christ the Fountaine*, p. 98. Jesper Rosenmeier has remarked this difference between the preparationist formulation of restoring man's senses in contrast to Cotton's remaking. See "New England's Perfection: The Image of Adam and the Image of Christ in the Antinomian Crisis, 1634 to 1638," *William and Mary Quarterly*, 3d ser., 27 (1970), 435–459.

46. Sibbes, *Works*, 6:541; see also 1:60; 2:454, 463; 3:14, 25; 4:167, 517; 7:440, for a mere sampling of this pervasive theme of the sermons. Compare with Preston's address to the saint who "commest indeed to perform holy duties from day to day . . . though he fail exceedingly in many things, yet his delight is still in the Lord, he desires exceedingly to please him," he has a new relish for divine things. This is in contrast to they that "have no taste, no relish, [they] doest them not with livelinesse, and quicknesse"; *New Covenant*, p. 391.

47. Cotton, *Christ the Fountaine*, pp. 134–135.

48. Sibbes, *Works*, 2:454. Davenport frequently uses the same language: "rellish is wrought in the renewed soul, by the spirit of faith"; it is a taste for "the sweetness of Gods grace" (*Saints Anchor-hold*, pp. 65, 87). It is this relish or desire which further energizes the growth in grace: "The rellish which believers have of the sweetness of Gods grace in Christ, turneth the eye of their soul towards him" (p. 87).

49. Sibbes, *Works*, 3:444.

50. Ibid., 1:130–131.

51. Ibid., 1:253.

52. Ibid., 3:195.

53. Ibid., 1:247.

54. Cotton, *Way of Life*, p. 213.

55. Cotton, *Christ the Fountaine*, p. 148.

56. Ibid., p. 50.

57. Davenport, *Saints Anchor-hold*, p. 92.

58. Cotton, *Christ the Fountaine*, pp. 52–53.

59. Sibbes, *Works*, 1:253.

60. Ibid., 1:253.

61. Cotton, *Christ the Fountaine*, p. 138. Like Sibbes and Preston, Cotton abhorred stasis and torpor.

62. Ibid., pp. 144–145, 148.

63. Cotton, *Way of Life*, p. 89.

64. Davenport, *Saints Anchor-hold*, p. 10.

65. The elders' position was that Cotton was limiting God's freedom by insisting on the absolute. They claimed "that Gods free grace may be reveiled and received as freely in a conditional (where the Condition is first wrought by Gods free grace and not trusted to, as we desire ever to be understood when we mention conditional promises) as in an absolute promise . . . For it is grace that works the Condition, it is Grace that reveals the Condition, it is grace that makes the promise, it is grace that sets on the promise; and what danger is there hereby, to a well instructed Christian of derogating from free grace?"; Hall, *Antinomian Controversy*, p. 67. Bulkeley, however, proved the lie in this statement; for by 1646 he was prepared to insiste upon the conditional. The elders complained that "to take our first Assurance to arise from the Spirit in an absolute promise only, is not only difficult to us to believe (and therefore desire your grounds) but seems dangerous to maintain, as straitning the freeness of Gods Spirit in working and destroying the comfort of many" (pp. 66–67). The elders, then, as well as Cotton himself, recognized in 1636 that when they used the word *covenant* they meant vastly different things.

66. Hall, *Antinomian Controversy*, p. 51. See also the 1636 "Sermon Delivered at Salem," in Ziff, *Cotton on the Churches of New England,* for an exposition of the absolute rather than the conditional promise.

67. Hall, *Antinomian Controversy*, p. 91.

68. Ibid., p. 134.

69. Ibid., pp. 102, 221. Cotton cites a passage from Ames in which he insists upon the immediate action of the Spirit. Though on balance, Ames focused on mediations that did accord agency to the saint, Cotton quite effectively marshalls this passage to support his own argument. This tactic is equivalent to hoisting the enemy by his own petard, since Ames was regarded by the elders as their own authorizing text. For the difference between Christ and Adam as a model for the saint, see Rosenmeier, "New England's Perfection."

70. Echoing Hutchinson's more radical Christology, Cotton stated his credo plainly: "For I do believe, as Christ is the first and last in other respects, so in this that he is the first and last condition of/in the promises"; Hall, *Antinomian Controversy*, p. 99. To Shepard, Cotton wrote: "I looke at all Promises as given us by the covenant of grace, and the covenant of grace as given us by christ. So that I doe not satisfy my selfe in closeing with a Promise, or with the covenant of grace but as I first close with christ, in whom the covenant, and the Promise is made, and confirmed" (ibid., pp. 29–30). For Cotton, then, covenant is secondary to Christ. There could be no greater disparity between this position and that of Shepard, who roundly condemns enthusiasts who seek the naked Christ. Moreover, as stated above, in formulating the double covenant Bulkeley not only abjures

the personal Christ but also Christ as the testator; he emphasizes instead the covenant of Abraham.

71. Hall, *Antinomian Controversy,* p. 103.

72. Ibid., pp. 133–135. Cotton says: "to seek our first Assurance of our Justification by Christ, or to seek the Assurance of Faith of our Justification in Christ by our works of Sanctification is to make such an use of Works as for which the Lord hath not sanctified them in the Covenant of Grace, but is peculiar to the Covenant of Works" (p. 132).

73. Ibid., p. 46.

74. Cotton urged similar tactics of strategic secrecy or duplicitous compliance on Wheelwright. See Sargent Bush, "'Revising what we have done amisse': John Cotton and John Wheelwright, 1640," *William and Mary Quarterly,* 3d ser., 45 (1988), 733–750.

75. In fact, just as critics like Bush and Shuffleton have argued that Hooker refined his formulation of the *ordo salutis* in response to Cotton's resistance, it might be argued that Cotton became more adamant in pressing for prevenience in response to the debates of these years. Here, the dialogic mode produced both a refinement of terms and a polarizing of positions. This might account for the shift in Cotton's theology on which Pettit and Kendall remark. But refinement of terms or heightened emphasis resulting from conflict is not equivalent to fundamental change. English sermons like *Christ the Fountaine* and *The Way of Life,* as well as the American "Sermon Delivered at Salem, 1636," and *A Treatise of the Covenant of Grace* (the later title given to *The New Covenant*) (London, 1671), reveal that Cotton was strong on prevenience and perseverance throughout his career. This last treatise offers further substantiation of the fundamental disagreements at stake: on the preeminence of absolute over conditional promises, see pp. 7, 19–21, 26, 35, 56, 66, 101, 111–113, 216–223. Notwithstanding, Cotton is also careful in this treatise to rescue his brand of spiritism from its misconstrual by those who tilt too much toward antinomianism: see pp. 87–88 and 130, where Cotton distinguishes the controversy as being "not about *grace,* but about the *discerning* of grace." This characterization is in keeping with his dockside admonition to religionists returning to England in 1637, yet rendered in a more conciliatory tone.

76. Cotton Mather, *Magnalia Christi Americana; or, the Ecclesiastical History of New England,* 2 vols., ed. Thomas Robbins (London, 1702; rpt. Hartford: Silas Andrus and Son, 1855), 1:288–289. Mather reports that Sibbes "did earnestly solicite him" to accept a fellowship at St. Catherine's, but Norton declined because he feared having to compromise his nonconformist practices.

77. This is not such a departure from Cotton's high stance as might be thought. After all, Cotton also advocated the use of signs in *Christ the Fountaine.* It was in the immediate context of the controversy that he became the most adamant about the illegitimacy of efficient causes and conditional means. Though he would not retreat from the emphasis on the absolute, he too allowed for the utility, though

never the efficacy, of pricking the conscience. See *Way of Life*, p. 134. Norton is not so far from this position in *The Orthodox Evangelist* (London, 1654).

78. Norton, *Orthodox Evangelist*, pp. 153–154, 159–160.

79. In "Preparation for Salvation," Perry Miller argues that Norton "carried the analysis [of preparationism] so far beyond Hooker that not only was he able to describe preparation as part of the process of conversion but to dissect preparation itself into a process"; Miller, *Nature's Nation* (Cambridge: Harvard University Press, 1967), pp. 71–72. Andrew Delbanco, on the other hand, sees Norton as a representative of "Puritan piety at its purest"; *Puritan Ordeal*, p. 24. Frank Shuffleton offers a balanced and insightful reading of Norton's ambivalence in *Thomas Hooker, 1586–1647* (Princeton, N.J.: Princeton University Press, 1977), pp. 293–296.

80. For Norton's disputes with Pynchon, see Philip Gura, *A Glimpse of Sion's Glory: Puritan Radicalism in New England, 1620–1660* (Middletown: Wesleyan University Press, 1984), chap. 11. For his writings against the Quakers, see Norton, *The Heart of New England Rent at the Blasphemies of the Present Generation* (Cambridge, Mass., 1659). For an interesting discussion of Norton's positions on radicalism and the Half-Way Covenant, see Stephen Foster, *The Long Argument: English Puritanism and the Shaping of New England Culture, 1570–1700* (Chapel Hill: University of North Carolina Press, 1991), 195–200.

81. Norton, *Orthodox Evangelist*, p. 160.

82. Ibid., p. 228.

83. Ibid., p. 228.

84. Ibid., p. 228.

85. Ibid., pp. 85–86.

86. Ibid., p. 98. The exiled John Wheelwright saw in Norton a fellow pietist. Sargent Bush reports that in his last writings Wheelwright cited the *Orthodox Evangelist* as supporting a spiritist position against the legalist encroachments of the other orthodoxy. Even after 1658 Wheelwright argued "the Faith of Gods Elect . . . is not grounded upon a conditional Promise," and that in the first motions of faith "we are altogether passive." See Bush, "John Wheelwright's Forgotten *Apology:* The Last Word in the Antinomian Controversy," *New England Quarterly*, 64 (1991), 28, 35.

87. Hall, *Antinomian Controversy*, p. 67.

88. Cotton's "Introduction" to Norton's *Orthodox Evangelist*. As evidence of the continued polarization, it should be recalled that Thomas Shepard provided the authorizing introduction to Bulkeley's *Gospel-Covenant*. The precariousness of Cotton's position may be registered in his anxiety about the disposition of his personal papers. There are few extant papers that would give us a sense of Cotton's most forthright utterances about the Antinomian Controversy or the evangelical practices in First Church. Thomas Hutchinson reports, "Upon his death-bed he ordered his son to burn all his papers relative to the religious disputes began in the time of Sir Henry Vane's year. He had bundled them all up, with an intention to do it himself, but death prevented his going into his study for that purpose.

His son, loth to destroy what appeared to him valuable, made a case of conscience to Mr. Norton whether he was bound to comply. Mr. Norton determined against the papers." Hutchinson, *The History of the Colony of Massachusetts Bay*, vol. 1 (rpt., New York: Arno Press, 1972), p. 152n. Similarly, Davenport requested the return of all of his correspondence with Cotton, apparently destroying all but one letter. See Isabel Calder, *Letters of John Davenport, Puritan Divine* (New Haven: Yale University Press, 1937), pp. 83n, 212.

89. Norton, *Orthodox Evangelist*, p. 227. Norton adds: "A condition improperly (so called, or a Consequent Condition) is such a condition, whose performance by the Covenantee, is absolutely undertaken for, and irresistibly wrought by the Covenantor, and not left in suspense upon the Covenantee, to be performed by his own strength" (p. 227). Again, in principle Shepard would certainly agree. But in the aftermath of the antinomian dispute, neither he nor Bulkeley pressed this line of argument. Rather, the discipline of consequent conditions buttressed their version of social and religious order.

90. Ibid., p. 160.

91. Ibid. Like Cotton before him, Norton cites those passages from Ames and Perkins which support prevenience and skips over their modifications in the direction of human agency. See *Orthodox Evangelist*, p. 168.

92. Norton distinguishes between the habit and the act of faith, as does Cotton, and argues that the habit comes only with the infusion of grace and not after it: "the soul is passive, as a vessel is a passive receiver of oyl powred therinto"; ibid., p. 252.

93. Ibid., p. 209. Norton usually presents sin as privative, a lack to be made up only by and with Christ's indwelling, not a blot to be removed by prior preparation: "The In-come of grace to, and the out-going of sin from the soul, is not in strictness, to be compared unto two things, (for sin is not a thing, but a corrupt privation of a thing) succeeding one another in the same place, after the order of a local mutation properly; where one of those things must give way, by being outed from its place, before the other can come in: But the In-come of the Spirit of grace into the soul, is after the manner of a habit, succeeding in the room of its contrary privation . . . the privation doth not first go out, and the habit come in: but the in-come of the habit, causeth the out going of the privation: as we see in knowledge, and ignorance in the soul; sight and blindness in the eye; light and darkness in the air; life and death in the body" (p. 187). Norton takes exception to an *ordo salutis* that would insist on the healing of sin *before* Christ's entry into the soul.

94. Ibid., p. 160.

95. Ibid., Norton's "Epistle Dedicatory" to the *Orthodox Evangelist*.

96. Ibid., pp. 195–196.

97. Ibid., p. 159.

98. See Giles Firmin, *The Real Christian* (1670; rpt., Boston, 1742), pp. 2–4. Norton, *Orthodox Evangelist*, p. 165.

99. Norton, *Orthodox Evangelist,* pp. 165–166.

100. Ibid., p. 319.

101. Ibid., p. 13.

6. CHARITY AND ITS FRUITS

1. Jonathan Edwards, *Charity and its Fruits* (rpt., Philadelphia: Presbyterian Board of Publications, 1874), p. 2.

2. Ibid., p. 1.

3. Charles Cohen claims contra Weber: "One's willingness to labor for God grows in light of His special love"; see *God's Caress: The Psychology of Puritan Religious Experience* (New York: Oxford University Press, 1986), p. 124. I concur with Cohen's claim but would add that it applies most fully to the Spiritual Brethren.

4. The literature of Puritan millennialism is vast. Bercovitch's chapter on the "Typology of America's Mission" in *American Jeremiad* (Madison: University of Wisconsin Press, 1978) is a good initial summary. Bernard S. Capp, in *The Fifth Monarchy Men: A Study in Seventeenth-Century English Millenarianism* (London: Faber, 1972), has argued that as much as 70 percent of Puritan sermons between 1640 and 1653 contained millennial themes (p. 38). See also Christopher Hill, *The Experience of Defeat: Milton and Some Contemporaries* (London: Faber, 1984); David Smith, "Millenarian Scholarship in America," *American Quarterly,* 17 (1965), 535–549; Peter Toon, ed., *Puritans, the Millennium, and the Future of Israel: Puritan Eschatology 1600 to 1660* (London: Clarke and Company, 1970); John F. Wilson, *Pulpit in Parliament: Puritanism during the English Civil Wars, 1640–1648* (Princeton: Princeton University Press, 1969); James Maclear, "New England and the Fifth Monarchy: The Quest for the Millennium in Early American Puritanism," *William and Mary Quarterly,* 3d ser., 32 (1975), 223–260; Joy Gilsdorf, "The Puritan Apocalypse: New England Eschatology in the Seventeenth Century," diss., Yale University, 1965; Jesper Rosenmeier's superb essay, "New England's Perfection: The Image of Adam and the Image of Christ in the Antinomian Crisis, 1634–1638," *William and Mary Quarterly,* 3d ser., 27 (1970), 435–459; Avihu Zakai, *Exile and Kingdom: History and Apocalypse in the Puritan Migration to America* (Cambridge, England: Cambridge University Press, 1992); and, most important, Theodore Dwight Bozeman, *To Live Ancient Lives: The Primitivist Dimension in Puritanism* (Chapel Hill: University of North Carolina Press, 1988), and Andrew Delbanco, *The Puritan Ordeal* (Cambridge: Harvard University Press, 1989).

5. Bercovitch marks the distinction in this way: "Technically speaking, the seventeenth-century colonists (like most Protestants of their time) were pre-millennialists. That is, they believed that the descent of New Jerusalem would be preceded and attended by a series of cataclysmic divine judgments and followed by a universal change in all things." In his reading this position contrasts that of Jonathan Edwards, who "posited a final golden age within history, and thereby freed humanity, so to speak, to participate in the revolutions of the apocalypse";

American Jeremiad, p. 94. Edwards is designated a postmillennialist. Bercovitch goes on to argue that a preacher could be both pre- and postmillennial, but that in general all seventeenth-century thinkers participate in the optimism and the faith in process characteristic of Edwards. Edwards merely applied the concept of progressive unfolding with "greater consistency of its logic," and thus his thought is not a transformation but a continuation of seventeenth-century chiliasm (ibid., p. 98). This is both accurate and deceptive. Edwards did continue the postmillennial tradition of Cotton, but he in large measure overturned the conservative premillennialism of the preparationists. [For the most thorough and provocative reading of Edwards, see Alan Heimert, *Religion and the American Mind: From the Great Awakening to the Revolution* (Cambridge, Mass.: Harvard University Press, 1966).] The orthodox mainstream tended to be amillennial or premillennial, as will be shown. See also Bozeman, *To Live Ancient Lives,* chap. 3, for arguments in support of this assertion.

6. Bozeman, *To Live Ancient Lives,* offers the most complete and subtle reading of this issue. I am pleased to find confirmation for much of my argument in Bozeman's text. The difference between our claims rests on the issue of partisan opinion. In general, Bozeman argues that Cotton and John Eliot were somewhat alone in considering the possibility of an unfolding kingdom in human time—a period that Bozeman calls the "Middle Advent." This period of earthly regeneration and enjoyment was expected as "the penultimate coming . . . and its effect [was] upon world history for a privileged interval long before the Second Coming" of judgment. (p. 233). Moreover, Bozeman sees Cotton's millennialist optimism as a product of the 1640s. I would argue that Cotton's early sermons on Canticles and I John General express the same general optimism as the later sermons. Moreover, though Sibbes, Preston, and Davenport do not elaborate their eschatology, they thought and wrote about the last days with excited anticipation. Bozeman remarks in a footnote that Richard Sibbes was interested in the millennium but that "he did not develop a full millennial conception" (p. 214). Davenport's millennialism is also remarked in passing (pp. 232–233, 262). I would argue that though their views on the matter were not fully or consistently developed, the Sibbesians in general were far more committed to millennialism than the Amesians. Though they may sometimes voice conflicting opinions, the Brethren thought, wrote, worried about, and eagerly anticipated the end time to a far greater degree than their preparationist counterparts. Again, without making a claim for affinity, Bozeman argues that Ames, Shepard, and Hooker expressed little optimism about the last days (pp. 224, 234).

7. Ibid., pp. 232–233.

8. *The Complete Works of Richard Sibbes,* 7 vols., ed. Alexander Grosart (Edinburgh: James Nichol, 1862), 1:185.

9. Ibid., 2:200. Canticles, their favorite text, was sometimes viewed as seductive: "ungodly men might take offence at it, yet the godly may be bettered by it." Cotton also defended the reading of Canticles: "The amorousness of the dittie will not

stirre up wantonness in any age, if the words be well understood, but rather by
inflaming with heavenly love, will draw out, and burne up all earthy and carnall
lust; and, even as fire in the hande is drawne out by holding it to a stronger fire,
or as the light and heat of the sunne extinguisheth a kitchen fire, so doth heavenly
love to Christ extinguish base kitchen lusts"; John Cotton, *A Briefe Exposition with
Practical Observations Upon the Whole Book of Canticles* (London, 1655), p. 8.

10. Sibbes, *Works,* 2:13.

11. John Cotton, *Christ the Fountaine of Life* (London, 1651), p. 33.

12. Sibbes, *Works,* 3:23.

13. Preston, *The New Covenant or the Saintes Portion* (London, 1630), p. 438. My
standard caveat holds: Preston frames such injunctions with reminders that "the
active part is committed to the Messiah" (p. 419).

14. Preston, *New Covenant,* pp. 435–436.

15. Cotton, *Christ the Fountaine,* pp. 134, 138. Goodwin also maintains: "Grace
is an active thing, and it is a growing thing also; and because the more it is acted
the more it grows. Therefore its growth is expressed as motion"; Thomas Goodwin,
The Tryall of a Christian's Growth . . . (London, 1643), p. 59.

16. Sibbes, *Works,* 3:321; 2:13.

17. Sibbes, *Works,* 5:494. See also Cotton, *Christ the Fountaine,* p. 99.

18. John Cotton, *A Practical Commentary . . . upon the First Epistle Generall of
John* (London, 1656), p. 12 (hereafter cited as *I John Generall*). See Jesper Rosenmeier, "'Clearing the Medium': A Reevaluation of the Puritan Plain Style in Light
of John Cotton's *A Practical Commentary Upon the First Epistle Generall of John,*"
William and Mary Quarterly, 3d ser., 37 (1980), 586–590, for a compatible exposition
of Cotton's doctrine of the Trinity.

19. Cotton, *I John Generall,* p. 12. Sibbes describes the Trinity similarly: "as they
have a perfect unity in themselves in nature, for they are all one God, so they have
a most perfect unity in their love, and care, and respect to mankind" (*Works,* 4:294).

20. Cotton, *I John Generall,* p. 365.

21. Sibbes, *Works,* 4:294.

22. Ibid., 6:113.

23. Ibid., 6:113. Sibbes's rhetoric, which could be interestingly glossed as ho-
mosocial, also appropriates images of female generativity: God's desire to communicate is analogized as "the breast that loves to ease itself of milk."

24. Ibid., 6:113.

25. Ibid., 3:194.

26. Ibid., 3:218.

27. Preston, *New Covenant,* pp. 437–438.

28. Sibbes, *Works,* 6:113. Compare to Cotton, *Christ the Fountaine,* p. 59.

29. Preston, *New Covenant,* p. 438; *Breast-plate of Faith and Love* (London,
1632), p. 212.

30. Cotton, *I John Generall,* p. 3.

31. Cotton, *Christ the Fountaine,* p. 148.

32. Sibbes, *Works*, 3:194.

33. Ibid., 5:214.

34. Ibid., 3:432.

35. Ibid., 1:122.

36. Ibid., 2:53.

37. Preston, *Saints Qualification* (London, 1637), pp. 30, 31.

38. Sibbes, *Works*, 3:13.

39. Jesper Rosenmeier has argued powerfully and eloquently that there was a shift in Cotton's second series to practical application reflecting a decline in his millennial expectations. See Rosenmeier, "The Teacher and the Witness: John Cotton and Roger Williams," *William and Mary Quarterly*, 3d ser., 25 (1968), 408–431. Bozeman, on the other hand, argues that Cotton discovers his millennialism in the 1640s. I would argue that Cotton remains interested in millennialism throughout; though Cotton does turn to matters of individual salvation in the second series, he does not abjure historical considerations. Cotton says there are three parts to Canticles: "1. Of the affection and relation between Christ and his Church in generall. 2. Of the affection and relation between Christ and every sincere Christian soul. 3. Of the estate and condition of every church." He goes on to explain his shift in emphasis: "now because in the former exposition this last sense and use was chiefly attended, and not so the two former . . . therefore now I thought good to go over it again, to supply what was then omitted"; *Briefe Exposition*, p. 2. Moreover, countering assertions of his chastened millennialism, Cotton preached his greatest millennial sermons on Revelation in the 1640s.

40. The inextricability of the work of redemption as it is manifested ontologically in each heart and temporally in the history of the church was the theme of Goodwin, Davenport, and Preston as well. Goodwin describes these two kinds of Christ's love: "his love to his *Church Mysticall* or his Saints simply considered as such," and his "love of his Churches." These two affections are wholly united in Goodwin's narrative, *Zerubbabels Encouragement to Finish the Temple* (London, 1642), p. 29.

41. Sibbes, *Works*, 2:117. Again, in response to those who might be tempted to argue that such a passage represents a pure preparationist perspective, it is worthwhile to quote the whole in context: "We must go through all means to seek Christ, not one must be left. Thus if we will seek him, undoubtedly he will make good his promise. Nay, in some sort, 'he is found before he is sought,' for he is in our souls to stir up desire of seeking him. He prevents us with desires, and answers us in some sort before we pray, Isa. lxv. 24. When he gives us a spirit of prayer, it is a pledge to us, that he means to answer us."

42. Cotton, *I John Generall*, p. 3.

43. Cotton, *Christ the Fountaine*, p. 181. Cotton goes on to add that the epistles of the apostles were preached, not read. Faith comes only by hearing and in the company of others.

44. Sibbes, *Works*, 5:507.

45. Ibid., 5:507.

46. For the importance of sermons in the life of New England, see Harry S. Stout's brilliant study of *The New England Soul: Preaching and Religious Culture in Colonial New England* (New York: Oxford University Press, 1986). Stout estimates that New Englanders listened to seven thousand sermons in their lifetimes (p. 4).

47. Sibbes, *Works*, 5:434, for discussion of the Spirit's acting on the soul; 5:506, for the function of the preacher. Cotton in *I John Generall*, p. 75, describes the ministry in a similar way; see also *The Way of Congregational Churches Cleared*, pp. 334–342, in *John Cotton on the Churches of New England*, ed. Larzer Ziff (Cambridge, Mass.: Harvard University Press, 1968); Preston, *New Covenant*, p. 458; and Sargent Bush, Jr., *The Writings of Thomas Hooker: Spiritual Adventure in Two Worlds* (Madison: University of Wisconsin Press, 1980), p. 258.

48. Cotton, *Briefe Exposition*, p. 128.

49. *The Work of William Perkins*, ed. Ian Breward (Abingdon: The Sutton Courtenay Press, 1970), pp. 214–215.

50. David D. Hall, ed., *The Antinomian Controversy, 1636–1638: A Documentary History* (Middletown, Conn.: Wesleyan University Press, 1968), p. 380.

51. Sibbes, *Works*, 1:19–20.

52. Ibid., 2:167.

53. Ibid., 5:507.

54. Ibid., 2:167.

55. Cotton, *Christ the Fountaine*, p. 99.

56. Sibbes, *Works*, 2:167.

57. Cotton, *I John Generall*, p. 75.

58. Cotton, *The True Constitution of a Particular Visible Church* (London, 1642), p. 4.

59. Sibbes, *Works*, 1:20.

60. Cotton, *I John Generall*, p. 75.

61. Winthrop, "A Model of Christian Charity," as cited in Alan Heimert and Andrew Delbanco, *The Puritans in America* (Cambridge, Mass.: Harvard University Press, 1985), p. 82.

62. *The Works of Thomas Shepard . . . with a Memoir of his Life and Character*, 3 vols., ed. John Albro (Boston, 1853; rpt., New York: AMS Press, 1967), 1:38, 39.

63. Sibbes, *Works*, 1:20–21.

64. Cotton, *Christ the Fountaine*, p. 59.

65. Preston, too, consistently addresses his auditors as "Beloved in Christ." See for example *The New Covenant*, pp. 324–325, 424.

66. Sibbes, *Works*, 1:231.

67. Cotton, *Christ the Fountaine*, p. 14. David Leverenz has noticed this difference between ministers who use the first- or third-person form of address; see *The Language of Puritan Feeling: An Exploration in Literature, Psychology, and Social History* (New Brunswick, N.J.: Rutgers University Press, 1980), p. 179.

68. Cotton, *Christ the Fountaine*, p. 59.

69. Sibbes, *Works*, 2:168.

70. John Preston, *The Golden Scepter Held forth to the Humble* (London, 1625), p. 10. As Preston explains, "My Beloved, it is a thing that we cannot expresse, it is a certain divine expression of light, a certain unexpressible assurance that we are the sons of God, a certain secret manifestation that God hath received us, and put away our sins: I say, it is such a thing, that no man knows but they that have it"—i.e., to those endowed with the new sense; *New Covenant*, p. 340.

71. Cotton, *Christ the Fountaine*, pp. 177–178.

72. Cotton, *I John Generall*, pp. 169–170.

73. Cotton, *Christ the Fountaine*, p. 178. Like Hawthorne's Arthur Dimmesdale, Cotton's sermons are for the initiated heart, "wherever educated." Nathaniel Hawthorne, *The Scarlet Letter* (Boston: Houghton Mifflin, 1960), p. 242. Hawthorne is said to have modeled Dimmesdale after Cotton, and his description of Dimmesdale's sermon style is not unlike that of his seventeenth-century forebear. Dimmesdale's voice "was in itself a rich endowment; insomuch as that a listener, comprehending nothing of the language in which the preacher spoke, might still have been swayed to and fro by the mere tone and cadence. Like all other music, it breathed passion and pathos, and emotions high or tender, in a tongue native to the human heart, wherever educated." Though Cotton would object to the total negation of sense by sound, he comes close to proving what Hawthorne suggests— that in the moment when communication becomes communion, the need for language disappears. For a lovely discussion of this parallel, see Teresa Toulouse, *The Arte of Prophesying: New England Sermons and the Shaping of Belief* (Athens: University of Georgia Press, 1987).

74. Hall, *Antinomian Controversy*, p. 141.

75. See Edward H. Davidson, "John Cotton's Biblical Exegesis: Method and Purpose," *Early American Literature*, 17 (1982), 119–137, for Cotton's use of syllogisms. See also Alfred Habegger, "Preparing the Soul for Christ: The Contrasting Sermon Forms of John Cotton and Thomas Hooker," *American Literature*, 41 (1969), 342–354; Norman Grabo, "John Cotton's Aesthetic: A Sketch," *Early American Literature Newsletter*, 3 (Spring 1968): 4–10; and Teresa Toulouse's *Arte of Prophesying* and her superb article, "'The Art of Prophesying': John Cotton and the Rhetoric of Election," *Early American Literature*, 19 (1985), 279–299.

76. Once again, these differences are suggested by the contrasting readings offered by William Haller and Perry Miller. Miller, pursuing that lineage rooted in the theology of Ames, and before him Perkins, attributed Puritan sermonic form to the twin influences of Ramus and Perkins; see Perry Miller, *The New England Mind: The Seventeenth Century* (Cambridge, Mass.: Harvard University Press, 1939), chaps. 11 and 12. Miller argued that logic rather than rhetoric, argument rather than affect, provided the foundation for these sermons. "Rhetoric was to be used as though it were the juice of a poisonous herb." Rhetoric was to come after logic, in the interest of preserving the purity of doctrine in the context of an unregenerate audience (p. 362). For a discussion of the "rigid dialectical structure"

of these sermons, see p. 334. The fear of ornament is directly related to a conception of the audience as fallen: "Puritans were always acutely conscious of rude and unformed auditors, of the constant necessity that the preacher reach the minds and hearts of the vulgar, that he employ ornaments not for the sake of ornament, but for the humbling of the mass of sinners" (p. 324). No preacher, according to Miller, could "any longer pour out his thought in sinuous word patterns that echoed and reechoed the phraseology of his texts, or that coiled around the fervid imagery of the Bible in reiterative incantations" (p. 327).

Haller, by contrast, understood that the success of the Cambridge preachers did not lie in "a greater power of lucid and coherent thought but in their command of the art of suggestive, provocative, poetic speech"; see William Haller, *The Rise of Puritanism* (New York: Columbia University Press, 1938), p. 256. Though he does not analyze theories of language as does Miller, Haller's Puritans win their audience by the power of their rhetoric, not their logic. Once again, these two readings are not so much in conflict as they are supplementary, applicable to different wings of the Puritan party. All that Miller described illuminates the sermonic mode of the circle of Ames. In much sketchier form, Haller adumbrates the essential qualities to be discovered in the preaching of the Cambridge Brethren. (Bercovitch in *The American Jeremiad*, p. 18, notes this difference between Miller and Haller on the issue of rhetorical analysis as well.)

77. Leverenz, *Language of Puritan Feeling*, p. 179.

78. Sibbes, *Works*, 2:168; 3:420; 5:505–515; 1:38.

79. Ibid., 3:420.

80. Ibid., 5:505.

81. Cotton, *Some Treasure Fetched out of the Rubbish* (London, 1660), pp. 9, 12. Only the first part of this treatise is now believed to be Cotton's work.

82. Consider Herbert's method of collation: "This verse marks that, and both do make a motion/Unto a third, that ten leaves off doth lie." From "The H. Scriptures II", in *The English Poems of George Herbert*, ed. C. A. Patrides (London: Dent, 1974), p. 77.

83. Eugenia Delamotte, "John Cotton and the Rhetoric of Grace," *Early American Literature*, 21 (1986), 58, argues: "by means of that technique he developed a rhetoric of grace which could liberate Puritan theology—for his own followers, at least—from that 'nervous, incessant activism' of language in which it was usually purveyed."

84. Sibbes, *Works*, 1:4.

85. Ibid., 1:4–6.

86. Ibid., 1:5.

87. Toulouse, "'Arte of Prophesying,'" p. 289.

88. James Guetti discusses the effects of repetition in *Word-Music: The Aesthetic Aspect of Narrative Fiction* (New Brunswick, N.J.: Rutgers University Press, 1980), p. 5: "One of the effects of this music, and of this subordination, is the staying of imaginative progress. The recurrence of images and rhythms not only seems to

make the pursuit of new images impossible, it also suggests that such a pursuit is no longer important. The imaginative action of following has been halted here and perhaps may even seem satisfied. The pressure toward intelligibility has eased." For a similarly evocative discussion of repetition, see Roland Barthes, *The Pleasaure of the Text* (New York: Hill and Wang, 1975).

89. To paraphrase Whitman, it is "not words" but the lull these preachers like, the hum of the Spirit's valved voice. Walt Whitman, "Song of Myself," Chant 5.

90. Sibbes, *Works*, 2:168.

91. William Hubbard, *General History of New England*, as cited in Leverenz, *Language of Puritan Feeling*, p. 179.

92. Cotton Mather, *Magnalia Christi Americana; or, the Ecclesiastical History of New England*, 2 vols., ed. Thomas Robbins (London, 1702; rpt., Hartford: Silas Andrus and Son, 1855), 1:275.

93. Ibid., 1:248.

94. Thomas Manton, "To the Reader," an introduction to Sibbes's *Exposition of Second Corinthians*, in *Works*, 3:6.

95. Toulouse says auditors "are not . . . asked to connect images logically but emotionally . . . Cotton's language calls up a certain state in his hearers but this state is never clearly defined by the preacher"; "Arte of Prophesying,'" p. 290. Though Toulouse is talking about Cotton's abjuring of applications, the argument is relevant to his use of repetition as well.

96. Guetti, *Word-Music*, p. 180.

97. Guetti, *Word-Music*, p. 171.

98. Sibbes, *Works*, 1:20.

99. The structure in Puritan sermon style has generated the same kind of scholarly interest that attended the study of typology ten years ago. As with so many aspects of his thought, Cotton's sermon style is being viewed as not only unique but somewhat anomalous in the New England context. Toulouse, for example, demonstrates the ways in which his style differs from Hooker's and argues that Cotton's underlying purpose is to subvert or deconstruct the model set out in Perkins's *Arte of Prophesying*. Yet, perhaps Cotton's motive should not be phrased in the negative. It may well prove fruitful to look for a positive precedent in Sibbes's own rhetoric and form. All the distinctive marks of Cotton's style are to be found in abundance in the architecture of Sibbes's sermons. Cotton was perhaps less bent on subverting Perkins than he was inspired by the example of his self-acknowledged mentor.

100. On the conversion narrative, see Edmund S. Morgan, *Visible Saints: The History of a Puritan Idea* (Ithaca, N.Y.: Cornell University Press, 1965); Stephen Foster, *The Long Argument: English Puritanism and the Shaping of New England Culture, 1570–1700* (Chapel Hill: University of North Carolina Press, 1991), chap. 4; Owen Watkins, *The Puritan Experience* (New York: Schocken Books, 1972); Patricia Caldwell, *The Puritan Conversion Narrative: The Beginnings of American Expression* (Cambridge: Cambridge University Press, 1983); and Cohen, *God's Caress*.

101. Cotton, *Way of Congregational Churches Cleared*, in Ziff, *Cotton on the Churches of New England*, pp. 357, 341; for full discussion see pp. 357–360. See also Cotton, *The Way of Churches in New England* (London, 1645), pp. 54–58, for a discussion of the testimony.

102. Caldwell says "something significant happens *between* the speaker and the hearers that validates the profession" (*Conversion Narrative*, p. 107). That something is the communal bond attendant upon aural performance—a bond of empathy and memory. Profession is good not just for the witness but for the auditor who is resealed in grace.

103. Cotton, *Christ the Fountaine*, pp. 93–94. As Caldwell has pointed out, it is "not the words but the music" that is essential in the narratives (*Conversion Narrative*, p. 96.)

104. Cotton, *Christ the Fountaine*, p. 93.

105. Cotton, *Way of Churches in New England*, p. 58.

106. Preston, *Breast-plate*, pp. 212–213; Sibbes, *Works*, 1:170; 2:133–134; 3:106–107.

107. Cotton, *Christ the Fountaine*, p. 247.

108. Sibbes, *Works*, 3:225; Davenport, *Saints Anchor-hold . . . and Sundry Sermons* (London, 1682), p. 187.

109. Preston, *Breast-plate*, p. 212.

110. Sermons focusing on millennial themes include Sibbes, "The Brides Longing," in *Works*, 6:535–560; Davenport, *Saints Anchor-hold*, pp. 180–190; Cotton, *Briefe Exposition, The Churches Resurrection* (London, 1642), and *the Powring out of the Seven Vialls* (London, 1642); Preston, *Breast-plate;* Goodwin, *Zerubbabels Encouragement*. Far more than their preparationist counterparts, the Sibbesians unfolded the meaning of current events within the divine timetable. Moreover, they attached communitarian desires with an optimistic providentialism.

111. Davenport, *Saints Anchor-hold*, p. 187.

112. Sibbes, *Works*, 1:376. See also 2:169.

113. Goodwin, *Zerubbabels Encouragement*, p. 29.

114. Sibbes, *Works*, 6:547.

115. Late in his career, Cotton remained adamant in his definition of the church as essentially spiritual. Defending New England polity against attacks by Robert Baille and the Presbyterians, Cotton nonetheless still argued for a spiritual understanding of church forms: "whence is all that spirituall power and life, which the people of God do ordinarily finde in all the visible Churches of the Saints . . . if the holy Ghost dwell not in them? . . . why do men stand so much upon visible churches, and their purity? They are neither temples of the holy Ghost, nor members of Christ, nor children of God almighty." Rather, "these glorious stiles" belong "to an hidden invisible company of Saints scattered universally, and invisibly all the world over." Though Cotton is defending the value of the visible church, he also maintains that ordinances are "husks, and shels," while Christian fellowship and union are the "very vitals, and cordials" of the church. Cotton, *Of the Holiness of Church Members* (London, 1650), p. 49, as cited in Caldwell, *Conversion Narratives*, p. 106.

116. See also Davenport, *Saints Anchor-hold*, pp. 181–193, for the role call of the Palatinate and the chastising of New England's complacency; and Cotton, *Churches Resurrection*, p. 15.

117. Sibbes, *Works*, 3:108.

118. Preston, *Breast-plate*, p. 216.

119. Ibid., p. 213.

120. See Irvonwy Morgan, *Prince Charles's Puritan Chaplain* (London: Allen and Unwin, 1957), pp. 174–183.

121. Sibbes, *Works*, 3:180–181, 3:187; 7:471.

122. Ibid., 7:471.

123. Ibid., 3:181.

124. Hooker, *The Danger of Desertion* (1641), as cited in Heimert and Delbanco, *Puritans in America*, pp. 15, 62–69.

125. It is important to note that members of the Sibbes circle were both more active on behalf of the church international and more loathe to abandon the cause in England. The degree to which Cotton and Davenport postponed, agonized over, and rationalized their departures indicates a level of anxiety largely absent in the writings of Ames, Hooker, and Winthrop.

126. Sibbes, *Works*, 5:53, 198.

127. Ibid., 7:307.

128. For a reading of difference within Puritanism along this axis of migration, see Foster, *Long Argument*.

129. Cotton's "Reasons for Departure" are recorded in Alexander Young's *Chronicles of the First Planters of the Colony of Massachusetts Bay from 1623 to 1636* (Boston: Charles C. Little and James Brown, 1846), pp. 438–444.

130. Cotton, "An Apologetical Preface for the Reader of Mr. Norton's Book," in John Norton, *The Answer to the Whole Set of Questions . . .* (London, 1648).

131. Heimert and Delbanco, *Puritans in America*, p. 71.

132. For fuller information, refer to note 6 of this chapter. Delbanco (*The Puritan Ordeal*) and Bozeman (*To Live Ancient Lives*) argue that the first generation of New English Puritans clung to the purity of the primitive churches, correcting Bercovitch's claim for the general postmillennial fervor and sense of errand in the first generation. However, as argued above, Cotton's millennialism was strong throughout his career and rejected local or national allegiance in favor of internationalism; Cotton was not especially devoted to a peculiar American mission, contrary to the claims of Sacvan Bercovitch. Other writers taking part in this debate include Zakai (*Exile and Kingdom*), who returns to and amplifies Perry Miller's claims for a fully articulated sense of sacred mission in the founding generation.

133. Cotton, *An Exposition upon the Thirteenth Chapter of the Revelation* (London, 1655), p. 93: "but so far as God helps by Scripture light, about the time 1655 there will be then such a blow given to this beast."

134. Bercovitch, *American Jeremiad*, p. 42–43, 32, 39. Rosenmeier takes up these issues in the "The Teacher and the Witness."

135. Mather, *Magnalia*, p. 325. For Cotton's typology see Bercovitch, "Typology in Puritan New England: The Williams-Cotton Controversy Reassessed," *American Quarterly*, 19 (1967), 166–191, as well as Rosenmeier, "The Teacher and the Witness." Maclear, "New England and the Fifth Monarchy," also argues that Cotton's typology led to a radical millenarianism, one adopted by William Aspinwall, Thomas Venner, and other English spiritists.

136. Cotton, "God's Promise to his Plantations," p. 7.

137. Ibid., p. 7.

138. Cotton, *Churches Resurrection*, p. 20.

139. Cotton, *Exposition upon the Thirteenth Chapter*, p. 21. Cotton's position anticipates the preaching of the Westminster divines, many of whom were his disciples. John Wilson in *Pulpit in Parliament* insightfully observes that though the "profound discipline of personal piety" has long been recognized in Puritan studies, the concern for "corporate piety" has been overlooked (p. 166). His argument that a collective eschatology of the new Zion emerges in the 1640s with the Independents does not, however, give proper credit to Cotton's influence (p. 223). Though Wilson recognizes that it is Cotton and not Hooker who represents early millenarian thought in England, he does not trace Cotton's possible influence on later radicals such as Thomas Goodwin (p. 225).

140. Cotton, *Churches Resurrection*, p. 26.

141. Cotton, *Churches Resurrection*, p. 21.

142. Ibid., p. 22. This contradicts Bercovitch's argument for Cotton's boosterism of the New England Way and as justifying the capitalistic motives of the colonists. See *American Jeremiad*, pp. 21–23.

143. Cotton, *Churches Resurrection*, p. 17.

144. Ibid., p. 22.

145. Davenport, *Saints Anchor-hold*, pp. 192–193.

146. Though Davenport did not match Cotton's copiousness on the subject, he made his devotion to the Middle Advent clear in his preface to Increase Mather's treatise on the end times. See "Epistle to the Reader," preface to Increase Mather's *The Mystery of Israel's Salvation* (London, 1669). Moreover, Davenport's letters, as well as his treatise on *The Saints Anchor-hold* are seasoned with millennial readings of current events. See Isabel Calder, *Letters of John Davenport, Puritan Divine* (New Haven: Yale University Press, 1937), pp. 82, 84, 137–140, for examples. Apparently (p. 84), Davenport preached a set of sermons on Revelation that has been lost.

147. Sibbes, *Works*, 6:543.

148. Ibid., 6:547.

7. The Heart of New England Rent

1. The subtitle of the treatise advertises Firmin's intent: "wherein the work of God in drawing the Soul to Christ being opened according to the holy Scripture, some Things required by our late Divines as necessary to a right Preparation for Christ and true closing with Christ, which have caused, and do still cause much

Trouble to some serious Christians, are with due Respects to those worthy Men, brought to the Ballance of the Sanctuary, there weighed, and accordingly judged"; Giles Firmin, "Preface," *The Real Christian* (1670; rpt., Boston, 1742), pp. A2, iv, v.

2. Ibid., pp. iv, v.

3. Thomas Goodwin and Philip Nye, "To the Reader," in Thomas Hooker, *The Application of Redemption, Ninth and Tenth Books* (London, 1656; rpt., New York: Arno Press, 1972), n.p.

4. Ibid. For an alternative reading of Goodwin's assessment, see Sargent Bush, Jr., *The Writings of Thomas Hooker: Spiritual Adventure in Two Worlds* (Madison: University of Wisconsin Press, 1980), p. 154.

5. Bush, *Writings of Thomas Hooker*, p. 252. Bush offers a superb reading of this issue of stylistic decline (pp. 252–253). Of the sermons dealing with the life of sanctification, he observes that they "often present carefully sharpened explanations of fine theological points but . . . sometimes lack the convincing concreteness, the metaphorical richness, and often the dramatic scene painting and character sketching so abundantly present in the volumes on the earlier stages of grace" (p. 252).

6. Ibid., p. 73.

7. Sacvan Bercovitch, *The American Jeremiad* (Madison: University of Wisconsin Press, 1978), pp. 49, 64.

8. See Theodore Bozeman, *To Live Ancient Lives: The Primitivist Dimension in Puritanism* (Chapel Hill: University of North Carolina Press, 1988), chap. 3, for a similar reading.

9. The term *genetics of salvation* is from Bercovitch, *American Jeremiad*, chap. 3. Werner Sollors, in *Beyond Ethnicity: Consent and Dissent in American Culture* (New York: Oxford University Press, 1986), p. 86, discusses the Half-Way Covenant as formalizing the shift from active consent to the pure church to de facto descent within the tribe.

10. *The Marrow of Theology: William Ames, 1576–1633*, trans. John D. Eusden (Boston: Pilgrim Press, 1968), p. 251.

11. Ibid., p. 252.

12. Ibid., p. 301.

13. Ibid., p. 302.

14. Ibid., p. 302.

15. Ibid., pp. 302–303.

16. Ibid. Eusden remarks that Ames recognizes the impossibility of unrestrained Christian love: "in practical living a moment of calculation must enter—even a moment of shrewdness. We should love our neighbor according to certain orders of comparison inherited from the scholastic tradition"; "Introduction," *Marrow of Theology*, p. 16.

17. Bush, *Writings of Thomas Hooker*, p. 258. John S. Coolidge, in *The Pauline Renaissance in England: Puritanism and the Bible* (Oxford: Clarendon Press, 1970), p. 148, observes that concern for community is the general context in which to understand Puritan thought: "Christian liberty as Paul conceives it, and the Puri-

tans after him, knits the individual conscience to communal consciousness indissolubly." Yet Coolidge also notes that this original aspect of Puritanism is in conflict with the individualism inherent in covenantal doctrine. While it is true that Ames and Hooker participate in the general spirit of communalism, their brand of preparationism promotes greater focus on the individual and on self-help. See also John Wilson, *Pulpit in Parliament: Puritanism during the English Civil Wars, 1640–1648* (Princeton: Princeton University Press, 1969), p. 166, for observations concerning the conflict between individualism and communalism.

18. *The Works of Thomas Shepard . . . with a memoir of his Life and Character,* 3 vols., ed. John Albro (Boston, 1853; rpt., New York: AMS Press, 1967), 1:clxxxvi (hereafter cited as Shepard, *Works*).

19. John Cotton, *Of the Holinesse of Church Members* (London, 1650), p. 49.

20. Laurence Chaderton, as quoted in Peter Lake, *Moderate Puritans and the Elizabethan Church* (Cambridge, New York: Cambridge University Press, 1982), pp. 35–36.

21. Sibbes asks, "What is the use of the sacraments but to help our souls by our senses, our faith by imagination?" Similarly preaching was to stir the soul experimentally. See *The Complete Works of Richard Sibbes,* 7 vols., ed. Alexander Grosart (Edinburgh: James Nichol, 1862), 1:185.

22. Ames, *Marrow of Theology,* p. 254. Yet the Sibbesian sense of meaningful difference is confirmed by Walter Ong: "Oral communication unites people in groups. Writing and reading are solitary activities that throw the psyche back on itself." See Ong, *Orality and Literacy: The Technologizing of the Word* (New York: Methuen, 1982), p. 69.

23. Ong, *Orality and Literacy,* p. 69.

24. John Wilson has noted the predominance of the "discipline of personal piety"; *Pulpit in Parliament,* p. 166. Ursula Brumm has noted the preparationists' fondness for the practice of private meditation. See Brumm, "Meditative Poetry in New England," in *Puritan Poets and Poetics: Seventeenth-Century American Poetry in Theory and Practice,* ed. Peter White (London: The Pennsylvania State University Press, 1985), pp. 337–357. See also Brumm, "The Art of Puritan Meditation in New England," in *Studies in New England Puritanism,* ed. Winfred Herget (Frankfort: Lang, 1983), pp. 137–167.

25. Ames, *Marrow of Theology,* p. 191.

26. Shepard, as quoted by Firmin in *The Real Christian,* pp. 19, 56. See Grosart, "Introduction," p. clxxxvii.

27. *Thomas Hooker: Writings in England and Holland, 1626–1633,* ed. George H. Williams et al. (Cambridge, Mass.: Harvard University Press, 1975), p. 213 (hereafter cited as Hooker, *English Writings*).

28. Ibid., pp. 213, 214. See Shepard, *Works,* 1:32. While in earlier writings and in his private notebooks, Shepard often speaks with the same benevolence as Sibbes, the Cambridge preachers, on the other hand, almost never adopt the vituperative mode that characterizes preparationist rhetoric.

29. Hooker, *English Writings*, p. 214.

30. See Shepard, *Works*, 1:36, 138, 328, for a few examples of this same tone.

31. Hooker, *The Soules Preparation for Christ* (London, 1632), p. 160; *The Soules Implantation* (London, 1637), pp. 71–72.

32. See Hooker, "The Faithful Covenanter," *English Writings*, pp. 190–221, for anxieties about rebellion; and for more on John Wilson, see A. W. M'Clure, *Lives of the Chief Fathers of New England* (Boston, 1846), p. 146.

33. Hooker, *Soules Implantation*, p. 91, 73.

34. From a preface to Shepard's sermons, cited in *Works*, 1:clxxxvii.

35. Sibbes, *Works*, 1:41; Shepard, *Works*, 1:clxxxvii.

36. Hooker, *Soules Implantation*, pp. 73–74. Ames also rails against ministers who "propound a certain text in the beginning as the start of the sermon and then speak many things about or simply by occasion of the text but for the most part draw nothing out of the text itself" (*Marrow of Theology*, p. 191). Of course, the main target of such criticism is Anglican sermonizing. But in this rejection of the more affective mode of collation, there might be an implicit criticism of the Sibbesian style. For Shepard, of course, the criticism of "tiffany and silken sermons" was directly aimed at men like Cotton. See Shepard, *Works*, 3:113.

37. *The Work of William Perkins*, ed. Ian Breward (Abingdon: The Sutton Courtenay Press, 1970), pp. 325–351. For commentary see Perry Miller, *The New England Mind: The Seventeenth Century* (Cambridge, Mass.: Harvard University Press, 1939), chaps. 11 and 12; Teresa Toulouse, "'The Arte of Prophesying': John Cotton and the Rhetoric of Election," *Early American Literature*, 19 (1985), 279–299.

38. Ames, *Marrow of Theology*, p. 191.

39. Here the distinction between Miller and Haller on the point of favoring logic or rhetoric is essential. While the brethren's oral mode is pre- or alogical, the preparationist sermons emphasize Ramean logocentricism. Ong argues, "in his dialectic or logic Ramus provided a virtually unsurpassable example of logocentrism." This is a method that "proceeded by cold-blooded definition and divisions leading to still further definition and more divisions, until every last particle of the subject had been dissected and disposed of"; *Orality and Literacy*, pp. 57, 144, 167. The benevolence of this impulse to comprehensibility should be acknowledged, however.

40. For amplification of this point, see Toulouse, "Art of Prophesying,'" p. 292.

41. Ames says, "Not all the doctrines which may be drawn out of the text are to be propounded or all the uses set forth but only those are to be selected which the circumstances of place, time and person suggest as most necessary"; *Marrow of Theology*, p. 192–193.

42. For Hooker's sermon plots, see Bush, *Writings of Thomas Hooker*, p. 165; Toulouse, "'Arte of Prophesying'"; and Alfred Habegger, "Preparing the Soul for Christ: The Contrasting Sermon Forms of John Cotton and Thomas Hooker," *American Literature*, 41 (1969), 342–354. Ong observes that narrative rests on a developmental structure suited to arguments. Incantation, on the other hand, has

an alogical structure that is of an additive and/or circular structure; *Orality and Literacy*, pp. 144, 37. This observation neatly describes the differences between Cotton and Hooker.

43. Hooker, *Application of Redemption*, p. 3.

44. Ames, *Marrow of Theology*, p. 192.

45. Hooker, *Soules Implantation*, pp. 8–9.

46. David Leverenz says of Hooker's style, "Everything floats, almost bounces, in apposition . . . The very short phrases, when put together to make up one of Hooker's typically mammoth sentences, give a cumulative effect wholly justifying the Ramist theory that particles, if arranged in their natural order, will form a whole . . . The arrangement also shows the static, well-regulated 'nature' behind Hooker's order"; *The Language of Puritan Feeling: An Exploration in Literature, Psychology, and Social History* (New Brunswick, N.J.: Rutgers University Press, 1980), p. 165. See also Habegger, "Preparing the Soul For Christ," p. 349.

47. Norman Grabo first made the observation many years ago in "John Cotton's Aesthetic: A Sketch," *Early American Literature*, 3 (1968), 4–10. Ong argues that Ramean logocentrism "reduces all sensation and indeed all human experience to visual analogues." If Cotton's appeal is to the ear, Hooker's concrete metaphors appeal to the eye; Ong, *Orality and Literacy*, p. 77.

48. Hooker, *Application of Redemption*, p. 4.

49. Hooker, *The Soules Preparation*, p. 70–71. See also p. 60 for images of breaking the heart and tearing down the will. Also *The Soules Implantation*, pp. 70–72.

50. Hooker, *Survey of the Summe of Church Discipline* (London, 1648), part 3, chap. 1, p. 6. As Patricia Caldwell, *The Puritan Conversion Narrative: The Beginnings of American Expression* (Cambridge: Cambridge University Press, 1983), pp. 125–138, and Charles Cohen, *God's Caress: The Psychology of Puritan Religious Experience* (New York: Oxford University Press, 1986), point out, few of the congregants could testify to a completed conversion. On the other hand, Cotton's insistence on the testimony of a union with Christ may reflect his own happy religious experience.

51. Hooker, *Summe of Church Discipline*, pt. 3:1, p. 5.

52. Ibid., pt. 3:1, p. 6.

53. Caldwell argues that Hooker's sense of the narrative betrays a profound distrust of Cotton's communitarianism and an assertion of clerical hierarchy. See *Conversion Narrative*, pp. 99, 110.

54. Shepard, *Works*, 1:cxxix; Thomas Shepard, *God's Plot: The Paradoxes of Puritan Piety: Being the Autobiography and Journal of Thomas Shepard*, ed. Michael McGiffert (Amherst: University of Massachusetts Press, 1972), p. 111 (hereafter cited as Shepard, *Journal*). Michael McGiffert's "Introduction" to Shepard's journal suggests the importance of anxiety in his conception of conversion, and it claims that this stress on doubt is offset by spiritual joy (see pp. 20, 26). See also Baird Tipson, "The Routinized Piety of Thomas Shepard's Diary," *Early American Literature*, 13 (1978), 64–80. Scholars Caldwell and Cohen are surprised, however, to discover

that few saints testify to a completed conversion. Yet, since they base their study on narratives of Shepard's church from a period after the Antinomian Controversy, it seems reasonable that auditors would testify to the anxiety rehearsed in preparationist sermons. For a fuller discussion of these texts see my review of *God's Caress* in the *Journal of the History of the Behavioral Sciences* (July 1988), 288–292.

55. John Albro, "Life of Thomas Shepard," in *Works*, 1:cxxvi. Shepard, *Wine for Gospel Wantons or Cautions against Spirituall Drunkenness* (London, 1668), pp. 9, 14. While this sermon (preached in 1645) was directed as much to the sins of Old England as New, the explicit accusations against antinomians must have had painful resonance for Cotton.

56. For the history of these new practices, see John Winthrop, *The History of New England from 1630 to 1649*, ed. James Savage (rpt., New York: Arno Press, 1972), vol. 1, pp. 179–194; Albro, in Shepard, *Works*, pp. cxxvi–cxxx. See also B. Richard Burg, *Richard Mather of Dorchester* (Louisville: University of Kentucky Press, 1976), pp. 28–37; Michael G. Hall, *The Last American Puritan: The Life of Increase Mather, 1639–1723* (Middletown, Conn.: Wesleyan University Press, 1988), pp. 17–21. For an alternative reading of the admissions tests as regulatory but also accommodating spiritist impulses, see Stephen Foster, *The Long Argument: English Puritanism and the Shaping of New England Culture, 1570–1700* (Chapel Hill: University of North Carolina Press, 1993), pp. 160–163.

57. Shepard, *Works*, 1:cxxviii–cxxix.

58. Ibid., p. cxxx. Stephen Foster argues that Shepard rejected the testimonies because they "revealed the putative saints to be still under a covenant of works." Yet, Shepard's distaste for enthusiasm seems to suggest the opposite reading. Foster's additional claim that the ritual of narration regulated but also accommodated spiritism seems over-generous. See Foster, *Long Argument*, pp. 161–166. See also Edmund Morgan, *Visible Saints: A History of a Puritan Idea* (Ithaca, N.Y.: Cornell University Press, 1965), pp. 99–105, for the Dorchester history.

59. The additional question of how much Shepard may have edited the narratives to conform to his version of the *ordo salutis* is worth considering. The uniformity of the handwriting in the original journal notebook, as well as the less thoroughly edited testimonies recently discovered, suggest that Shepard may have actively shaped—even ventriloquized—the narratives in his recording of them. See Mary Rhinelander McCarl, "Thomas Shepard's Record of Relations of Religious Experience, 1648–1649," *William and Mary Quarterly*, 3d ser., 48:3 (1991), 432–466. I have argued for a more suspicious reading of the testimonies, as well as the text of Winthrop's *History*, in two papers delivered at the Modern Language Association: "The Winner's Tale: The Politics of the Puritan Archive" (1992) and "The Case of the Ending: Conversion Narratives and the Pieties of Discipline" (1990).

60. Jesper Rosenmeier, in "New England's Perfection: The Image of Adam and the Image of Christ in the Antinomian Crisis, 1634–1638," *William and Mary Quarterly*, 27 (1970), 435–439, first made the argument for orthodox primitivism that Bozeman has recently elaborated.

61. Keith Sprunger, *The Learned Doctor William Ames* (Chicago: University of Illinois Press, 1972), p. 185. Sprunger goes on to add: "While some of his friends were espousing the hope of millennialism, particularly Joseph Mead of Christ's College, Ames remained unconvinced" (p. 185).

62. Bush, *Writings of Thomas Hooker*, p. 24.

63. See Hooker, *English Writings*, p. 217, for a vivid portrait of the personal apocalypse of the deathbed.

64. Ibid., pp. 228–252. Hooker observes: "all things are ripe to destruction" (p. 232). The signs of the times are filled with "prophecies . . . of its destruction" (p. 232). "God will be God over thee in destruction" (p. 241). Absent is any of the optimism Bercovitch remarks as characteristic of preparationist doctrine.

65. Hooker, "Preface," *Summe of Church Discipline*.

66. Bulkeley, "The Reader," *The Gospel-Covenant: or the Covenant of Grace Opened* (London, 1646), p. A4.

67. See Peter Toon, *Puritans, the Millennium, and the Future of Israel: Puritan Eschatology 1600–1660* (Cambridge, London: Clarke and Company, 1970), pp. 14, 35; Wilson, *Pulpit in Parliament*, pp. 189, 223, 225. Wilson recognizes Cotton as the premier influence on radical millenarian thought (p. 225), as do Maclear, Gura, and Bozeman.

68. Jonathan Mitchell, "Preface," in Shepard, *Works*, 2:8–9.

69. Ibid., 2:169, 44.

70. Ibid., 2:14–15.

71. Ibid., 2:375–378.

72. Ibid., 3:74–75.

73. Ibid., 3:259–260. Shepard rails against those religionists who typologize the Sabbath and therefore "have spiritualized it out of the decalogue." He laments that "the times are now come, wherein, by the refined mystical divinity of the old monks, not only the Sabbath, but also all the ordinances of Christ in the New Testament, are allegorized and spiritualized out of the world." Shepard rejects not only radical typology, however, but also denies the more orthodox practice of Cotton (3:257, 178).

74. Ibid., 3:260.

75. Ibid., 2:25.

76. Ibid., 3:74.

77. Ibid., 3:259.

78. Ibid., 3:260.

79. Ibid., 2:25.

80. As Rosenemeier says, "Whatever happened in each man's soul had its clear analogies in God's universal drama." See "New England's Perfection," p. 445.

81. Shepard, *Works*, 2:25.

82. Ibid., 2:510.

83. See Joy Gilsdorf, "The Puritan Apocalypse: New England Eschatology in the Seventeenth Century," Ph.D. dissertation, Yale University, 1965, p. 108. She

finally concludes that Shepard repudiated the thousand-year reign of the saints on earth.

84. Shepard, *Works*, 2:633.

85. Ibid., 2:154.

86. Ibid., 2:169–171.

87. Ibid., 2:509–514.

88. In his preface to Bulkeley's *Gospel-Covenant*, Shepard again alludes to apocalyptic punishment, unless the churches reform: "aske and search diligently, what should be the reason for this sore anger and hot displeasure, before they and theirs be consumed in the burning flames."

89. Shepard, *Works*, 2:431.

90. For fuller discussion of this topic, see Williston Walker, *Creeds and Platforms of Congregationalism* (1893; rpt., Philadelphia: Pilgrim Press, 1960), pp. 238–339; Perry Miller, *The New England Mind: From Colony to Province* (Cambridge, Mass.: Harvard University Press, 1953), chap. 7; Bercovitch, *American Jeremiad*, chap. 3; Morgan, *Visible Saints*, chap. 4; Robert Pope, *The Half-Way Covenant: Church Membership in Puritan New England* (Princeton: Princeton University Press, 1969); E. Brooks Holifield, *The Covenant Sealed: The Development of Puritan Sacramental Theology in Old England and New, 1570–1720* (New Haven: Yale University Press, 1974); and Foster, *Long Argument*, chap. 5. Debate over church membership was also a part of the Williams-Cotton controversy. See Williams, "The Bloudy Tenent of Persecution," in *Puritan Political Ideas*, ed. Edmund S. Morgan (Indianapolis: Bobbs Merrill, 1965), pp. 203–218. Of the founding generation, Hooker's *Survey of the Summe of Church Discipline*, Cotton's *The True Constitution of a Particular Church* (London, 1642), and *The Way of the Churches of Christ in New-England* (London, 1645) deal with the saint's qualifications.

91. Though many ministers supported such measures in the 1640s they were unable to implement them, perhaps because the problem had not yet become sufficiently acute to offset the specter of certain controversy. By 1650, disputes emerge in the Connecticut churches over this issue. In general, the laity resisted the innovation. See Pope, *Half-Way Covenant*, pp. 23–33, and Foster, *Long Argument*, chap. 5, for this history.

92. "Mr. Chauncy, Mr. Mayo, and Mr. Eleazer and Increase Mather Dissent from the Return of the Synod of October, 1662," in "Papers Relating to the Synod of 1662," transcribed by David Pulsifer (MSS, Beineke Library, Yale University), pp. 29, 34. The documents in the Pulsifer Papers include: Chauncy, E. Mather, I. Mather, and Mayo, "The Judgement of the Dissenting Brethren of the Synod" and "A Plain Proposall of the Dissenting Messengers"; Davenport, "A Reply to the 7 Propositions Concluded by the Synod Setting at Boston June the 10th. 1662"; Nicholas Street, "Considerations upon the 7 Propositions Concluded . . . June 10: 1662"; and "Mr. Davenport's and Mr. Street's Papers Contra . . . the late Synod." Cited by permission of the Beineke Rare Book and Manuscript Library, Yale University. Part of these texts are published in Davenport, *Another Essay for the*

Investigation of the Truth (London, 1663), and Chauncy, *Anti-Synodalia Scripta Americana* (London, 1662). See Robert Pope, *Half-Way Covenant,* for supplementary readings of these papers.

93. Davenport distinguished between mediate and immediate church members. Children baptized under the parent's covenant are mediate members who must either offer a personal testimony or pass out of the covenant. See manuscript, "Davenport's Answer to 21 Questions put to ye Revd. Author," in the John Davenport Papers, American Antiquarian Society, pp. 2, 8.

94. Many of Davenport's polemical writings deal with this issue. See *A Just Complaint Against an Unjust Doer* (Amsterdam, 1634); *An Apologeticall Reply to a Booke Called an Answer to the Unjust Complaint of W.B.* (1636; rpt., Amsterdam: Walter Johnson, Inc., 1976); *Another Essay;* and Pulsifer, "Papers Relating to the Synod of 1662."

95. Pope, *Half-Way Covenant,* pp. 170, 264, documents lay opposition. Cotton Mather, in *Magnalia Christi Americana; or, the Ecclesiastical History of New England,* 2 vols., ed. Thomas Robbins (London, 1702; rpt., Hartford: Silas Andrus and Son, 1855), 2:312–313, observed that in 1692 most churches still had not adopted the measures. For another version of these party allegiances, see Foster, *Long Argument,* pp. 201–205. Foster claims that defenders of the Synod were anti-tolerationists and accommodationists with respect to the restored monarchy. Anti-Synodists resisted crown authority and favored toleration of baptists.

96. Morgan, *Visible Saints,* pp. 124, 133; Pope, *Half-Way Covenant,* chap. 10; and David Hall, *Worlds of Wonder, Days of Judgment: Popular Religious Belief in New England* (New York: Alfred A. Knopf, 1989), view the measures as both a reaffirmation of high ideals and a recognition of the claims of continuity.

97. The Miller school, including Andrew Delbanco, view the Half-Way Covenant as a betrayal of idealism. See Delbanco, *The Puritan Ordeal* (Cambridge, Mass.: Harvard University Press, 1989), pp. 229–230.

98. Bercovitch has been cited above as making the most persuasive case for the links between preparationism, the Half-Way Covenant, tribalism, and finally American exceptionalism. See *American Jeremiad,* p. 49: "preparation was a sort of personal analogue to the tribal concept of errand"; p. 64: "This genetics of salvation . . . may be seen as the doctrinal counterpart of the concept of errand."

99. The fullest reading of the transatlantic context for Puritan culture is Stephen Foster, *Long Argument.*

100. Davenport, "The Third Essay Containing a Reply . . . ," manuscript, John Davenport Papers, p. 43, by permission of the American Antiquarian Society.

101. Davenport, "Reply," p. 75; Chauncy et al., "Judgement of the Dissenting Brethren," p. 13; both in Pulsifer, "Papers Relating to the Synod of 1662."

102. Street, "Considerations," p. 90, in Pulsifer, "Papers Relating to the Synod of 1662."

103. Bercovitch, *American Jeremiad,* pp. 64–65.

104. Pulsifer, "Papers Relating to the Synod of 1662," pp. 34, 57.

105. Ibid., p. 29.

106. Davenport, "A Vindication of the Treatise Entitled Another Essay," pp. 5–6, in the John Davenport Papers, American Antiquarian Society.

107. For an account of Davenport's late career and the founding of Third Church, see Hamilton Hill, *History of the Old South Church, Boston, 1669–1884* (Boston: Houghton Mifflin, 1890). Miller, in *New England Mind: From Colony to Province,* pp. 93–118, gives an extremely insightful reading of the events. See also Pope, *Half-Way Covenant,* pp. 152–184; Foster, *Long Argument,* chap. 5; Richard C. Simmons, "The Founding of the Third Church in Boston," *William and Mary Quarterly,* 3d ser., 26:2 (1969), 241–252; Thomas Hutchinson, *The History of the Colony of Massachusetts Bay,* vol. 1 (rpt., New York: Arno Press, 1972), pp. 270–275; John Hull, *The Diary of John Hull,* vol. 3, *Transactions* of the American Antiquarian Society (Boston, 1857); Mather, *Magnalia,* 2:302–315 (Book 5, part 3).

108. Hill, *Old South Church,* p. 4.

109. In New Haven Davenport and Eaton had adopted the biblical code Massachusetts had commissioned Cotton to draft but then had refused to implement. See Isabel Calder, "John Cotton and the New Haven Colony," *New England Quarterly,* 3d ser., 3 (1930); Isabel Calder, *The New Haven Colony* (New Haven: Yale University Press, 1934), p. 208.

110. Calder, *New Haven Colony,* p. 209, 211; *Letters of John Davenport, Puritan Divine,* ed. Isabel Calder (New Haven, Conn.: Yale University Press, 1937), p. 90.

111. Calder, *New Haven Colony,* pp. 222–223. Calder reports that the regicides stayed in Davenport's home for eight weeks. See Calder, *Letters of John Davenport,* pp. 191–193.

112. Calder, *Letters of John Davenport,* pp. 137, 197.

113. *Collections,* Massachusetts Historical Society, 4th ser., vol. 8 (Boston, 1868), pp. 1, 7, 10. Davenport wrote to Goffe in 1662 that "there are to the No. of 8 or 9000 protestant people, Banished out of some other country"; Calder, *Letters of John Davenport,* p. 207.

114. Calder, *Letters of John Davenport,* p. 177.

115. Hull, *Diary,* pp. 156, 195. Hull despaired that it was "as if, when they had been now twenty years conflicting, and a great part of them in bloody war, for reformation, they should all upon a sudden be sent back again, as sometime Israel in the wilderness, ready to enter into Canaan, yet for unbelief and disobedience sent back to the Red Sea, and to wandering for forty years, to consume that generation that would not learn and do the work of their generation" (p. 197).

116. Hull wrote that though there was "present peace in all Europe . . . the protestants much oppressed in France . . . The nonconformists in England have no liberty to preach . . . many fears of a massacre from the popish party in England"; *Diary,* p. 228.

117. Calder, *Letters of John Davenport,* p. 178.

118. Ibid., pp. 248, 178, 212–247; Calder, *New Haven Colony,* pp. 230–250.

119. Calder, *Letters of John Davenport,* p. 248.

120. Davenport had a history of this kind of behavior. He departed Coleman Street Church in 1633 without the proper letters of dismissal. Calder speculates that this incident, along with his policy on baptism, contributed to Paget's successful block of Davenport's appointment in Amsterdam; *New Haven Colony*, p. 24.

121. Pope, *Half-Way Covenant*, p. 156; Hill, *Old South Church*, pp. 11–13; Calder, *Letters of John Davenport*, pp. 271–288.

122. Hutchinson, *History*, pp. 270–271; Miller, *New England Mind: From Colony to Province*, p. 106.

123. Hill, *Old South Church*, pp. 24–28, chaps. 1 and 2; Pope, *Half-Way Covenant*, chap. 6.

124. Mather, *Magnalia*, 2:312–313. In an act of particular rancor, the First Church refused to allow wives of the dissenters to join their husbands in the Third Church, even after its formation was allowed. Formal release was never extended to the women; again the consociation of outside ministers had to release them against First Church's objections. See Hill, *Old South Church*, pp. 170, 203–204.

125. Hill, *Old South Church*, pp. 60, 90.

126. See Hall, *Last American Puritan*, pp. 80–81.

127. Hutchinson, *History*, p. 270. The upshot was that "antiministerial spirit had thereby been strengthened and emboldened, the hearts and hands of those who labored in the ministry weakened, the spirits of many being filled with groundless jealousies and suspicions against the ministrations of the elders" (p. 273).

128. Quoted by Hill, *Old South Church*, p. 93.

129. Since Davenport's own confession of faith was printed as an appendix to Cotton's sermon, this echo was quite possibly an unconscious bid to recall the fallen congregants to the true New England way, as set down by John Cotton.

130. Davenport, "A Sermon preached at the Election of the Governor, at Boston, in New England, May 19, 1669," in *Publications of the Colonial Society of Massachusetts*, vol. 10, pp. 12–13.

131. Ibid., p. 15. Davenport's sermon, "God's Call to His People to Turn Unto Him" (Cambridge, Mass., 1669), preaches a similar lesson.

132. Davenport, "God's Call to His People," pp. 15–16.

133. Ibid., p. 4.

134. From a passage signed by Chauncy, Mayo, and Increase and Eleazer Mather, in Pulsifer, "Papers Relating to the Synod of 1662," p. 38.

135. Davenport, *Saints Anchor-hold . . . and Sundry Sermons* (London, 1682), pp. 192–193.

136. Hutchinson, *History*, p. 272; Hill, *Old South Church*, p. 94–98.

137. Hutchinson, *History*, p. 272; Hill, *Old South Church*, p. 102.

138. Hill, *Old South Church*, p. 102.

139. Hill, *Old South Church*, p. 105.

140. The outraged magistrates had refused to vote the customary thanks to Davenport for his 1669 election sermon and sent a remonstrance to the Deputies,

declaring that "many passages in the said sermon being ill-resented by the Reverend Elders of other churches." See Hill, *Old South Church,* pp. 94–98. Needless to say, they were no happier with the deputies' report.

141. Ibid., p. 110.

142. Pope, *Half-Way Covenant,* pp. 159–69.

143. Hill, *Old South Church,* p. 107.

144. Miller, *New England Mind: From Colony to Province,* p. 108. Miller calculates: "at the election of May 1671 fourteen Deputies (all opponents of the Third Church) were defeated, nineteen (all 'safe') were reelected, and thirteen new names were chosen (all amenable)."

145. The new court was quick to issue a remonstrance of their predecessors, a "full and complete vindication" of the orthodox position and of the members of Third Church. See Hill, *Old South Church,* p. 110.

146. Miller, *New England Mind: From Colony to Province,* p. 66.

147. Miller, *New England Mind: From Colony to Province,* p. 107.

Epilogue

1. David Levin, *Cotton Mather: The Young Life of the Lord's Remembrancer, 1663–1703* (Cambridge, Mass.: Harvard University Press, 1978); Robert Middlekauff, *The Mathers: Three Generations of Puritan Intellectuals, 1596–1728* (New York: Oxford University Press, 1971), could serve as points of origin for such study.

2. Williston Walker, *The Creeds and Platforms of Congregationalism* (1893; rpt., Boston: The Pilgrim Press, 1960), pp. 283–287. Edwards rejected preparationism, arguing: "'Tis to be feared that some have gone too far towards directing the Spirit of the Lord, and marking out his footsteps for him and limiting him to certain steps and methods"; *Religious Affections,* in *The Works of Jonathan Edwards,* vol. 2, ed. John E. Smith (New Haven, Conn.: Yale University Press, 1959), p. 162.

3. Alan Heimert, in *Religion and the American Mind: From the Great Awakening to the Revolution* (Cambridge, Mass.: Harvard University Press, 1966), has brilliantly shown that Edwards was a thoroughgoing postmillennialist, whose commitment to the international body of saints, practice of unions in prayer, and doctrine of benevolence fueled the American Revolution.

4. It should be noted that in the *Religious Affections* Edwards cites Thomas Shepard more than any other theologian. This may be because Cotton, identified with antinomianism, was too controversial to cite in what was a period of dispute over the marks of true religion. Certainly, Chauncy's repeated analogy between antinomianism and the revivals might prove a caution against citing Cotton as an authority. See Chauncy's introduction to *Seasonable Thoughts on the State of Religion in New England* (Boston, 1743). Shepard's conservative reputation may have appealed to Edwards at a time when his own evangelical movement was being closely scrutinized by the Boston orthodoxy. Moreover, Shepard possessed an evangelical zeal that may have made him appealing to Edwards. Though this chapter stresses an evangelical sweetness and a millennial optimism that links Edwards to Sibbes

and Cotton, he also preached the terrors of sin in a way graphic enough to have been inspired by Shepard. In many ways, then, Edwards is as complex and contradictory as Shepard himself. His repudiation of preparationism and his emphasis on signs of grace received rather than on steps to the altar, however, do separate Edwards from the marrow of Shepard's doctrine. On these important issues Edwards rearticulates the faith as it was delivered to Richard Sibbes.

5. For Edwards's debt to Sibbes, see John E. Smith, "Introduction," in Edwards, *Religious Affections,* pp. 69–70; and Douglas Elwood, *The Philosophical Theology of Jonathan Edwards* (New York: Columbia University, 1960). James Hoopes has also argued that Edwards is best understood in terms of a Puritan rather than Enlightenment tradition.

6. For a summary of the disputes over Edwards's debt to Enlightenment models, see Janice Knight, "Learning the Language of God: Jonathan Edwards and the Typology of Nature," *William and Mary Quarterly,* 3d ser., 48 (1991): 533–537. *Jonathan Edwards and the American Experience,* ed. Nathan O. Hatch and Harry S. Stout (New York: Oxford University Press, 1988), offers a good collection of recent scholarship. See also Norman Fiering, *Jonathan Edwards's Moral Thought and Its British Context* (Chapel Hill: University of North Carolina Press, 1981); Mason Lowance, *The Language of Canaan: Metaphor and Symbol in New England from the Puritans to the Transcendentalists* (Cambridge, Mass.: Harvard University Press, 1980).

7. Edwards, *Charity and its Fruits* (Philadelphia: Presbyterian Board of Publications, 1874), Lecture One.

8. *The Philosophy of Jonathan Edwards from His Private Notebooks,* ed. Harvey G. Townsend (Eugene: University of Oregon Press, 1955), p. 130 (hereafter cited as *Miscellanies*).

9. See Sang Lee, *The Philosophical Theology of Jonathan Edwards* (Princeton, N.J.: Princeton University Press, 1988), for a complementary reading of Edwards's conception of God's dynamic, communicative nature. I am pleased to find that a number of the ideas suggested here are confirmed and elaborated there, but I dissent from Lee's formulation in one fundamental respect: Lee argues that Edwards's dynamism exemplifies not a return to traditional pietism, but a more radical modernism than even Miller suspected (p. 3).

10. Edwards, *Religious Affections,* p. 255.

11. Ibid., p. 255.

12. Ibid., pp. 179, 256.

13. *Dissertation I. Concerning the End for which God Created the World,* in *The Works of Jonathan Edwards,* vol. 8: *Ethical Writings,* ed. Paul Ramsey (New Haven, Conn.: Yale University Press, 1989), p. 429.

14. Ibid., p. 433.

15. Ibid., pp. 512–513.

16. "Treatise on Grace," p. 62; "An Essay on the Trinity," p. 118, both in Jonathan Edwards, *Treatise on Grace and other Posthumously Published Writings,* ed. Paul Helm (Cambridge, Mass.: Harvard University Press, 1971).

17. Ibid., p. 99.

18. Ibid., pp. 99–100.

19. Ibid., p. 63.

20. Ibid., p. 78.

21. Ibid., p. 118.

22. Cotton, *A Practical Commentary . . . upon the First Epistle Generall of John* (London, 1656), p. 12 (hereafter cited as *I John Generall*).

23. Edwards, *Miscellanies*, p. 152.

24. Edwards, *Dissertation I*, p. 422.

25. Ibid., p. 422; *Treatise on Grace*, p. 97.

26. Edwards, *Dissertation I*, p. 513.

27. Jonathan Edwards, *Images or Shadows of Divine Things*, ed. Perry Miller (New Haven, Conn.: Yale University Press, 1948), p. 64.

28. Edwards, *Images or Shadows*, p. 64; Edwards, "Types of the Messiah," in *The Works of President Edwards with a Memoir of His Life*, vol. 9 (New York, 1830), p. 110. I would like to thank Mason Lowance and David Watters for generously sharing their typescript of this document, now available in the Yale series.

29. Edwards, *Dissertation I*, pp. 105, 12.

30. Edwards, *Miscellanies*, p. 129.

31. Edwards, *Dissertation II: The Nature of True Virtue*, in *The Works of Jonathan Edwards*, vol. 8, ed. Paul Ramsey (New Haven, Conn.: Yale University Press, 1989), p. 551. For other examples see *Religious Affections*, p. 205, and *Dissertation I*, p. 422.

32. Clarence H. Faust and Thomas H. Johnson, eds., *Jonathan Edwards: Representative Selections*, rev. ed. (1935; New York: Hill and Wang, 1962), pp. 324–325.

33. Ibid., p. 325.

34. Edwards, *Treatise on Grace*, p. 74; *Religious Affections*, pp. 256–257.

35. Ibid., pp. 205, 206, 248.

36. *The Complete Works of Richard Sibbes*, 7 vols., ed. Alexander Grosart (Edinburgh: James Nichol, 1862–1864), 1:60, 2:34, 2:463.

37. Cotton, *Christ the Fountaine of Life* (London, 1651), pp. 135, 99

38. Edwards, *Religious Affections*, pp. 205–206.

39. Ibid.

40. Ibid., pp. 200, 201–208.

41. Ibid., pp. 114–116.

42. Sibbes, *Works*, 1:185.

43. See Perry Miller's "Introduction" to Edwards's *Images or Shadows of Divine Things*. Mason Lowance in *The Language of Canaan* also stresses innovation rather than continuity in Edwards's reading of types. For an extended version of this argument see Knight, "Learning the Language of God."

44. Jonathan Edwards, "Notebook on the Types," manuscript, Andover Collection, cited in Lowance, *Language of Canaan*, p. 198.

45. Edwards, *Images or Shadows*, p. 70.

46. Edwards, *Religious Affections*, p. 343.

47. Edwards, *Charity and its Fruits* (Philadelphia: Presbyterian Board of Publications, 1874), p. 226.

48. Ibid., pp. 226, 227, 243, 248.

49. Ibid., p. 7. In the "Treatise on Grace," Edwards flatly declares, "A Christian love to God, and a christian love to men, are not properly two distinct principles in the heart." They are "the same principle flowing forth towards different objects according to the order of existence"; *Treatise on Grace*, p. 48.

50. Edwards, *Dissertation II*, p. 548; *Dissertation I*, pp. 422–423.

51. Sibbes, *Works*, 5:214.

52. Edwards, *Charity and its Fruits*, p. 36.

53. Alan Heimert has traced the links between communitarianism and revolution in *Religion and the American Mind*. Edwards's millennialism is everywhere in his works, but most notably in *The History of the Work of Redemption*, *The Humble Attempt*, and *Notes on the Apocalypse*. See *The Works of Jonathan Edwards*, vol. 5: *Apocalyptic Writings*, ed. Steven J. Stein (New Haven, Conn.: Yale University Press, 1977).

54. Edwards, *A History of the Work of Redemption*, in *The Works of Jonathan Edwards*, vol. 9, ed. John F. Wilson (New Haven, Conn.: Yale University Press, 1989), p. 149.

55. For Edwards, the telescope, with its penetration of distance, is a type of the coming union in which man's understanding will draw ever nearer to God's nature. See Edwards, *Images or Shadows*, p. 102.

56. Edwards, *An Humble Attempt*, in *Apocalyptic Writings*, p. 338.

57. Ibid., p. 339.

58. Sibbes, *Works*, 6:543.

59. Ibid., 6:543, 547, 549.

60. Edwards, *Dissertation II*, p. 549.

61. Edwards, *Dissertation I*, p. 534.

62. Edwards, *Apocalyptic Writings*, p. 339.

63. For full rehearsal of these issues and the critics involved, see Knight, "Learning the Language of God." Perry Miller is the critic most identified with this reading of Edwards in light of Locke and Newton. See his "Introduction" to Edwards, *Images or Shadows*, as well as his many essays and monograph on Edwards.

64. There are notable exceptions, however, including John F. Wilson and Stephen Stein (see their articles in Hatch and Stout, *Edwards and the American Experience*).

65. Deploying the discourse of Newtonian science, Edwards described a diffusive God: "that being who has the most of being, or the greatest share of universal existence"—the Entity of greatest possible mass; *Dissertation II*, p. 550. Inherent in the mass of entities was an attractive force, an emanation of energy. In God's nature, too, this property of emanation or communication is implicit. Marrying ancient faith to modern metaphor, Edwards provided a supplemental translation of *kavod* as gravity; *Dissertation I*, pp. 512–513.

66. For counter-arguments see Mason Lowance, *Language of Canaan;* R. C. De Prospo, *Theism in the Discourse of Jonathan Edwards* (Newark, Del.: University of Delaware Press, 1985), pp. 12–13, 59, 68, 75, 83.

67. See Bercovitch, *The American Jeremiad* (Madison: University of Wisconsin Press, 1978), and, more recently, *The Rites of Assent: Transformations in the Symbolic Construction of America* (New York: Routledge Press, 1993).

68. Patricia Tracy, *Jonathan Edwards, Pastor: Religion and Society in Eighteenth-Century Northampton* (New York, Hill and Wang, 1980), is one example of such local study. Other studies, perhaps more sensitive to issues of rhetoric and doctrine, await their authors.

69. Among philosophical readings are Roland Delattre, *Beauty and Sensibility in the Thought of Jonathan Edwards* (New Haven, Conn.: Yale University Press, 1968); Conrad Cherry, *The Theology of Jonathan Edwards: A Reappraisal* (Garden City: Doubleday, 1966; Gloucester, 1974).

70. Charles Olson, "Maximus to Gloucester, Letter 27 [withheld]," in *The Maximus Poems,* ed. George F. Butterick (Berkeley: University of California Press, 1983), p. 185.

Index

Ward, Samuel, 48
Warwick, Earl of, Robert Rich, 39, 46, 62–66, 68
Weber, Donald, 215n3
Weber, Max, 4, 67, 98, 104, 106, 108, 129, 131, 186, 266n3
Weld, Thomas, 55, 57; on Antinomian Controversy, 18; career and influence of, 55, 65
Whalley, Edward, 24, 189
Wheelwright, John, 16, 19, 22, 25, 27, 28, 70, 192, 264n86; in Antinomian Controversy, 18; fast-day sermon, 18, 25; banishment of, 19, 27; Cotton and, 28–29; career of, 57, 70
Whitman, Walt, 199, 212
Williams, John, 45, 48, 60, 64, 65, 188
Williams, Raymond, 5, 8, 219n23
Williams, Roger, 6, 13, 19, 73, 184, 231n2
Wilson, John, 16, 18, 22, 25, 26, 53, 57, 62, 70, 180; alliance with Shepard and Winthrop, 24, 25, 28, 57; career and influence of, 54, 62, 65, 67; and Ames, 54, 55, 57; on millennium, 276n39
Winthrop, John, 2, 10, 15, 17, 19, 23, 25, 26, 27, 54, 61, 70, 254n61; on Antinomian Controversy, 10, 14, 15, 16, 17, 19, 26, 28, 223n15; dispute with Dudley, 23; challenged by Vane, 23–24; defends General Court, 27; condemns Hutchinson, 29; on preparation, 31, 53, 56–57; career and influence of, 28, 56, 70; ties of Ames to, 57; on Communion of Saints, 143; on charity, 143; on migration, 158
Winthrop, John, Jr., 189
Work, Christian, 3, 76, 89, 93–96, 99, 101–104, 106–108, 118–120, 207; as love, 115, 119–120, 127, 129, 131, 134; and preparation, 126, 253n33, 254n47, 255n77, 257n87, 269n41

York House debate, 49, 51

Zwingli, Ulrich, 91